Preface   xi

DECIDING ON THE PURPOSE OF AN EDUCATIONAL TEST

1   **Perspectives on Purposes- Past and Present**   3

Prominent Applications of Educational Tests, 6
The Purposes of Testing, 9
Prior Purposes of Testing: A Capsule History of Educational Measurement, 10
Related Issues, 18
Practice Exercizes, 20
Answers to Practice Exercises, 21
Discussion Questions, 21
Suggestions for Additional Reading, 22

Contents

2   **Norm-Referenced and Criterion-Referenced Measurement**   24

The Fundamental Distinction, 25
Targets for Educational Tests, 33
Matching the Measurement Strategy with the Mission, 34
Practice Exercises, 38
Answers to Practice Exercises, 39
Discussion Questions, 40
Suggestions for Additional Reading, 41
And For Those Who Tire of Reading, 41

EVALUATING EDUCATIONAL TESTS

3 **What to Look for in an Educational Test** 45

Evaluative Factor One: Description of Measured Behavior, 47
Evaluative Factor Two: Items per Measured Behavior, 50
Evaluative Factor Three: Scope of Measurement, 56
Evaluative Factor Four: Reliability, 58
Evaluative Factor Five: Validity, 59
Evaluation Factor Six: Comparative Data, 60
Other Considerations, 61
Organizing the Test Evaluation, 62
Practice Exercises, 63
Answers to Practice Exercises, 64
Discussion Questions, 64
Suggestions for Additional Reading, 65

4 **Statistical Concepts Needed to Evaluate Tests** 66

Frequency Distributions, 68
Graphic Displays, 71
Indicators of Central Tendency, 75
Indicators of Variability, 79
Indicators of Relationship, 85
Practice Exercises, 95
Answers to Practice Exercises, 96
Discussion Questions, 97
Suggestions for Additional Reading, 97

5 **Establishing the Validity of Educational Tests** 98

Content Validity, 101
Criterion-Related Validities, 108
Construct Validity, 113
Practice Exercises, 123
Answers to Practice Exercises, 124
Discussion Questions, 124
Suggestions for Additional Reading, 124

6 **Reliability** 126

Stability, 128
Equivalence, 132
Equivalence and Stability, 134
A Simple-Minded Explanation of Rasch Test Equating, 135
Internal Consistency, 141

The Standard Error of Measurement, 146
Illustrations of Published Reliability Data, 148
Practice Exercises, 152
Answers to Practice Exercises, 154
Discussion Questions, 154
Suggestions for Additional Reading, 154

7   **Comparative Data**   156

The Normal Curve, 157
Percentiles, 160
Standard Scores, 162
Norms, 172
Practice Exercises, 178
Answers to Practice Exercises, 179
Discussion Questions, 179
Suggestions for Additional Reading, 180

8   **Test Bias**   181

Culture-Fair Tests, 184
Evaluating for Test Bias, 190
Practice Exercises, 197
Answers to Practice Exercises, 197
Discussion Questions, 198
Suggestions for Additional Reading, 198

CREATING EDUCATIONAL TESTS

9   **Specifying What a Test Should Measure**   203

A Range of Assessment Options, 205
Test Specifications for Norm-Referenced Tests, 206
Test Specifications for Criterion-Referenced Tests, 211
Two Functions of Test Specifications, 230
Practice Exercises, 232
Answers to Practice Exercises, 233
Discussion Questions, 233
Suggestions for Additional Reading, 233
And For Those who Tire of Reading, 234

Selected-Response Tests   235

Binary-Choice Items, 241
Matching Items, 247
Multiple-Choice Items, 251
Practice Exercises, 262
Answers to Practice Exercises, 263
Discussion Questions, 264
Suggestions for Additional Reading, 264

Constructed-Response Tests   266

Relative Merits of Selected and Constructed Response Items, 268
Short-Answer Items, 271
The Essay Item, 274
Practice Exercises, 283
Answers to Practice Questions, 283
Discussion Questions, 284
Suggestions for Additional Reading, 284

Improving Test Items   286

Judgmental Improvement of Test Items, 289
Empirical Improvement of Test Items, 293
Practice Exercises, 305
Answers to Practice Exercises, 306
Discussion Questions, 307
Suggestions for Additional Reading, 308

Observations and Ratings   309

Systematic Observations, 311
Ratings, 315
Practice Exercises, 325
Answers to Practice Exercises, 326
Discussion Questions, 326
Suggestions for Additional Reading, 326
And For Those who Tire of Reading, 327

Creating Affective Measures   328

Isolating the Attribute to be Measured, 333
Assessment Options, 335
Individual and Group Affective Assessment, 345
Practice Exercises, 349
Discussion Questions, 349
Suggestions for Additional Reading, 349
And For Those who Tire of Reading, 350

USING EDUCATIONAL TESTS

Administering Educational Tests   353

Preparing Effective Test Directions, 355
Administering the Test, 357
Scoring the Tests, 361
Correcting for Guessing, 363
Additional Considerations, 365
Recording Test Results, 365
Test Security, 367
Practice Exercises, 369
Discussion Questions, 369
Suggestions for Additional Reading, 370

Setting Performance Standards   371

General Considerations, 375
Major Factors in Setting Standards, 377
Alternative Standard-Setting Procedures, 384
Appraising the Alternatives, 392
Separate or Aggregate Standards, 394
Practice Exercises, 396
Answers to Practice Exercises, 398
Discussion Questions, 398
Suggestions for Additional Reading, 398

Using the Results of Educational Tests   400

Grading, 400
The Design and Improvement of Instruction, 412
Practice Exercises, 422
Answers to Practice Exercises, 425
Discussion Questions, 426
Suggestions for Additional Reading, 426

Index   429

"Why on earth write another measurement book?" That question, or a more saltily paraphrased version of it, escaped my lips when I was initially approached by a suave Prentice-Hall editor with the idea that I author a textbook on educational testing. After all, my bookshelves were already bursting with textbooks on measurement. Who needed another measurement text? And, besides that, there was a paper shortage.

Relentlessly, however, the cunning editor kept tossing Socratic-like inquiries at me. "Tell me, Jim," he continued, "are you altogether satisfied with the textbooks you're using in the introductory measurement classes you teach?" I had to confess that I wasn't. "And isn't there anything new in the field of educational measurement that's worth writing about?" he inquired. I responded in the affirmative. There was, after all, plenty of new stuff regarding criterion-referenced measurement that wasn't included in the available measurement texts. "And don't you believe," he persisted, "that today's educators really need to know about these modern advances?" He had me hooked. Education editors are a diabolical lot.

Thus, thoroughly conned, I set out to write this introductory text on educational measurement. Its title, *Modern Educational Measurement,* hope-

Preface

fully conveys my intent. I have tried to collect recent advances in the field of educational measurement and fold them ever-so-gently, just like beaten egg whites in a cake recipe, into a traditional measurement context.

I wish to get a personal bias out in the open early on, namely, that I believe strongly in the power and utility of *criterion-referenced* approaches to educational measurement. Since the late '60s I have been a continuing advocate of criterion-referenced measurement strategies, often urging that they be used instead of more traditional measurement schemes *for certain purposes.* I still cherish criterion-referenced tests. I still believe that there are scores of educational decisions which will be better serviced by criterion-referenced tests than by more traditional tests.

But this text is *not* a polemic in favor of these newer tests and opposed to traditional, *norm-referenced* testing approaches. I believe that there are crucial roles which norm-referenced tests can play in the securing of decision-relevant data for educators. There are many time-honored psychometric techniques that are eminently deserving of honors. This text will not short-change those norm-referenced notions, not at all. Instead, an honest attempt has been made to render a balanced approach to educational testing. For certain purposes, norm-referenced tests are espoused. For other purposes, criterion-referenced tests are advocated. In no instance are the distinguishing features of these two testing approaches masked over because of the possibility of offending the proponents of either testing strategy. The time has come, indeed, the time is long overdue, to abandon petty bickering about whether norm- or criterion-referenced assessment strategies are "better." There are obvious and important roles for both testing orientations. I have attempted to point out these applications in this text.

This text, incidentally, makes no pretense of serving audiences for which it was not intended. It is customary at this point in an author's preface to cite the galaxy of audiences that might profit from reading the book. Publishers just love such listings. It makes a book seem ever so much more marketable. And authors usually satisfy their publishers by listing as potential audiences any group of people who might remotely have a need for the text, almost including inhabitants of yet undiscovered planets.

This text, however, was written for a limited market. It was written for educators who want to learn about measurement as it applies to their work. The text is *not* intended to serve simultaneously the needs of psychologists. In spite of the many measurement texts written for "education and psychology," it's really impossible to address effectively the requirements of educators and psychologists *at the same time.* Neither is this a text that treats measurement *and evaluation.* Despite the many textbooks around that purport to deal with both educational measurement and evaluation, none really do a defensible job on the topic of educational evaluation. That's really a subject that needs to be addressed in a separate volume. Since I wrote such an evaluation book, I confess a bit of prejudice on that score. In sum, the book will appeal only to those who wish to learn about what its title indicates, that is, *Modern Educational Measurement.*

The text is designed to promote three major competencies, namely, an educator's skill in (1) *evaluating,* (2) *developing,* and (3) *using educational tests.* Each of these three topics is addressed in one of the text's major sections, that is, Parts II, III, and IV. In Part I an orientation is provided to the *purposeful* use of educational tests.

I am indebted to a number of colleagues and students who waded through early versions of many chapters and, baffled by the obscurities contained therein, offered solid suggestions for improvement. Joan Orme transformed my suggestions into honest-to-giggle cartoons. I am also in-indebted to a first-rate team of stenographic wizards who were able to make occasional sense out of my hand-scrawled, cryptic initial drafts. Any stylistic virtues the volume possesses are due to the editorial liberties that the following folks took when they couldn't figure out what in blazes I wrote: Joan Morley, Barbara Trelease, Beth Rytkonen, and Robert Fugini.

Finally, I am grateful to Robert Sickles, former Education Editor of Prentice-Hall, Inc., who gave me one year's additional grace in my deadline for the book. During the year that I had hoped to get most of the writing done, I found myself serving as President of the American Educational Research Association. While substantially less demanding than being President of General Motors or of the United States, that responsibility did take much more time than I had anticipated. I pleaded with Bob for an extra year, and he acceded. It appears that editors can be kind as well as cunning.

I do hope that the extra year's preparation time allowed me to turn out a text that will be of use to educators who wish to learn about modern measurement.

W.J.P.
Los Angeles

MODERN
EDUCATIONAL
MEASUREMENT

part 1

DECIDING ON THE PURPOSE OF AN EDUCATIONAL TEST

Educational tests are employed for particular purposes. Testing devices, unlike random raindrops, do not descend on the educational scene without a discernable mission. In the first two chapters of this book an attempt is made to emphasize the centrality of *purpose* in working with educational tests. The first chapter considers the purposes to which educational tests are put today and the purposes to which such tests have been put during the past. The second chapter analyzes two major categories of tests, that is, norm-referenced and criterion-referenced measures, in relationship to the educational purposes which those two assessments might best serve.

A persistent and important theme throughout the entire volume is introduced in Part One, namely, that educational tests are no different from any other sorts of tools that human beings employ. Whether it's a crosscut saw, a crescent wrench, or an intelligence test, a tool can be used properly or improperly. A major determinant of whether a tool is used properly is the extent to which the tool matches the purpose for which it is being employed. Effective users of educational tests, therefore, will have to become as clearheaded as possible about the degree to which their measures and their missions actually mesh.

1

Today's educators have a choice when it comes to measurement. Either they become familiar with what's involved in educational measurement, or they don't. However, today's *truly competent* educators have no choice at all in this regard. An educator who fails to become conversant with the current considerations in educational measurement is an educator destined to deal unsatisfactorily with a host of educational problems.

So many of our recent educational issues have been inextricably tied to the use and interpretation of tests that it would be foolhardy for an educator to neglect the field of educational measurement. This text is designed as an introduction to educational measurement, chiefly for those aspirant professionals who intend to become educational specialists of one sort or another. After having read the book with reasonable attentiveness, such fledgling professionals should, for most purposes, be able to amble out into the real educational world and successfully wrestle with educational problems involving measurement. Furthermore, in education, measurement-related problems are myriad.

Perspectives on purposes - past and present

Why Get Involved with Measurement?

Mastering the ins and outs of educational measurement is not fool's play; it's hard work. Why, the reader might reasonably ask, should every educational professional engage in such an arduous effort? After all, this volume contains plenty of pages, and it's going to be tough reading at times. Beyond that, most of the chapters are decisively less thrilling than those describing a James Bond or Sherlock Holmes caper. Quite naturally, a reader might speculate about the ultimate utility of a love affair with educational measurement.

To supply yourself with a smidge of internally generated motivation for the task at hand, try this little experiment. Tick off a list of a dozen or so major problems that today's educators must tussle with, then decide how many of those problems hinge, focally or peripherally, on matters of measurement. It would be most surprising if half your listed problems didn't depend, in a major or minor way, on educational testing. In today's educational milieu just about 50 percent of the problems we encounter do, in fact, involve test use, test construction, or test interpretation. Consequently, just about any kind of specialist who, lacking knowledge about measurement, goes out to do battle with today's educational problems is almost certain to come back a loser. For the present and foreseeable future, educators who wish to be effective in their work simply must master the major tenets of educational measurement. This text is specifically designed to promote tenet mastering.

What About the Measurement Wizards?

Not every physician need be a dermatologist or a neurologist. After all, one finds specialists in all fields—in medicine as well as education. This being the case, doesn't it seem more appropriate for most educators to steer clear of testing and its terrors, leaving such matters to those bizarre folks who get their kicks from assessing people?

Well, just as in medicine, there are surely specialties in education. Moreover, just as in medicine, each of these educational specializations has its own idiosyncratic sack of truths, its own jargon, and its own identity. But just as in medicine, almost all of these specializations in education are dependent on the *unique* application of *common* techniques. In medicine we find a variety of specializations employing basic diagnostic and prescription strategies, laboratory analytic methods, and the like. Similarly, in education we find that almost all major specializations have occasions where they must rely on routine *measurement* practices.

Of course, these measurement practices will often need to be adapted. Individuals who work in special education, that is, those who deal with atypical learner populations, must modify traditional measurement techniques. Counselors and school psychologists will find greater need than will classroom teachers for individual diagnostic devices that yield clinically relevant data. Classroom teachers will need tests that help them in their day-to-day struggles with the dark and venomous forces of ignorance, disinterest, and despair. Oh yes, in educational measurement as in all aspects of life, for different folks we must employ strokes of a decisively nonuniform nature.

But even educational philosophers and historians, ignorant of measurement fundamentals, would be obliged to place themselves at the mercy of educational measurement specialists—as would all educational professionals. Yet, such situations should not be.

Although educational measurement wizards rove the land, these people should be called on only when special, aberrant measurement problems arise. Such special measurement problems quite naturally should fall to educational specialists. To face routine decisions involving measurement, educators need to become comfortable with such fundamental concepts as reliability, validity, test bias, and norms. Most importantly, educators need to understand that for differing educational purposes, one must employ different educational tests. We shall deal with this point in greater detail a bit later. For the moment let's consider why it is that so much recent attention has been showered on educational measurement issues.

Must Everything Be Tested?

We live in an era when everybody adores *evidence*. We want evidence that patent sleeping pills do indeed send us off to the Land of Nod. We want evidence that food additives are not carcinogenic. We want evidence that our space program is worth the money we spend on it. Moreover, most relevant to an educator, we want evidence that the nation's schools are effective.

Citizens are no longer merely requesting such evidence; they are demanding it. With respect to public schooling, this demand for evidence of effectiveness is most typically translated into a demand for satisfactory student test performance. During the past decade or so we have seen the increasing enactment of federal and state legislative decrees demanding that educators deliver tangible evidence their educational programs are worth what they are costing taxpayers.

The spirit of *educational accountability,* born in the late sixties, lingers today. Though perhaps less virulent than in those days, there are still informal and formal pressures to hold educators accountable for their efforts.

The public has, with proper cause, become incredulous regarding the effectiveness of educational enterprises. Plummeting test scores and accusations of student incompetence abound. No longer are citizens assuaged by a school superintendent's glib assurances that "Our educational program is one of the finest in the nation!" No, the public wants less rhetoric and more evidence. Invariably, that evidence turns out to be test scores of one type or another.

No more startling evidence of citizen disenchantment with public education need be found than the massive number of states which in the late 1970s enacted laws and regulations obliging high school students to *demonstrate* minimum competencies in the basic skills prior to receiving a high school diploma. In almost all cases, these mandated demonstrations took the form of test performance. In this instance, as in many others, citizens were registering incredulity regarding educational quality. They wanted proof.

In many other sectors of our day-to-day endeavors, the quest for evidence of effectiveness is at hand. In many health professions, for example, we see increasing pressures for *competency assurance,* namely, the display of evidence that a professional is indeed competent to render health services to the public. Indeed, the licensing and relicensing of many health professionals may soon be dependent on measured displays of competency.

There is little doubt that we are living smack in the middle of an evidence-oriented era. That evidence orientation, having intruded most dramatically on the educational enterprise, should force educators to consider a fundamental truth. *In an evidence-oriented enterprise, those who control the evidence-gathering mechanisms control the entire enterprise.* Since, in education, tests constitute our chief evidence-gathering mechanisms, it is apparent that all educators should become knowledgeable regarding the fundamentals of educational measurement. They should at least learn enough about the conduct of educational measurement so that they will not permit only the measurement specialists to devise responses to contemporary pressures for educational evidence. All educators need to get into that act.

PROMINENT APPLICATIONS OF EDUCATIONAL TESTS

Looking around the educational landscape will reveal a highly assorted application of educational tests. We have the traditional in-the-classroom tests, such as Miss Jones's midterm exam on Mr. Hill's weekly quizzes, that most of us spent a dozen or more years enduring. We also have the traditional aptitude tests, such as the *Graduate Record Examination* or the *Scholastic Aptitude Test,* that anyone aspiring to higher educational levels has had to hurdle. Oh yes, most of us have become pretty well innured to the frequent intrusion of testing on our educational lives.

However, there are some applications of educational tests which have toddled onto the educational scene only recently. Since one adjective in the title of this text is, after all, *modern,* it seems only fitting to spend a few paragraphs in consideration of these more recent uses of tests.

Individual Assessment

Over the decades the most frequent applications of educational tests have been to assess individual students in order to make instructional and/or counseling decisions about those students. This form of individual assessment still predominates in education, where if we could magically get a count on how many tests were used for what kinds of purposes, the odds-on winner would be using tests to decide upon youngsters' class grades or their advancement to the next grade.

Dominantly, of course, this type of educational measurement activity is based on the use of teacher-made tests, such as Mr. Jergen's end-of-unit exams in his fifth-grade class, Ms. Bell's semester examination in her high school chemistry class, and Mrs. Pringle's surprise quizzes in her twelfth-grade "Mathematics for Muttonheads" class.

All of these teacher-made tests, although they may be administered simultaneously to an entire classroom full of students, are employed to make individual decisions about individual pupils. Teachers characteristically score such exams, decide upon grades for the students, record those grades in some kind of record book, and return the exams to the students. It is a familiar ritual, and as students we went through such testing operations uncountable times. At the end of the school year or semester, teachers usually tally up each student's collection of isolated exam results, coalesce them somehow, then issue that one big end-of-course grade that finds its way into the pupil's permanent record folder.

Although employed far less frequently, there are also many tests used for individual student assessment by counselors and school psychologists. These educators usually focus their attention less on a student's in-class achievements and more on a student's intellectual aptitude, interests, and personality. Tests used for such purposes are, of course, still employed to help make decisions about individual learners. In some instances such tests are used to allow individual learners to make decisions about themselves, for example, in choosing a career goal or a curriculum emphasis.

It is apparent that educational tests not only have been used dominantly for individual assessment, but that for some time to come they will continue to be used in that manner.

Program Evaluation

When the Elementary and Secondary Education Act of 1965 (ESEA) was passed by Congress, we witnessed the first truly large-scale federal subsidies for public education. Because many congressional legislators were dubious about the wisdom of such federal expenditures, stipulations were included in the law which forced local educators to *evaluate* one year's ESEA program if they wished to get next year's federal dole.

Almost overnight educational evaluation was born. Perhaps one could argue that ESEA's evaluation requirements simply surfaced latent evaluation tendencies that had existed in education for decades. After all, a number of educational writers had previously extolled the virtues of educational evaluation. However, in spite of occasional advocacy, few American educators had really attempted to evaluate their instructional programs with any rigor until ESEA's financial incentives goaded them to do so. A financial carrot, as we have seen time and again, is a powerful motivator.

In the late sixties and early seventies, therefore, American educators became almost preoccupied with educational evaluation.[1] Most of that attention was devoted to *program evaluation,* that is, a formal attempt to assess the merits of a specific instructional program, such as the innovative instructional schemes funded under ESEA's Title III.

Almost without exception, these program evaluations focused on the test performance of students. Indeed, because so many American educators had been thrust into the role of educational evaluator without adequate preparation for that thrusting, some educators naively equated measurement with evaluation. To test, they assumed, was to evaluate. In order to evaluate, such beginners believed that all one had to do was test kids before a program, test them after the program, and report the results.

Although there's a good deal more to educational evaluation than administering a test or two, it is true that measurement of pupil performance plays a crucial role in most educational evaluations. Moreover, unlike the traditional educational testing which focused so heavily on individual assessment, the use of tests in program evaluation typically results in the aggregation of *grouped* test results, not individual student-by-student results. Thus, for example, educational evaluators try to report the *average* results of a group of students who have been taught by means of a particular instructional approach. In some cases the tests may be identical to those employed for purposes of individual assessment. However, the decision to retain or eliminate a given instructional program is typically made in such a way as to influence an entire group of students. Accordingly, the test results are typically summarized for the total group.

Educational evaluation as a specialization has grown substantially since its ESEA-spurred beginnings in the mid-sixties. Now, because so many educators have become habituated to expecting educational evaluations to accompany not only the introduction of new programs but also the continuing appraisal of existing programs, we shall surely see a continuing emphasis on evaluation in education for many years. We can also expect that educational testing will continue to play a pivotal role in the conduct of educational evaluations.

Catalysts for Instructional Improvement

For well over a half a century, almost everybody involved in educational measurement believed it was the job of educational measurers to determine

---

[1]For a year or two your congenial author became almost preoccupied with writing a text about the same topic; see W. James Popham, *Educational Evaluation* (Englewood Cliffs, N.J.: Prentice-Hall, Inc., 1975).

students' status with respect to each other or to particular skills and knowledge. Until recently, this *status-determination orientation* to educational measurement has totally dominated the educational measurement scene. Measurement specialists believed it was their job to isolate what an individual pupil (or, because of program evaluation requirements, a group of pupils) could do. The student's status having been determined, measurement folks turned their test results over to someone else, such as curriculum and instruction specialists, whose task it was to help pupils learn. However, that view, ever so incrementally, is beginning to fall into disrepute.

Because of the integral link between today's instruction and the measurement of its effects, more and more teachers and other instructional personnel are recognizing that their efforts will ultimately be appraised in relationship to pupils' test performance. Furthermore, they are becoming aware that there are certain kinds of tests which can abet the *design* of effective instruction more than other kinds of tests can. An increasing number of educational measurement specialists are moving toward an *instructional-improvement orientation* in their work.

Tests that are constructed chiefly as status-determination devices may or may not prove helpful to instructional designers. It is possible, however, to construct tests so that they not only permit more effective instructional design, they actually *promote* improved instructional design. As we shall see, the chief factor in such tests is the clarity with which they describe the attributes being measured. Teachers who are designing lessons on the basis of clarified expectations regarding tests have an eminently better chance to put together on-target lessons than teachers who are aiming toward amorphously described measures.

The implications of attempting to employ tests as catalysts for instructional improvement are clear. No longer should educational measurement wizards insulate themselves from principles of curricular and instructional design. No longer should tests be put together with a view to finding out merely what a student's status is. Measurement specialists and instructional specialists must join forces in creating tests that stir up the instructional stew so that it tastes much better.

Although there is considerable controversy about the extent to which our schools are carrying out their tasks effectively, it seems likely that instructional improvements will always be needed. That being the case, this recently perceived mission of educational measurement as a stimulus to instructional improvement will doubtlessly receive considerable attention in years to come.

THE PURPOSES OF TESTING

From the foregoing discussion, it should be clear that educational tests can serve numerous functions. Now be alert, for here comes one of Chapter 1's blockbuster truths: *Different educational purposes require differing educational tests and differing uses of those tests.*

There are too many educators who unwarrantedly assume that "a test is a test is a test." Even though this phrase possesses enticing poetic and metaphysical qualities, it is also in error. To employ a test for instructional improvement that was created to sort out youngsters for other assessment purposes can be a serious mistake. Similarly, to use a test designed for instructional improvement to try to evaluate a program's instructional effectiveness may turn out to be a major blunder.

Even if educators are adroit in their efforts to mesh particular tests with particular purposes, there will still be some mistaken inferences drawn from the application of educational tests. When tests are *not* matched to purposes, those mistaken inferences multiply exponentially. Thus, anyone who is truly conversant with educational measurement should become familiar, not only with the differing purposes to which educational tests can be put, but also with the differing kinds of tests that are available for such purposes. Most importantly, beyond merely *knowing* that different purposes require different sorts of tests, an astute educational measurer will *act* on that knowledge by continually attending to the specific purposes called for in the situation at hand.

In fact, as a constant and routine initial operation, educational measurement specialists should ferret out the purpose of the testing that's going on. Having done so, it's then necessary to see that the proper tests are used *for that purpose* and that the proper interpretations of test performance are made *for that purpose.*

PRIOR PURPOSES OF TESTING: A CAPSULE HISTORY OF EDUCATIONAL MEASUREMENT

One of the best ways to understand the diversity of purposes that today's educational tests are expected to serve is to consider the prior purposes that such tests were asked to accomplish. The astute reader will discern that the previous sentence subtly sets the stage for a close-up peek at educational measurement history. Now why, the reader might ask, are we going to be put through this consideration of historical measurement milestones? Surely there is more important stuff going on today.

It's no doubt true that some authors perceive an almost moral commitment to toss in a section on the history of the textbook's subject. However, that's not the reason that a discussion of measurement history is being offered here. Frankly there are too many educators who see the whole field of measurement as a body of sacrosanct, quantitative truths beyond question and usually beyond comprehension. Well, that just isn't true. Educational measurement techniques were not carved out by deities on some psychometric Olympus. On the contrary, those techniques were devised by terribly mortal men and women who, though brighter than your run-of-the-mill chowderhead, were much like you and your more able colleagues.

Some of the schemes devised through the decades by these measurement folks turned out to be such turkeys that, having been introduced, they disappeared after a few years—or a few hours. Other schemes worked, and those are the ones that you'll be reading about in later pages. However, please disabuse yourself of any ideas that these past measurement specialists were annointed prophets. They were simply creative people who were vexed by the same kinds of practical problems that we face today in education. They simply figured out some clever ways to solve those problems.

Going Back

Testing has been around for centuries, for longer than most people today realize. In biblical times Jephthah used the term *Shibboleth* as a test word by which to distinguish the fleeing Ephraimites (who couldn't pronounce the *sh*) from his own Gileadites. We are told that those who failed to pass Jephthah's test had their heads lopped off. Alternatively, phrasing it in suitably awesome educational parlance: In relationship to their pretest status, the posttest status of deficit Ephraimite examinees was significantly less cerebral.

Chinese civil service examinations. However, formal testing had its origins well before Ephraimites were displaying pronunciation inadequacies. The historian Dubois informs us that as far back as 2200 B.C. Chinese emperors examined their key officials every three years to verify their fitness for office.[2] In fact, for more than 3,000 years the Chinese, who unlike European nations had no hereditary ruling class, employed a sophisticated system of competitive examinations to select personnel for government positions. After three of these every-three-year exams, officials were either dismissed or promoted.

Records indicate that by 1115 B.C. applicants for governmental jobs were assessed to detect their competency in each of the *six arts*, that is, writing, arithmetic, music, archery, horsemanship, and the ceremonial rites of private and public life. Later, during the Han dynasty, 202 B.C. to A.D. 200, written examinations were based on the *five studies*, namely, agriculture, civil law, military affairs, revenue, and geography of the empire.

The Chinese civil service examination system continued to undergo

---

[2]For a fascinating account of educational and psychological testing through the ages, see Philip H. Dubois, *A History of Psychological Testing* (Boston, Mass.: Allyn and Bacon, 1970).

many modifications through the centuries, more or less settling down around the year A.D. 1300. At that point an individual seeking a high government office was obliged to pass three highly competitive examinations. The first of these, administered annually in the chief city of the district in which the candidate resided, required candidates to spend a day and a night in a tiny, isolated booth. Candidates were obliged to write a poem plus one or two essays on assigned topics. Assignments emphasized the candidate's ability to recall and interpret Confucian classics. The candidate's efforts, judged according to penmanship and diction, resulted in a failure rate of between 93 and 97 percent.

Every three years candidates who passed the district examinations gathered in the provincial capitals where for three sessions, each consisting of three days and three nights, compositions in verse and prose were required. For provincial-level exams no credit was given for penmanship since a special bureau of examination copyists, established around A.D. 1000, copied all papers in another hand prior to the examinations being

FIGURE 1–1 *Hundreds of Individual Civil Service Examination Rooms at Nanking, China.* © 1927, National Geographic Society. (Photographed by Maynard Owen Williams about twenty years after testing stopped in 1905.)

"Is it true that the first recorded instance of student cheating on a test involved the use of 3 chopsticks?"

read independently by two graders. A third grader received and reconciled the grades from the first two graders. The failure rate for the provincial examinations ranged between 90 and 99 percent.

Finally, for those candidates surviving the provincial tests, similar examinations were held the following spring in the imperial capital, Peking. For these examinations the failure rate was 97 percent or higher. Those passing the examinations became mandarins and were thus eligible for public office.

A detailed but delightful account of the Chinese civil service examinations, published in 1976, is *China's Examination Hell*.[3] In that treatise the author provides a vivid picture of what it must have been like for the nervous young Chinese candidates who, after a cannon was fired three times, were admitted to an agonizing examination experience. When today's critics of testing contend that some tests are too long, they might take

[3]I. Miyazaki, *China's Examination Hell,* trans. Conrad Schirokauer (New York: Weatherhill, 1976). (It should be noted that because this book about China's exams was written by a Japanese scholar and translated into English by someone with a Germanic background, its syntax is delightfully unpredictable.)

solace from a consideration of the Chinese system, in which an uninter-
rupted 72-hour bout with an examination was customary.

As the Chinese civil service examinations flourished, certain elements
of those examinations became more and more ritualistic. For example, by
the time a successful candidate had passed the preliminary exams and
reached the prestigious Palace examinations, a set form was to be written by
each candidate at the close of the examination: "I, your humble servant, a
superficial scholar newly advanced, not realizing where I was, have ven-
tured to state my own views and am so ashamed of offending the Majesty of
the Emperor that I do not know where to hide. I respectfully submit my
answer."[4] Although this version of abject student humility may seem appealing to certain teachers, we will probably have to wait a thousand years or
so before such language starts popping up at the close of our students'
exams.

The Chinese civil service examinations retained their three-tiered,
district-province-capital structure until 1905 when they were officially
abolished. In the 3,000 years during which the Chinese civil service examination flourished, there were no universities or public school systems in
China. The system, stressing classical scholarship, nevertheless, made it
possible for one's demonstrated competence to lead to public responsibility
and honor. The examination system was a major element in Chinese life.

During the sixteenth century, as European contacts with China developed, the Chinese system of competitive written examinations as a vehicle for entering public service was noted and admired by several scholars,
including Voltaire, who advocated such a system for France. Early in the
nineteenth century the newly established British open civil service examination system was influenced by diplomats and missionaries familiar with
the Chinese examination enterprise.

It would seem difficult for today's educators to remain unmoved
upon contemplating the ancient Chinese examination system. There were
the Chinese, centuries before Socrates, wrestling with the same kinds of
problems that sometimes cause today's educators to stumble. One is struck
with numerous similarities to present-day testing practices, including the
use of two independent readers and a third reader who settles differences
of opinions.

The idea of locking up students in isolated examination booths all day
and all night might seem particularly appealing to today's teachers for
whom students' cheating on examinations poses a problem. To cut down
on the pupil-teacher ratio, of course, selected students could be kept locked
up for an entire semester or two.

This account of the Chinese testing exploits was intended to reveal the

[4]Ibid, p. 79.

parallels in the measurement problems faced, for example, by officials of Hunan Province in A.D. 1400 and officials of the State of Michigan in the 1980s. The Hunan officials, like their ancestors hundreds of years before, did the best job they could in devising fair tests and testing procedures. The Michigan officials, like their Chinese counterparts, will do the best job they can in devising fair tests and testing procedures. If they make mistakes, then just as their Chinese predecessors did, they'll revise their testing procedures and try again.

U.S. Civil Service examinations.   Noting the successful experience of the British Civil Service Commission which was established in the 1850s, several prominent United States legislators attempted to create comparable testing operations on this side of the Atlantic in the 1860s. Senator Charles Sumner of Massachusetts and Representative Thomas Jenckes of Rhode Island introduced bills to establish a civil service examining commission, and in 1868 Jenckes submitted to Congress a 220-page report about the possibilities of civil service examinations in the United States. The report included detailed descriptions of civil service examining procedures employed in China, Prussia, and France.

In 1871 a Civil Service Board was established by President U. S. Grant as a rider to an appropriations bill. Although the board went out of existence four years later in 1875, a permanent Civil Service Commission was subsequently created in January 1883. Typical of the examination items created by the 1871 board and the 1883 commission is the following three-item excerpt from a twenty-item civil service examination for examiners of trademarks, U.S. Patent Office used in early 1873:

1. What is a trademark, and to what is it applicable?
2. Who may obtain one?
3. What is the geographical extent of a trademark?

A wide range of such examinations was developed for dozens of occupations from postal clerk to maritime meteorological expert. In addition to the examinee's answers to questions similar to the preceding, other factors used in determining competence were (1) biographical information supplied by the candidate's application form and (2) on-the-job performance during a six-month's probationary period.

University examinations.   We have no records to indicate that any formal examinations existed in Greek and Roman schools or in the cathedral and monastery schools of medieval Europe. However, during the later Middle Ages oral examinations became popular in European universities. Among the earliest of these were the law examinations at the University of

Bologna which commenced in 1219. Formal oral exams were also described by the chaplain of Louis IX, Robert de Sorbon, who founded in 1827 the community of scholars that evolved into the Sorbonne.

Louvain University employed a widely acclaimed competitive examination system in the mid-1400s. In the Louvain scheme candidates were ranked in four classes: *rigorosi* (honors), *transibiles* (satisfactory), *gratiosi* (charity passes), and failures. Many of today's teachers surely believe they are moving along some of their less able students on a *gratiosi* basis.

The Jesuit order, established by St. Ignatius of Loyola in 1540, made extensive use of written examinations for placement and evaluation of students. In 1599 the *Ratio Studiorum*, a set of prescriptions for educational procedures, including the conduct of examinations, was published. Some of the guidelines set forth in that sixteenth-century document seem eminently pertinent today. For example, here is one of the test administration rules from the *Ratio Studiorum:*

> All should be present in the classroom in good time to receive the assignment and instructions, given either by the prefect himself or his substitute, and they must finish the assignment before the end of school. After silence has been enjoined, no one may speak to another, not even to the prefect or his substitute.[5]

In England oral examinations for the B.A. and M.A. degrees were introduced at Oxford in 1636. Written examinations were used at Oxford as early as 1803, having been introduced at Cambridge some years earlier. Written examinations, as used in English universities, were generally considered to be successful and a legitimate basis for making significant decisions about candidates for degrees.

Rice, Thorndike, and the origins of standardized testing.

An influential pioneer in the U.S. testing movement was Joseph Mayer Rice who in the late 1880s abandoned his medical practice to study methods of augmenting the efficiency of schooling. After studying psychology and pedagogy, he carried out the first major comparative studies of U.S. school children's academic accomplishments. In 1897 Rice reported the results of some 33,000 pupils' efforts on a standardized test of spelling. In 1902 he tested 6,000 children with an arithmetic examination, and in 1903 Rice tested over 8,000 pupils with a language examination.

By administering his tests to substantial samples of school children and establishing the average scores to be expected at different grade levels, Rice's work contributed heavily to early thinking about the use of standardized tests in education.

[5]W. J. McGucken, *The Jesuits and Education* (Milwaukee: Bruce, 1932).

Rice's efforts greatly influenced the work of E. L. Thorndike whose insights and creativity helped establish Teachers College, Columbia University as the early twentieth-century center for the creation of new educational achievement measures. Thorndike and his students not only refined some of Rice's approaches to measurement, they also evolved a host of important technical advances. Many of the standardized achievements tests developed in the early 1900s were created by Thorndike-trained measurement specialists.

Binet's intelligence scales.   A giant in the history of educational measurement was Alfred Binet, a French physiological psychologist, who in 1905 created the first successful intelligence scale. His work with young children, featuring the creation of isolated testing procedures as early as 1890, ultimately resulted in the 1905 scale which coalesced thirty of these separate testing approaches into a cohesive, individually administrable intelligence test. The subtests used in the 1905 Binet intelligence scale were varied in the content they covered, obliged the examinee and the examiner to remain in contact, and focused on tapping the examinee's judgment. Many of the items employed in the 1905 scale were used in subsequent revisions of the Binet, some in revisions of the Stanford-Binet as recently as the 1960s.

The success of Binet's assessment strategies was to prove enormously influential on a number of later American measurement specialists and, as a consequence, on American education itself.

The impact of World War I on group testing.   Given the widely acclaimed success of Binet and his colleagues in devising effective intelligence tests administerable to individuals, it did not take too long until American psychologists began flirting with intelligence tests which were administerable simultaneously to groups of examinees.

Interestingly enough, it was World War I that spurred interest in group intelligence tests. Even prior to the United States' entry into the war in 1917, Arthur S. Otis had developed a group intelligence test that could be scored objectively. The Otis test became a prototype for the U.S. *Army Alpha,* the assessment instrument first employed in large-scale testing.

In order for the United States to effectively staff its military operation, an efficient procedure had to be developed which would facilitate the identification of likely officer candidates. Robert M. Yerkes, then president of the American Psychological Association, assembled a committee on the psychological examination of recruits in May 1917. This committee of seven psychologists met at the Vineland Training School and in seven working days, drawing on the prior efforts of Binet, Otis, and others, created ten forms of a group intelligence test—each consisting of ten different subtests. After several revisions, based on tryouts with fairly small samples of examinees, this test became the famous *Army Alpha*. Examples of the eight subtests included in the *Army Alpha* were Following Oral Directions, Analogues, Arithmetic Reasoning, and Synonym-Antonym.

In all, over 1.7 million men were examined during the World-War-I Army testing program under the direction of Yerkes. Of these, more than 1.25 million were tested with one of the five forms of the *Army Alpha*. The testing program was rather sophisticated for its time, with considerable attention being given to technical measurement considerations. Highly quantitative analyses were used extensively, and the technical merits of such tests as the *Alpha* and its nonverbal counterpart, the *Army Beta*, were carefully studied.

The success of the Army testing program was unprecedented. The *Alpha*, which featured the first widespread use of multiple-choice test items, stimulated an explosive growth in the number of educational tests that were produced in subsequent years. Whereas only a handful of copyrighted standardized tests existed prior to World War I, after that time the Copyright Office was besieged by creators of standardized tests. Just about anyone who could crank out multiple-choice items and tie them together, or so it appeared, began publishing group aptitude or achievement tests. America's educational testing movement was underway.

Regular problems, regular people.   Clearly, in our rapid-fire journey through measurement history, a galaxy of stalwart contributors have been neglected. Those individuals who were discussed rank among the most prominent contributors, but there were many more. It is important, from the reader's perspective, to recognize that the types of problems these people were tangling with are remarkably similar to the types of problems that today's educators face. Many of the measurement strategies provided by our predecessors were flagrantly faulty and have long since sunk into the psychometric seas. The surviving measurement schemes constitute our current educational measurement technology.

It is not a sacred technology, created without the possibility of modification. Instead, it is a convention-laden, malleable set of tools and rules that are still subject to alteration and improvement.

RELATED ISSUES

Compatibility of functions.   In looking back over the history of educational measurement, we saw that many insightful and inventive individuals tossed in their two cents as America created its educational measurement currency. For most of these individuals, however, their mission was primar-

FIGURE 1–2 *Recruits Taking Examination at Camp Lee, 1917.* (U.S. Signal Corps photo number 11–SC386 in the National Archives.)

ily *status-determination.* Putting it another way, their chief goal was to detect the current functioning of individual examinees, in particular with respect to other examinees. This function of measurement is most pronounced in connection with the historical *individual-assessment* efforts of measurement people. However, it is possible that to a considerable extent the *program evaluation* and *instructional-improvement* missions of educational measurement are not well served by tests created to assess individuals. There is currently considerable disagreement as to the extent to which those three missions are compatible. Many of today's substantive disagreements over educational measurement stem from differing perceptions of the role of educational measurement.

> ***Governmental expansion of measurement's technology.*** Another observation that you might have made as we wandered down the psychometric trail was that with the exception of World War I (and later, although it wasn't described, in World War II), educational measurement advances

have occurred largely without governmental support. There are many educators who think this is as it should be. Private enterprise, they are convinced, will ultimately result in the creation of an adequate technical base for educational measurement.

Other educators, however, contend that given the critical role measurement is playing in our nation's educational enterprises, federal and state governments have a responsibility to provide financial subventions specifically to foster the emergence of a more sophisticated, hence more useful, educational measurement technology. Only recently, for example, has the federal government shown any serious interest in subsidizing empirical and analytical research dealing with the expansion of educational measurement's technical base. Resolution of this issue will play a pivotal role in determining the nation's educational measurement capabilities.

PRACTICE EXERCISES

Since the initial chapter was chiefly historical and orientational, few tidy constructs present themselves for self-test purposes. One exception, however, was the distinction drawn between two perceptions of testing, namely, testing as *status determination* and testing as a vehicle for *instructional improvement.* Consider the following five vignettes of educators in action, then decide in each instance whether measurement is being primarily used in a manner consonant with a *status-determination orientation* or an *instructional-improvement orientation.*

The correct answers, as will be the case with all practice exercises, follow the exercises immediately. Be sure to make your response to each practice exercise before looking at the correct answer.

1. A new academically oriented high school was recently opened in Detroit, Michigan. Enrollment in Renaissance High School was initially limited to two hundred students per grade level. Because more than five times that number of students wanted to enroll in the new school, officials obliged all applicants to complete a comprehensive aptitude test battery. Decisions regarding which students to accept were made, in large measure, on the basis of these test results. (Which of the two orientations is operative here?)

2. An Oregon school district has devised a graduation competency program which calls for students to pass a test measuring fifteen well-described competencies prior to graduation. Throughout the high school program, starting in grade nine, teachers are supplied with multiple copies of diagnostic tests and practice exercises for use in the classroom. Each of these measures consists of test items similar to those used in the district's annual competency tests. Each year for grades nine through twelve, the competency test is given in May. A competency-by-competency profile of each

student's performance is provided for all teachers. (Which of the two orientations is reflected here?)

3. Mrs. Rogers always "whips up" a brand new end-of-course exam for her biology classes the day before the course concludes. She contends that this gives her the "best insights on what the little organisms have learned." (Which orientation is Mrs. Rogers using?)

4. Members of a law school faculty have built an end-of-program screening exam designed to help students discover whether they are ready for the state-administered bar examination. For each skill isolated in the end-of-program exam, practice quizzes are made available for use by faculty and/or students who often prepare for their courses or study groups. (Which orientation is operative here?)

5. The university's graduate school uses student scores on the *Miller Analogies Test* (a verbal aptitude measure) as a factor in deciding which students will be admitted to graduate school. (Which orientation dominates here?)

ANSWERS TO PRACTICE EXERCISES

1. In this vignette the primary purpose of the testing is to find out what skills students currently possess, hence the orientation reflective here is that of status determination.

2. This Oregon school district appears to be using its competency tests in a manner designed to promote student mastery of the competencies. An instructional-improvement orientation is dominant here.

3. Because her last-minute exam can hardly supply much guidance for instructional design, it appears that she is employing a status-determination orientation.

4. In this vignette we see how the two orientations can often overlap. Although the end-of-program exam appears to serve a status-determination purpose, the practice quizzes derived from it are intended for instructional improvement. Overall, then, in this situation, the instructional-improvement orientation is somewhat more dominant.

5. This is a traditional use of aptitude tests, and it reflects without question a status-determination orientation.

DISCUSSION QUESTIONS

1. Can a test which was created for one purpose be used for another purpose? If so, can you supply an illustration?

2. Why was the measurement activity associated with World War I so influential on educational testing in the U.S.?

3. Do you have any friends or colleagues who typify either the status-determination or instructional-improvement orientations? If so, what attributes do they seem to possess?

4. What role, if any, should the federal government take in enhancing the quality of educational measurement technology?

SUGGESTIONS FOR ADDITIONAL READING

CHASE, CLINTON I., "How We Got Where We Are," Chapter 2, *Measurement for Educational Evaluation* (2nd ed.), pp. 18–29. Reading, Mass.: Addison-Wesley, 1978. This is a brief, readable history of educational assessment including a consideration of intelligence testing, achievement testing, and personality testing.

DUBOIS, PHILLIP H., *A History of Psychological Testing.* Boston: Allyn and Bacon, 1970. The author has written a thoroughly readable description of psychological testing which bears on the concerns of educational measurement personnel. Although some of the topics are more focally relevant to psychologists than educators, the bulk of the material is directly pertinent to the field of educational measurement. Highly personalized in its orientation, the treatment features sketches of the chief figures in educational and psychological measurement. A book which must be read by those who would become conversant with the origins of educational measurement.

EBEL, ROBERT L., "Educational Measurement: Current Developments," Chapter 1, *Essentials of Educational Measurement* (3rd ed.), pp. 1–17. Englewood Cliffs, N.J.: Prentice-Hall, Inc., 1979. This is an up-to-date analysis of recent developments in the field of educational measurement. Ebel deals with such issues as mandated assessment, criticisms of test and testing, and the problem of test bias. It serves as a highly readable introduction to an eminent authority's views of important concerns in educational measurement.

KARMEL, LOUIS J., and MARYLIN O. KARMEL, *Measurement and Evaluation in the Schools* (2nd ed.). New York: Macmillan, 1978. This offers an exploration of the various purposes for which educators give tests. The authors offer a consideration of the pros and cons of using standardized tests.

MEHRENS, WILLIAM A., and IRVIN J. LEHMANN, "Public Concerns about Future Trends in Evaluation," Chapter 19, *Measurement and Evaluation in Education and Psychology* (2nd ed.), pp. 667–687. New York: Holt, Rinehart & Winston, 1975. This concluding chapter in a recent revision of a measurement text deals with a number of current purposes to which tests are put. The use and misuse of test scores are explored, as well as a series of issues, such as state legislation on testing and the competence of consumers of educational test results.

MIYAZAKI, ICHISAD, *China's Examination Hell,* trans. by Conrad Schirokauer. New York: Weatherhill, 1976. This study is authored by a prominent historian of Chinese civil service examination systems. The examination system was a key ingredient in China's bureaucratic apparatus for almost 1,400 years in its final elaborated phase. All aspects of the examinations are explored, including the types of questions, the style and form in which they were to be answered, the problems of cheating, and the psychological impact on the examinees.

STANLEY, JULIAN C., and KENNETH D. HOPKINS, "A Brief History of Educational Measurement," Chapter 7, *Educational and Psychological Measurement and Evaluation* (5th ed.), pp. 155–169. Englewood Cliffs, N.J.: Prentice-Hall, Inc., 1972. A succinct treatment of educational measurement in American education is related to more current educational measurement operations, such as the National Merit Scholarship Program and the National Assessment of Educational Progress.

AND FOR THOSE WHO TIRE OF READING

The American Educational Research Association (AERA), 1230-17th Street, N.W., Washington, D.C. 20036, offers tape recordings of sessions from the AERA annual meetings. For a complete and up-to-date listing, write to AERA. Here are some illustrations of recent taped sessions from the 1979 annual meeting:

A Criterion-Referenced Approach to the Measurement of Reading Comprehension. Winsor A. Lott, New York State Education Department; Stephen H. Ivens, The College Board; Bertram L. Koslin, Touchstone Applied Science Associates; Carolyn A. Byrne, New York State Education Department; Thomas P. Fitzgerald, New York State Education Department; E. R. Rothkopf, Bell Labs.

Intelligence Tests in the Year 2000: What Forms Will They Take and What Purposes Will They Serve? Douglas K. Detterman, Case Western Reserve University; Ulric Neisser, Cornell University; John Horn, University of Denver; Lauren Resnick, University of Pittsburgh; Ann Brown, Lucia French, University of Illinois; William Turnbull, Educational Testing Service; Robert J. Sternberg, Yale University.

The Consequences of Standardized Testing: Results of a Four-Year Experiment. Roger Lennon, Psychological Corporation; Thomas Kellaghan, St. Patrick's College, Dublin, Ireland; Peter Airasian, Boston College; George F. Madaus, Boston College; Benjamin Bloom, University of Chicago; Walter Haney, National Consortium on Testing.

2

For well over a decade educators have been hearing about a supposedly new approach to testing, namely, *criterion-referenced measurement.* Criterion-referenced tests are, of course, relatively recent additions to our measurement tool kit. Until archaeologists unearth some evidence indicating that the ancient Chinese had stumbled across criterion-referenced testing a few thousand years ago, we're going to assume that with few exceptions (such as Jephthah's Shibboleth test) criterion-referenced testing is a Johnny- or Joanie-come-lately on the measurement scene.

Criterion-referenced tests are so designated in order to distinguish them from the more traditional educational tests, which people now usually refer to as *norm-referenced* tests. Although there are a few allusions to such nontraditional tests in earlier times, credit for drawing our attention to this distinction goes to Robert Glaser. In 1963, Glaser authored a brief but provocative essay on testing entitled "Instructional Technology and the Measurement of Learning Outcomes." Stemming from his concerns regarding the impact of more effective instructional techniques on traditional measurement tactics, Glaser introduced the concepts of norm-referenced and criterion-referenced measurement.[1]

Norm-referenced and criterion-referenced measurement

Although a period of several years' dormancy followed, in the early seventies educational interest in criterion-referenced measurement almost

[1]Although Glaser used the expression *criterion-referenced measurement* for the first time in a chapter coauthored one year earlier with David Klaus, it was his 1963 article that caught the attention of the educational community. The earlier coauthored piece was Robert Glaser and David J. Klaus, "Proficiency Measurements: Assessing Human Performance," in *Psychological Principles in Systems Development,* ed. Robert M. Gagne (New York: Holt, Rinehart & Winston, 1962), pp. 419–474. The 1963 essay that stimulated the interest in criterion-referenced measurement uses Robert Glaser, "Instructional Technology and the Measurement of Learning Outcomes: Some Questions," *American Psychologist,* 18 (1963), 519–521. Because of its landmark qualities, the diligent reader should consult Glaser's 1963 remarks. It is a widely reprinted essay, for example, in W. James Popham, ed., *Criterion-Referenced Measurement: An Introduction* (Englewood Cliffs, N.J.: Educational Technology Publications, 1971), pp. 5–14.

literally exploded. "Criterion-referenced" was the fashionable word among avant garde educators who applied it in adjective form to just about every unescorted noun in the neighborhood. We saw workshops, speeches, and conferences on such topics as *criterion-referenced testing, criterion-referenced evaluation,* and *criterion-referenced instruction.* It is reported that one group of school librarians even staged a seminar on *criterion-referenced references!* Criterion-referencing was high up on the fashionability charts.

Fashionable notions, of course, attract all sorts of followers. Soon we saw the emergence of a small but vocal cult of criterion-referenced test devotees who, with the characteristic zeal of recent converts, totally repudiated their former objects of adoration (norm-referenced tests) in favor of this new deity. "Criterion-referenced tests," these proponents of a new order enunciated, "are education's only salvation."

I'm overdramatizing a trifle, but it is true that in the mid- and late seventies, many educators were admonished to abandon norm-referenced tests altogether. Criterion-referenced tests were being touted as an answer to most educators' wish lists.

Some of the contestants in this educational measurement contest engaged in wholesale rejection of the other folks' testing tools. Sweeping castigations such as the following found their way onto the podium and into print: "Norm-referenced tests, having outlived their usefulness, should be abandoned completely." "Criterion-referenced tests must, of necessity, deal only with piddling outcomes." "Critics of norm-referenced (or criterion-referenced) tests were born under conditions of debatable legitimacy." The latter allegation was often phrased in a more earthy manner.

These disputations were marked by far more heat than light. However, after the partisan struggle diminished to some extent, a fundamental truth was recognized by most of the testing debate's contestants; namely, that *both norm-referenced and criterion-referenced testing approaches are needed to accomplish the full range of purposes necessary in educational measurement.*

THE FUNDAMENTAL DISTINCTION

Norm-Referenced Tests

Let's turn to a consideration of the fundamental distinction between norm-referenced and criterion-referenced tests. Basically, it depends on the manner in which we *interpret* the results of an examinee's test performance. If you were to be given a particular test, for example, a test of mathematical computation skills, it might be impossible for you to discern merely from inspection of the test itself whether it was norm- or criterion-referenced. The test items used on norm- and criterion-referenced tests often appear to be pretty similar. To find out whether you had a norm- or criterion-referenced test, you would need to consult the technical and descriptive materials accompanying the test to see what constitutes the basis by which the test's scores are to be interpreted. Just as you can't tell a book by its cover, you typically can't distinguish between criterion-referenced tests or norm-referenced tests merely by inspecting the test items.

In the case of a norm-referenced test, we interpret someone's test performance according to the performances of others; in the case of a criterion-referenced test we interpret someone's test performance in relationship to a well-described class of skills, attitudes, and the like. In a very real sense, interpretations are made *relatively* for norm-referenced tests and *absolutely* for criterion-referenced tests.

Here's a reasonable working definition for a norm-referenced measure:

> *A norm-referenced test is used to ascertain an individual's status with respect to the performance of other individuals on that test.*

In a typical situation, a student completes a norm-referenced test and, for example, obtains a score of 72 items correct out of 85 possible. The *raw score* of 72 is interpreted by use of a table of normative data which summarizes the performances of a group of other students who have previously completed the same exam. As it turns out, let's say the student's 72 items correct is equivalent to the 91st percentile rank, which means that the student equaled or exceeded the performances of 91 percent of the students in the norm group. It is because we make our interpretation of examinees' scores by relating or *referencing* them to that of examinees in the norm group that we refer to such tests as *norm-referenced.* In Chapter 7 we spend plenty of time becoming conversant with normative data, more specifically, how to gather and make the most sense out of test norms.

Now a norm-referenced test obviously yields more interpretive information than an examinee's raw score or its percentile equivalent. For example, we know that we're using a test of reading comprehension, a test of arithmetic skills, or a test of verbal aptitude. However, whereas most norm-referenced tests are accompanied by at least some general descriptive information regarding the global attribute they're attempting to measure, the emphasis with most norm-referenced tests is on the *relative* interpretation, that is, the interpretation of an examinee's performance in relationship to the performance of the examinees in the normative sample.

Criterion-Referenced Tests

Although a norm-referenced test focuses on the relative status of an examinee's test performance, a criterion-referenced test endeavors to tie down the nature of an examinee's test performance more tightly or, if you prefer, *absolutely*. Here's our definition for a criterion-referenced measure:

> *A criterion-referenced test is used to ascertain an individual's status with respect to a defined behavioral domain.*

Whereas a norm-referenced test references an examinee's performance to that of a norm group, a criterion-referenced test references an examinee's performance to a defined set of criterion behaviors, that is, a behavioral domain. An example of such a behavioral domain would be the ability of a student to select from multiple-choice alternatives the best statement of the main idea for written selections that display specified characteristics.

However, we cannot swoop by this notion too swiftly, since lasting confusion can result if the reader fails to understand why it is that the term "criterion," in the phrase, "criterion-referenced test," refers to a behavioral domain.

Going back many years, the term *criterion* was usually employed to signify a desired level of proficiency. Instructors might say, for example, that "It took two weeks to get my students up to criterion." We can think of this as the *criterion-as-a-level* conception.

There is another substantially different sense in which the term criterion is employed to signify the target behaviors themselves. For instance, when a gymnast is finally able to perform a particularly difficult and long-sought maneuver, we sometimes assert that the gymnast has mastered the criterion (behavior). We can think of this as the *criterion-as-a-desired-behavior* conception.

Unfortunately, in Glaser's classic 1963 article which popularized the notion of criterion-referenced tests, *both* of these two meanings of criterion were present. Sometimes Glaser referred to "specific behaviors" and to "what the individual can or cannot do." In doing so, he conveyed the idea that a criterion-referenced test referenced an examinee's performance to a defined behavioral domain. At other points in the article, Glaser referred to a "continuum of knowledge" and "desired performance at any specified level." By such comments he conveyed the idea that a criterion-referenced test references an examinee's performance to a level of proficiency.

In spite of the significant and lasting contribution represented by Glaser's 1963 essay, we must conclude that there are some points imbedded in that piece which warranted further clarification. The notion of *criterion* was one. But, after all, few people criticize the Wright brothers because their original Kitty Hawk model was incapable of transoceanic flight. Glaser's contribution quite naturally required some polishing. We must recognize, however, that the confusion resulting from the dual meaning of

criterion in Glaser's 1963 essay has led some measurement specialists down decidedly dead-endish pathways.

Although not really foreseeable in the mid-sixties, it is now apparent that to interpret *criterion* as a level of examinee proficiency yields almost no dividends over traditional testing practices. In fact, by using that conception of criterion, one could magically transform any norm-referenced test into a criterion-referenced test merely by setting a specific proficiency level for the test. If criterion-referenced tests are going to constitute a unique contribution to our measurement arsenal, it will be because they yield a more accurate depiction of an examinee's performance, not in relative terms, but in absolute terms. In other words, if criterion-referenced testing is going to provide any substantial educational payoff, it will be because we can secure a more precise notion of an examinee's status with respect to a clearly delimited domain of behaviors. The contribution to educational measurement that criterion-referenced tests are supposed to make is predicated on their *increased descriptiveness*.

Other phrases are sometimes used to describe criterion-referenced tests. Because confusion can result if we inadvertently confuse such descriptors, a bit of term defining is in order. Let's consider the two most popular of these expressions, that is, *objectives-based tests* and *domain-referenced tests*.

Objectives-based tests. Sometimes referred to as *objectives-referenced* tests, objectives-based tests are those whose items have been constructed to measure an instructional objective. Usually such objectives have been formulated behaviorally, that is, they describe the type of postinstruction behavior being sought of learners. Quite often the objectives on which such tests are based possess qualities similar to the *behavioral objectives* so strongly advocated by many educators during the late sixties and early seventies.

However, behavioral objectives are, of necessity, fairly terse mechanisms for describing intended learner outcomes. Their brevity, while helpful for purposes of short-hand communication, fails to supply the degree of descriptive detail necessary to tie down satisfactorily just what it is that an examinee's test performance really means.

As a consequence, although some educators would like to classify all objectives-based tests as bona fide criterion-referenced tests, most objectives-based tests fall far short of carving out the well-defined behavioral domain that constitutes the essence of any truly virtuous criterion-referenced test.

It is probably wiser to view objectives-based tests in the same way that we sometimes think of teacher-made classroom tests. All such measuring devices can, if well constructed and sensibly interpreted, serve highly useful educational functions. But to consider them as genuine exemplars of criterion-referenced measurement reflects more generosity than accuracy.

Domain-referenced tests. During the late sixties Wells Hively and his colleagues at the University of Minnesota were wrestling with the problem of how best to define curricular content in science and mathematics for purposes of instructional design. The scheme they came up with, first referred to as an *item form,* consisted of a detailed set of specifications which limited the form of items that measured a particular skill.[2] In later work Hively and his colleagues described their approach to measurement as *domain-referenced testing* because an examinee's performance was referenced to a defined domain of learner behaviors.[3] The definition of criterion-referenced measurement supplied earlier in this chapter is essentially equivalent to Hively's conception of domain-referenced testing. Most people who have been working in the field of criterion-referenced measurement (your author included among them) have been influenced substantially by Hively's pioneering efforts to create a scheme for circumscribing the class of behaviors on which examinees are measured.

[2]W. Hively, H. L. Patterson, and S. A. Page, "A Universe-Defined System of Arithmetic Achievement Tests," *Journal of Educational Measurement,* 5 (1968), 275–290.

[3]W. Hively, and others, *Domain-Referenced Curriculum Evaluation: A Technical Handbook and a Case Study from the Minnemast Project,* CSE Monograph Series in Evaluation, no. 1 (Los Angeles: UCLA Center for the Study of Evaluation, 1973).

Then, you might ask (if you're being alert—and if you're not, start the chapter over again), why not simply refer to such tests as domain-referenced tests instead of criterion-referenced tests? After all, not only was Hively there first, but think of all the paper to be saved because there are three less letters in the word *domain* than in the word *criterion*. If for no other reason than to save forests, it would appear we should opt for *domain* over *criterion*.

Well, conservation considerations aside, there is a straightforward practical reason that I've opted for the expression *criterion-referenced measurement* over *domain-referenced measurement,* even though for me those two notions are essentially interchangeable. During the seventies our educational world became attuned to criterion-referenced measurement. Even though in many educators' minds there was more confusion than clarity regarding that measurement notion, it was generally conceded that in criterion-referenced measurement educators had found a new approach to assessment which, for certain purposes, offered advantages over traditional measurement strategies.

Given that situation, namely, fairly widespread acceptance of criterion-referenced measurement, it seemed impolitic, if not impolite, to say, "Hold it educators; what most of you have been calling criterion-referenced tests for a decade or so must now be referred to as domain-referenced tests." Busy educators would hear such an admonition, giggle quietly, and go on about their business. The impact of such a renaming crusade would be acutely underwhelming.

Accordingly, it seems to make more strategic sense to mold the still unrigid understanding of what it is that constitutes a criterion-referenced test into a useful conception. The idea of a domain-referenced test is such a conception. Throughout the remainder of the text, although we shall no longer be talking about domain-referenced tests, the reader with first-rate powers of recall will remember that the notion of a domain-referenced test is imbedded solidly in our conception of criterion-referenced measurement.

Reprise on Distinctions

We've spent more paragraphs in describing what's meant by a criterion-referenced test than we did on norm-referenced tests. That doesn't signify that criterion-referenced tests are any more praiseworthy. It only means that most people are less familiar with criterion-referenced assessment approaches than they are with norm-referenced measurement schemes. For particular purposes both approaches to measurement have much to offer. More about these purposes later in this chapter.

Comprehensiveness of the test.   Let's review, for a bit, two key distinctions between these two testing strategies. A norm-referenced test typically measures a more *general* category of examinees' competencies (for example, reading comprehension), knowledge (for example, familiarity with the U.S. government system), or aptitude (for example, problem-solving potential).

A criterion-referenced test, on the other hand, typically focuses on a *more specific domain of examinee behaviors.* In the next chapter we shall consider just how large or small a domain of behaviors can be measured by a criterion-referenced test. But at this point, it's certainly safe to say that several criterion-referenced tests would typically be required to tap the skills and knowledge being assessed by a norm-referenced test. In Figure 2–1 you can see a graphic depiction of how the two testing strategies would attempt to deal with the field of reading comprehension.

The 100-item norm-referenced test would attempt to cover the entire range of a learner's reading comprehension skills. In contrast five separate twenty-item criterion-referenced tests would focus only on five well-defined skills within the overall realm of reading comprehension.

Reflected in Figure 2–1 is a major difference in the two approaches to measurement. A norm-referenced measure will attempt to use a wide range of different test items to sample a general field, such as reading comprehension. If there are distinctive subskills represented in that general field, those subskills are typically represented in the overall test with

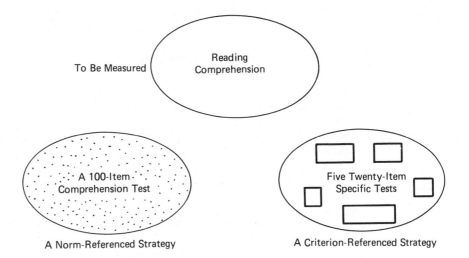

FIGURE 2–1   Norm-referenced and criterion-referenced strategies for coping with the measurement of a substantial field of examinee skill.

only a few items each. Because of the breadth of its coverage, the norm-referenced test can provide an overall estimate of how well the examinee has done in the general field of skill and/or knowledge being measured.

A criterion-referenced test, on the other hand, will not attempt to assess comprehensive mastery of a field. Instead, major discrete subskills within a field will be measured. Because these subskills will be measured with more precision (better descriptions of the attributes being measured and more items per attribute), a greater degree of clarity is associated with each test (as represented by the darker borders around the five subskills measured in Figure 2–1's criterion-referenced tests). The more general norm-referenced test must be satisfied with less descriptive precision (as represented by the lighter border for the norm-referenced strategy).

On the other side of the coin, however, note that because the five twenty-item criterion-referenced tests focus on much, but not all, of the overall field of reading comprehension, there are clear gaps in the content coverage of the five criterion-referenced tests. Because the norm-referenced test's 100 items are designed to sample more broadly, that test can tap segments of the reading comprehension field not measured by the five criterion-referenced tests.

So there you have the first of many trade-offs that must be confronted by users of norm- and criterion-referenced tests. Criterion-referenced tests provide better descriptions of the attributes they do measure, but they do not measure as broadly as a norm-referenced test. Clearly, the educational purpose for which a test will be used should influence your decision as to whether you need a more comprehensive and less well-described test or a series of less comprehensive but better described tests.

Percentiles versus percentage correct.   A second significant difference in the way we deal with an examinee's performance under the two testing strategies hinges on the type of interpretation typically associated with norm-referenced versus criterion-referenced tests. For both a criterion- and a norm-referenced test we first secure an examinee's raw score, that is, the number of items answered correctly. However, it's what we do then with the raw score that makes the difference.

With norm-referenced tests there are normative tables that accompany the test so that we can quickly find out what the percentile equivalent of each raw score is. For instance, if Jane Jones answered 37 out of 60 items correctly on a norm-referenced vocabulary test, we would whip out the test's norm tables and discover that Jane's 37 raw score was equivalent to a percentile rank of 73. This would indicate that Jane's raw score equaled or exceeded the performance of 73 percent of those examinees in the norm group.

With criterion-referenced tests, however, let's say Jane answered 20 items correctly out of a 25-item spelling test. Since we are chiefly interested in how well Jane has mastered the behavioral domain defined by the test, we would report that she achieved an 80 percent correct score, that is, 20 out of 25 items.

Obviously, the two kinds of interpretations offer two substantially different ways of thinking about an examinee's performance. With the percentile interpretation, we are employing a totally *relative* interpretative strategy. With the percentage-correct approach, since we are describing the examinee's status in relationship to total mastery, our interpretation more closely resembles an *absolute* explanatory strategy.

To reiterate a point made earlier, although there will be other differences that we point to in the way that criterion- and norm-referenced tests are built, polished, and reported, the most telling distinction between the two testing approaches lies in the notion of the *interpretation* that we give to an examinee's test performance. For the past several paragraphs we have been emphasizing two key distinctions in those interpretations: (1) the *general versus specific scope of the measurement focus* and (2) the *percentile versus percentage correct* interpretation of raw score performances.

TARGETS FOR EDUCATIONAL TESTS

We have thus far been attending to the differentiation between norm- and criterion-referenced assessment approaches by attempting to stress the importance of the distinction between the interpretations given to examinees' test performances. There are some educators who believe that the major determiner in whether a norm- or criterion-referenced test should be used is the nature of the content or skill that is being measured. Such a view is incorrect.

Let's consider the major categories of behavior in which educators are interested, namely, *cognitive, psychomotor,* and *affective* behaviors. *Cognitive* tests attempt to tap an examinee's intellectual skills, such as one's capacity to solve verbal or mathematical problems. *Psychomotor* tests attempt to measure an examinee's physical competencies, either small muscle skills (such as using a typewriter) or large muscle skills (such as pole vaulting). *Affective* tests attempt to gauge examinee's attitudes, values, and interests, such as the attributes measured by a test of one's self-esteem.

Tests in the cognitive or psychomotor realm are often focused on an examinee's *attainments* at a given point in time; these tests are usually referred to as *achievement* tests. Tests of a cognitive or psychomotor sort may be focused on an examinee's *potential* to perform well, in which case we refer to the tests as *aptitude* tests.

We are far more familiar, of course, with cognitive than psychomotor tests, most of us having been reared on a steady diet of cognitive aptitude and achievement tests since we sauntered through the kindergarten door. We've less frequently encountered psychomotor tests unless they turned out to be the exams in a typing class or the performance tests required in a physical education class. For both cognitive and psychomotor tests, we ordinarily are concerned with measuring *optimal performance,* that is, getting an answer to such questions as, "How well can you perform this skill?"

For affective measures, we are more anxious to get a fix on an examinee's *typical performance.* We are less interested in the question, "What *can* you do?" and more interested in the question, "What *will* you do?" To secure a reasonable idea of a student's attitudes toward school, for example, we need to find out how the student typically feels about school. We don't really want to know if the student has the ability to create positive or negative impressions of attitudes toward school (unless we're in a drama class), we want to know how the student *truly* feels about school. For affective measures, therefore, the conventional distinction between aptitude and achievement makes little sense. What educators usually want to get at in the affective realm is a good idea of the student's current affective status in order to determine what the student's future affective dispositions are apt to be. To illustrate, educators may wish to assess students' current *attitudes* regarding government so that reasonable predictions can be made concerning students' future *behaviors* regarding government (after school has been completed).

Irrespective of whether we're assessing affective, cognitive, or psychomotor behaviors, there are instances in which we'll need *both* norm-referenced tests and criterion-referenced tests. The important distinction rests more directly on the specific purpose we're attempting to accomplish. We can illustrate that point by considering some of the more common purposes for which educators employ tests, then discussing whether norm- or criterion-referenced measures best fit the bill.

MATCHING THE MEASUREMENT STRATEGY WITH THE MISSION

The purposes to be described for the next few paragraphs will not, obviously, exhaust the missions on which educational tests might be sent marching. The educational world is a big one, and this chapter (almost concluded) is a small one. Nevertheless, it should prove illuminating to cite several instances where norm- or criterion-referenced measurement strategies would or would not be suitable.

Selection Decisions

Educators are frequently faced with the necessity to make selections among students. For example, decisions must be made about which students should be admitted to college or other sorts of advanced training programs. At the other end of the spectrum, decisions must be made about which poorly performing students warrant special remedial attention. It's difficult to imagine a week's time in a typical school that wouldn't be well sprinkled with decisions involving the selection of students. However, there are two quite different contexts in which such choices are made, and those contexts will determine whether we should opt for norm- or criterion-referenced measures.

Fixed-quota settings.   One category of selection decisions arises from situations in which there are more applicants than openings. For example, let's say a prestigious law school has only 100 openings in next year's class, yet it is deluged with over 500 applicants for those slots. Even though there are numerous candidates, there is a *fixed quota* of openings. Accordingly, decisions must be made among the candidates so that only 100 of the more than 500 applicants end up as would-be Perry Masons.

In these types of fixed-quota settings, it is requisite to sort out individuals according to their relative abilities, hence norm-referenced tests are needed. Indeed, norm-referenced tests have typically been honed to perform precisely this sort of "spread-'em-out-and-spot-the-best" function. By the same token, if we were trying to make selections at the low end of the ability continuum, for instance, when we were trying to identify the most instructionally needy in a group of retarded children, then norm-referenced measures would again be more appropriate than criterion-referenced measures.

To illustrate, let's suppose that a criterion-referenced test, rather than a norm-referenced measure, had been used by the law school, but that almost 150 of the 500 applicants attained essentially the same high scores (that is, scores within a point or two of each other). Since the criterion-referenced test was not deliberately constructed to detect variability in examinees' scores, this type of result is quite possible. Since the quota is fixed at 100 and the law school's faculty is unable to distinguish among 150 applicants, the criterion-referenced test failed to provide the necessary information to do the required sorting job. A well-constructed norm-referenced test will do the job better.

Requisite-skill settings.   There are other contexts in education where the decision revolves not around who is best or worst, but rather *who is qualified.* For example, let's say a medical school has just put the finishing touches on a crop of fledgling physicians. Before the medical school faculty releases these successors of Hippocrates on an unsuspecting public, it is decided to give them a comprehensive "everything-a-patient-would-like-you-to-know" examination. On the basis of the exam's results, some students will receive their white coats and stethoscopes while others will continue training until they improve their medical abilities.

In such a setting a norm-referenced test would not be appropriate, since if this year's crop of medical students was truly cruddy, the medical school would be sending out the best of an unqualified lot. Would you want some slow-witted surgeon probing for your appendix who was licensed by virtue of being at the 75th percentile among a class of incompetents? No, this would be an instance where the *requisite skills* needed by an individual should be identified, then measured by a criterion-referenced test. Only those candidates who displayed the requisite skills should be let loose on the public. Only criterion-referenced measures that accurately reflect the necessary skills will work in such situations.

Counseling Decisions.   Many educators, particularly school psychologists and counselors but also classroom teachers, find themselves giving advice to students regarding educational, vocational, or psychological choices. First off, of course, educators should be aware of their own limitations. People who are not fully qualified to render psychological advice should avoid dabbling in any serious emotional problems their students happen to present. Assuming suitable professional assistance is available, for instance, a licensed school psychologist or counselor, then this would be a delightful time for the teacher to engage in a bit of highly responsible buck passing.

To some extent the situations faced when one is counseling students approximate the two classes of situations just described in the case of *fixed-quota* and *requisite-skill* selection decisions. Sometimes students will seek advice based on whether they "do or do not possess the necessary skills" for a given role, such as a future educational training program. In such cases, *if* the necessary prerequisite skills for the training program have been well defined and a criterion-referenced test exists that measures these skills, then a criterion-referenced test would be suitable.

However, more often than not, a student will seek counseling advice based on "how capable am I in relationship to other people?" In those kinds of situations, clearly, norm-referenced tests would be more suitable. In fact, since there will be relatively few instances in which the necessary skills (or interests, attitudes, and the like) for a future assignment have been well explicated—and still fewer instances in which an on-target criterion-referenced test is at hand, in most counseling settings norm-referenced tests will currently prove more useful than criterion-referenced tests.

Program Evaluation.   In attempting to appraise the worth of an instructional program, that is, in trying to evaluate the program, there are few instances in which norm-referenced tests will prove appropriate. Oh, in some situations, of course, *any* test is better than no test, but if a suitable criterion-referenced test can be located, it will almost always be preferable.

In brief, although the deficits of norm-referenced tests for program evaluation purposes are treated elsewhere,[4] there are three weaknesses of norm-referenced tests for program evaluation pruposes. First, since norm-referenced tests are often so general, they frequently fail to mesh satisfactorily with the curricular emphases of the program being evaluated. Even worse, these mismatches between what is being tested and what is being taught are often unrecognized by the evaluators who use the tests.

Second, because of their generality of description, few cues for instructional amelioration are provided by norm-referenced tests. When an instructional program is evaluated and found wanting, it is assumed that efforts should be made to improve it. The typical diffuseness of norm-referenced tests renders them largely useless for such improvement guidance.

Finally, there are some technical item-production and item-refinement procedures employed in the generation of norm-referenced tests which tend to make such tests less sensitive to detecting instructional effects than their criterion-referenced counterparts. We shall delve into these norm-referenced test-development practices in later chapters.

Because a well-constructed, criterion-referenced test effectively dodges these three deficits, that is, (1) it is specific enough to match an instructional program's curricular emphasis, (2) it provides cues for instructional amelioration, and (3) it is more instructionally sensitive, a criterion-referenced test should almost always be selected for program evaluation.

Instructional Design and Diagnosis.   For designing an instructional sequence to promote a desired end, or for discovering which particular skills a student lacks, criterion-referenced tests are definitely superior to norm-referenced measures. The descriptive rigor that characterizes a properly fashioned criterion-referenced test is ideal for planning on-target instructional activities. After all, who can create on-target instructional activities without a decent idea of what the target is?

In the same vein, if a teacher is trying to pinpoint a student's deficits in order to supply a dash of remediation, it is necessary to get a solid fix on the particular skills that a student has not mastered. The teacher is less interested in how a student stacks up against other students and more interested in what it is that the student can or can't do. Criterion-referenced tests supply such information. Norm-referenced tests don't.

---

[4]W. James Popham, *Criterion-Referenced Measurement* (Englewood Cliffs, N.J.: Prentice-Hall, Inc., 1978), Chapter 4. See also, W. James Popham, "The Case for Criterion-Referenced Measurement," *Educational Researcher,* November 1978, pp. 6–10.

Large-Scale Resource Allocation   There are situations in which educators need to decide how to allocate resources, for example, financial or personnel, on a large scale. In one example, a state board of education might be deciding whether to spend most of its program development dollars to support curriculum work in mathematics or science. Suppose the board plans to carry out a large-scale needs assessment, one element of which is to find out how the state's youngsters are performing in math and science.

At such a general level of information, a more broadly oriented norm-referenced test would probably be more suitable than a series of separate, less easily aggregated criterion-referenced tests. The situation is similar to that illustrated earlier in Figure 2–1 where we saw that a general, if not too well-defined, estimate of a broad field of learner accomplishment is better provided by a norm-referenced than a criterion-referenced test.

A Matter of Degree.   The discussion of the last several pages has implied that in most educational settings (and obviously there are many more than the few treated here), there is a clear choice as to whether we should select norm- or criterion-referenced tests. While in some cases that will be true, in most instances it won't. The choices between norm- and criterion-referenced tests are often difficult.

In many cases it is a matter of degree. For instance, in some settings, although a criterion-referenced test could be used, a norm-referenced test will yield results at least as useful and probably better. That being the case, the evaluator should opt for a norm-referenced strategy. Sometimes the odds will favor a criterion-referenced test rather than a norm-referenced test. Sometimes the educator's decision will be made not on the basis of the differences in measurement strategies but instead on the basis of costs, ease of scoring, and so on. If all else fails, the perplexed educator can always flip the ever-present coin: "Heads, criterion-referenced; tails, norm-referenced." Hopefully, the remaining chapters of this text reduce the necessity of resorting to the coin-tossing method of selecting an educational testing strategy.

PRACTICE EXERCISES

Presented below are some typical educational situations in which tests are needed. Read each situation, then decide whether you would recommend the use of a *norm-referenced test* or a *criterion-referenced test*.

1. Mr. Josephson wishes to sharpen his teaching program in high school geometry by employing an end-of-course examination as an instructional target. He has asked the school district's evaluation coordinator to supply copies of commercially available norm- and criterion-referenced tests.

2. As part of a new "quality assurance" program adopted by its national convention, members of the Physician's Assistants Association are recommending that a new exam be constructed and administered to all practicing physician's assistants, so that those who fail to display the necessary competencies must undertake a retraining program.

3. Admissions officers at a newly established College of Cuddles and Warmth, a private and self-professed "institution reflecting the finest of neohumanism's insights," find that they have 1,272 applicants for their first semester and space for only 550 students. Assuming they can come up with an aptitude measure tapping one's neohumanist potential, should they go for a norm- or criterion-referenced testing strategy?

4. A school counselor wishes to rank students according to their "interests in quantitatively oriented professions." What sort of a test, that is, norm-referenced or criterion-referenced, should she try to use?

5. In a large metropolitan school district in North Dakota (obviously, a fictitious setting), extra resources are dispersed by the district to school staffs which are successful in designing and refining programs that improve elementary school children's reading skills. The district wishes to employ pupil test performance as the tangible index of reading achievement. Schools that reach a specified level of accomplishment will get extra funds and personnel; schools that don't—won't.

ANSWERS TO PRACTICE EXERCISES

1. Because good descriptions of the desired behavior will be needed so that Mr. Josephson can design on-target instructional sequences, a criterion-referenced test should be the choice here. Almost any time there are specific instructional decisions at stake, criterion-referenced tests are preferable to norm-referenced tests.

2. Here's another case where a criterion-referenced test is needed. This is a clear instance of the *requisite-skills* situation described in the chapter.

3. Any self-respecting College of Cuddles and Warmth will be hard pressed to find a humanistically acceptable aptitude measure, but if they do, it certainly ought to be norm-referenced in nature. This is a case when the fixed quota will force the admissions officers to do some choosing. In such situations it is necessary to spread out applicants on one or more dimensions. Norm-referenced tests do this best.

4. This is a case where students need to be spread out in order to be ranked, hence, it's clearly a case for a norm-referenced test.

5. This is a program evaluation application of tests, since the task will be to discern which schools have promoted the requisite level of student skills in reading. It is a case when criterion-referenced tests should be employed.

DISCUSSION QUESTIONS

1. If you were asked to explain to a school board what the essential differences were between norm- and criterion-referenced testing strategies, how would you go about it?
2. Can you think of situations in which it makes no real difference which of the two testing strategies is employed? If so, what are the distinguishing features of such situations?
3. Is it possible to make norm-referenced interpretations with a typical criterion-referenced test? How about the reverse, that is, can one make criterion-referenced interpretations with a typical norm-referenced test?
4. Which sort of test, that is, norm-referenced or criterion-referenced, do you think would be most expensive to develop? Why?

SUGGESTIONS FOR ADDITIONAL READING

BERK, RONALD A., ed. *Criterion-Referenced Measurement: The State of the Art.* Baltimore: The Johns Hopkins University Press, 1980. This is a collection of individual papers treating various aspects of criterion-referenced measurement. Many of the chapters are extremely useful; a few require a fair amount of mathematical sophistication on the part of the reader.

GLASER, ROBERT, "The Instructional Technology and the Measurement of Learning Outcomes: Some Questions," *American Psychologist,* 18, no. 7 (August 1963), 519–21. This is the classic article by Glaser which initiated the considerable interest now present in criterion-referenced measurement. As the kick-off article, it is worth the attention of anyone interested in the field of criterion-referenced measurement.

HAMBLETON, RONALD K., and others, "Criterion-Referenced Testing and Measurement: A Review of Technical Issues and Development," *Review of Educational Research,* 48, no. 1 (Winter 1978), 1–48. This is an absolutely first-rate review of research regarding criterion-referenced measurement. The authors have done an outstanding job in rounding up a good deal of disparate literature and synthesizing it in relationship to key issues faced by the developers and/or users of criterion-referenced tests.

MEHRENS, WILLIAM A., and IRVIN J. LEHMANN, "Norm- and Criterion-Referenced Measurement," Chapter 3, *Measurement and Evaluation in Education and Psychology* (2nd ed.), pp. 48–61. New York: Holt, Rinehart & Winston, 1975. Although the conception of criterion-referenced measurement proffered by Mehrens and Lehmann in their text differs from that given in the text you are now reading, these authors provide a useful description of the differences between norm- and criterion-referenced measurement from the perspective of measurement traditionalists.

MILLMAN, JASON, "Criterion-Referenced Measurement," in *Evaluation in Education: Current Applications,* ed. W. James Popham. Berkeley, Calif.: McCutchan, 1974. This is a useful exploration by Millman of different conceptions of criterion-referenced measurement. Millman treats a number of topics related to criterion-referenced measurement, such as standard setting and test length.

POPHAM, W. JAMES, ed., *Criterion-Referenced Measurement.* Englewood Cliffs, N.J.: Prentice-Hall, Inc., 1978. In this text the author presents a somewhat less balanced (from that of the current text) perspective regarding the relative merits of criterion-measurement versus norm-referenced measurement. The nuts and bolts of criterion-referenced measurement are explored in some detail.

POPHAM, W. J., ed., *Criterion-Referenced Measurement: An Introduction.* Englewood Cliffs, N.J.: Educational Technology Publications, 1971. This is a somewhat older book which, because of your current author's obvious bias, is still thought to contain some useful sections. The book includes the classic Glaser 1963 article and a 1969 article by Popham and Husek which has been widely cited, even by someone other than Popham!

AND FOR THOSE WHO TIRE OF READING

EBEL, ROBERT L., and POPHAM, W. JAMES, A videotape *Debate on the Relative Merits of Criterion-Referenced and Norm-Referenced Measurement.* The American Educational Research Association, 1230-17th Street, N.W., Washington, D.C. 20036. In the videotape, a live debate takes place between Professor Ebel and your author at the 1978 Annual Meeting of the American Educational Research Association in Toronto. It is a formal debate complete with rebuttals and pointed barbs on the part of both presenters. The videotape can serve as a useful stimulus for classroom discussion (70 minutes).

Modern Measurement Methods. Distributed by Vimcet Associates, Inc., P.O. Box 24174, Los Angeles, Calif. 90024. This is a thirty-minute filmstrip-tape program describing the difference between norm-referenced and criterion-referenced testing procedures.

What to Look for in a Criterion-Referenced Test. Distributed by Vimcet Associates, Inc., P.O. Box 24174, Los Angeles, Calif. 90024. Six characteristics of a well-constructed criterion-referenced test are described in this thirty-minute illustrated filmstrip-tape program.

Why Standardized Achievement Tests are Inappropriate Measures of Educational Quality. Distributed by Vimcet Associates, Inc., P.O. Box 24174, Los Angeles, Calif. 90024. This thirty-minute illustrated filmstrip-tape describes four reasons why norm-referenced achievement tests may be unsuitable for evaluating the quality of instructional programs.

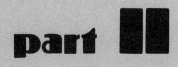

part II

EVALUATING EDUCATIONAL TESTS

In Part One's two chapters we saw that the purpose for which an educational test is used is the most significant element in determining what sort of test to employ. However, once the purpose of testing has been isolated, there is still the necessity of choosing among alternative testing instruments.

It is virtually impossible today to conceive of an educational purpose for which two (and usually many more) tests are not apparently suitable. The task facing educators, therefore, is how to choose the best test among several contenders. In Part Two's six chapters, we probe a number of considerations which can assist you in deciding whether you'll select Test *A,* Test *B,* or Test *C.* At the conclusion of Part Two, you hopefully acquire the first of the three major competencies being promoted by the text, namely, the ability to evaluate educational tests so that the best tests will be selected for the purposes those tests must fulfill.

There are dozens of dimensions on which almost any commodity can be judged. When people buy a new automobile, for example, they may attend to such factors as style, safety, gasoline mileage, and so on. In the same way, when educators attempt to judge the appropriateness of a testing device, they can focus on all sorts of considerations. Some of these considerations, naturally, are more defensible than others. In this chapter we consider six factors that are pivotal in deciding whether or not an educational test is suitable. Because the last three of these factors to be described are treated at greater length in separate chapters, they are only introduced at this time.

It must be noted at the outset of this discussion that the six factors to be discussed in this chapter do not, obviously, exhaust the range of considerations that prospective test users will wish to apply when evaluating educational tests. We will not, for example, do much more than mention the cost of a test. Yet, quite obviously, if you're a school principal who needs 100 tests and you have only $200 to make a purchase, it becomes significant whether the tests cost more than $2 each.

There are other things to consider in evaluating educational tests, such as the ease with which they can be administered and scored. All of

these practical considerations are genuinely important. However, in attempting to cover all the possible points to review when evaluating a test, the reader would soon be overwhelmed. This is another instance where more would surely turn out to be less.

As a consequence, there will be a deliberate effort to focus your attention on only six significant factors to employ while judging the quality of an educational test. If you become truly conversant with these half dozen dimensions and apply them more or less systematically when scrutinizing educational tests, you should be able to do a decisively better job in distinguishing between winning and losing tests.

Surely, choices can be made among educational tests. In a very common case, for example, teachers at a particular school (or officials for an entire school district) will find themselves obliged to select a test for determining the effectiveness of a language arts program. Obviously, because a number of different commercial test publishers have language arts tests to peddle, a choice must be made among them. Whether that choice will be made wisely or whimsically depends in large measure on the sophistication that the test choosers bring to their task.

Although the act of choosing among commercially published tests presents a fairly common and straightforward instance where one's test evaluation skills should be sharp, there are numerous other occasions when educators will need expertise in deciding whether a test is laudable or laughable. To illustrate, in recent years a good many large and middle-size school districts have, sometimes rather energetically, gone into the test development business. Most often these tests are intended exclusively for use in the local district, although there are some cases in which a school district has created a test for local use but has subsequently turned the test over to a commercial publishing house that distributes the test nationally, with royalties going back to the district. The Los Angeles Unified School District, for example, developed a test of high school students' reading skills in the late seventies, then turned that test over for distribution purposes to a commercial publisher, CTB/McGraw-Hill.

These school district test development efforts often result in the production of first-rate tests. In other cases, because district personnel lack either the test development expertise or the financial resources to do the job properly, the resulting tests make better scratch paper than assessment devices. The trick is to figure out which tests are which. An educational test should not be considered as a decent assessment tool, even if it is produced by local test developers. After all, even some of mother's homemade apple pies may have been baked too long.

Teachers and administrators who are supposed to employ these district-developed assessment tools have a professional responsibility to judge whether the tests are good ones. To make these kinds of judgments sensibly requires educators to bring a set of defensible standards to the test evaluation enterprise. If a test is found wanting, it is the responsibility of teachers and administrators to call those deficits to the attention of the district's officials who, often because of parental pride, fail to see the flaws in their locally sired assessment devices.

At an even more personal level, many teachers create their own tests. Some of these tests are, of necessity, churned out in a hurry to meet the requirements of an end-of-unit exam or a once-a-week quiz scheme. Such tests, as any harassed teacher will tell you, are not intended to serve as inspired examples of assessment at its best.

However, there are other tests that classroom teachers develop which reflect substantially more work. Some of these tests are employed to make significant decisions about students. For instance, an end-of-course examination in many cases may help the teacher decide whether a student gets an A, B, C, D, or F. In some classes a course grade can be the deciding factor in whether a student moves to the next class or grade level. Oh yes, the test-based stakes in many classes are truly high ones.

Now in such settings it should be apparent that considerable attention should be given by teachers to the quality of their examinations. Teachers who possess the skills necessary to detect flaws in their own tests can then set about rectifying those defects. Teachers who do not possess the skills needed to evaluate tests will, in all probability, continue to employ flawed assessment tools. As a consequence, they will often make inappropriate decisions about the students who must suffer through those tests.

In these and other instances, it should be clear that the educator who knows how to evaluate testing instruments is going to be a more effective professional than one who is intimidated by such tests. Let's turn, therefore, to a consideration of six factors which will elevate the reader from the status of Test Evaluation Tyro to that of Test Evaluation Tiger.

EVALUATIVE FACTOR ONE: DESCRIPTION OF MEASURED BEHAVIOR

The initial factor to consider in appraising an educational test stems from the reason that such tests were created in the first place, namely, to allow us to draw inferences about an examinee's status. However, that examinee's status, of course, is being assessed with respect to a particular focus. We obviously can't measure everything about examinees at one time. No, we attempt to assess a limited sphere of the examinee's skill, aptitude, and the like. It is imperative, therefore, that an educational test be accompanied by a description of just what it is that the test is attempting to measure.

A *description of measured behavior* is available for every commercially published test and, almost without exception, for district-developed educational tests as well. With most teacher-made tests designed for classroom use, the description of learner behavior usually bounces around in teacher's heads rather than on paper, although some teachers do take the trouble to explicate in writing what it is that their major examinations are supposedly measuring.

A description of measured behavior can range in length and detail from a terse, almost telegramlike behavioral objective (that is' supposedly measured by the test) to a detailed, highly elaborate set of test specifications, setting forth the permissible operations that can be used to generate test items. In all cases, although certain of these descriptions are obviously more communicative than others, the intention of the description is to convey to the user of the test a notion of what it is that the test is allegedly measuring.

The attentive reader will have noted the use of the term *allegedly* in the previous sentence. As we shall see later in this chapter, not every test that is called a cow by its creators can, in fact, give milk. For example, some tests that are described as "measures of higher-order problem solving" turn out to be little more than tests of one's vocabulary and short-term memory skills. The match between what a test says it's measuring and what the test actually measures constitutes a key aspect of the test's *validity*. Validity of a test will be the fifth factor we consider in this chapter.[1]

Before we can discern whether a test's description of measured behavior is accurately representing what the test is measuring, we must have the description itself. Because there are no hard and fast rules (or even soft and slow ones) regarding how test developers should describe their wares, there is enormous variability in the nature of the test descriptions that accompany educational assessment devices.

Norm-Referenced Measures

As a rule, since norm-referenced tests rely more heavily on percentile comparisons as the chief mechanism for interpreting one's test score, the descriptive language accompanying such tests is not intensely delimiting in its nature. More often than not, a somewhat general statement will be made about what it is that the test measures. In some cases these general statements will be backed up by a list of topics (content) that the test covers or a list of fairly general skills that the test attempts to tap. In some manuals for norm-referenced tests, a more detailed breakdown is provided of number of items per topic or skill.

Indeed, as one surveys the range of descriptive literature available with norm-referenced tests, it soon becomes apparent that the degree of descriptive detail accompanying these tests can range from an extremely terse description, perhaps little more than a thumbnail sketch, to a fairly elaborate and detailed effort to let test users know what it is that the test's developers hoped to measure.

Criterion-Referenced Measures

In view of their relatively recent arrival on the educational scene, it is not surprising that the quality of the descriptions accompanying criterion-referenced tests is even more variable. In a sense this is somewhat dis-

---

[1]The reader will, hopefully, not be too distressed if I occasionally treat tests anthropomorphically. Now everyone knows, well almost everyone, that tests really don't talk, hence, when I refer to what "a test says it's measuring," this represents literary license. I have, however, known some colleagues who, after working with educational tests for many years, assert with substantial conviction that many educational tests can indeed speak—but only when the moon is full.

couraging, since the major contribution that a good criterion-referenced test can make is its more sharply delimited description of what it is that examinees can or can't do. Yet, as matters currently stand, many creators of criterion-referenced tests attempt to get by with descriptions of measured behavior no more detailed, that is, no more limiting, than those of their norm-referenced counterparts.

A good description of measured behavior for a criterion-referenced test, as we shall see in Chapter 9, may be several pages in length, rather than the sentence or two sometimes associated with behavioral objectives. The essence of an effective set of descriptive information for a well-constructed criterion-referenced test is that it communicates, with as little ambiguity as possible, what it is that the test is supposedly measuring. Because we must rely, for the most part, on *words* as we attempt to explain what it is that the test measures, our efforts will sometimes fall short of our expectations. Words, even well-woven words, sometimes fail to capture the complexity of behaviors that educators are attempting to assess. By and large, however, a criterion-referenced test's description of measured behavior will tend to be more detailed than is a norm-referenced test's description.

Now that we've stressed the importance of appraising a test's description of the behavior it's attempting to measure, what does one do about it? In other words, how does a person evaluating an educational test decide whether a test's description is sufficiently explicit to be acceptable?

As always the answer to this question hinges directly on the *purpose* to which the educational test is to be put. Tests to be used for examinee selection in fixed-quota settings, situations for which norm-referenced measures are well suited, need not contain inordinately explicit descriptions of measured behavior. Tests to be used for instructional design or program evaluation should contain really tight descriptions of what the tests are measuring.

In the case of judging whether a test's description of measured behavior is sufficiently precise for the measurement task at hand, it depends on the purpose for which the test is being used. As a test evaluator, your job will be to consult the test's description of the behavior it's ostensibly measuring, then judge whether—for the intended purpose—that description is sufficiently explicit.

Here, for example, is a description of a social studies subtest in a widely used, commercially published norm-referenced achievement test:

> Test 1 contains 60 four-option multiple-choice items at each grade level. The items were selected to reflect the most current content and objectives of the social studies curriculum at each grade. The test items include items on American history, world history, government, geography, economics, sociol-

ogy, and study skills. Some items test knowledge of fact; many test ability to use factual knowledge of social studies in unfamiliar situations.[2]

Now suppose you were a teacher who was attempting to design a relevant instructional sequence to improve students' scores on this test. Would the previous description of what the test measures give you a decent idea of what you should be striving to accomplish? Well, not unless you possessed the gift of prophecy, the test's description of measured behavior offers you scant guidance for instructional design. Different social studies teachers would read the preceding paragraph and come up with substantially different interpretations. For purposes of aiding instructional designers, this test's description of measured behavior falls way short of the mark.

Yet, for other purposes, the test's fairly general description may be acceptable. Suppose as a school administrator you were only trying to get a very general fix on what your students knew about social studies. Under such circumstances, the fairly ink-blotty description may prove sufficient.

The best way to determine whether the test's description of measured behavior is adequate is to have different individuals, those who may use the test for the purpose at hand, read the description, then independently write out what they think is really being measured, for example, what the test items will be like. If these independently prepared interpretations coincide fairly well, for this purpose the test's description of measured behavior is suitable. If the interpretations are markedly different, the test's description of measured behavior is not clear enough.

EVALUATIVE FACTOR TWO: ITEMS PER MEASURED BEHAVIOR

A second factor to consider when evaluating an educational test is the number of items being employed to assess the behavior, or behaviors, being measured by the test. To make this point, perhaps ludicrously, let's imagine that a sales representative from a commercial testing firm tries to persuade you to buy the firm's brand new test of political science knowledge. The sales rep might extol with rapture the new test's "up-to-date content, its subtle diagnostic potential, the first-rate consultants who participated in its creation, and its remarkably low cost." When you ask how many total items are in this new instrument of assessment wizardry, the sales rep replies, "Only two; but they're damned good ones!"

It is apparent, of course, that only a handful of test items will not permit educators to get an accurate fix on what it is that students can or

---

[2]*Tests of Academic Progress*, Form S, Manual for Administrators, Supervisors, and Counselors. (Boston: Houghton Mifflin 1972), p. 11.

can't do. There's just too much chance that results on a test with so few items will be nothing more than a fluke. Students' examination performance is too apt to be due to chance, rather than their true capabilities (attitudes, and so on).

Tests, Subtests, and Sub-Sub-Subtests

Before proceeding to a consideration of the tricky question regarding "How many test items are sufficient," it's necessary to take a brief side excursion dealing with the number of behaviors that a test sets out to measure. Let's think of a typical norm-referenced achievement test which attempts to assess a primary child's "reading comprehension ability." Although there might be a number of different kinds of items on the test, with those differences reflecting fairly distinctive sorts of comprehension subskills, the test yields a total score that is a *composite* index of a student's reading comprehension ability. Although the test's developers intend it to assess a medley of varied comprehension subskills, there is no attempt to provide separate indices of those subskills. Thus, if the test consists of 100 items, all of those items can be counted as measuring that test's single measured behavior, namely, reading comprehension ability.

Other tests, however, attempt to measure a series of distinctive subskills in such a way as to yield separate scores for each subskill. For example, suppose a test of basic mathematical skills has 80 items, 20 each on the four fundamental calculation skills (addition, subtraction, multiplication, and division). Each of these 20-item sets yields a separate score for each of the four calculation skills. In other words, an examinee earns a separate score for addition skill, another for subtraction skill, and so on. Whether or not there is a total score reported for the examinee's performance on the 80 items (sometimes there is and sometimes there isn't), the test is surely attempting to measure each of the four calculation skills with 20 items per skill. Hence, for that test there would be 20 items for the smallest behavior the test purports to measure.

So far so good, but let's now consider a test that allegedly measures 55 separate decoding skills in reading with 55 items. For readers with less than fundamental mathematical prowess, it can be noted that the test is supposedly measuring each decoding skill (separately listed in the test's manual), with one item per skill. One item per skill, most would agree, is pretty skimpy. Since the test permits the reporting of results on a skill-by-skill basis, there's no doubt that the test's publishers are really trying to peddle it as 55 separate tests. And one-item tests at that!

You can see that when you evaluate a test to discern whether it provides a sufficient number of items per measured behavior, you must isolate the smallest units of behavior which the test supposedly measures, then see how many items the test provides for measuring those units. In the preceding paragraphs we've seen examples of tests containing 100 items, 20 items, and one item per measured behavior.

What about tests that not only report subscores but *also* provide a composite, total score? For example, if our 55-item test of decoding skills provides a total "overall decoding skill" score, for that measured behavior the test would possess 55 items. In such instances, therefore, one might conclude that there were enough items when the test is used as a composite instrument but not when the test is viewed as 55 separate subtests.

As always, the purpose for which the test will be used turns out to be the chief determiner of how many items are needed. Let's suppose we want to use our 55-item decoding skills test to gain an overall estimate of whether a given set of textbooks helps youngsters acquire the decoding skills of reading. For such a purpose, with no need to move to a more precise level of reporting, the 55-item test would appear to have enough items.

On the other hand, if we wished to use the test for some sort of diagnostic purpose, for instance, to get an idea of the particular decoding skills that pupils did or did not possess, then one item per skill is too paltry. It is absurd to contend that with a single item (or even a married one) we could detect whether a child possesses a specific decoding skill.

For this reason, of course, we see that the purpose for which the test is to be used must be clearly understood prior to engaging in any sensible sort of test evaluation. In educational testing, as in other realms of human endeavor, form *should* follow function.

The Number of Items

One would think, given so much messing around with educational measurement over the decades, that by now we would have available a delightfully succinct and satisfyingly solid answer to the question: ("How many test items are really necessary?" Distressingly, there is no simple answer to that important question; "It depends.")

In the case of deciding how many test items per measured behavior are needed, it is fairly easy to demonstrate why it is that the requisite number of test items depends on the purpose for which the test's results are to be used. Let's dabble with a couple of common situations to illustrate that point.

Imagine that you were using a written test to certify whether clinical psychologists knew their stuff, that is, knew it well enough to allow them to practice on a neurotic world. Since the stakes are quite high, you would want plenty of items on the test, maybe 100 or so, to make sure that the actual clinical skill of the examinees is well sampled. To give those clinical psychology candidates a four- or five-item exam, then expect to have any confidence in the exam's results, would be patently silly (or a bit psychotic).

However, let's say you're a classroom teacher of first-grade pupils, and you want to find out which of the youngsters need an extra hour's worth of instruction on how to pronounce consonant-vowel-consonant words. Your plan is to assemble a subgroup of those children and give them an extra 60-minute practice session. In this instance, when the stakes are decisively lower than in the clinical psychologist example, and where today's errors in measurement can be rectified during tomorrow's reading instruction, you can undoubtedly get by with a test that has only a few items, as few as two or three, to provide you with the rough estimates of student skill.

These two examples should, hopefully, highlight one key question that must be considered when deciding how many test items per measured behavior are needed, namely, how important is the decision at hand? High-stakes, difficult-to-reverse decisions require more items than low-stakes, easy-to-reverse decisions.

There are other considerations involved in deciding upon test length, and these include the level of proficiency required of examinees in relationship to their expected level of functioning. That sounds fairly complex, and it is. Let's analyze it. Suppose you were using an exam for a placement decision and had determined that only those examinees who earned a score of 80 percent correct or better would be selected. Now if most of the examinees are actually functioning around a 20 percent correct score, it will be the exceptional examinee who scores at the required (80 percent) level. An exam performance at that level will be a rare event and not apt to be attributable to chance. For example, if you had five fill-in-the-blank, short-answer test items, most students would only be getting one out of five items correct, and those getting four or five (out of five) correct would display an exceptional (and believable) performance. You'd have confidence that such high-scoring examinees really were knowledgeable.

However, let's imagine that with the same required performance level, that is, 80 percent correct, we expected that most students would actually be performing around 75 percent to 85 percent correct.[3] In that setting an examinee's performance might be expected to fluctuate around the 80 percent cut-off level more often, merely as a function of the imprecision of our measurement device. Consequently, we would want more items per measured behavior in order to increase our confidence that those who topped our required 80 percent-level were doing so because of true skill, rather than chance.

---

[3]We'll treat the establishment of such performance levels in Chapter 16, so be patient.

I am not arguing that the passing standard should be set at a point substantially different from examinees' average performance merely to allow us to use fewer items. However, if a standard is set at a point which *turns out* to be near the group's typical performance, more items are certainly requisite.

Once more we see that the educational measurement world is far more complex than it ought to be. The decision as to how many items per measured behavior constitutes an acceptable minimum is much more difficult than most people imagine. Although some psychometricians (a fancy term to describe those folks who measure psychologically or educationally relevant variables) have addressed this problem, so far we do not have any tidy answers to the question: "How long should a test be?"

Promising approaches.   Two of the more encouraging strategies for dealing with the test-length issue have been proposed by Millman[4] and by Novick and Lewis.[5] Millman has prepared a series of tables which, for specified passing score percentages, permit us to identify how many students would be misclassified if tests of different lengths were used. Millman's approach is based on the binomial probabilities associated with an examinee's likelihood of passing or failing each item in a behavioral domain of test items. It is easy to use, although it fails to take account of certain factors involved in the approach recommended by Novick and his colleagues.

Novick's solution strategy employs a Bayesian statistical model. Bayesian statistical approaches, to oversimplify outrageously, allow one to pick up greater analytic precision with less actual data by making experience-based assumptions regarding the nature of such variables as examinees' current level of skill. The Bayesian solutions to the test-length problem take into consideration several subtle elements, including how much more serious an error it is to misclassify false-positives (examinees who appear to possess a skill but really don't) than to misclassify false-negatives (examinees who appear to lack a skill they really possess). The *estimated* relative gravity of these two sorts of misclassification errors is referred to as the *loss ratio* and is built into a Bayesian formula which helps us decide how many test items are needed.

In general the binomial model requires somewhat longer tests than the Bayesian model. The Bayesian approach, however, is more complicated

[4]J. Millman, "Passing Scores and Test Lengths for Domain-Referenced Measures," *Review of Educational Resources,* 43 (1973), 205–216.

[5]M. R. Novick and C. Lewis, "Prescribing Test Length for Criterion-Referenced Measurement," in *Problems in Criterion-Referenced Measurement,* ed. C. W. Harris, M. C. Alkin, and W. J. Popham, CSE Monograph Series in Evaluation, no. 3 (Los Angeles: UCLA Center for the Study of Evaluation, 1974).

to use. Familiarity with both approaches is recommended for anyone who has to get serious about *developing* a test, particularly a criterion-referenced test. For those who must *evaluate* a test, and that's what we're focusing on here, conversance with Millman's and Novick's recommendations will induce warranted humility regarding the difficulty of deciding just how many test items are requisite.

A rule of thumb.   Faced with a currently less-than-adequate set of techniques for tussling with the test-length problem (both Millman and Novick concede that their efforts are only beginning approximations of suitable solution strategies), what is a well-intentioned test evaluator to do?

As a test evaluator you should be most attentive to the dangers of *too few items* per measured behavior. Some test publishers, caught up with the fervor of free enterprise and the profit motive, will try to make their tests potentially appealing to any educator who might conceivably ever want a test of any kind whatsoever. These unscrupulous testing tycoons will contend that their tests assess everything in sight—with only an item or two per measured behavior. These are the tests that should be evaluated as losers, even without a sophisticated set of procedures for singling out a suitably long test. Quite clearly, as always, the purpose to which the test's results will be put turns out to be the decisive factor in deciding whether a test is too terse.

As a very rough rule of thumb, based chiefly on the writings of Millman and Novick, plus a healthy dose of practicality, I suggest that ten items per measured behavior constitute an absolute minimum number of items for any reasonably important educational decision. That minimum should be increased, say to twenty or more items, when the stakes get higher, and decreased, say to five or so items, when the stakes get lower. For instance, if you're developing a test that is to be used for a high school graduation competency requirement, and those students failing the test will be deprived of a diploma, that's a pretty high-stakes decision context. If your test is measuring six different competencies, use at least ten items per competency. If you're using a test to certify a neurosurgeon's right to go out and start probing between people's ears, then maybe twenty or more items per measured behavior makes more sense. If you're using an exam's results only to alert a pupil's parents to the fact that more focused home study is needed, then five or so items per measured behavior may be more than sufficient.

This rule of thumb interacts very decisively with the next evaluation factor to be described, namely, scope of the test. To illustrate, if you are creating a single test of a broadly defined competency, such as reading comprehension, then ten items won't prove sufficient. However, if you're trying to get at a student's reading comprehension skills by using six separate, yet related, criterion-referenced tests, then ten items per test might just do it. Clearly, there's a good deal of judgment that goes into one's estimate of whether a test has enough items per measured behavior to do the job it's supposed to do. However, by being attentive to this factor, you'll at least be able to spot the most egregious test-length offenders.

EVALUATIVE FACTOR THREE: SCOPE OF MEASUREMENT

All of the evaluative factors we'll be describing in this chapter interact to some extent. In particular the initial two factors, that is, a test's descriptive accuracy and its number of items per measured behavior are directly intertwined with the third evaluative factor, namely, *scope of measurement.* By scope of measurement we refer to the breadth of the attribute being measured by the test. At one extreme, for example, we could think of a test that attempted to tap a student's "total knowledge." That, of course, is a fairly hefty target. Developers of such a broad-scope test would have to labor mightily to create an accurate description (evaluative factor one) of what's being measured and would find that, unless they tested examinees for several weeks at a time, they probably wouldn't have enough items per measured behavior (evaluation factor two). Indeed, a broad-scope test of that sort (and this is only, after all, a fictitious example) illustrates quite graphically that as one moves toward tests of broader scope, one must expect less accurate descriptions. There's simply too much being measured by the test to describe the behavior well. Broad-scope tests, because they cover a wider terrain, also require many more items than narrow-scope tests.

At the other extreme, an exceedingly narrow-scope test might be one that would assess a student's ability to spell the words *to, too,* and *two.* Given the number of words that people are obliged to spell, we would surely be obliged to build a bushel basketful of such narrow-scope tests if we were going to secure a decent estimate of how well someone could spell.

It is the test *developers* who determine whether a test's scope will be broad or narrow. In a sense it is they who decide "how big a chunk of examinee behavior we should bite off." It is the test *evaluator* who must decide whether the scope of measurement is suitable for the purpose to which the test's results will be put. Let's illustrate that point with a few examples.

Suppose you are a classroom teacher whose instructional effectiveness is being evaluated for purposes of the district's making a decision as to whether you should be granted tenure. Suppose further that a key factor in the evaluation of your teaching skill is the extent to which your pupils perform well on an end-of-semester examination. Suppose, finally, that you want your pupils to do well on the test so that you can gain tenure. Should you push for the use of a narrow-scope or broad-scope test?

Well, if you have your wits about you, you'll request a narrow-scope test, since such tests will invariably focus on more limited sorts of learner behaviors, the sort that would constitute a reasonably attainable instructional target. Broad-scope tests, on the other hand, are difficult to teach toward since they cover such a wide terrain.

However, let's flip that situation a bit by supposing you are a member of a school board who is trying to get the best teachers for the district so that the district's youngsters receive a decent education. If you were using pupils' test performance as one index of a teacher's skill, would you want tests with a narrower or broader scope? Well, if you still had your wits about you, you ought to lean toward tests of a somewhat broader scope. After all, you don't want the district's teachers to be teaching toward trifling targets, then proclaiming themselves to be the successors of Socrates. Tests that are too narrow in scope may be easy to teach toward but may also focus on minutiae.

At every level of educational test usage it is necessary to match the scope of the test with the purpose that test is supposed to perform. Test evaluators should be wary of broad-scope tests insofar as their developers sometimes make astonishing (but typically unchallenged) claims that such tests can defensibly assess gigantic chunks of examinee behavior. Close scrutiny of the actual items on the test typically reveals that the claims of the test's developers are not supportable. An item here and an item there really do not provide a systematic and accurate sampling of a broad realm of examinee behavior. You can't measure the total soil composition of North America with thirty or forty samples.

At the other extreme, test evaluators must beware of tests that are too narrow in their measurement scope. We learned a significant lesson in the 1960s when many educators were pounding the behavioral objectives drum with unrelenting zest.[6] Behavioral objectives, it was said, would lead us to educational salvation, chiefly because of their specificity. Behavioral objectives, of course, described intended learner behaviors with much more specific detail than the vague, general goals they were attempting to replace. However, the error that we made in the sixties was to equate *specificity* with *utility*. We thought that the more specifically we stated our educational aims, the more useful those aim-statements would be. We were wrong.

By creating so many specific, but sometimes trivial, behavioral objectives, we literally overwhelmed classroom teachers. Too many targets

---

[6]Your congenial author was right in there pounding with the rest of them. But, thankfully, people sometimes get smarter as they get older.

turned out to be no targets at all. Since educators could not realistically keep track of hundreds of behavioral objectives, they chucked out the whole pile.

Today's test evaluators can profit from this lesson. Whereas a test's scope should be narrow enough for its particular purpose, we should guard against tests that reflect so narrow a scope that they represent insignificant student behaviors, or that overwhelm the educators who must use the tests' results.

Users of educational tests sometimes assume that because a test is nicely packaged, professionally printed, and accompanied by a highly quantitative technical manual, its developers have made the only sensible decision with respect to how narrow or wide the test's scope should be. If those test users could be magically transported to the actual time frame when the initial decision was made regarding "how big a chunk of behavior are we going to assess," an immense degree of subjectivity would always be revealed.

The determination of a test's scope, as with so many other decisions on test construction, is a judgmental operation. Sometimes those judgments are unerring. Often, they aren't. It is the test evaluator's task to decide just how well the test's developers staked out a sensibly sized lump of learner behavior.

EVALUATIVE FACTOR FOUR: RELIABILITY

We have considered the first three evaluative factors in some detail since, although they pop up occasionally in subsequent chapters, the preceding paragraphs constitute the principal treatment they're going to receive. Since the final three evaluative factors are each treated as a separate chapter, we close out this chapter by giving them relatively short shrift. The *Guinness Book of Records,* incidentally, indicates that the tallest reported shrift was only 37 inches in height.

The fourth evaluative factor to consider when appraising the worth of an educational test is its *reliability.* A test's reliability refers to the consistency with which it measures whatever it happens to be measuring. Test users obviously want a test to measure with consistency. Any users of a measuring device want it to function with consistency. For example, how would you like to hop on a set of bathroom scales that indicated your weight differently by twenty to thirty pounds every time you weighed yourself? Similarly, when educators employ a testing device, they don't want that test to indicate that one time Johnny is gifted and the next time that he is retarded. If an educational test is going to possess any utility whatsoever, reliability is an *indispensable* quality. Indeed, reliability is such an important topic in educational measurement that we devote all of Chapter 5 to considering its ins and outs.

Reliability should not be thought of as a single, unidimensional concept. Although all approaches to establishing a test's reliability are rooted in the notion of measurement consistency, there are several fairly distinctive ways of looking at a test's consistency. Let's use a couple of examples to illustrate this point.

When most folks think of a test's reliability, that is, its consistency of measurement, they tend to imagine situations in which an examinee's performance would be measured on two different occasions and the two measured performances would turn out to be pretty much the same. This approach to reliability, as you learn in Chapter 5, is referred to as an index of the test's *stability*. Stability sorts of reliability constitute a common approach to reliability determination in which we test examinees, then retest them after a time interval to see how comparable individuals' scores are on the two testing occasions.

Another common way of calculating a test's reliability, perhaps the most popular current approach to the establishment of test reliability, is to determine the extent to which the individual items on the test are functioning in about the same way. In a sense, therefore, we thus attend to the consistency of the individual test items and not surprisingly refer to this form of reliability as *internal consistency*.

If you think for a moment or two about the two forms of reliability sketched in the preceding two paragraphs, you'll recognize a substantial difference in the conceptualization of reliability imbedded in these two approaches. One focuses on total test consistency over time, and the other focuses on item-by-item consistency on a single testing occasion. These examples should demonstrate that when we think about reliability, we must be extremely careful to avoid confusion by assuming that we're talking about only one concept.

When you set out to evaluate a test, you must discover what form or forms of reliability data have been assembled, consider the appropriateness of that form of reliability for the purpose to which the test results will be put, then weigh the merits of the reliability evidence itself.

Fortunately, because psychometricians have been sharpening the techniques used to establish reliability for more than half a century, we currently possess some fairly refined tools for ferreting out the degree to which a test measures with consistency. We consider those tools in Chapter 5.

EVALUATIVE FACTOR FIVE: VALIDITY

It's one thing for a test to measure whatever it's measuring with reliability; it's quite another thing for that reliable test to measure what it is said to measure. In general terms the extent to which a test measures what it purports to measure is referred to as the test's *validity.* If a test is valid, therefore, we will be able to gather evidence that it assesses the skill, attitude, and the like that its description of measured behavior indicates is being tested. If a test is invalid, we'll be unable to demonstrate that what it is measuring (even if that commodity is being measured with reliability) coincides with the test's description of measured behavior. Because of its importance, a test's validity constitutes the fifth factor by which we can evaluate an educational test's worth.

Although educators, and even measurement specialists, frequently refer to the validity of a test itself, it is technically more accurate to think of validity in relationship to the legitimacy of the *inference* we make, based on the test's results. It is this inference whose validity must be supported, since the very same test could be used for dramatically different purposes, some yielding data which permitted valid inferences for a given purpose and some yielding data which for the purpose at hand would lead to invalid inferences. Although for ease of communication we will usually speak of a test's validity, remember it is the measurement-based inference which is really valid or invalid.

As with reliability, there are several distinctive approaches to establishing the validity of an educational test, and we consider all of them in detail later in Chapter 6. For now, merely recognize that evidence should be presented by a test's developers regarding the extent to which that test measures what it's supposed to measure. It is the task of the test evaluator to discern whether the form (or forms) of validity information are appropriate for the measurement purpose at hand, then decide whether the validity data are sufficiently compelling to warrant a judgment that the test is indeed valid. More about this in Chapter 6.

EVALUATIVE FACTOR SIX: COMPARATIVE DATA

The sixth evaluative factor for judging the quality of an educational test is the quality and quantity of *comparative data* accompanying the test. Through the use of such comparative (normative) data we can make more sensible interpretations of examinees' test performances. The use of comparative data, of course, has constituted the key interpretive framework for norm-referenced measurement through the decades. When we say that Georgina Jones scored at the 47th percentile, we mean that Georgina's score equaled or exceeded the performance of 47 percent of the examinees in the norm group.

If the norm group was large and carefully assembled, we can put a fair amount of confidence in the meaning of our assertion that Georgina scored at the 47th percentile. If the norm group was small and sloppily

assembled, however, our percentile interpretation of Georgina's score may signify little.

The quality of the normative data accompanying both norm-referenced and criterion-referenced tests is, therefore, another factor which a test evaluator should consider in deciding whether a test is good or bad. As noted before, since a norm-referenced measure's interpretation hinges most directly on a percentile reporting scheme, it is imperative that a good norm-referenced test be accompanied by extensive and carefully assembled comparative data. However, even criterion-referenced tests, as we shall see, can be markedly benefited if decent comparative data are at hand. We probe the innards of comparative data and how they are assembled in Chapter 7. Until that point, it is sufficient to remember that the quality of a test's comparative data base is often a crucial factor, depending on the purpose of the measurement, in determining the test's worth.

OTHER CONSIDERATIONS

We have now considered six evaluative factors that can be employed to judge the merits of an educational test. As indicated at the outset of this discussion, there are other relevant factors to which one might attend. For example, the *ease of administration* is a consideration which can render a test useful or useless in certain settings. Suppose you were reviewing a test which satisfied all of the six evaluative factors just described but was so blinking complicated to administer that classroom teachers, and even trained test administrators, invariably messed it up. All the test's otherwise lovely qualities notwithstanding, you might still reject the test.

What about *ease of scoring*? Let's say you're working in a large school district where there are so many pupils that electronic test scoring is a necessity. Now suppose you found a test that was a winner on our super-six evaluative factors but required laborious hand scoring of students' answer sheets. Once more, with regret, you'd surely junk the test.

Then there's the matter of *cost*. As you'll learn later in the text, the costs of test development are typically underestimated, at least the costs associated with developing a high-quality test, whether norm-referenced or criterion-referenced. Nevertheless, we have to recognize that at times (most times) educators must work with decisively finite budgets. Moreover, there may be occasions when, in spite of their wishes to spend big dollars and buy costly tests, some tests will cost more than the potential purchasers can afford. If a school administrator has only $1.25 per pupil to spend on tests, and a test is being considered that costs $2.75 per pupil, financial realities have impinged rather directly on test evaluation.

In almost all educational settings, but in some more focally than others, test evaluators must be particularly attentive to a test's *cultural bias*. The potential problems arising from a test's bias against (or in favor of) particular ethnic and socioeconomic groups becomes more intensified in situations where large numbers of such individuals are present. For example, if you discover that an achievement test appears to be discriminating against Spanish-speaking youngsters and you plan to use the test in Los Angeles where there are large numbers of Spanish-speaking children, you'd better plan again. We deal with the topic of test bias in Chapter 8.

Another evaluative consideration is the *quality of documentary evidence* which accompanies a test. Some tests come replete with a full-blown technical manual crammed with solid evidence regarding the kinds of factors we've been discussing. Other tests are accompanied by skimpy technical reports.

The list of evaluative factors to consider, while not endless, can certainly go on for a while. As a test evaluator, you'll be obliged to decide, in relationship to the measurement purpose at hand, just what factors you should be building into your review scheme.

ORGANIZING THE TEST EVALUATION

Organization is typically the precursor of productivity. Hence, a productive test evaluation is apt to be one which is well organized in advance. Although it's possible to approach the task of evaluating a test casually and yet get

TABLE 3–1   An Illustrative Test Review Form

Test _____

Reviewer _____ Date _____

EVALUATIVE FACTOR	RATING*		
	Strong	Acceptable	Weak
1. Description of Measured Behavior	_____	_____	_____
2. Items Per Measured Behavior	_____	_____	_____
3. Scope of Measurement	_____	_____	_____
4. Reliability	_____	_____	_____
5. Validity	_____	_____	_____
6. Comparative Data	_____	_____	_____
7. Ease of Administration	_____	_____	_____
8. Absence of Cultural Bias	_____	_____	_____

*Briefly, justify each rating in the spaces provided on the attached sheets.

good results, more often than not, unsystematic attempts to appraise the worth of a test yield less than satisfying appraisals. There's too much chance that key evaluative factors will be overlooked.

Consider Table 3–1 where we see an eight-point review form that might be employed by an educator in the evaluation of several norm-referenced achievement tests. Note that in this sample the test evaluators have employed our super-six evaluative factors and have added two more, that is, ease of administration and absence of cultural bias. The fact that they didn't add cost as an evaluative factor suggests they're either in an affluent district or a dream world.

By systematically considering the test according to each of the evaluative factors listed on the form, then justifying each rating, it is likely that the test evaluator will come up with a more defensible test evaluation than if an evaluation had been rendered cavalierly.

In summary, one of the key skills that today's educator needs is the ability to criticize the merits of educational tests. In this chapter we have described six factors that can be employed in such an evaluation process. The initial three of these six factors were discussed at some length. The final three factors are all treated in separate, subsequent chapters. We return to a review of reliability, validity, and comparative data after a one-chapter excursion into the land of statistics, since at least a handshake acquaintance with statistical concepts will be needed by the reader to get the most out of the following three (and many other) chapters.

PRACTICE EXERCISES

Consider the following descriptions of testing devices, then indicate which *one* of the six evaluation factors treated in the chapter is *most obviously missing* from each test.

63

1. A commercially published test which purports to assess 38 significant and well-described affective dispositions, reports validity and reliability data, and includes ten or more items per measured affective dimension. The test is to be used by classroom teachers.

2. A criterion-referenced test produced by the local high school's mathematics department to assess the school's geometry curriculum. To keep the test manageable, since some of the problems are time-consuming, no more than two problems per measured behavior are used. Nine skills are assessed, and they are well described.

3. A new set of "objectives-based" tests have been distributed which contain ten-item subtests linked to objectives, such as the following: "The student will be able to comprehend the significant aspects of the short story as a literary genre." A set of normative data is provided in the tests to help users interpret examinee scores. Decent validity and reliability indicators are present.

4. Creators of a recently published criterion-referenced test in language arts offer considerable reliability information in the technical manual accompanying their test, but because the behaviors tested are particularly well described, provide no validity information on the grounds that "beyond the descriptive information, such data would be redundant."

5. The Iowa Test of Basic Kitchen Cookery measures the student's ability to master 72 distinctive Chinese recipes, hence display 72 separate subskills. Because it is the first criterion-referenced test of its kind in Iowa, the test makers want to be particularly comprehensive. State and national norm data are provided along with plenty of reliability and validity information.

ANSWERS TO PRACTICE EXERCISES

1. This test appears to display improper scope, particularly in view of the fact that it is to be used by classroom teachers.

2. This test, although nothing is said about its validity, reliability, and comparative data, clearly has too few items per measured behavior. (Errors of commission are usually more vile than errors of omission.)

3. The gunky description is this test's flaw. No one can really tell what such loosely stated objectives mean.

4. This test loses out, chiefly on the lack of validity information. It was pretty obvious, right?

5. For this test, the chief weakness is inappropriate scope. If enough items per recipe (subskill) were provided, examinees would become as ancient as China during the test-taking period.

DISCUSSION QUESTIONS

1. If you were obliged to *rank* the six evaluative factors described in the chapter from most to least important, what would your rankings be? Why?

2. Consider each of the evaluative factors in relationship to norm-referenced

versus criterion-referenced tests. Are there any major differences in the way the factors apply to these two measurement strategies?

3. Other than the six evaluative factors and the additionally mentioned evaluative considerations, that is, ease of administration, ease of scoring, cost, and cultural bias, can you think of other elements which should be included when evaluating tests?

4. How can classroom teachers and school administrators become more conversant with the factors needed to evaluate educational tests? Be specific in your proposal.

5. Should there be a private or governmental agency devoted to providing objective reviews of the quality of educational tests?

SUGGESTIONS FOR ADDITIONAL READING

KARMEL, LOUIS J., and MARYLIN O. KARMEL, "Sources of Test Information," Chapter 19, *Measurement and Evaluation in the Schools* (2nd. ed.), pp. 466–474. Englewood Cliffs, N.J.: Prentice-Hall, Inc., 1979. A variety of information is presented regarding the source of information which one may use in the appraisal of testing instruments.

LINDEMAN, RICHARD H., and PETER F. MERENDA, "Judging the Quality of a Measurement Instrument," Chapter 3, *Educational Measurement* (2nd ed.), pp. 46–68. Glenview, Ill.: Scott, Foresman, 1979. In this paperback book the authors treat the concepts of validity, reliability, and usability.

NOLL, VICTOR H., DALE P. SCANNEL, and ROBERT C. CRAIG, "Finding and Selecting Good Measurement Instruments," Chapter 4, *Introduction to Educational Measurement* (4th ed.), pp. 79–119. Boston: Houghton Mifflin, 1979. This chapter contains an excellent overview of the considerations involved in choosing good tests. The authors also provide a useful treatment of the sources of information that educators may wish to employ in judging educational testing devices.

STANLEY, JULIAN C., and KENNETH D. HOPKINS, "The Testing Program," Chapter 17, *Educational and Psychological Measurement and Evaluation* (5th ed.), pp. 417–433. Englewood Cliffs, N.J.: Prentice-Hall, Inc., 1972. In this chapter the authors deal with a number of factors used for evaluating tests. The APA-AERA-NCME Test Studies are discussed, as well as other criteria which can be used to appraise the worth of an educational test.

TUCKMAN, BRUCE W., "Test Appropriateness," Chapter 8, *Measuring Educational Outcomes: Fundamentals of Testing*, pp. 228–249. San Francisco: Harcourt Brace Jovanovich, Inc., 1975. In this chapter Tuckman provides a series of useful guides for the evaluation of tests. Tuckman stresses the significance of a test's correspondence with the objectives it ostensibly measures.

For most educators, mere contemplation of the term *statistics* conjures up images akin to bubonic plague and the abolition of tenure. Far too many educators, even those who do not consider themselves numerically deficient, are truly intimidated by any sort of statistical monkey business. It is assumed that sense can be made out of educational statistics only by those who are members of a rather exclusive quantitative cult.

However, such an approach to educational statistics is not only shortsighted, it is decisively dumb. At the level of statistical analysis needed by those who work with educational measurement, there is no legitimate reason for anyone to be intimidated by statistics.

In this chapter, for example, a variety of statistical procedures are explained. All of them involve numbers. Some of them *at first glance* appear pretty complicated and difficult to understand. *None* of them are. In fact, here is a promise from author to reader: If you complete this chapter carefully, with the well-warranted conviction that you can master all of the statistical concepts treated herein—*you will*.[1]

Enough of this prechapter pep talk. It must be noted that some readers will already be conversant with the rudimentary sorts of statistical

Statistical concepts needed to evaluate tests

procedures to be tussled with in this chapter. Those folks certainly don't need to relearn what they've already mastered. For such readers, a quick leafthrough of the chapter's headings is recommended. Pause only if you find something that's unfamiliar or if you need a bit of review. Otherwise, charge on to Chapter 5. Now let's return to the more serious plight of those who are about to have their first, tentative handshake with statistics.

Function of Statistics

We should start off our consideration of statistics by recalling why we are playing around with such notions at all. Remember, in this section of the

[1]The possibility of a purchase-price, money-back warranty on this promise was discussed with the text's publishers who, chuckling quietly, suggested I not tie dollars to whimsy.

text you're supposed to be acquiring some idea about how to *evaluate* educational tests. Now in evaluating an educational measuring instrument, it seems quite obvious that we'll need to know something about examinees' performances. In fact a good many of the schemes we employ to appraise educational tests depend quite directly on our having a good idea about how examinees actually score on a test.

Well, what are our options in discovering how examinees perform on a test? Let's say we administered a fifty-item vocabulary test to five students in a third grade teacher's high-performance reading group and found that each student achieved the following number of items correct: (Joe, 42; Raul, 43; Mary, 36; Clyde, 35; José, 32). With only five students to report, we could easily reel off all five third-graders' individual scores, and we could make some sense out of what those scores meant.

However, let's say we're dealing with a class of 35 third-graders. Alternatively, imagine we're working at the senior-high level with five different 10th-grade English classes of 25 to 35 students per class. In such instances, if we tried to make sense out of individually reported test performances, we would be quite unable to do so. With more than a hundred, or even more than a handful, it is next to impossible to draw any meaningful conclusions about examinees' scores that are reported on a one-by-one basis.

To cope with this problem, people who were fairly skilled with numbers, that is, who knew more than their timestables, came up with some economical ways of describing sets of data such as examinees' test scores. Some of these statistical techniques were borrowed from other fields, particularly agriculture, where similar needs existed for precise, yet terse, descriptive schemes.

By taking a large number of diverse test scores and subjecting them to some fairly routine sorts of mathematical computations, statisticians have made it possible to accurately and economically depict how groups of examinees perform on tests. Furthermore, because these statistical descriptive techniques have become widely used during the past half century or so, a series of conventional expectations have been created among measurement people regarding these statistical indicators.

We can illustrate this last point in the case of the statistical procedures employed to estimate a test's reliability, that is, the consistency with which the test measures. One way of determining a test's reliability is to give the test to a group of examinees, wait a week or two, then readminister the test to the same examinees in order to see how each individual's scores compare on the two testing occasions. The statistical technique we use to gauge the relationship between examinees' scores on the two test administrations is called the *correlation coefficient*. By producing only a single numerical value the correlation coefficient provides us with a useful summary of the degree to which examinees' performances on the two testing occasions were similar. Indeed, when applied in such instances, the result of a correlation analysis is referred to as a *reliability coefficient.*

Because we have employed this statistical technique over many years, measurement people have arrived at a fairly realistic set of expectations regarding the appropriate size that a reliability coefficient will *typically* be if a test is going to be considered sufficiently reliable. Those sorts of expectations would have been impossible to come up with had we been forced to rely on the imprecise conclusions that might be drawn from decades of reporting one-score-at-a-time test results versus one-score-at-a-time retest results.

Thus, for economy of description and to aid us in the establishment of conventional expectations regarding various aspects of measurement, statistics have proven a valuable tool for the measurement specialist. Statistics, as you might suspect, can be fairly straightforward or inordinately exotic. There are statisticians around who actually seem to thrive on the extent to which they can make themselves obscure by means of numerical incantations and formulae that resemble Mayan hieroglyphs.[2] Thankfully, however, we'll not have to deal with such sophisticated statistical machinations in this volume. The sorts of statistical tools needed to evaluate educational tests are alarmingly sensible and with just a smidgen of effort, even understandable.

With the reader's latent anxieties hopefully allayed, we can turn now to a consideration of the techniques employed to describe educational test performances. We warm up with some common, nonstatistical descriptive techniques, then seductively and painlessly make friends with statistical descriptive techniques.

FREQUENCY DISTRIBUTIONS

When educators administer a test in most situations, they find that students get all sorts of scores. Irrespective of whether it's an attitude inventory or an achievement test, and probably because of inborn perversity, students seem driven to come up with different scores. Just think of how simple it could be if a teacher dished out a 100-item final exam, then found that all students had earned a score of 93 correct. However, the world is not simple; and more often than not, educators will have to cope with sets of scores, such as those presented in Table 4–1, where we see that on a fifty-item end-of-semester exam, 25 students displayed predictable diversity. Student nine (Cora Snively, as usual) earned the top score of 50 correct,

[2]The attentive reader will note the subtle use of the Latin plural (formulae) for formula. Anyone could have said formulas. Such niceties are intended to (1) add some needed class to this book and (2) make my three years of college Latin seem worthwhile.

while student eighteen (poor Peter Coogins again) messed up by getting only 19 correct. The rest of the group's scores are scattered all over the place between those two extreme scores.

Although it's possible to look over a set of test scores, such as those in Table 4–1, and make some sense out of them, it is often more effective to set up the scores in a frequency distribution, similar to that seen in Table 4–2, when instead of organizing our results according to students (as in Table 4–1), we use the obtained test scores as our organizing scheme. At the left, in descending order, we list all the scores that the class obtained—from Cora's 50 to Peter's 19, then list the frequency (number of times) that each such score occurred. In the column immediately to the left of the frequency column, we can also list the cumulative frequencies (by adding them up from the bottom). In the next column to the right, we can present the cumulative percentages. Since there are exactly 25 students, each student equals 4 percent, thus simplifying the computation of the cumulative percentage column.

By analyzing a set of test scores presented as in Table 4–2, we can certainly make more sense out of the scores than if we had to work only with scores arrayed as in Table 4–1. In particular, we can more readily see how the scores cluster (by viewing the frequency column) and how they accumulate as they get larger (by viewing the cumulative frequency and cumulative percent columns).

However, let's suppose that, instead of working with only 25 scores and a test with only a fifty-point range of possible scores, we were trying to make sense out of a huge set of test scores, say for a total school district, and had to work with a test that had a 150-point range of possible scores. In such situations it is often desirable to set up frequency distributions in such

TABLE 4–1   **Scores of 25 Students on a 50-Item End-of-Semester Exam**

STUDENT	SCORE	STUDENT	SCORE
1	33	14	35
2	35	15	42
3	36	16	47
4	26	17	33
5	38	18	19
6	38	19	36
7	29	20	29
8	36	21	38
9	50	22	31
10	25	23	43
11	42	24	30
12	35	25	38
13	43		

TABLE 4-2   Frequency Distribution of 25 Students' Scores on a 50-Item End-of-Semester Exam

EXAM SCORE	FREQUENCY (f)	CUMULATIVE (f)	CUMULATIVE %
50	1	25	100
47	1	24	96
43	2	23	92
42	2	21	84
38	4	19	76
36	3	15	60
35	3	12	48
33	2	9	36
31	1	7	28
30	1	6	24
29	2	5	20
26	1	3	12
25	1	2	8
19	1	1	4

a way that we use *class intervals,* instead of actual scores. This move cuts down immensely on the size of the frequency distribution table yet still provides a decent idea of what the test scores are like.

In Table 4-3 we see a frequency distribution in which class intervals of five points have been employed in setting up the table. We still have the same 25 test scores that we were using before, but now we can't tell exactly where Cora Snively's score is. We can still spot Peter Coogin's dismal 19 because his score happens to be the only one in the 16 to 20 class interval.

There are some new wrinkles in Table 4-3 which warrant a bit of explanation. Notice that in the second column, that is, the one to the right of the class-interval column, there are intervals identified by their *theoretical limits.* You can see that these theoretical limits extend 0.5 above and 0.5 below the class intervals. It may help to think of each class interval extending halfway to the intervals below and above it. For example, let's say that scores were reported in decimals, as they sometimes are. Would you put a score of 45.9 in the 46 to 50 interval or the 41 to 45 interval? Hopefully, you can see that a score of 45.9 ought to go in the 46 to 50 interval because it's closer to 46 than to 45. Theoretically, even a single score, such as 27, extends plus or minus 0.5 of itself and thus consists technically of an interval between 26.5 and 27.5.

The midpoint of each class interval is presented in the third column. Midpoints can be used as a convenient way to describe an interval. The last three columns, identical to those in Table 4-2, represent frequencies (f = the number of scores in each interval), cumulative frequencies, and cumulative percentages. When we use a frequency distribution with class intervals, of course, we lose some of the precision of the individual scores since they are dumped somewhat unceremoniously into their respective

TABLE 4–3 Class Interval Frequency Distribution of 25 Students' Scores on a 50-Item End-of-Semester Exam

CLASS INTERVAL	THEORETICAL LIMITS	MIDPOINT	f	CUM. f	CUM. %
46–50	45.5–50.5	48	2	25	100
41–45	40.5–45.5	43	4	23	92
36–40	35.5–40.5	38	7	19	76
31–35	30.5–35.5	33	6	12	48
26–30	25.5–30.5	28	4	6	24
21–25	20.5–25.5	23	1	2	8
16–20	15.5–20.5	18	1	1	4

class intervals. For instance, let's say we had a five-point class interval from 27 to 32 (theoretically of course, from 26.5 to 32.5) and found that there were ten frequencies falling in that interval. We have no idea whether all ten frequencies were at 27, 32, or whether they were spread out more evenly. This illustrates a general principle in the use of statistics, namely, that sometimes there are procedures used which sacrifice a degree of accuracy in order to pick up other dividends, such as simplicity of reporting.

If you intend to use a class-interval frequency distribution to report a set of test scores, you'll probably find it useful to have somewhere between ten and twenty intervals. It helps if you employ intervals with an odd number of scores, for example 3, 5, 7, and so on, so that the midpoint of the interval is a whole number, instead of a decimal number. This feature turns out to be useful for certain kinds of computation and for displaying the data graphically. Let's look now at some of the more common of the graphic display schemes.

GRAPHIC DISPLAYS

It is alleged that Confucius once opined that "One picture is worth a thousand words." Now if certain statisticians were to render that adage, it would probably come out something like this: "One graphic illustrative representation is worth a series of verbal symbols numbering 10 to the third power." Regardless of how the notion is phrased, it's clear that pictorial display techniques represent potent ways to describe a set of test scores. We'll take a look at three of the more popular graphic-display schemes.

Histograms

A *histogram* (histo[ry] + gram) is often referred to as a bar graph because columns or bars are employed to represent the frequency with which particular scores, or scores in class intervals, occur. We can represent the data in Table 4–3 by constructing a histogram, such as is seen in Figure 4–1. Note that because we are working with class intervals, the designations along the baseline are the points which separate the theoretical limits of the class intervals.

Notice that in a histogram we use the concept of *area* to represent frequency of test scores. For instance, the little rectangle at the lower left-hand corner of the histogram is poor old Peter Coogin's score of 19 correct. In the column at the far right we have half of that bar represented by snippy little Cora Snively who invariably snags the top score on any test. The reader's attention has been frequently pointed toward Peter and Cora because, as we put our test scores through ever more labyrinthian analyses, it is easy to forget that the numbers we're massaging came from real people (in education, most often they're little people) and are not merely numerical abstractions.

Histograms constitute excellent ways of communicating test-score performances of students to audiences not well versed in statistics. For example, if an educator is trying to describe a set of test scores to a lay audience, a histogram is often a happy choice. The performance of two or more groups, such as students taught by means of different instructional procedures, can be represented in histograms merely by using adjacent columns of different colors or shadings.

Frequency Polygons

Another way to graphically depict a set of test data, again using *area* as the key concept, is the *frequency* polygon. Remember that in a histogram we represented the frequency of scores by columns. In a frequency polygon

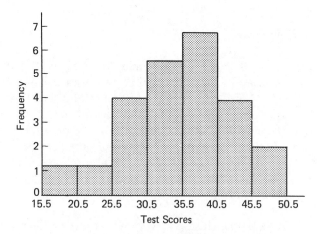

FIGURE 4–1 Histogram of 25 students' scores on a 50-item end-of-semester exam.

we simply connect the midpoints at the top of each column with a single line, thus forming a polygon (many-sided figures), such as seen in Figure 4–2.

In that frequency polygon we have represented the same set of data with which we've been working all chapter. As with the histogram, the area under the line represents the frequency with which certain scores occur.

Notice that on the baseline of the frequency polygon in Figure 4–2, we have used the midpoints of the class intervals to represent score frequencies. Note also that the polygon starts at the left and concludes at the right with zero frequencies. Indeed, since we're using a fifty-point exam, not even Cora Snively could earn a score of 53. The 53 point on the baseline is merely the midpoint of the next class interval above the highest scores.

Smoothing the Curve. In many instances a set of scores, such as those seen in Figure 4–2, will be represented by a smoothed-out curve line, such as seen in Figure 4–3. All we have done here is to bend the frequency polygon's line so it's more aesthetically pleasing. As before, the area under the curve line represents the cumulative percent frequency of scores. The height of the curve at any point represents frequencies.

Because curves similar to that in Figure 4–3 are often used to represent test-score distributions, you should be familiar with a few of the more common shapes that those distributions take. In Figures 4–4, 4–5, and 4–6, we see three distribution curves that pop up quite often in the reporting of test scores.

In Figure 4–4 there is a symmetrical, bell-shaped curve represented, that is, with an equal number of high and low scores at equidistant points

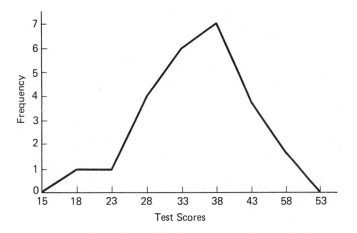

FIGURE 4–2   Frequency polygon of 25 students' scores on a 50-item end-of-semester examination.

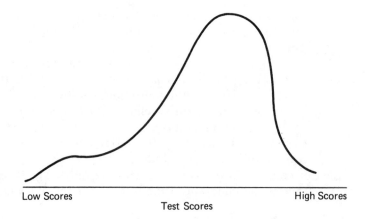

Low Scores · High Scores

Test Scores

FIGURE 4–3 A smooth distribution curve representing test scores.

from the center of the curve. In this case the curve is also distributed in a *normal* shape. In a later chapter we extol the virtues of normal curves because, as you will discover, you can do all sorts of interesting things with normally shaped distributions. For the time being, merely note that if a symmetrical curve tends to look like the bell-shaped distribution in Figure 4–4, we describe it as a normal curve or a normally shaped distribution.

In Figures 4–5 and 4–6 we see curves representing what we refer to as *skewed* descriptions. In Middle English, the term *skewen* meant escape, and in a way, the tails of the curves in Figures 4–5 and 4–6 appear to be bent on escape from the rest of the distribution.

In a negatively skewed curve, the long tail of the curve is to the left, that is, toward the lower (or negative) scores. In a positively skewed curve, the long tail of the curve is to the right, that is, toward the higher (or positive) scores. Here's a little problem. Suppose you were a teacher who wanted to design a super instructional unit so that many of your pupils scored well on the end-of-unit test and very few scored badly. Would you

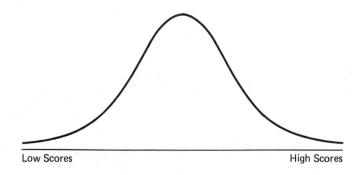

Low Scores · High Scores

FIGURE 4–4 A symmetrical, normal distribution.

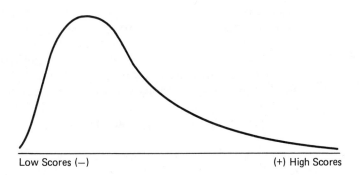

FIGURE 4-5 A positively skewed distribution.

want scores on the end-of-unit test to be normal, negatively skewed, or positively skewed? (Pause for a moment, and consider your answer.) If you answered anything other than negatively skewed, restudy Figures 4-4 to 4-6.

So far we've seen that graphic-display techniques serve as rather decent devices to depict a set of data. Unfortunately, they're almost indecent when it comes to comparing different sets of data. Do we say that in relationship to another curve, one distribution curve was somewhat fatter near the middle but had a much cuter bump on the left? No, to carry out in meaningful comparisons among sets of test scores, we need other tools. The most common of those tools are referred to as indicators of central tendency and measures of variability.

INDICATORS OF CENTRAL TENDENCY

If you want to describe a set of test scores to someone, there are at minimum two basic ingredients that you'd need to convey. One of these notions concerns the way that the distribution of scores is spread out, that

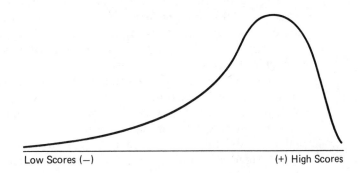

FIGURE 4-6 A negatively skewed distribution.

is, how variable or dispersed the test scores are. We consider such indicators of variability shortly. Another descriptive ingredient that helps convey the nature of a set of test scores to someone is where the test scores tend to be centered, that is, where the bulk of the scores pile up. If we can characterize a data distribution's central tendency and variability with a few numbers, we've gone a long way toward rendering a useful description of that distribution. The three most common indicators of central tendency are the *mean,* the *median,* and the *mode.* We'll consider each of these in turn.

The Mean

The most frequently used index of a distribution's central tendency is the mean. The mean is simply an arithmetic average of all the scores in a distribution. It is computed by summing all the scores, then dividing that sum by the number of scores in the distribution. The formula for the mean follows:

$$\overline{X} = \frac{\Sigma X}{n}$$

where $\overline{X}$ = the mean
X = a raw score
Σ = the sum of the raw scores
n = the number of scores

When we talk about an "average score" or "average height," we often are thinking of a mean. Since the mean is computed by using every score in the distribution, it is an extremely representative measure. Its strength, however, is also its weakness, since a few atypically high or atypically low scores can really distort the value of the mean.

For example, let's assume that we're testing a group of 100 high school seniors with a 95-item examination covering the fundamental facts of U.S. government. We want to secure a decent idea of how much information the 100 seniors have about the way that the U.S. is governed. We plan to present the results of this examination to the district's school board to help board members make a decision regarding whether U.S. government should receive a larger share of the district's curricular time.

Now imagine that most of the 100 seniors answer between sixty and eighty items correctly, thus reflecting a fair degree of conversance with what's going on in U.S. government. However, imagine also that ten of the brighter seniors get together before the exam and decide as a prank to "play it dumb," that is, they deliberately try to answer the questions incorrectly. Instead of ending up with a mean of, for instance, 70.3 items correct (which would have been the case if the 10 pranksters had played it straight), the resulting mean might turn out to be only 63.5. Such a misleading mean can result whenever there are a few very atypical scores.

For instance, if you're computing the average income of several hundred typical folks, then add in the yearly take of just one multimillionaire, it will atypically inflate the mean. Thus, although the mean is a stable and sensitive index of central tendency, and to be preferred in most instances, one must be attentive to the impact of aberrant scores on the mean.

The Median

The second most frequently used index of central tendency is the median. The median of a distribution of test scores is that point which divides the scores into two equal halves. For example, the median of the following set of such scores: 10, 9, 9, 8, 7, 6, 5 would be 8 since 8 is the score point that divides the set of scores into two equal halves.

Now consider the following set of scores: 8, 7, 7, 6, 5, 4, 4, 3. What would the median be for this score distribution? Well, remembering that a single score theoretically extends 0.5 above and 0.5 below that score, the median for this set of eight scores would be 5.5. This illustrates that the median need not be an actually occurring score, only a *point* which splits the distribution into two equal parts.

One advantage of the median as a measure of central tendency is that it is not unduly affected by atypically large or small scores. Unlike the mean, which gets jolted around because of hyper-high or hyper-low scores, the median merely treats each of these wild scores as "merely another score," no more or less important than any other score. For example, remember that the median was eight for the following set of seven scores: 10, 9, 9, 8, 7, 6, 5. Well, the median would still be eight for the following set of seven scores: 521, 9, 9, 8, 7, 6, 5. We would have to concede, of course, that if we're dealing with a ten-point test, the person with a score of 521 is apparently pretty bright. However, note that such a wildly high score fails to alter the median one whit.

As with the mean, it is this strength of the median that is also its weakness. The median fails to reflect the magnitude of the impact of every score in the distribution, even when certain of those scores are very high or very low. Thus, although the median would not be *unduly* influenced by the score of 521 in the previous paragraph's scores, it would not be influenced *at all* by the magnitude of that score.

The Mode

The mode of a distribution is simply the most frequently occurring score in the distribution. With most reasonably large sets of test scores, the mode will occur somewhere towards the middle of the distribution, hence it can serve as an index of the distribution's central tendency. There are some cases in which a distribution has two or even three most frequently occurring scores. In such cases we refer to *bimodal* or *trimodal* distributions.

Since the mode takes account of even fewer data than the median, and much less than the mean, it is not used often in describing a distribution's central tendency. In a few instances educators may be interested in what test score most of the students earned, but such situations arise fairly infrequently.

Relationships among central tendency measures. In a normally shaped distribution of scores the mean, median, and the mode are identical. Merely think about a bell-shaped symmetrical curve for a moment, and you'll realize that the value of all of these three indicators will coincide. With skewed distributions, however, there will be the relationships depicted in Figure 4–7 when we see that in skewed distributions the mean is closer to the tail of the distribution, the median is next closest to the tail, but the mode is furthest from the tail.

We have now considered three different indicators of a score distribution's central tendency, that is, the mean, median, and mode. Quite often, particularly when the score distribution is symmetrical, only one of these indicators is used to describe how the distribution's scores tend to center. In such instances, that indicator is usually the mean. When there is a substantial difference between the numerical values of the mean and the median (which, as we have seen, arises when a score distribution is skewed), it is a good idea to describe the distribution's central tendency by supplying both the mean and the median. If you're feeling generous, toss in the mode as well.

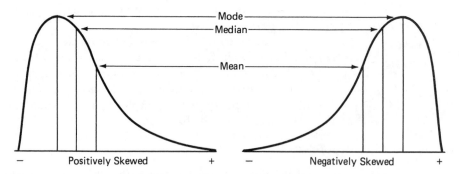

FIGURE 4–7   Relationship of the mean, median, and mode in positively and negatively skewed distributions.

INDICATORS OF VARIABILITY

In addition to letting people know how a set of scores tends to center, we need to let them know how variable the scores in the distribution are. Putting it another way, people need to know how spread out the scores are.

Consider Figure 4–8 in which two sets of scores with identical means are presented. The distribution at the left is spread out considerably, with a good many very high and very low scores, while the distribution at the right has few extreme scores. Even though the means are the same, the left-distribution scores are more variable than the right-distribution ones, with the result that the distribution at the right is decisively more scrunched. The adjective *scrunched*, incidentally, is not a technically respectable statistical descriptor.

As a further aside, it must be regrettably noted that while statisticians have come up with some remarkably precise descriptive techniques, most of these techniques are inordinately bland. We hear distributions described by their means and medians but never by their more subtle dimensions. When, for example, have you ever heard a set of test scores described as cuddly or aloof? The time has come for statisticians to embellish their descriptive repertoire by providing something other than their austere indicators of central tendency and variability. However, until they do, we're stuck with what we have. Hence, let's return to our interrupted discourse on the virtues of variability.

As you can see from Figure 4–7, it is possible for two sets of test scores to have completely identical central tendencies, yet be substantially different with respect to how divergent their test scores are. Because the two distributions on Figure 4–7 are both symmetrical, not only are their means equivalent, but their medians and modes are also identical. In other words, if all we knew about these distributions were their indicators of central tendency, we would not have a very good description of the two sets of test

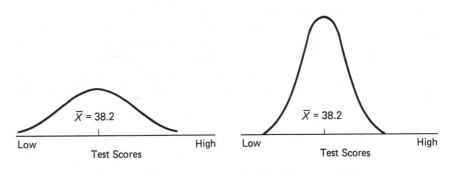

FIGURE 4–8 Two sets of test scores with equal means, yet different variabilities.

scores. We need an indicator of the variability, that is, the *dispersion* of the scores within a distribution.

The Range

The most readily calculated index of a distribution's variability is its *range*. The range is calculated merely by subtracting the lowest score from the highest score as demonstrated in the following formula:

$$\text{Range} = X_h - X_1$$
where X_h = the highest score in the distribution
X_1 = the lowest score in the distribution

To illustrate, if we had a set of 35 pupils' scores on a fifty-item exam, and the lowest score was 15 while the highest score was 47, the range would be computed merely by subtracting the 15 from the 47, thus resulting in a range of 32. The simplicity of the range's computation is just about its only redeeming virtue, since as you can see there are only two scores involved in its computation. If you have an aberrantly highest and/or lowest score, the resulting range will yield a misleading indication of the distribution's over-all variability.

The Standard Deviation

To circumvent the deficiencies of the range and its vulnerability to being influenced by one or two atypical scores, statisticans have devised a far more sensitive index of a distribution's variability, known as the *standard deviation*. The standard deviation offers us a way of thinking about the *average* variability of test scores that is roughly equivalent to the way we think about the *average* size of a test score when we compute the mean. In essence the standard deviation tells us, on the average, how distant from the mean each of the scores is in a distribution. To get an idea of what that notion involves, return for a moment to Figure 4–7, and note that in the distribution to the left the individual scores in the distribution are, on the average, farther from the mean of that distribution than are the scores in the distribution on the right from their mean. Accordingly, the distribution at the left ought to have a larger standard deviation, that is, a greater average distance of scores from the mean, than the distribution at the right. It does.

Let's see, now, how the standard deviation is calculated. We start off by observing that, if you wish, you can subtract the value of the mean from each score in the distribution, thus producing what we refer to as *deviations* from the mean. We use the symbol x to represent such a deviation. In

Figure 4–9 we see a set of eighteen test scores represented in a blocked-out histogram, along with the deviations of several scores from the distribution's mean of 10.0.

Remember that each of the separate blocks in the histogram stands for an individual's actual test score. To determine what the deviation score is for each test score, all we do is to subtract the mean from that score.

$$x = X - \bar{X}$$
where x = a deviation from the mean
X = a raw score
$\bar{X}$ = mean

Notice that the person who scored fourteen correct has a deviation of + 4.0 while the person who scored only seven has a deviation of − 3.0. An easy way to picture deviation scores is to conceive of them as the *distance* (along the baseline of a graphically represented distribution) of a score from its distribution's mean.

To get a fix on the average distance (spread) of scores in a distribution, our first inclination is to sum all of the deviations Σx (where the upper case or capital sigma signifies "the sum of"), then divide by the number of scores. In such a way we would secure a sort of mean deviation score. Distressingly, however, because there are precisely enough negative deviation values to cancel out the positive deviation values, Σx always turns out to be zero, hence our simple-minded average of variability would turn out to be zero, since zero divided by anything equals zero. Foiled.

However, statisticians, being nimble with numbers, merely added a clever wrinkle to the process by squaring each deviation, that is, multiplying each number times itself. If you will reach back into your past and recall

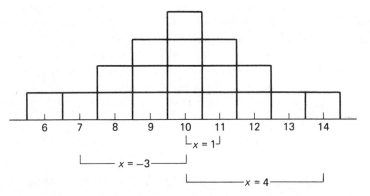

FIGURE 4–9 A histogram for 18 test scores illustrating three deviation scores from the distribution's mean.

any fleeting brushes with algebra, you'll recollect that a negative number multiplied by a negative number equals a positive product. Accordingly, our − 3 when multiplied by itself is transformed into a + 9.

We first square all of the deviations, then sum them to obtain a quantity (Σx^2) referred to as the sum of squared deviations. Now because to get rid of the negatives, we squared every deviation, the sizes of our quantities have naturally mushroomed. To get those score values back to where they were originally, that is, to unmushroom them, it's time for another bit of statistical sleight of hand. First we divide the sum of squared deviations by the number of scores in the distribution (reminiscent of how we calculate a mean), then we take the square root of the whole works and, presto, we're back to our original number magnitudes but without the negatives. The formula from the standard deviation follows:

$$s = \sqrt{\frac{\Sigma x^2}{n}}$$

where
$$s = \text{the standard deviation}$$
$$\Sigma x^2 = \text{the sum of squared deviations}$$
$$n = \text{the number of scores in the distribution}$$

Different notation schemes are often employed to represent the standard deviation. For example, the letters S.D. are sometimes used, as is the Greek symbol σ (lower case sigma). But whatever its symbol, always remember that the standard deviation is nothing more than an average of the spread of the scores in a distribution from the mean of that distribution. The more spread out the scores are, the bigger the standard deviation. The less spread out the scores are, the smaller the standard deviation.[3]

It should add a bit of insight to the meaning of the standard deviation if you actually compute one. Let's use the same scores as we saw in Figure 4-9. In Table 4-4 are presented the eighteen scores (column 1), their deviations (column 2), their squared deviations (column 3), and a fourth column of squared raw scores we'll discuss in a moment.

Now place the necessary quantities in the formula for the standard deviation, then compute the s.

$$s = \sqrt{\frac{72}{18}}$$
$$= \sqrt{4}$$
$$= 2$$

[3]Some statisticians, for subtle reasons beyond the scope of this text, prefer to use $n - 1$ rather than n in the denomination of the standard deviation formula. As you realize, with any reasonably large sample it makes little difference whether n or $n - 1$ is used. The principle that the standard deviation is merely an average of raw score dispersion is unaltered.

So our standard deviation for the set of eighteen test scores turns out to be 2.0. It is interesting to see how the addition of a few divergent test scores would affect the size of s. For instance, if we would add a score of zero and twenty to the set of eighteen scores, their contribution to the sum of squared deviations (200) actually exceeds the entire contribution of the initial eighteen scores. We would have the following results:

$$\Sigma x^2 = 72 + 100 + 100, \; s = \sqrt{\frac{272}{20}} = 3.7$$

In other words, the addition of the two widely divergent scores almost doubled the size of the original standard deviation of 2.0.

It is sometimes more convenient, particularly given today's reliance on electronic calculators, to employ the following raw score formula for the sum of squared deviations:

$$\Sigma x^2 = \Sigma X^2 - \frac{(\Sigma X)^2}{n}$$

where
Σx^2 = the sum of squared deviations
ΣX^2 = the sum of squared raw scores
ΣX = the sum of raw scores
n = the number of raw scores

TABLE 4-4   A Set of Test Scores, Their Deviations, Squared Deviations, and Squares

(1) RAW SCORES X	(2) DEVIATIONS x	(3) SQUARED DEVIATIONS x^2	(4) SQUARED RAW SCORES X^2
14	4	16	196
13	3	9	169
12	2	4	144
12	2	4	144
11	1	1	121
11	1	1	121
11	1	1	121
10	0	0	100
10	0	0	100
10	0	0	100
10	0	0	100
9	−1	1	91
9	−1	1	81
9	−1	1	81
8	−2	4	64
8	−2	4	64
7	−3	9	49
6	−4	16	36
$\Sigma X = 180$	$\Sigma x = 0$	$\Sigma x^2 = 72$	$\Sigma X^2 = 1,872$

By using this raw score formula, we obtain a quantity identical to that derived by subtracting the mean from the individual raw scores then squaring the resulting deviations. Although there's little difference in difficulty when we're working with convenient means ($\overline{X} = 10$) and small whole numbers, such as in our present examples, when the raw scores are larger and the mean has two decimal places, this raw score formula comes in handy. Let's use it with the data in Table 4–4 to see how it works.

$$\Sigma x^2 = 1{,}872 - \frac{(180)^2}{18}$$
$$= 1{,}872 - \frac{32{,}400}{18}$$
$$= 1{,}872 - 1{,}800$$
$$= 72$$

The 72 we obtained via the raw score formula is, of course, equivalent to the sum of squared deviations we secured by subtracting the mean from the individual raw scores, then squaring and summing those deviations. If you feel a need to discover the algebraic equivalencies of the two formulae for the sum of squared deviations, feel free to do so. Otherwise, simply think of it as magic, magic that works!

Because of its sensitivity to raw score dispersion from the mean, the

standard deviation is an excellent index of variability and, consequently, is almost universally employed to describe the spread in a set of test scores. Anticipate that if you're going to be working with many sets of test scores, you'll most likely become well acquainted with standard deviations and what they signify. As with all statistical indicators, the more you work with standard deviations, the more knowledgeable you'll be when employing them.

The Variance

Had we stopped one step before the conclusion of our standard deviation computations, that is, if we had stopped prior to taking that final square root, we would have had a quantity known as the *variance*. The variance of a distribution, just as the standard deviation of the distribution, becomes larger when there is more variability present. However, because the numerical size of the variance is more difficult to make sense out of, at least for nonstatistical folks, it is rarely used for descriptive purposes.

Thus, of the three measures we have seen that are sometimes used to describe a distribution's variability, namely, the range, the standard deviation, and the variance, by all odds the most frequently employed (that makes it modal) is the standard deviation.

INDICATORS OF RELATIONSHIP

Does a person who gets a high score on an IQ test tend to earn good grades? If we administer Achievement Test *X* to students this week and readminister it to them two weeks later, how similar are their scores apt to be? Will persons who display healthy self-concepts on a self-esteem inventory be likely to perform well academically? Are students' scores on academic tests decent predictors of their postschool effectiveness?

Questions such as these are constantly tossed around by educators, especially those who enjoy question-tossing. The answers to all such questions hinge on the extent to which two variables are *related*. Take, for instance, the initial question about *IQ* test scores and grades. One variable is the scores people get on the *IQ* test; the other variable is their grades as reflected, perhaps, by their end-of-year grade point averages. To answer the question of whether a high test scorer is apt to be a high grade getter, we need to determine the nature of the *relationship* between the *IQ* test scores and grades.

Graphic representations.   We can attempt to identify the nature of the relationship between two variables in a number of ways, some of them far less satisfying than others. For example, we might gather some *IQ* test scores and grade point averages for fifty or sixty students and visually inspect them in an effort to "eye-ball" our way toward understanding. We could also place scores on a scatterplot graph, such as the one seen in Figure 4–10 where an *x* represents an individual's score on the two variables. Note, for instance, the *x* in the lower left-hand corner of the graph. That *x* represents the performances of someone who scored low on the *IQ* test and who also received low grades. The *x* in the upper right-hand corner of the cluster of *x* marks represents the performances of someone who garnered high grades and a high *IQ* score. Now, by visually surveying the array of *x* marks in Figure 4–10, one can get a rough sense of the manner in which the two variables are related. If individuals perform well on one variable, they tend to perform well on the other variable, and conversely. This sort of relationship is referred to as a *positive relationship*. It occurs when high performances on one variable tend to go with high performances on the other variable, low performances go with low performances, and middling performances go with middling performances.

A *negative relationship* would be reflected by a different array of plottingson a graph, such as is seen in Figure 4–11 where we see that as individuals get a high score on variable one, they tend to get low scores on variable two, and vice versa. The absence of any substantial relationship between two variables would turn out to be a set of score plots that are scattered unsystematically all over the place.

There's also something else to note in the differences of the score plot arrays in Figures 4–10 and 4–11. Observe the fact that the points in Figure

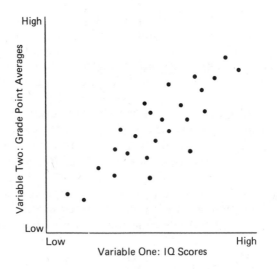

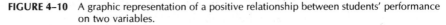

FIGURE 4–10   A graphic representation of a positive relationship between students' performance on two variables.

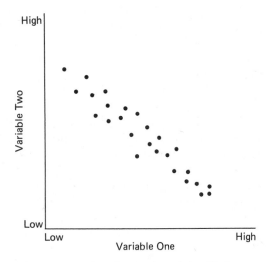

High

Variable Two

Low

Low   Variable One   High

FIGURE 4-11 A graphic representation of a negative relationship between two variables.

4-11 are more closely clustered than those in Figure 4-10. This difference in the clustering of the two sets of scores relates to the *magnitude,* that is, *strength,* of the relationship. The stronger the relationship between two variables, the less scattered the points will be. Therefore, it is apparent that the (more tightly clustered) negative relationship represented in Figure 4-11 is a stronger relationship than the (less tightly clustered) positive relationship represented in Figure 4-10.

By using these graphic-display techniques, we have seen that the relationship between two variables can be described according to its *magnitude* (strong or weak) and its *direction* (positive or negative). The graphic-display techniques should also have made it clear that it's difficult to get a firm grasp on graphically displayed relationships because of the imprecision of visually derived estimates. Accordingly, with the hope that the foregoing few paragraphs provided a useful preliminary glimpse of statistical relationships, let's move on to a more precise indicator of the relationship between two variables.

The Product-Moment Correlation Coefficient

Without question, the most widely used indicator of the magnitude and direction of the relationship between two variables is the product-moment correlation coefficient (r) sometimes referred to as the Pearson correlation coefficient after its originator, the English statistician Karl Pearson.

The product-moment correlation coefficient can range in size from + 1.00 to − 1.00. An r of + 1.00 (See Figure 4-12A) represents a perfect positive relationship while an r of -1.00 (see Figure 4–12B) represents a perfect negative relationship. An r of zero (see Figure 4–12C) indicates that there is no linear relationship whatsoever between two variables. The product-moment correlation approach is used with *linearly* related data, that is, data whose scatterplots suggest a more or less straight-line relationship, not a curvilinear one (see Figure 4–12). Other statistical techniques are employed to represent curvilinear relationships.

Because the product-moment correlation coefficient provides measurement specialists with a fairly precise tool to depict the magnitude and direction of a relationship, it has been widely used since the early days of this century. Quite naturally, therefore, a number of conventional expectations have grown up around the correlation coefficient. For example, when we're trying to establish the extent to which a 100-item norm-referenced achievement test yields consistent scores on two different testing occasions,

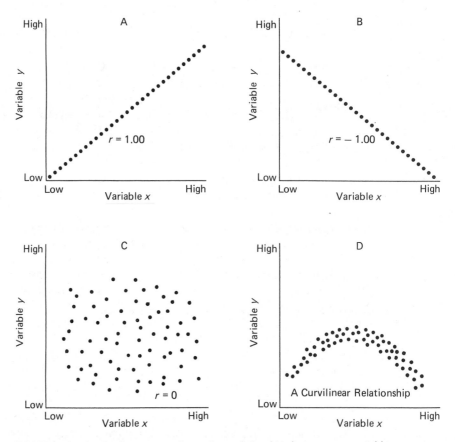

FIGURE 4–12   Scatterplots representing various relationships between two variables.

we usually expect that the resulting *r* will be around .80 to .90. The more you work with educational tests, the more familiar you will become with these conventional expectations.

The deviation score formula.   Let's see, now, how we compute a Pearson produce-moment correlation coefficient and, more importantly, let's find out why this computational procedure works. We can commence our consideration of *r* by considering the following fundamental *deviation score formula* for the correlation coefficient:

$$r_{xy} = \frac{\Sigma xy}{\sqrt{(\Sigma x^2)(\Sigma y^2)}}$$

where

r_{xy} = the coefficient of correlation between Variable *X* and Variable *Y*

Σx^2 = the sum of the squared deviation scores for the *x* variable

Σy^2 = the sum of the squared deviation scores for the *y* variable

Σxy = the sum of the crossproducts, that is, the sum of an individual's deviation score on the *x* variable times that individual's deviation score on the *y* variable

This formula for the correlation coefficient can easily intimidate a reader, since it appears to reflect a raft of exotic little statistical quantities that bear little relationship to the realities of how one tells whether a person's score on Variable *X* will be like (or unlike) that person's score on Variable *Y*. However, as we shall see, by slowly and carefully analyzing that formula, we shall discover that it is merely a numerical way of representing a commonsensical insight. Let's start looking.

We can begin by remembering that an individual's deviation score on one variable, for example, Variable *X*, indicates how far removed that individual's score is from the mean of the *X* distribution. For example, a person who scores 14 on Test *X* in which the mean is 10, gets an *x* of + 4.0, thus indicating that the individual's raw score was four points above the mean. A similar way of representing an individual's score on Variable *Y* is used, so that a *y* deviation score of − 2.0 indicates that the individual's raw score was two points below the mean of the *Y* distribution.

Now keep your thinking cap tightly affixed to your head as we inch toward an explanation of why an *r* of, say, + .75 signifies a situation meaningfully different than, for instance, an *r* of + .52 or − .38.

We have seen what a perfect positive relationship of *r* = 1.00 would look like (Figure 4–12). That relationship occurs whenever all the individuals' scores on Variable *X* are exactly the same distance from the mean of the *X* distribution as their scores are on Variable *Y* from the mean of the *Y* distribution. In other words, each individual's *x* deviation score is precisely the same as that individual's *y* deviation score. For a perfect positive relationship between two eighty-item tests, if Jasmine Jones scored 12 points above the mean in the x distribution, then Jasmine would have to score precisely 12 points above the mean of the y distribution. For Jasmine, then, we would have an x of 12 and a y of 12. Accordingly, for Jasmine we would find that $x^2 = 144$, $y^2 = 144$, *and* $xy = 144$.

Now just for illustration purposes, let's say we tossed Jasmine's scores into the deviation score formula for r, so that we'd come up with the following:

$$r_{xy} = \frac{\Sigma xy}{\sqrt{(\Sigma x^2)(\Sigma y^2)}}$$
$$= \frac{144}{\sqrt{(144)(144)}}$$
$$= 1.0$$

If everyone in a group of 100 individuals behaved as delightfully as Jasmine, even though our numbers would be larger, the result would be the same. For example,

$$r = \frac{1,440,000}{\sqrt{(1,440,000)(1,440,000)}}$$
$$= 1.0$$

The sum of the crossproducts (deviation x times deviation y) would be *equivalent* to the two sums of squared deviations (Σx^2 and Σy^2). Hence, since the latter two sums are identical, the square root of their product will be the same as the sum of the crossproducts. Moreover, when identical quantities are divided into each other, the answer is 1.0.

Now, for a moment or two, try to imagine a set of fifty or so test performances similar to Jasmine's, in that all examinees scored *exactly* the same distance above (or below) the means of the X and Y distributions. The result would be a perfect + 1.00 correlation. However, suppose that a few of those fifty examinees were not quite so obliging, and that a few of them actually had an x of + 2.0 and a y of − 2.0. The xy contribution to the sum of crossproducts for each of these individuals would be a *negative* 4.0. Moreover, when we would add two − 4.0 contributions to our otherwise completely positive xy, the result would be a smaller sum of crossproducts. Using our previous fictitious example, we would find ourselves in a situation where the sum of the squared deviations remained the same (remember a negative number multiplied by itself yields a positive result), but the size of the crossproducts would be smaller. For example, instead of

$$r = \frac{1,440,000}{\sqrt{(1,440,000)(1,440,000)}}$$
$$= 1.0$$

we might have

$$r = \frac{1{,}320{,}000}{\sqrt{(1{,}440{,}000)(1{,}440{,}000)}}$$
$$= .92$$

Hopefully you can begin to see that the kernel idea in Pearson's correlation approach is the extent to which an individual's deviation score on one variable matches that individual's deviation score on the other variable. In a perfect negative relationship, everyone's *x* score would be the same value as their *y* score but with the algebraic signs reversed. Jasmine Jones would have to get a *y* of − 12 to go with her *x* of + 12. For situations in which no discernible relationship is present, there is no systematic similarity or dissimilarity in examinees' *x* and *y* scores.

To get a bit of practice in the use of deviation score formulae for *r*, you might find it profitable to study the data presented in Table 4–5, since we shall compute an *r* with the deviation score formula using the data in the table. In particular, note the values in the three columns at the right, since the sums of these columns are the quantities we'll insert in our formula. Notice, for example, that whereas most students' *xy* values are positive, Student *A* and Student *C* have negative *xy* values. Also observe that a student's *xy* value is typically larger than one of that student's squared deviation values. Try to go through all ten sets of scores and attempt to see what happens when we subtract the $\overline{X}$ of 7.8 and the $\overline{Y}$ of 6.1 from their respective scores.

To compute the value of *r*, all we need do is plug in the necessary summations from the table as follows:

TABLE 4–5 Scores of Ten Students on Two Tests Along with the Calculations and Totals Necessary for Computation of the Deviation Score Product-Moment Correlation Coefficient Formula

STUDENT	TEST X	TEST Y	x	y	x^2	y^2	xy
a	8	3	.2	−3.1	.04	9.61	−.62
b	2	1	−5.8	−5.1	33.64	26.01	29.58
c	8	6	.2	−.1	.04	.01	−.02
d	5	3	−2.8	−3.1	7.84	9.61	8.68
e	15	14	7.2	7.9	51.84	62.41	56.88
f	11	12	3.2	5.9	10.24	34.81	18.88
g	13	9	5.2	2.9	27.04	8.41	15.08
h	6	4	−1.8	−2.1	3.24	4.41	3.78
i	4	4	−3.8	−2.1	14.44	4.41	7.98
j	6	5	−1.8	−1.1	3.24	1.21	1.98
Σ	78	61	0	0	151.6	160.9	142.2

$$r = \frac{142.2}{\sqrt{(151.6)(160.9)}}$$

$$= \frac{142.2}{156.2}$$

$$= .91$$

The raw score formula. Now that you hopefully understand the basic logic of the product-moment correlational method of describing a relationship, we can employ another formula for r which, though far more imposing, because it is simply brimming with letters and symbols, is much easier to use. It is the *raw score formula* for the product-moment correlation coefficient:

$$r_{xy} = \frac{\Sigma XY - \dfrac{(\Sigma X)(\Sigma Y)}{n}}{\sqrt{\left(\Sigma X^2 - \dfrac{(\Sigma X)^2}{n}\right)\left(\Sigma Y^2 - \dfrac{(\Sigma Y)^2}{n}\right)}}$$

If you will recall our earlier discussion of the standard deviation, we introduced (ever so politely) the raw score formula for computing the sum of the squared deviations (Σx^2). You'll recognize that the expression at the lower left of this new formula for r is the very same formula. The two other expressions in the raw score formula for r are merely the raw score equivalents of (Σy^2) and (Σxy).

We can apply the raw score formula to the same set of scores we used in our previous example with the deviation score formula. In Table 4–6

TABLE 4-6 Scores of Ten Students on Two Tests Along with the Calculations and Totals Necessary for Computation of the Raw Score Product-Moment Correlation Coefficient Formula

STUDENT	TEST X	TEST Y	X²	Y²	XY
a	8	3	64	9	24
b	2	1	4	1	2
c	8	6	64	36	48
d	5	3	25	9	15
e	15	14	225	196	210
f	11	12	121	144	132
g	13	9	169	81	117
h	6	4	36	16	24
i	4	4	16	16	16
j	6	5	36	25	30
Σ	78	61	760	533	618

those scores and the necessary quantities for the raw score product-moment correlation formula are presented.

Substituting the necessary values in the raw score formula, we have

$$r_{xy} = \frac{618 - \frac{(78)(61)}{10}}{\left(760 - \frac{(78)^2}{10}\right)\left(533 - \frac{(61)^2}{10}\right)}$$

$$= \frac{142.2}{156.2}$$

$$= .91$$

You will notice, of course, that since we are using the raw scores, their squares, and their crossproducts (as opposed to subtracting the two means from each of the scores), the calculations are usually more simple with the raw score formula. By working through the practice exercises at the close of the chapter, you should become quite comfortable in the use of either of these two formulae.

The Rank-Order Correlation Coefficient

Another technique for estimating the magnitude and direction of the relationship between two variables is the rank-order correlation coefficient introduced by Sir Charles Spearman. Spearman's correlation coefficient (r_s) is interpreted in essentially the same way as the Pearson product-moment r, but it is generally more simple to compute. Besides its computational simplicity, it may be used with data which represent only an *ordinal scale* and not necessarily an *interval scale*.

Measurement scales. It's necessary to spend a few sentences on the kinds of scales that we work with in educational measurement since, for the first time, we must be concerned about these scales. An *interval scale* is one which allows us to believe that there are actually equal intervals between equidistant points on the scale. For example, the ten-point difference between scores of 48 and 58 on a 100-item scale would be considered identical to the ten-point difference between scores of 88 and 98. If we are convinced that such is the case, then we have an interval scale. A *ratio scale,* incidentally, is an interval scale for which a zero point exists, such as a weight scale or a height scale in which it is possible to have a true zero. We encounter few ratio scales in educational measurement.

An *ordinal scale* needs no equal intervals between its points. Instead, only rank order is requisite. For instance, if a principal ranked five teachers in order of their effectiveness, this would be an example of data representing an ordinal scale. There are many situations in education in which we cannot confidently believe that equal scale intervals are present in our data, hence we choose to assume we're working with data on an ordinal, rather than interval, scale. Now the Pearson product-moment correlation coefficient requires *interval* data. The Spearman coefficient can be computed with data representing only an ordinal scale.

The formula for the rank-order correlation coefficient is the following:

$$r_s = 1 - \frac{6\Sigma d^2}{n^3 - n}$$

where

$\quad\quad n =$ the number of subjects
$\quad\Sigma d^2 =$ the sum of the squared differences between subjects' ranks

We can illustrate the application of the formula for r_s by using it with the data in Table 4–7 where seven students' scores on two attitude inventories have been presented.

$$r_s = 1 - \frac{6(8.6)}{7^3 - 7}$$
$$= .85$$

Obviously, the computation of r_s is almost fool's play in contrast to the laborious calculation of the deviation score and raw score product-moment correlation formulae.

Applications

Well, if you've survived this brief brush with numbers and notations, you have mastered the key statistical concepts that you need to evaluate educational tests. Particularly in the next two chapters we have frequent

TABLE 4–7   Scores of Seven Students on Two Attitude Inventories

STUDENT	INVENTORY 1		INVENTORY 2		d	d²
	Score	Rank	Score	Rank		
a	124	1	62	2	−1	1
b	123	2	59	3	−1	1
c	119	3	67	1	2	4
d	117	4	57	4.5	0.5	0.25
e	110	5	57	4.5	0.5	0.25
f	104	6	50	7	−1	1
g	94	7	52	6	1	1
						$\Sigma d^2 = 8.5$

need of these tools as we probe the ins and outs of reliability and validity. To deal with these two key constructs in measurement without the benefit of statistical tools would be genuinely difficult. With luck you're now ready to do battle with validity concepts in the next chapter and, one chapter later, with notions of reliability as well.

PRACTICE EXERCISES

1. For these test scores what is the mean?

   10, 8, 7, 6, 6, 6, 6, 3, 2, 1

2. For these exam scores what is the median?

   27, 24, 23, 23, 22, 20, 19, 18, 17, 9

3. For these test scores what is the mode?

   9, 9, 9, 8, 8, 7, 6, 5, 5, 3

4. For the following set of test scores, what are the mean, median, and mode?

   47, 45, 44, 44, 43, 42, 41, 39, 28

5. What is the standard deviation of the following set of test scores?

   6, 4, 3, 2, 0

6. What is the standard deviation of the following set of exam scores?

   20, 19, 18, 18, 17, 16, 15, 14, 14, 10

7. What are the mean, median, and standard deviation for the following set of scores?

69	64	56
68	63	56
68	62	54
67	61	54
65	60	51
64	58	50
64	58	48

8. What is the product-moment correlation between the X and Y measures?

X	Y	X	Y
49	42	40	38
46	42	38	39
44	44	38	40
44	40	36	29
42	43	34	37

9. What is the product-moment r between the following pretest and posttest scores?

STUDENT	PRETEST	POSTTEST	STUDENT	PRETEST	POSTTEST
1	23	82	11	20	95
2	20	90	12	21	81
3	15	78	13	20	69
4	20	74	14	19	84
5	21	84	15	17	69
6	22	78	16	21	77
7	20	82	17	19	78
8	12	80	18	18	85
9	15	84	19	23	90
10	15	54			

10. What is the rank-order correlation coefficient between the following two sets of test scores?

STUDENT	TEST A	TEST B
Joe	20	17
Tom	19	19
Ann	17	11
Lee	15	14
Jim	13	15

ANSWERS TO PRACTICE EXERCISES

1. mean = 5.5
2. median = 21
3. mode = 9 (wasn't that easy?)
4. mean = 41.4, median = 43, mode = 44
5. standard deviation = 2.0
6. standard deviation = 2.8
7. mean = 60.0, median = 61, standard deviation = 6.1

8. $r = .67$
9. $r = .35$
10. $r_s = .52$

DISCUSSION QUESTIONS

1. How skilled in statistics do you think that a measurement specialist should be? How about a classroom teacher? What about a school administrator, for example, a district superintendent? Why?
2. In what sorts of situations, if ever, do you think that graphic-display techniques are preferable to numerical indices, such as the mean and standard deviation?
3. Do you think it is possible to describe the statistical procedures treated in this chapter so that lay citizens can understand them? Will this be necessary for citizens to understand the results of large-scale educational assessment operations?
4. Why do you suppose so many educators register fear and mild loathing when the subject of educational statistics arises? Do you think such aversion tendencies can be eliminated? If so, how?
5. Can you explain to a nonmathematician in commonsense language how to understand intuitively the meaning of the standard deviation and the correlation coefficient? How would you do it?

SUGGESTIONS FOR ADDITIONAL READING

EBEL, ROBERT L., "Test Score Statistics," Chapter 11, *Essentials of Educational Measurement* (3rd ed.), pp. 202–206. Englewood Cliffs, N.J.: Prentice-Hall, Inc., 1979. An excellent exposition of the rudimentary statistics needed by measurement personnel is provided.

LINDEMAN, RICHARD H., and PETER F. MERENDA, "Basic Statistics," Chapter 2, *Educational Measurement* (2nd ed.), pp. 18–44. Glenview, Ill.: Scott, Foresman, 1979. A brief, introductory treatment of descriptive and inferential statistics in relationship to educational tests is presented.

MARTUZA, VICTOR R., *Applying Norm-Referenced and Criterion-Referenced Measurement in Education*, Chapters 2–8, pp. 15–121. Boston: Allyn and Bacon, 1977. Deeper analysis is provided than is typically the case in introductory measurement books. For example, an introduction to linear regression is provided, along with an introduction to classical measurement theory.

STANLEY, JULIAN C., and KENNETH D. HOPKINS, "Statistical Concepts in Test Preparation," Chapter 2, *Educational and Psychological Measurement and Evaluation* (5th ed.), pp. 14–79. Englewood Cliffs, N.J.: Prentice-Hall, Inc., 1972. This is an excellent treatment of the statistical concepts needed in connection with testing. One of the special features of the chapter is that there are programmed instruction segments designed to promote the reader's conversance with the statistical concepts treated.

In order to evaluate an educational test, we need to know whether the test is valid. If you were to ask most educators what is meant by a test's *validity*, they would probably respond with something like: "The validity of a test indicates whether the test measures what it's supposed to measure." If that educator had recently completed a course in tests and measurements, then the response might be: "The validity of a test indicates whether the test measures what it *purports* to measure." Measurement people don't find too many occasions to use the word *purport*, hence they love to employ it when defining validity.

Validity of Tests, Validity of Interpretations

Well, that's not a bad general description of test validity. However, if you're going to appraise tests rigorously, you have to become a little more sophisticated when considering the concept of test validity.

Let's use an example. Suppose you possess barely latent tendencies to be a French chef and harbor a hidden desire to spend the rest of your life spinning out soufflés. One of your chief measuring tools would be a *table-*

Establishing the validity of educational tests

spoon. With that highly useful measuring devide you could follow your favorite recipes by tossing in the requisite tablespoons full of spices, sugar, and so on. The measuring instrument, that is, the tablespoon, is doing what it is supposed to do. It would seem to be a valid measuring instrument.

However, let's say that, after nipping the cooking sherry a bit too frequenty, you try to measure the *temperature* of a sauce with your tablespoon. Obviously, you would be destined for disappointment. Your sauce would surely curdle. Although a measuring instrument can be valid for one purpose, it can be thoroughly invalid for another purpose.

Setting aside the soufflé-making metaphor, let's think about a more common educational example in which school counselors might use an *interest* inventory designed to gauge students' interests in various vocational pursuits. Now, whereas the inventory might yield meaningful data if the counselors are trying to identify the vocation in which students are interested, the inventory tells the counselors nothing about whether the students have the *ability* to succeed in certain vocations. In other words, we do not validate a test per se, since a test can be used properly or improperly. Indeed, the initial two chapters of this book stressed the importance of isolating the *purpose* for which an educational assessment device is to be used. Even though it is commonly asserted that a test is valid to the extent that it measures what it purports to measure, *the actual focus of validity should be on the interpretation of test scores,* not on the *test itself.*

Messick states it succinctly when he observes that "one validates, not a test, but an interpretation of data arising from a specific procedure."[1] Linn echoes that point when he asserts that "questions of validity are questions of the soundness of the interpretation of a measure."[2] As we saw from the previous discussion, a measurement tool, when employed, simply yields data—typically test scores. The *interpretation* of those test scores is the operation which may or may not be valid. Then, even though we may talk somewhat cavalierly about "the validity of a test," we must recognize that it would be technically preferable to discuss the validity of the *interpretation* of test results in connection with the purpose for which the test is being used. The latter phrase, of course, is a hefty mouthful. Hence, for ease of communication we will often employ the more terse expression, "test validity," or "the validity of a test."

Acceptable and Unacceptable Convictions

In a field, such as education, where educators face numerous situations in which test validity is at issue, it is only natural that different people would come up with different ways of thinking about test validity. By the 1950s matters were really getting out of hand, with all sorts of exotic validity types and validity terms finding their way into the measurement literature. People were writing about "intrinsic" validity, "extrinsic" validity, "divergent" validity, "convergent" validity, "face" validity, and in all likelihood, "two-faced" validity.

To quell this confusion, the professional associations most concerned with the quality of educational tests attempted to establish some order in the assessment field. In 1954 the American Psychological Association (APA) published *Technical Recommendations for Psychological Tests and Diag-*

---

[1]Samuel A. Messick, "The Standard Problem: Meaning and Values in Measurement and Evaluation," *American Psychologist,* 30 (1975), 955–966.

[2]Robert L. Linn, "Issues of Validity in Measurement for Competency-Based Programs" (Paper presented at the Annual Meeting of the National Council on Measurement on Education, New York, 1977).

nostic Techniques. One year later the American Educational Research Association (AERA) and the National Council on Measurements Used in Education (NCME) collaborated to publish (through the National Educational Association) *Technical Recommendations for Achievement Tests.* Later, in 1966, these three organizations (AERA, NCME, and APA) joined forces to publish (through APA) *Standards for Educational and Psychological Tests and Manuals.* In 1974 those standards were revised again by a committee of measurement experts representing the three organizations and published by APA as *Standards for Educational and Psychological Tests.* The three organizations have now initiated plans to revise and update the 1974 *Standards,* in particular to incorporate some of the advances in criterion-referenced testing that have taken place in the seventies.

Now, why all the fuss about professional associations and their attempts to reduce the terminological chaos with respect to such concepts as test validity? Well, as any student of language will tell you, the meanings we attach to words are basically conventions. We fly on an *airplane* and write at a *desk* because the terms *airplane* and *desk* have, through convention and custom, become widely accepted ways of describing things we fly on and write at.

In a technical field, such as education, where precision of communication is imperative, it makes sense to rely on widely used conventions. Otherwise, educators will be employing all sorts of aberrant expressions to describe technical phenomena, with the result that confusion, rather than clarity, ensues. As a consequence, it will be strategically sensible for us to rely on the terminology conventions most recently sanctified by APA, AERA, and NCME, and this means the terminology endorsed in the 1974 *Standards.*[3] Those who wish to become particularly conversant with the ins and outs of validity would do well to read carefully the entire 1974 AERA-APA-NCME *Standards.* Even though some of the concepts in the 1974 *Standards* now need refinement, it will be wiser for us to work with widely accepted terminology conventions than to whip up a host of potentially more accurate descriptors that would not be widely known.

In the remainder of this chapter, therefore, we deal with the three categories of validity endorsed in the 1974 *Standards,* that is, *content validity, criterion-related validity* (predictive and concurrent), and *construct validity.* The rest of the chapter is organized so that each of these three types of validity is first described in general; then a separate discussion will be provided of how that validity category pertains, first to norm-referenced measurement and, second, to criterion-referenced measurement.

[3]*Standards for Educational and Psychological Tests.* Prepared by a joint committee of the American Psychological Association, the American Educational Research Association, and the National Council on Measurement in Education (Washington, D.C.: American Psychological Association, 1974).

Reasons for Different Types of Validity

At first blush, persons making their initial pilgrimage to measurement land might legitimately wonder why it is that we are going to be talking about different sorts of validity. After all, a test either measures what it is supposed to, or it doesn't. Correct?

Incorrect. Even though a test's validity hinges on the extent to which the test measures what it purports to measure, there are legitimately different ways of viewing whether the test is fulfilling its purported purpose.[4]

Choosing an example from another field, suppose you were trying to judge how effective a new automobile was. You might conceive of effectiveness as the mileage, fuel-consumption ratio, an index of the auto's power and speed under stress conditions, or the auto's mechanical longevity. Each of these alternative perspectives deals with an aspect of the new automobile's effectiveness. Viewed in concert, they provide us with a richer notion of the auto's effectiveness than if we had focused only on one aspect of the auto's capabilities. In like manner, when we really think hard about the validity of a test, we discover that there are related, but substantially different, ways of conceptualizing whether a test measures what it is supposed to measure.[5] Now let's look at three variations on the test-validation theme.

CONTENT VALIDITY

How would a reasonable person approach the task of conceptualizing whether a test measures what it's supposed to? Well, one of the first questions that might come to someone's mind, particularly someone who was thinking about achievement tests (such as a test of one's mathematics skills), would be the following: "Does the test deal with the *content* it's supposed to be measuring?" For example, does a test supposedly measuring someone's knowledge of U.S. history cover the important particulars of history in the United States, rather than the history of Argentina or Greece? Because of this very sensible concern about the adequacy with which a test taps the topics it should, one form of validity is known as *content validity*.

Content Validity Defined

The 1974 *Standards,* pointing out that content validity is most often evaluated for tests of skill or knowledge, offers the following definition:

---

[4]Don't forget the earlier diatribe about validity technically referring to test score interpretations rather than to tests themselves.

[5]St. Thomas Aquinas loved to conclude his philosophical analogies with "in like manner," but I've resisted the temptation to emulate him, that is, until now.

To demonstrate the content validity of a set of test scores, one must show that the behaviors demonstrated in testing constitute a representative sample of behaviors to be exhibited in a desired performance domain. Definition of the performance domain, the user's objectives, and the method of sampling are critical to claims of content validity.[6]

All right, you might say, that's a pretty sophisticated way of saying, "does the test cover the content it's supposed to?" But how can we determine whether a test covers the content it's supposed to? Well, the answer is that somebody must render a judgment about whether the test is properly covering the content it should, and the *should* in this case applies to the *purposes* of the test *user*. The *Standards* put it this way: "a definition of the performance domain of interest must always be provided by a test user so that the content of a test may be checked against an appropriate task universe."[7] The key judgment to be made, then, is whether the use (inference) to which a test's results will be put coincides with the content the test actually measures. Set forth in these simple terms, content validity sounds easier to establish than is actually the case.

To ascertain a test's content validity properly, we need to do far more than merely ask experts to judge the match between (1) the test itself and (2) the performance domain about which the test's results will be used to make inferences. This type of superficial judgment, regarding whether the test *appears*, on the face of it, to be relevant for a given purpose, is sometimes referred to as *face validity*. Face validity is not a *Standards*-approved form of validity and should not, therefore, be employed by measurement people. Indeed, it was to extinguish the proliferation of such expressions as face validity that the *Standards* were originally produced.

Unlike face validity which rests on a single judgment of match between a test and its apparent use, content validity is properly established "by a set of operations, and one evaluates content validity by the thoroughness and care with which these operations have been conducted."[8]

Now what are these "operations" that must be carried out well if content validity is present? Well, it should be clear by now that really explicit descriptions must be created for both the content-behavior being measured by the test and the content-behavior domain to which inferences will be made. These descriptions must be highly detailed so that one can subsequently judge the match between test-sampled behavior and the performance domain of interest.

With some tests and performance domains the creations of crisp descriptions is fairly simple. For instance, if we're working with a fairly

[6] *Standards for Educational and Psychological Tests,* p. 28.
[7] Ibid.
[8] Ibid.

modest skill, such as an examinee's ability to multiply pairs of double-digit numbers, the construction of decent definitions is delightfully easy. However, when the behavior domains of interest start getting larger, such as when we're trying to tap an examinee's conversance with U.S. history, then it is devilishly difficult to construct a lucid description that accurately delimits such an immense chunk of content-behavior.

Whether Content Equals Behavior

The attentive reader will have noted that in the previous paragraphs your amiable author has been playing a bit fast and loose with two concepts, namely, "content" and "behavior." We've been focusing, of course, on content validity. But the committee of scholars who prepared the most recent revision of the *Standards,* when dealing with content validity, often rely on such phrases as "the behaviors demonstrated in testing" and "the performance domain." Doesn't this sound as if they should be describing something called "behavioral" validity or "performance" validity instead of "content" validity?

Well, here is where history confuses us a bit. At the outset, content validity was a notion applied almost exclusively to achievement tests and, as such, made a good deal of sense. Did the content, that is, the facts and principles in a test, adequately represent the subject-matter content it was supposed to sample? However, that rather limited conception of content coverage doesn't sit so happily when we start talking about tests dealing with attitudes or physical skills. In those sort of assessment situations we are more directly concerned with a class of examinee behaviors rather than subject matter content. This, of course, is where confusion can fester.

It is probable that as the various measurement experts who produced the current and prior *Standards* wrestled with this problem, they decided to retain the phrase "content validity" (by then, widely accepted) but to define it more broadly so that the focus was on behavior, rather than content. In the case of achievement tests, particularly tests of knowledge, the emphasis will still probably be on content. With many other types of tests, however, it will make more sense to think of content validity as an umbrella covering behavior as well as content.

Norm-Referenced Applications

Norm-referenced tests have been around for a half a century or more. With half a century of experience, one would surmise that for most norm-referenced tests, the quantity and quality of evidence regarding content validity would be pretty impressive. Sadly, it isn't.

For most commercially published tests there is a technical manual of some sort which offers information and evidence regarding the test's validity, reliability, and other psychometric qualities. In almost no instance will one find a really first-rate establishment of the content validity of a norm-referenced test.[9]

What is typically found in the technical manuals of norm-referenced tests is a description of how the test's developers attempted to make sure that all of the crucial content was included in their test. For example, the manual will describe the qualifications of the subject-matter experts who helped decide what content should be included. The manual might also set forth how the test developers surveyed the content included in widely used textbooks or, perhaps, in the curriculum syllabi of major school districts. In essence, the thrust of most norm-referenced test manuals is to describe the *process by which the test's content was selected,* then assume that this description adequately handles the matter of content validity. This casual treatment of such an important issue is regrettable.

There are undoubtedly a number of reasons why norm-referenced test developers have given only superficial attention to content validity. One reason is the absence of any generally accepted procedures for assembling evidence of a test's content validity. In spite of their efforts to illuminate what we mean by content validity, the writers of the *Standards* do not provide much in the way of step-by-step guidance regarding how test developers should gather content validity evidence.

In the same vein, there have been no agreed-upon schemes to represent the extent of a test's content validity in a quantitative manner. Other validity approaches, to be described later in the chapter, can be represented by tidy quantitative indicators, such as correlation coefficients. Not so with content validity. Perhaps the absence of these pithy numerical indicators has dissuaded norm-referenced test conductors from getting heavily involved with the establishment of content validity.

Another reason that creators of norm-referenced tests may have been a bit relaxed in their efforts to establish content validity is the dominant reliance on normative interpretation of an examinee's performance. As long as the test covers the content of concern (for instance, reading) in a general way, then to use the test effectively it is ordinarily sufficient to gather only the examinee's relative (percentile) status in relationship to that of the normative group. Accordingly, less attention need be given to the test's content boundaries.

There is yet another reason that commercial developers of norm-referenced tests have heretofore devoted scant attention to the generation

---

[9]I have obviously not read all the technical manuals for all the norm-referenced tests in the world. (Even if I had, I'd be ashamed to admit it.) However, I've read a good many of these manuals. I have *never* found a well-defended case of content validity.

of solid evidence supporting a test's content validity, and this reason is economic in nature. When I was young and naive (as opposed to being middle-aged and naive), I assumed that test-publishing companies were something like research and development appendages to a university. I conceived of the people running these enterprises as quantitatively facile scholars and technicians who, while advancing our knowledge about testing, were developing and distributing much needed assessment instruments. I never once thought about a test-publishing company as a real profit-making *business.*

Now I recognize that commercial testing houses are, like other businesses, obliged to make a profit. They must price their tests competitively so that their tests are as apt to be purchased as the next firm's. They must cut development costs to the point that the actual purchase price for the test is not prohibitive. Sometimes this means doing a less solid job in technical development than the test developers would prefer. Perhaps the harsh realities of the measurement marketplace have blunted the emergence of solid content-validity procedures for norm-referenced tests, since in consumers (that is, prospective test purchasers) there has historically been only casual interest in content validity. Until the purchasers of norm-referenced tests *demand* dependable data regarding a test's content validity, we can expect publishers of norm-referenced tests to give relatively little attention to content validity.

Criterion-Referenced Applications

Because the chief thrust of a criterion-referenced test is to provide a clear picture of what it is that an examinee can or can't do, it is only natural that, for criterion-referenced tests, content validity should be a matter of paramount importance. Since, as we saw earlier, the focus of content validity is on the behaviors being sampled by a test, the task in demonstrating a criterion-referenced test's content validity is to make sure that the *description* of the test's measured behavior is sufficiently accurate so that precise interpretations can be drawn from an examinee's test performance.

Elsewhere, and earlier, I took the position that for criterion-referenced tests a preferable way of thinking about content validity was to refer to it as *descriptive validity* since, after all, descriptive validity was a more accurate indicator of whether a test satisfactorily described an examinee's behavior.[10] However, while I still think that "descriptive" validity captures the intended notion more precisely, I'll have to abide by the discussion earlier in the chapter favoring the use of terms which have been officially

[10]W. J. Popham, *Criterion-Referenced Measurement* (Englewood Cliffs, N.J.: Prentice-Hall, Inc., 1978).

sanctioned in the *Standards.* For criterion-referenced tests, however, it will be helpful to think of content validity as an attempt to establish how well the test accurately describes the behavioral domain being measured.

A Quantifiable Procedure.   How, then, can criterion-referenced test developers go about establishing a test's content validity? Should they pattern their efforts after the somewhat casual approaches employed by norm-referenced testing folk? No, criterion-referenced test developers will need to create more rigorous ways of attesting to a test's content validity. In the following paragraphs one such procedure will be provided. It is essentially a judgmental procedure, but one in which the judgments that are rendered can be reported quantitatively.

First off, locate a group of individuals who are sufficiently familiar with the subject matter of the test that, if asked, they could comfortably write test items in that field. The number of individuals needed is not clear, but at least ten or so would seem to offer a reasonable degree of representitiveness. Next, present to these people whatever descriptive information accompanies the test. This descriptive information might be in the form of elaborate test-item specifications, brief paragraphs, or even behavioral objectives. Merely use whatever information is provided to test users in order for them to discern what the criterion-referenced test is supposed to be measuring. Then request the individuals to each prepare a specified number of test items that could legitimately be used to assess the described behavior. Collect these test items, and have another group of individuals judge the *homogeneity* of the independently prepared items. This completes the first step in a two-step content validation procedure.

Let's see how this initial step might actually work. Suppose we were attempting to establish the content validity of a twenty-item test of a youngster's ability to solve higher-order mathematics story problems. Ten mathematics instructors would be asked to read the descriptive information regarding what the test supposedly measures. Each of the ten math instructors would then be asked to generate four items in accord with the descriptive information. These forty items would be presented to a group of five other math teachers who independently (and without referring to the test's descriptive information) would (1) isolate the examinee behavior being measured by most of forty items and prepare written descriptions of that behavior and (2) indicate which items were congruent with the description (or, putting it another way, which items formed a homogeneous pool). If the written behavior descriptions are consonant with the test's actual description of measurement behavior, the percentage of items judged to be accurate indicators of this behavior should be reported. For instance, let's say that four of the five judges accurately identified the behavioral domain being measured. The fifth judge missed out badly. The four judges then indicated that of the forty items proposed by the ten judges, 36 (or 90 percent) were homogeneous indicators of the same behavior. At the close of step one, therefore, we would have established that the test's descriptive information is capable of guiding knowledgeable test writers to generate test items that are 90 percent homogeneous. The test's descriptive information, therefore, can be viewed as relatively unambiguous.

Having established the clarity of the test's descriptor, the second step in this process involves locating another collection of subject-matter knowledgeable judges, say ten again, and having them go through each item on the actual test to see if those items are congruent with the test's description. These new judges should first read the test's descriptive information then, one-by-one, see whether the test items are consistent with this descriptive information. The percentage of items judged to be congruent with the test description can then be determined.

To illustrate, suppose that ten judges were called in to assist in this second step of our content-validity procedure as the same twenty-item mathematics test is being analyzed. Although there was some variability in the judges' estimates, the average number of items judged congruent with the test's description was 17, that is, 85 percent.

As an easy but useful refinement, prior to giving the items to the judges, we could toss in a few deliberately incongruent (or "lemon" items), thus permitting us to identify and eliminate any ratings by judges who are not sufficiently attentive to spot these deliberately inserted incongruent items. It should be noted, of course, that such a safeguard procedure would help isolate judges who were being inattentive and/or excessively lenient. It would not help identify judges who were being excessively stringent, that is, were judging too many items as being incongruent.

In the next chapter we shall treat a commonly employed index of variability, that is, an estimate of a test's *internal consistency*. As we shall see, for criterion-referenced tests this index is better thought of as a reflection of the test's content validity since it indicates the extent to which the items are functioning in a homogeneous fashion.

In review, then, since content validity is perhaps the most crucial of the validity approaches which should be established for a good criterion-referenced test, it has been recommended that criterion-referenced test developers employ content-validation schemes which are capable of yielding quantitative indices. Not only should these indices be reported, but also the specific procedures employed in the content-validation effort should be made known.

In the illustration supplied here, for example, after carefully describing the procedures involved, the test developers could have reported that (1) 90 percent of independently authored test items constructed according to the test's descriptive information were judged homogeneous and (2) 85 percent of the items on the test itself were judged to be congruent with the test's descriptive information. It is much too early in the use of such quantitively oriented content-validation procedures to say, "what percentages are good enough?" In time, experience will guide our expectations so that for various types of behavioral domains we will possess some sort of idea as to how much descriptive clarity and item congruence test users have a right to expect. In the meanwhile, those using criterion-referenced tests should demand that test developers approach the task of demonstrating content validity with zeal uncharacteristic of their norm-referenced predecessors.

Rovinelli and Hambleton have commented favorably on the use of content specialists in judging the quality of criterion-referenced test items.[11] They indicate that "there is considerable evidence to suggest that content specialists can complete their ratings quickly, and with a high degree of reliability and validity." The respective merits of judgmental versus empirical approaches to item improvement was discussed in an earlier paper by Coulson and Hambleton, who concluded that "content specialists" ratings along with the empirical procedures provide an excellent basis for establishing content validity of domain-referenced test items.[12]

With either norm- or criterion-referenced applications of content validity, there is the necessity to attend to a test's *adequacy of content coverage*. Suppose the content domain being measured includes four importantly different types of "subcontent" or "subskills." In the generation of items to measure the overall content domain, test developers will need to create items which, insofar as is possible, measure all those subdomains. Schemes of stratified sampling are most useful in this regard. In some cases, of course, such stratified coverage of a behavior domain's subcomponents is less important than in others.

Before bidding farewell to content validity, it must be stressed one final time that both norm- and criterion-referenced test developers should give much more systematic and intense attention to this important, but characteristically underemphasized, form of validity.

CRITERION-RELATED VALIDITIES

Here's a switch. Instead of talking about a second approach to validity, it appears from this heading that it's bonus time; the reader will soon learn about *two* forms of *criterion-related validity*. Actually, the two variants of this

---

[11]R. J. Rovinelli and R. K. Hambleton, "On the Use of Content Specialists in the Assessment of Criterion-Referenced Test Item Validity," *Laboratory of Psychometric and Evaluative Research Report* No. 24 (Amherst, Mass.: University of Massachusetts, 1976).

[12]D. B. Coulson and R. K. Hambleton, "Some Validation Methods for Domain-Referenced Test Items," *Laboratory of Psychometric and Evaluative Research Report* No. 7 (Amherst, Mass.: University of Massachusetts, 1974).

type of validity differ only in a temporal manner, hence measurement specialists simply lump them under a simple generic heading. Let's see what the *Standards* say about criterion-related validities.

> *Criterion-related validities apply when one wishes to infer from a test score an individual's most probable standing on some other variable called a criterion. Statements of predictive validity indicate the extent to which an individual's future level on the criterion can be predicted from a knowledge of prior test performance; statements of concurrent validity indicate the extent to which the test may be used to estimate an individual's present standing on the criterion.*[13]

As we see, criterion-related validity is based on the extent to which an examinee's score on a test allows us to infer the examinee's performance on a criterion variable. The most common example of criterion-related validity occurs when we might employ a verbal aptitude test, administered in high school, to predict what kind of grades (the criterion) students will earn in college.

Predictive and Concurrent Validity

If we administer the predictor test (in the previous example this was the verbal aptitude test) in high school and wait, say two years, until students earned a two-year grade point average (the criterion), a correlation between students' grade point averages and their scores on the verbal aptitude test would bear on the test's *predictive validity*. With predictive validity it is requisite for a substantial time interval to occur between administration of the test (being validated) and the gathering of criterion data.

With *concurrent validity* no such time interval is present. For instance, let's say we administered the identical verbal aptitude test to college sophomores on the same day they received information on their two-year grade point averages. Even though the aptitude test was designed for high school students, not college sophomores, the resulting correlation coefficients between examinees' test scores and their grade point averages does provide us with some evidence regarding the test's validity. For instance, suppose these was only a 0.21 correlation between predictor (the test) and criterion (grade point averages), then that trivial relationship would certainly cast doubt on the inferences about college grades which one might draw from scores on the aptitude test.

Now in the practical world of education we typically want to make *future* predictions, for instance, about the chances that a high school student has for academic survival in college. That being the case, you might ask, why we don't always gather criterion-related validity data of the predic-

---

[13] *Standards for Educational and Psychological Tests.*

tive sort, since it so obviously coincides with our real world requirements. The most common reason for gathering concurrent-validity information, rather than predictive-validity information, is that people can't afford to wait.

While predictive inferences based on concurrent-validity data must be made most cautiously, it's better to make such inferences on the basis of concurrent-validity data than on the basis of no validity data whatsoever. Test developers sometimes adopt a strategy of creating a new test and disseminating it on the basis of concurrent-validity information, hoping to add predictive-validity information at a later point. Given the practicalities of real-world test development, this is often a sensible strategy.

Quality of the Criterion

When a test has been developed chiefly to make predictions regarding how someone will perform in a subsequent situation, then criterion-related validity is the most appropriate validation approach. The examinee's performance in the subsequent situation is typically indicated by some sort of variable which we refer to as the *criterion* variable. Indeed, it is because we want to see how the test being validated relates to this criterion variable that we refer to this type of validation as *criterion-related* validity.

It should be apparent, therefore, that the legitimacy of the criterion variable itself is pivotal in this validation approach. If test developers merely adopt the most convenient criterion measure at hand, the resulting validation effort will typically be of little worth. Great care must be taken to establish that the criterion variable itself is "valid." For example, if we want to see how well students perform academically in college or high school, then a grade point average (GPA) is a sensible indicator. However, let's say the test developers were in a hurry, so that rather than gathering official GPAs from the school's records, they relied on students' self-reported GPAs. Obviously, student recollections tend to be somewhat inaccurate (and typically inflated), hence the self-reported GPAs would constitute a less defensible index of academic achievement than would GPAs based on official transcripts.

Instead of going to the official records or asking students for self-reported GPAs, what if the test developers had asked parents to estimate how well (on a ten-point scale) their children were doing in school. While it would certainly be possible to compute a correlation coefficient between students' test scores and these highly partisan ratings—and the resulting r could be carried out to three or four decimal points—the coefficient would certainly contribute less to an appraisal of the test's validity than would a study involving a less biased criterion variable. Selection of a criterion measure on the basis of mere opportunism should be deplored.

Quality of the Validation Study

What sort of criterion variables are we usually interested in when we attempt to establish criterion-related validity, either of the predictive or concurrent variety? Well, grade point averages or teacher ratings often serve as criterion measures when we're trying to validate a test that's predictive of one's academic performance. For predicting vocational success, we sometimes use comprehensive skill tests as a criterion, such as an end-of-the-school exam. Supervisory ratings of on-the-job performance are also employed.

Sometimes we can employ less obvious, but indisputably sound, criterion variables. For instance, a colleague of mine was validating a predictor test being used to screen potential waiters and waitresses for a national restaurant chain. He chose as a criterion variable the size of tips given on credit card receipts as his criterion measure. Although he recognized that many tips were given in cash, hence would not be recorded, he inferred that the tips which were reported on credit card receipts would reflect customer satisfaction with the waiters and waitresses.

Had my colleague administered the survey test to already employed personnel and then correlated their performance on the test with the past month's tips, this would have been an instance of *concurrent* criterion-related validity. Had he administered the test to newly hired personnel, then waited six months to gather the information on tips, it would have been a case of *predictive* criterion-related validity.

Because criterion-related validity evidence is needed when we wish to be confident of the legitimacy of our inferences about someone's performance on a criterion variable, we must be certain that the individuals involved in the validation investigation are similar to those persons for whom we wish to make predictions. The less similarity there is between those in the validation sample and those for whom we wish to make predictions, the more tentative our predictions should be.

By the same token, the conditions surrounding the validation study (or studies) should be comparable to the conditions surrounding the situation in which one wants to make predictions. If these situations are markedly dissimilar, our predictions should be made with suitable caution.

Norm-Referenced Applications

As you will doubtlessly recall from Chapter 3's discussion of norm-referenced tests, the chief mission of a good norm-referenced instrument is to distinguish among examinees so that meaningful comparisons can be made between, for example, Billy and Bertha. Now the most typical situation in which educators will find need of such comparative information is when they select individuals in a *fixed quota* situation. For instance, suppose there is only room in a beginning law school class for 150 new law students but that 1,550 students have applied for admission. Some sort of law school aptitude test will usually be employed to sort out the potential Supreme Court jurists from the ambulance-chasing incompetents. The more fine-grained comparisons that the aptitude test permits, the better.

For any norm-referenced *aptitude* test, evidence of criterion-related validity is the most useful sort of validation data since these tests are invariably used for predictive purposes. Even norm-referenced achievement tests are sometimes used to make predictions about students, such as when we employ a test of a student's reading skills in the lower grades to predict the student's reading skills in higher grades. In such cases, of course, criterion-related validity information would be of great value in judging the test's potential value for that predictive purpose.

It is not surprising, therefore, that the vast majority of validation studies carried out on educational tests during the last half century have been of a criterion-related nature. Because the bulk of the tests available to educators were norm-referenced tests, and because these tests were typically used to make predictions in fixed quota settings, it is only natural that measurement personnel would have become preoccupied with criterion-related validity.

Criterion-Referenced Applications

Since in most cases a criterion-referenced test is employed to get a fix on what the examinee can do *now,* not predict what an examinee will do in a later setting, there are relatively few instances in which criterion-related validity bears focally on the worth of a criterion-referenced test. There are, of course, situations in which we might wish to ascertain an examinee's current status with respect to a well-defined behavioral domain, yet also use that status information to make predictions about the examinee's future status. For such situations, criterion-referenced test developers should approach the assembly of criterion-related validity in much the same way as their norm-referenced colleagues.

It should be noted that because there will often be fewer test items measuring a particular skill on a criterion-referenced test than would be the case with a norm-referenced test, any correlations based on the shorter test will most likely be lower than would have been the case if a longer test had been involved. To illustrate, our experience with criterion-related validity is typically drawn from fairly lengthy norm-referenced tests of 100 or so test times. The resulting correlations between these long tests and the criterion variables might run in the neighborhood of .50. With a short (fifteen-items) criterion-referenced test, that .50 correlation might shrink to .40 or below. Shorter tests are less stable than longer tests, hence, we had best prepare to alter our expectations regarding the size of validity coefficients we should expect to garner for criterion-referenced tests.

Finally, some people confuse criterion-related validity with criterion-referenced tests merely because these two phrases commence with a "criterion" and a hyphen. As we have seen, however, the two notions, while similar in their appearance, are related but substantially different creatures.

CONSTRUCT VALIDITY

Being a compassionate writer, I have saved the most complicated category of validity for the last. Besides that, I feared that if I embarked on a discourse on *construct validity* too early, you might never have forged ahead to discover the raptures of content validity and the criterion-related validities.

We can start off by seeing what the committee preparing the *Standards* had to say when they attempted to define a "construct."

> *A psychological construct is an idea developed or "constructed" as a work of informed scientific imagination; that is, it is a theoretical idea developed to explain and to organize some aspects of existing knowledge. Terms such as "anxiety," "clerical aptitude," or "reading readiness" refer to such constructs.*[14]

Construct Validation Considerations

Here's how construct validity evidence is assembled. (Oh yes, please read this and the next few paragraphs slowly, because the ideas presented therein may be a bit foreign to your experience.) First off, the test developer conceives of the existence of some hypothetical construct, such as "love of animals." Typically the creation of this hypothetical construct is based on prior research or plenty of experience. Then a test is developed which supposedly measures this construct. Let's say we have whipped up a thirty-item test entitled the Animal Lover's Inventory (ALI, for short, with no relationship to heavyweight boxing champions). High test scores on the ALI indicate that the examinees love animals, and low test scores indicate that the examinees find animals repugnant.

Now, with the ALI in hand, we want to see if it possesses construct validity. Based on our knowledge of what this construct is, we then design an investigation in which we predict that if the ALI is valid, individuals

---

[14]Ibid.

should obtain particular kinds of scores on the test. For instance, let's say one prediction is that if we administered the ALI to individuals entering and exiting the City Dog Pound, those people *leaving* the pound with a dog or cat in their arms will get higher ALI scores than those who are *entering* the pound with a dog or cat. This study would be based on the idea that animal lovers would tend to rescue pets from the pound where they are apt to be "put to sleep" while those who are dropping off animals at the pound are not doing so because the animals need a nap.

If we could get ALI scores on the two groups of examinees, that is, pet leavers and pet getters, and found that our hypothesis was confirmed (ALI scores of pet getters being significantly higher than ALI scores of pet leavers), we have produced evidence, not only of the validity of our test, but also of the legitimacy of the construct itself.

If the hypothesis had not been confirmed, then doubt is cast on (1) the validity of the test, (2) the legitimacy of the construct on which test was based, or (3) both of these. In situations where the predicted results do not occur, it is the task of the test developers to determine whether there are defects in the construct, the test, or perhaps in the design of the construct-validity study which was carried out.

As the authors of the *Standards* make clear, "evidence of construct validity is not found in a single study; rather, judgments of content validity are based upon an accumulation of research results." In a sense, since we're dealing with a covert, unobservable attribute, we need to marshal a host of data to support the authenticity of the inferred construct and the validity of the test that we believe is assessing it.

Construct-Validation Strategies

There is no one, single way to gather construct-validity evidence. The kinds of empirical data that can bear on the validity of a test (and the construct on which it is based) are truly myriad. The only limiting factor is the ingenuity of the construct validator.

More often than not, construct validation studies are of the following sorts:

1. *Intervention Studies:* Attempts to demonstrate that examinees respond differently to the measure after receiving some sort of treatment.
2. *Differential-Population Studies:* Efforts to show that individuals representing distinct populations score differently on the measure.
3. *Related-Measures Studies:* Correlations, positive or negative depending on the measures, between examinees' scores on the test and their scores on other measures.

Let's briefly illustrate each of these approaches to construct validation. There are, of course, many others.

To illustrate the *intervention studies* approach, we might be validating a new inventory measuring a person's test anxiety, that is, the extent to which people become anxious prior to taking tests. From 100 prospective college students taking a math test, we randomly select fifty and inform them that their scores on the approaching test will be "crucial." We tell the other fifty students that the test will be "no big deal." Then we give all 100 people our test-anxiety inventory prior to their taking the mathematics test. Our prediction is that the fifty students who received the "crucial" treatment will display greater test anxiety on our inventory than the other fifty students.

Turning to an illustration of the *differential-population* approach, let's imagine that we have created a self-report questionnaire designed to measure one's preoccupation with their own skin quality. We then administer the new test to (1) 100 adolescent boys and girls besieged by acute acne attacks and (2) residents of a retirement community, all of whom are at least sixty years old. Our prediction, not surprisingly, would be that the teenagers would display higher scores (reflecting greater preoccupation with skin quality) than would the senior citizens. Had our inventory dealt with "skin wrinkles," of course, the prediction would have been reversed.

Finally, to illustrate a *related measures* approach, we might predict that scores on a new development problem-solving test would be negatively correlated with scores on a rigidity test. That is, better problem solvers would display less rigidity while weaker problem solvers would tend to possess stronger perseveration tendencies. As this example illustrates, the notion of the predicted conclusion can be positive or negative, depending on the measures involved.

There is one sort of correlational evidence that is often confused by educators, and it occurs when we correlate a new test of, for instance, intelligence with a previously established test of that same attribute. Suppose, for example, that you had developed a nifty new IQ test that was culturally unbiased, delightfully inexpensive, and could be administered in less than 6.5 minutes. Now if you had 100 students tested with your new IQ test, named the *Shorty* for obvious reasons, then correlated these *Shorty* scores on the widely accepted *Stanford-Binet Intelligence Scale,* what sort of validity would you have?

Well, too many people think that this scenario constitutes an instance of criterion-related validity. It doesn't. It's an example of construct validity, because you're assuming that the *Stanford-Binet* already has been validated as a measure of intelligence, and you're simply trying to piggyback on the established test's assessment of the construct your new test is trying to tap. It is *not* an instance of criterion-related validity, because the *Stanford-Binet* is not an index of a criterion behavior which you wish to predict. Why, after all, would someone go to the trouble of whomping up a test of Construct *X* merely to predict someone's score on another test of Construct *X*? If the previously established test of the construct is good enough for you to use in your validation effort, it's probably good enough to already measure the construct in which you're interested. Intelligence tests are created in order to predict how individuals will perform in some criterion situation, such as in college or on the job. Intelligence tests are not created to predict one's scores on another intelligence test.

Thus, whenever for validity purposes we attempt to correlate two measures of the same attribute, we are adopting a construct-validation strategy. It is typically a fairly weak form of construct validation because the creators of the new test are buying into the established test's validity. If that test's validity is less than perfect—and it will be—then the new test's construct validity is thereby itself weakened.

What we are attempting to do when we attempt to assess a test's construct validity is to build a network of relationships and understandings such that we have confidence our test legitimately taps the attribute we're trying to measure. To establish such networks is a nasty, complex business. The more elusive the attribute being measured is, the more nasty and complex. One does not confirm a test's construct validity merely by churning out a correlational study or two. It's a tough job.

Eligible Targets for Construct Validation

Measurement experts usually drag out construct-validation strategies when they are attempting to validate elusive attributes, such as those found in the affective domain, for example, anxiety, self-concept, and locus of control. For the more routine tests of a student's ability to read, we rarely see full-blown construct-validation efforts. Yet, it is only because we are more comfortable in our belief that an individual possesses "skill in reading" that we fail to employ construct-validation strategies here too. There is no *fundamental* difference between the constructs of (1) self-confidence and (2) skill in solving simultaneous equations. Neither of these entities is observable. Both must be inferred. As a consequence, test developers would do well to assemble the necessary network of relationships and data needed to establish the legitimacy even of a skill as prosaic as "the ability to read with understanding."

Norm-Referenced Applications

We have a long history of construct-validation applications for norm-referenced tests, particularly in efforts to validate the kinds of measures used for clinical work with individuals. These investigations, because of the admitted elusiveness of the constructs being assessed, have often been marked by considerable care on the part of those carrying out the validations. As indicated earlier, however, less attention has been given by norm-

referenced test developers to the construct validation of traditional tests designed to measure skills and knowledge.

With the emergence of more exacting validation methods for criterion-referenced tests, it is likely that we shall soon see intensified efforts on the part of those developing norm-referenced tests to supply improved validation evidence of all three varieties, that is, content, criterion-related, and construct.

Criterion-Referenced Applications

(As we shall see in a subsequent chapter, developers of criterion-referenced tests must typically select one particular measurement strategy from several contenders, then describe this measurement strategy in great detail so that test items congruent with the strategy can be produced, more so than with a norm-referenced test, where the attributes being assessed are often broader and described much more generally. It is apparent to the developer of criterion-referenced tests that a clear choice among assessment strategies has been made.)

For instance, should a student's ability to write be assessed by (1) a multiple-choice test dealing with the rules of usage, (2) a completion-type test in which partial sentences are to be completed, or (3) a requirement that the student compose an original essay? If one of these three assessment strategies is selected as an index of the student's "ability to write," its validity needs to be verified just as much as attitudinal or emotional constructs, such as "attitudes regarding other ethnic groups" or "insecurity." The verification that a sensible domain of test behaviors has been selected needs to be validated for criterion-referenced tests, and such validations will be of a construct variety.

It should also be noted that if criterion-referenced tests are to be employed to make educational decisions regarding *groups* of students, as opposed to *individuals,* there are instances in which the validity evidence to be gathered need not demonstrate that the test possesses validity for individuals, but only validity for groups. We delve more deeply into this topic in the chapter dealing with affective measurement.

Illustrations of Validity Reports

We conclude the chapter by providing actual examples of the way commercial test publishers report their validity evidence. Incidentally, if one really wishes to become familiar with the sort of topics treated in this text, there are few activities more illuminating than analyses of the tests and accompanying technical manuals distributed by commercial test houses.

Construct Validity of an Aptitude Test.   What follows is an excerpt from the *Technical Manual* of the *Cognitive Abilities Test,* a test appropriate for use from grade three to the first year in college.[15] A portion of the discussion of validity has been presented here.

Construct Validity

For any test which aspires to provide a measure of some trait or psychological construct, we may inquire what the nature of the trait or construct is that the test signifies and how meaningful and useful a description of a person it yields. The term *construct validity* has been used to designate this approach to evaluating a test. The term is inevitably a somewhat slippery one. Evidence on the construct validity of a measure is found in the way in which it fits into a meaningful structure of relationships—relationships among the parts of the test, relationships with other tests designed to measure the same attribute, relationships with a variety of criterion variables, relationships to various experimentally manipulated independent variables. A cognitive abilities test is valid as signifying intelligence, then, insofar as it shows the

---

[15]R. L. Thorndike and E. Hagen, *Technical Manual, Cognitive Ability Test,* Multilevel Edition (Boston, Mass.: Houghton Mifflin, 1974), pp. 30–31.

complete pattern of correlates that we should expect of a measure of our construct "effective cognitive functioning."

The data on relationships to school achievement presented in the previous section are relevant to the construct "effective cognitive functioning." Certainly, we should expect such a measure to show a substantial correlation, but far from a perfect correlation, with academic success.

Correlations with Intelligence Tests

A second expectation for any measure of cognitive functioning is that it should show substantial correlation with measures that have been developed for, and have some acceptance as, measures of intelligence. Correlations between the *Lorge-Thorndike* tests and other tests of intelligence have been reported in a number of studies and the results are summarized in the Technical Manual for that test. Since, as has been pointed out, the item types and subtest organization in the Verbal Battery of the *Cognitive Abilities Test* remain much the same as those in the *Lorge-Thorndike,* the results for the earlier batteries should be quite representative of those to be expected from the current test.

This is less true of the Quantitative and Nonverbal, which do not have a close parallel in the previous *Lorge-Thorndike* battery.

An individual ability test that has long stood as the yardstick against which other tests are measured is the *Stanford-Binet Intelligence Scale.* As a by-product of the 1972 restandardization of the *Stanford-Binet,* it was possible to identify 554 individuals who had been tested with the Binet during the 1971–72 school year, and who had taken the *Cognitive Abilities Test* in the fall of 1970. The correlations are shown separately for three age groups in Table 1. Judging from the standard deviations, this group was slightly more variable than the national standardization group, and the correlations may be slightly raised by this fact. Perhaps representative figures would be 0.75 for the Verbal score, 0.68 for Quantitative and 0.65 for Nonverbal.

A further set of data on the relationship of the *Cognitive Abilities Test* to other ability measures is presented in Table 2. Correlations are based on a sample of 173 ninth grade students in a midwestern community, who took the CAT in grade 9 and had taken certain tests of the *Differential Aptitude Tests* in grade 8. The correlations are substantial, though clearly the tests are not identical. The pattern of relationships is about as we would expect, Verbal correlating highest with Verbal and Quantitative with Numerical, but the relatively high correlation of the CAT Nonverbal score with DAT Numerical Ability is a little surprising.

TABLE 5-1   Correlations of Binet with CAT

			VERBAL		QUANTITATIVE		NONVERBAL	
AGE GROUP	N	BINET S.D.	r	S.D.	r	S.D.	r	S.D.
9–11	197	17.8	.72	19.7	.65	17.4	.60	17.7
12–14	238	17.6	.77	19.2	.68	18.5	.68	17.3
15+	119	17.2	.78	16.5	.68	18.0	.65	17.6

	COGNITIVE ABILITIES TEST		
DAT	*Verbal*	*Quantitative*	*Nonverbal*
Verbal Reasoning	.74	.55	.54
Numerical Ability	.54	.70	.65
Abstract Reasoning	.59	.59	.65
Space	.40	.45	.61

Criterion-Related Validity of a Reading Test

Presented next is the discussion of criterion-related validity found in the
technical manual of the *Nelson Reading Skills Test* (RST), a reading achievement test for grades 3 to 9.[16]

Criterion-Related Validity

A small northeastern school district which participated in the March
1976 spring standardization program also made available to the publisher
end-of-year grades in reading, language, and spelling for the examinees. The
teachers had not yet seen the RST scores when they assigned the final grades.
These school grades were used to compute criterion-related validity coefficients.

Table 3 reports the means and standard deviations of RST scores for
each of grades three through nine for this validity sample. A comparison of
corresponding standard deviations between this sample and the spring standardization sample (reported in Table 3) reveals that scores in this district
were less variable than scores from across the nation. Therefore, the obtained
correlation coefficients from the present validity sample are smaller than
would be expected from a district in which student variability more nearly
approximated that of the national sample.

Table 3 reports the correlations between RST scores and grades in the
subjects for which grades were available. Across grades three through nine,
the median correlation of reading grade with Word Meaning score was .59;
with Reading Comprehension score .55; and with Total Reading score .58.
Language grades had median correlations with the correlations with the same
scores of .53, .52, and .51, respectively. The corresponding median validity
coefficients for spelling grades were .53, .41, and .49. The absolute levels of
these correlation coefficients provide evidence of the criterion-related validity
of the RST.

The data reported in Table 3 also shed light on an aspect of construct
validity. The fact that each of these three scores has a higher median correlation to reading grades than to grades in either language or spelling provides
evidence of the RST's discriminate validity.

[16]Gerald Hanna, L. Schell, and R. Schresner, *Technical Manual, The Nelson Reading Skills
Test,* Levels A, B, and C, Forms 3 and 4 (Boston, Mass.: Houghton Mifflin, 1978), pp. 9–12.

TABLE 5-3   Correlation of RST Scores with School Grades

LEVEL	GRADE	N	SUBTEST	RST M	RST SD	Reading	Language	Spelling
						CORRELATION WITH GRADES IN		
A	3	71	WM	18.0	5.8	.74	.60	.62
			RC	20.9	6.8	.68	.52	.54
			TR	59.7	18.8	.72	.56	.58
			SS	12.5	2.9	.72	.63	.59
			RW	15.4	4.3	.44	.30	.49
			Syl	12.7	3.0	.49	.38	.52
	4	65	WM	19.3	4.3	.59	.48	.27
			RC	23.1	4.2	.54	.44	.22
			TR	65.4	11.8	.60	.49	.26
			SS	13.4	2.1	.24	.19	.30
			RW	15.9	3.4	.35	.24	.05
			Syl	14.2	0.9	.13	.33	.33
B	5	47	WM	21.3	6.9	.63	.69	.67
			RC	22.9	7.5	.67	.74	.71
			TR	67.0	21.2	.68	.75	.72
	6	76	WM	23.7	6.7	.58	.53	.44
			RC	26.6	6.5	.32	.32	.23
			TR	76.8	19.2	.52	.50	.40
C	7	90	WM	22.2	8.2	.46	.54	
			RC	22.1	6.5	.49	.55	
			TR	66.3	20.0	.51	.58	
	8	88	WM	24.0	7.6	.59	.46	
			RC	22.2	6.8	.48	.47	
			TR	68.5	19.9	.55	.50	
	9	85	WM	26.9	6.5		.37	
			RC	25.5	5.8		.52	
			TR	77.9	16.5		.51	

Content Validity of a Criterion-Referenced Test

The final illustration of validity reports from a commercially published test is taken from the test manual of the *IOX Basic Skill Tests,* a criterion-referenced test of high school students' skills in reading, writing, and mathematics.[17]

A brief discussion of the validation approach employed with the *IOX Basic Skill Tests* will conclude the manual. It should be noted, of course, that

[17]*Test Manual, IOX, Basic Skills Tests* (Los Angeles: Instructional Objective Exchange, 1978), p. 13.

the 14 separate skills being measured were first defined with intense specificity. Having created detailed test specifications of far greater precision than is typically employed in the development of such achievement tests, the IOX staff created test items that were continually referenced to those specifications. These items were, in essence, the vehicles for operationalizing the reading, writing, and mathematics skills that the test specifications were designed to assess.

The congruence between items and test specifications was continually monitored by internal and external reviewers, for it is the basic premise of IOX test development efforts that a criterion-referenced test is only as useful as the clarity with which the examinee's test performance is described.

This validation approach has been characterized by Popham as *descriptive validity*, a concept basically comparable to the more traditional notion of *content validity*.[18] Although content validity is usually established by test development agencies merely by verbal assertion, IOX recognizes that the internal congruence reviews of items and specifications need to be corroborated by external, independent reviews. Because of our desire to make the *Basic Skill Tests* available to educators as soon as possible, we chose to publish the tests with only our internally conducted descriptive validation analyses to support the tests' validity. It is our intention, however, to initiate a number of external validation efforts, and to report these investigations in the next revision of this manual.

Another type of validity that is relevant to criterion-referenced tests hinges on the defensibility of the attributes being measured, in this case the skills that are assessed in the IOX tests. Equally important as the skills themselves are the particular assessment schemes which—through the test specifications—have been chosen to operationalize those skills. Both of these factors are involved in what has been referred to as *domain-selection validity*.[19] Considerable attention was given to the domain-selection validity of the IOX tests.

Regarding the skills themselves, as indicated earlier, over 300 teachers and administrators supplied IOX with rankings of potential competencies necessary for high school graduation. Having selected the most highly ranked of these skills, the IOX staff generated the test specifications, that is, the particular assessment strategies employed, by considering three major factors.

The first of these was *probable generalizability* of the measured behavior, that is, would an examinee who mastered the skill (as we were operationalizing it) be apt to display mastery of other measurement tactics that might be employed to measure that skill. The second factor considered was *teachability, that is, the extent to which the skill as measured was amenable to improvement as a consequence of instruction. Finally, we considered practicality* of measurement, that is, the logistical and temporal requirements of the measurement strategy selected. All three of these factors were continually used to guide the selections of the behavior domains which are defined by the test specifications for the *IOX Basic Skill Tests*.

In sum, then, although the IOX tests were developed with considerable attention to both descriptive validity and domain-selection validity, it is our

---

[18]For a further discussion of this approach to the validation of criterion-referenced tests, see Popham, *Criterion-Referenced Measurement.*
[19]Ibid.

intention to supplement the amount of objectivity of our validity analyses as soon as possible, and to incorporate such supplementation into future versions of the *Test Manual.*

Having considered the topic of validity in some detail, we can turn in the next chapter to a discussion of reliability.

PRACTICE EXERCISES

There were four types of validity described in the chapter. To give you some practice in distinguishing among them, see if you can decide in each of the following ten vignettes whether a (a) *content*, (b) *predictive criterion-related*, (c) *concurrent criterion-related*, or (d) *construct-validation* strategy is being employed.

1. A test of high school study habits and attitudes, supposedly predictive of how well high school students will perform academically, is administered to twelfth graders during the same week that their cumulative grade point averages in high school are made available. The resulting "validity coefficient" is .56.
2. A group of college English professors judge the adequacy of coverage of a newly developed test of students' knowledge of grammar and syntax. The professors conclude that the coverage is "excellent."
3. Scores on a new version of the *Miller Analogies Test* (MAT) taken during college students' senior year are correlated with their grades in graduate school two years later. The MAT versus GPA correlation is .49.
4. Scores on a sixth-grade achievement test in basic skills are used as a predictor of high school achievement as reflected by high school teachers' rankings of students. The rank-order correlation coefficient between these two variables is .55.
5. Scores on a newly developed self-esteem test are correlated with scores on the widely used Coopersmith *Self-Esteem Inventory.* The correlation between the two sets of scores was quite high ($r = .84$).
6. Teachers who will ultimately be using results of a newly developed math test review it, item by item, to make sure that all of the key topics have been tested. They are divided in their opinions.
7. A test publisher predicts that the firm's new vocational interest test will show that those scoring high on various subscales (such as "clerical" or "sales") are more likely to hold "real life" positions in those job categories than are those scoring low on such subscales.
8. A screening test administered to applicants for medical school correlates .63 with end-of-program grades earned by medical students.
9. A new quantitative aptitude test is administered to high school juniors two days before they take the districtwide test of mathematical skills. The resulting correlation between the two measures is .71.
10. A group of content specialists judge the contents of a new test in history

and conclude that its content coverage was so splendid that they are "thoroughly contented."

ANSWERS TO PRACTICE EXERCISES

1. This would be an instance of criterion-related validity of the concurrent type.
2. Content validity.
3. Criterion-related validity (predictive).
4. This is another case of predictive criterion-related validity.
5. This is a case of construct validity. If it caused you any problems, reread the section dealing with construct validity of this type (page 00).
6. Content validity.
7. Construct validity.
8. Predictive criterion-related validity.
9. Concurrent criterion-related validity.
10. This was a tough one: content validity.

DISCUSSION QUESTIONS

1. If you were asked to explain in jargonless English the three basic validity categories for educational tests to a group of citizens on a school advisory council, how would you do it?
2. Which of the three types of validity do you think is most important for norm-referenced tests? Why?
3. Which of the three types of validity do you think is most important for criterion-referenced tests? Why?
4. Which of the various types of validity is the most expensive for a test publisher to gather? Why do you think so?
5. What is the conceptual relationship, if any, among the three types of validity? Can you think of situations in which all three types of validity information should be gathered?

SUGGESTIONS FOR ADDITIONAL READING

GRONLUND, NORMAN E., "Validity," Chapter 4, *Measurement and Evaluation in Teaching* (3rd ed.), pp. 79–104. New York: Macmillan, 1976. A comprehensive consideration of validation approaches used in education is presented here.

HAMBLETON, RONALD K., "Test Score Validity and Cut-off Scores," in *Criterion-Referenced Testing: State of the Art,* ed. Ronald Berk. Baltimore: The Johns Hopkins University Press, 1980. In this paper Hambleton deals with validity issues as they relate to criterion-referenced measures.

MEHRENS, WILLIAM A. and IRVIN J. LEHMANN, "Reliability and Validity,"

Chapter 5, *Measurement and Evaluation in Education and Psychology* (2nd ed.), pp. 87–132. New York: Holt, Rinehart & Winston, 1975. The authors treat both reliability and validity. The description of various types of validity is relatively comprehensive.

Standards for Educational and Psychological Tests. Prepared by a joint committee of the American Psychological Association, American Educational Research Association, National Council on Measurement in Education. Washington, D.C., The American Psychological Association, 1974. This is mandatory reading for educators who wish to understand completely the notions of validity as they are employed in the field of education.

TUCKMAN, BRUCE W., "Test Validity," Chapter 9, *Measuring Educational Outcomes: Fundamentals of Testing*, pp. 228–251. San Francisco: Harcourt Brace Jovanovich, Inc., 1975. The chapter provides a lucid exposition of the major types of validity which are of concern to educators.

6

Validity and reliability are the meat and potatoes of the measurement game. In the previous chapter you received a fairly hefty serving of meat; now it's potato time.

From the chapter on validity you learned that the concept of validity is not unitary. There are different sorts of validity, depending on what functions the test is designed to serve. Not surprisingly, reliability is also a multimeaning concept. There are different sorts of reliability, depending on the way the reliability evidence is gathered. In general, of course, when we think about the reliability of a test, we focus on the *consistency* with which the test is measuring whatever it's measuring. Moreover, as indicated during the brief introduction to reliability in Chapter 3, most educators probably conceive of consistency as *consistency over time.* In other words, if you asked a run-of-the-mill group of teachers and administrators to tell you what is meant by a test's reliability, odds are they'd respond with something like this: "Test reliability indicates whether students would get essentially the same scores if they took the test at different times." The sort of reliability these folks are talking about is referred to as *stability,* and it constitutes one of the more important types of reliability. Later, we'll look carefully at ways

Reliability

of securing stability estimates, as well as several other types of reliability. Before doing that, however, let's spend a moment or two considering the relationship between a test's reliability and its validity.

Can Validity Find Happiness if Reliability Is Unfaithful?

If a test is valid, must it also be reliable? If a test is reliable, does that mean it's valid? If a test is neither reliable nor valid, should it be cherished or fed to a paper shredder?

Answers to these and similar questions depend on the relationship between reliability and validity. That relationship can be set forth succinctly: *Test reliability is a necessary, but not sufficient, condition for test validity.*

In order for a test to be valid, it must be reliable. Unreliable tests cannot possibly be valid. Merely because a test is reliable, however, does not guarantee its validity. Let's see why this is so.

First off, please recall the discussion at the outset of the previous chapter, where it was noted that technically, it is not the test that is valid, but the *inference* that we make based on the test score. In that discussion we described a test which yielded scores that though perfectly valid for drawing the sorts of inferences for which the test was designed, would be totally invalid if we tried to draw absurdly irrelevant inferences based on the test scores.

In much the same way, we can think of a test which might yield delightfully reliable scores, yet whose results might be employed in drawing zany and incorrect inferences. Such a test, while reliable, would not be valid. To illustrate, suppose we prepared a fifty-item vocabulary test that yielded very consistent scores, even if students took the test again several weeks after their initial bout with it. Thus, of course, the test possesses reliability of the stability sort. However, let's say we used students' scores on the vocabulary test to draw inferences about their aptitude to pole vault. Clearly, those inferences would be invalid. Even if we had the fifty-item test entitled in boldface letters at the top, *A Really Swell Pole-Vaulting Aptitude Test,* the test would not be valid for purposes of predicting one's pole-vaulting prowess. Thus we see that a test can be reliable without necessarily being valid.

But how about valid tests? Do they *really* have to be reliable? Well, let's think of a newly created aptitude test whose criterion-related concurrent validity we're trying to establish. Let's say we're attempting to correlate scores on the new aptitude test with 200 students' current grade point averages. We administer the aptitude test, then calculate the grade point averages, and are just about ready to compute the correlation coefficient between these two sets of data when a violent but remarkably selective tornado bursts through the door, swoops up only the aptitude test scores, and carries them off to the Land of Oz. Distressed by these developments, although cooled by the breeze, we readminister the tests to the 200 students. Now we once more sit down to crank out the correlation coefficient, only to discover that in the meanwhile the guilt-ridden tornado had swooped in to redeposit the original aptitude test scores. Pleasantly surprised by the beneficence of Mother or Father Nature, we glance at the two sets of aptitude test scores and discover, to our surprise, that students' scores fluctuate wildly. Gwendolyn, who earned a high score on the first testing, earned a low score on the second testing; and Tulliver, who earned the top score on the initial test administration, only scored near the mean on the second test administration. A cursory consideration of the remaining test scores confirms our suspicion: The test is not reliable.

Now, can you see that if we ran the correlation between grade point averages and the first batch of aptitude test scores, we would get a correlation coefficient which would be radically different from the one we would get if we used the second set of aptitude test scores. Unreliable, that is, inconsistent, test scores can never yield a consistent relationship with a criterion variable, hence, no consistent validity coefficient is attainable. A test that is unreliable can never be valid.

Hopefully, the discussion of the past few paragraphs will help confirm the original contention that reliability is a necessary, but not sufficient, condition of validity. To establish a test's worth, we need evidence of its reliability *and* validity.

As indicated before, there are different ways of securing evidence regarding the reliability with which a test measures whatever it's measuring. We now consider the four most commonly used approaches to test reliability and, as a consequence of those considerations, assume that the reader will come to the inescapable conclusion that different approaches to test reliability yield substantially different ways of viewing the consistency with which the test is measuring. The four approaches to reliability which are described are *stability, equivalence, equivalence and stability,* and *internal consistency*. As with the previous chapter's discussion of types of validity, after describing each of these four approaches to reliability in general, we point out any differences which might arise if we were attempting to establish the reliability of norm-referenced or criterion-referenced tests.

STABILITY

Already alluded to, *stability* estimates of reliability are based on the consistency of a test's measurement *over time*. In the most common way of securing a test's stability, we administer a test to a group of examinees, wait for a reasonable interval (say two or three weeks), then readminister the test to the same examinees. By correlating examinees' scores on the two occasions, we secure a reliability coefficient, in this case a stability coefficient (often called a *test-retest* coefficient). If the coefficient is high, for instance, .80 to .90, then the test developer and test user can take some solace in the fact that individuals will apparently obtain comparable scores on the test even though it is administered at different times.

This sort of stability information would be of interest to a test user if, in fact, there was the likelihood that the test might have to be administered to individuals at different times. Suppose, for example, that a high school graduation test was being administered by a school district under such strict security conditions that if a student was absent, that student would be obliged to wait three weeks until the test was readministered. Under such circumstances, we should definitely be interested in the test's stability.

The length of the interval between the two testing occasions is, of course, an issue of significance. If we wait only minutes or seconds to readminister the test, the examinee's second test performance is likely to be influenced by the initial test performance. Too short a between-testing interval is obviously unsound. At the other extreme, if we wait a decade or two between testings, all sorts of intervening events in the lives of the examinees will act to mess up the resulting correlation between the two sets of test scores. The selection of the between-testing interval's length should be made so as to reduce the influence of the first testing on the second but also to reduce the likelihood that intervening events in the lives of the examinees will distort the second set of test results. Between-testing intervals of weeks are common when establishing the reliability of achievement tests whose results might be influenced by intervening instruction. Longer between-testing intervals are often seen with aptitude tests, since such measures are thought to be less influenced by instructional interventions.

A problem with the stability approach to reliability determination is that teachers and students often view the readministration of a test as a less than superlative use of their time. Students who are instructed to "retake the same old dumb test" will often score lower on the second testing merely because they view the activity as meaningless. Care must be taken to create an atmosphere where students will devote comparable zeal to both test administrations.

Norm-Referenced Applications

For many widely distributed norm-referenced tests, one does not see efforts to secure evidence of stability reliability, chiefly because of the costs involved. Large samples of examinees are usually employed to secure normative data for such tests, hence the costs and logistical difficulties of readministering tests to large numbers of examinees often incline norm-referenced test developers toward other reliability strategies.

Sometimes, however, only samples of the normative population are readministered the test in order to secure a stability estimate. With well-developed norm-referenced measures and a reasonably short between-testing temporal interval, the stability coefficients often range between .70 and .90. In some instances, tests of verbal aptitude have been readministered after an interval of one or two years and yield stability coefficients as high as .80.

As with other approaches to reliability, the longer the test, the more reliable the test tends to be. A one- or two-item test is obviously subject to chance error, while a test of 100 items will yield a much more representative estimate of an examinee's performance. Most norm-referenced tests, since they typically deal with somewhat general skills, knowledge, or aptitudes, are relatively long instruments and, therefore, tend to yield relatively high reliability coefficients such a those associated with a test's stability.

Criterion-Referenced Applications

Users of criterion-referenced tests are often concerned about the stability with which their tests are measuring. In this regard there is little difference between the users of norm- and criterion-referenced tests. There are settings, however, in which those employing criterion-referenced tests are fearful that examinees' scores on their tests will not be sufficiently variable to produce reasonable reliability coefficients. The reader should know that when the variability among a group of test scores is low, it is much less likely to secure a high correlation (with *any* other variable) involving those test scores than if the scores displayed considerable variability. Users of criterion-referenced tests in instructional settings often hope that as a consequence of effective instruction, most students will earn high test scores. The resulting *range restriction* would make it impossible to secure the sorts of reliability coefficients that one would obtain with norm-referenced tests in which there was considerable score variability.[1]

Even though this fear of range restriction and its consequent depression of the magnitude of reliability coefficients (and, in some cases, validity coefficients) has been a subject of discussion for well over a decade, the experience of most educators is that instructional interventions are rarely sufficiently effective to get most students up to mastery. As a consequence, whenever there is a reasonable degree of score variability present, traditional correlational methods can usually be employed to secure an index of a criterion-referenced test's stability over time.

Because criterion-referenced tests are often employed in connection with impending decisions about students and/or instructional programs, it has been proposed that a *decision-consistency,* rather than a score-consistency, approach to reliability might be sensibly employed with such tests. For instance, suppose you were placing low-scoring students in a remedial reading program if they earned a score of less than 60 percent correct on a criterion-referenced reading test. If Griselda earns a score of 55 percent correct on the test, she goes into the remedial class. She'll go in the remedial class if she only scored 40 percent or even 59 percent. Now

[1]See, for example, W. J. Popham and T. R. Husek, "Implications of Criterion-Referenced Measurement," *Journal of Educational Measurement,* 1969 6(1), 1–9.

one way of conceptualizing a criterion-referenced test's stability is to categorize examinees according to the *decisions* made about them in order to see, if the test were administered at a different time, how many students would be classified in the same manner.

To illustrate this *decision-consistency* approach, let's use the example of the reading test with 60 percent correct being used as the cut-off score. Assume that the test was administered to 100 youngsters in early February and that 72 percent earned a score on the test of 60 percent or better, so that the remaining 28 percent would be targeted for the remedial class. Then in mid-February the test was readministered, and students were once more assigned according to the 60 percent correct standard. Let's say that of the 28 percent who originally scored below the designated cut-off, all but five youngsters still scored below 60 percent correct. Of the 72 percent who hit 60 percent correct or better on the initial test, however, seven students fell below that standard on the second test administration. Thus for 88 percent of the youngsters, consistent decisions were made. That is, the same 23 percent fell below the standard, and the same 65 percent were above the standard on both testing occasions.

In using the decision-consistency approach to the determination of test reliability, it is important to note that the extent of decision consistency is strongly dependent on *where the cut-off standard is,* that is, where the score is which will be used to make decisions, *in relationship to the average performance of the group.* This point can be illustrated by considering the two situations depicted in Figure 6–1. In which of these two situations would we get a higher test-retest percentage of decision consistency?

Consideration of the two situations should allow you to see that in Situation Z there would be a greater degree of decision consistency because there are fewer scores close to the cut-off point (45); thus the predictable score fluctuations that would occur with the second test's administration would find few students crossing over the cut-off score. In Situation *X*, however, the proximity of the mean (25) to the cut-off score (27) would indicate that more students would fluctuate around the cut-off score merely because there are more students close to that point. The principle to be drawn here is that the proximity of the distribution's mean to the cut-off score will play a significant role in determining the magnitude of decision consistency. In general, test developers who employ a decision-consistency approach would do well to provide decision-consistency percentages based on different (but likely) cut-off levels.

A final point about the reliability of criterion-referenced tests depends on the *length* of these tests in comparison to the traditional norm-referenced tests with which we are familiar. Because criterion-referenced tests will sometimes have only ten to twenty items per measured behavioral domain, we can expect lower reliability coefficients than would be found if

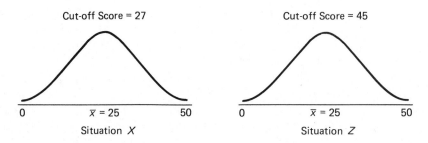

Cut-off Score = 27   Cut-off Score = 45

| 0 $\bar{x} = 25$ 50 | | 0 $\bar{x} = 25$ 50 |
Situation X Situation Z

FIGURE 6–1   Two fictitious distributions of test scores with equal means and standard deviations, but dissimilar cut-off scores.

longer tests were being employed. If, for example, test users have come to expect stability coefficients of .80 or better for traditional norm-referenced tests of 50 to 100 items, they should alter their expectations when the test-retest reliability coefficient of a ten-item criterion-referenced test is being reported. Although we do not yet have the experience with short-test reliability coefficients to establish reasonable expectations for such reliability coefficients, it is certain they will dip well below the customary .80 to .90 levels.

EQUIVALENCE

A second form of reliability is associated with the use of two or more forms of the same test. Since it is generally hoped that the two or more forms will yield consistent information regarding examinees, there is a necessity to secure information regarding the *equivalence* of the two or more test forms.

In the most straightforward manner of securing equivalence information, we simply administer two forms of the same test, then correlate examinees' scores on the two test forms. The resulting coefficient is referred to as the *equivalence coefficient of reliability* or sometimes, as the *equivalent forms reliability* coefficient.

Typically, publishers of tests, whether norm- or criterion-referenced, will supply information regarding the extent to which two or more forms of the test are parallel with respect to the content or skills they cover. These comparable forms of the test can either be presented by publishers as content-parallel, meaning they supposedly cover the same content, or as difficulty-parallel, meaning both forms of the test are equidifficult. Information will usually be supplied regarding each test form's mean and standard deviation (often based on an administration to some examinees used during the norming of the test). Finally, the correlation between examinees' performances on the two forms will typically be supplied.

Evidence of the equivalence of different test forms is needed whenever multiple forms are being employed as essentially interchangeable tools. This is often the case when educators use tests for making important decisions about individuals and there is the need for *test security.* For example, the *Miller Analogies Test* (MAT) is a widely used test of one's verbal aptitude, typically employed as a screening test for those students applying to graduate schools. Because students are permitted to retake the MAT on different occasions, it is either necessary to have different forms of the MAT or to count on an examinee's forgetting everything about the first administration of the test prior to the second test administration. However, as every graduate school professor will attest, although graduate students are a forgetful lot—they aren't *that* forgetful. Obviously, multiple MAT forms are requisite. Furthermore, just as requisite is information regarding the extent to which individuals taking two different MAT forms will earn consistent scores.

Norm-Referenced Applications

Many norm-referenced tests are not prepared with multiple forms and hence, have no need for equivalence-reliability data. For those which do supply multiple forms, it is recognized that information regarding the equivalence of the forms should be supplied. Sometimes, typically because of limited financial resources, multiple test forms are made available but *only* assertions, such as the following, are found in the test's technical manual: "Content-parallel test forms are available." Now, although we should applaud efforts to develop forms that possess content which is parallel, assertions about content similarity will not suffice. Correlational evidence is also needed regarding how examinees perform on the two test forms. In addition, examinee means and standard deviations on the two forms are needed.

You can get a strong, positive *r* between two test forms, yet one form can be much more difficult than the other. For instance, let's say you gave fifty youngsters a 100-item test, then pretended you were administering a much more difficult second form of the test by knocking off ten points from each student's score. If you ran a correlation between the two sets of scores (that is, the original scores and the set of "scores minus ten points"), the resulting correlation coefficient would be 1.00. It is for this reason, that is, to check for *difficulty disparities,* that we also need descriptive statistics on the two forms, such as the test form means. A few paragraphs later we describe a much niftier way of establishing test-form equivalence than the typically employed approaches.

The equivalence coefficients for most well-established norm-referenced tests, as was the case with such tests' stability coefficients, tend to hover between .80 and .90. Some equivalence coefficients even get as high as .95.

Criterion-Referenced Applications

One substantial difference between norm- and criterion-referenced tests is the rigor with which the measured domains of examinee behaviors are described. Whereas norm-referenced test developers typically provide only rather general descriptions of what these tests are measuring, developers of high-quality, criterion-referenced tests set forth extremely detailed descriptions of the rules employed to generate the tests' items. This increased rigor of description, typically cast in the form of test specifications, makes it much easier to create truly equivalent forms of a criterion-referenced test.

Think of it like this—a set of specifications for a criterion-referenced test makes explicit the item-generation rules which define a domain of examinee behavior. By using these item-generation rules, we can theoretically create an almost unlimited number of test items to tap the behavior thus defined. To get equivalent forms of a criterion-referenced test, in theory, all we need do is randomly sample from the item pool.

However, theory, in measurement as elsewhere, is often messed up by practice. So even with criterion-referenced tests that spring from delightfully detailed test specifications, we still need to garner the customary empirical data regarding test form equivalence.

As we saw in the discussion of stability reliability, this information is often best represented in the form of decision-consistency data. If possible, both decision-consistency data with more traditional correlational data should be presented.

EQUIVALENCE AND STABILITY

A third form of reliability arises from combining the two previously discussed. Since those two forms were *stability* and *equivalence,* it should not come as a stunning surprise that this third form of reliability is referred to as *equivalence and stability.*

We have the need to secure such reliability information when we administer different forms of a test after a temporal delay. In Figure 6–2 we see the three reliability approaches depicted that we've been discussing so far. Of the three approaches, the lowest reliability coefficients will arise from the equivalence and stability approach since there are two factors (the time delay and any differences between the two forms) that operate to reduce the consistency of measurement. Thus, whereas all test developers strive for .80 to .90 reliability coefficients when dealing with stability or

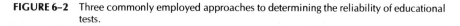

(1) Test + Time Delay vs. Retest =   Stability

(2) Form A vs. Form B =   Equivalence

(3) Form A + Time Delay vs. Form B =   Equivalence and Stability

FIGURE 6–2   Three commonly employed approaches to determining the reliability of educational tests.

equivalence approaches, they may be well satisfied with a solid .70, or lower, for estimates of equivalence and stability.

The norm- and criterion-referenced applications of equivalence and stability estimates are similar to those discussed earlier under the separate treatments of stability and equivalence. However, before turning to the fourth and final form of reliability, that is, *internal consistency*, we're going to deal with a technique for developing equivalent forms that has been receiving considerable attention in recent years, namely, the *Rasch* method of developing equivalent forms. Because this approach offers considerable advantages over more traditional test-equating schemes, it is worthy of your attention.

A SIMPLE-MINDED EXPLANATION OF RASCH TEST EQUATING

I have attempted to provide a relatively understandable explanation of how the Rasch model can be employed to create equivalent test forms. Because the mathematics associated with Rasch procedures are relatively abstruse, a formula-ridden explanation would be of little assistance to most readers.

We are dealing here with an intensely practical problem currently being encountered by many educators, such as those responsible for the implementation of minimum competency testing programs. Since not all students will pass any given administration of a test, those failing the test will have to retake the same test or another version of it. Because such failing students might recall items from their initial interaction with the same test, most often it is recommended that an equivalent form of the test be used for the second administration of the test.

Equivalent test forms are also needed if the test is being administered often, for example, annually, because of the probable breaches of test security that will occur. Suppose a statewide minimum competency test is to be given at the end of each academic year. If the identical test is used every year, then it would be feared that certain teachers might soon be teaching directly to the particular items on the test. To forestall such security violations, new forms of the test can be given each year.

Clearly, there will be many situations in which we would like to have access to test forms that are not only equivalent in the content or skills they assess, but are also equivalent in the *difficulty* of the test items they contain. How can these equivalent test forms be obtained?

Well, one way would be *marathon testing*. In this approach we would generate huge item pools, corral a large number of students, then have all the students complete all the items so that for each item we would obtain a *p* value (the proportion of examinees answering an item correctly). Different forms of the test would then be constituted which were equal both in content as well as difficulty (as reflected by equal item *p* values).

The difficulties with this approach are several. First off, it is very costly to generate huge item pools at one time. If we could produce those additional items over an extended period of time, the costs would typically be spread out and thus more tolerable. Second, fatigue factors might be operative after students had completed a hundred or so test items, thereby rendering their responses atypical. Finally, because the students would realize that their marathon test-taking session was not the "real thing" and only of use in test equating, their unmotivated responses to items would often be less accurate than would be the case if the stakes (for example, a high school diploma) were real. The marathon approach to test equating is, obviously, fraught with problems.

Another scheme for equating tests is to administer one form of a test, then subsequently generate enough new items so that they could be field tested on a different population of examinees in order to secure test items of equivalent difficulty (*p* values).

For example, suppose a sixty-item test of mathematics achievement had been given as part of a minimum competency testing program to all of the 2,000 eleventh-graders in a school district, with a resulting *average p* value of 0.71. In other words, the *p* value for each of the items had been calculated (if 82 percent of the students answered item nine correctly, its *p* value would be 0.82), then the mean *p* values had been calculated by summing all the individual *p* values and dividing that sum by the number of items.)

Let's say we cranked out 100 new items and administered them to a different sample of 300 eleventh-grade students so that we could put together a new form of the test whose content coverage matched that of the first test and whose average *p* value was also 0.71. Doesn't that sound pretty good so far?

However, there is a flaw. If the 300 students used in the new tryout of the 100 items are not identical in ability to the original 2,000 eleventh-graders, misleading *p* values will be yielded. Thus, even if the second test has an average *p* value of 0.71, it may be substantially different than the first version of the test. For instance, suppose the 300 youngsters were much less bright than the original 2,000. Then a second test with a mean *p* value of 0.71 (based on weaker students' performances) would be a markedly easier test than the earlier test.

Similarly, let's say that there had recently been highly effective mathematics instruction in the district so that the 300 eleventh-graders (although equal in mathematics ability to the 2,000 students) really performed well on the test. Again, even though the average *p* values on both tests are 0.71, the second test will turn out to be even tougher because the second sample of students is much more knowledgeable than the original students who didn't have the benefit of the improved instruction. A similar situation would also arise if the second test had been tried out on 300 students who were much brighter than the original 2,000.

The dilemma, then, is trying to develop equivalent test forms so that the artificiality or the exhaustion associated with a single group of students' taking many test items fails to yield *p* values of comparable meaning. On the other hand, when we use different samples of examinees in an effort to secure comparable *p* values, differences in the ability or training of those samples can lead to noncomparable *p* values.

Rasch as the Remedy

The Rasch model, developed some years ago by the Danish mathematician Georg Rasch, provides us with a way of overcoming these difficulties and therefore developing different test forms which are truly equivalent in difficulty.

The Rasch model is the most popular of several *latent trait* models which deal with such latent (hidden) traits as ability. Latent trait models are beginning to receive substantial attention from psychometricians. Here's how the Rasch approach to test equating works.[2]

First off, one form of the test is administered to a reasonably large group of examinees. Rasch devotees differ as to how many responses per item they think are needed, but somewhere between 200 and 500 responses are apparently required for each item. Then all of the items are analyzed to see if they "fit" the Rasch model, that is, to see if they behave the way that items are supposed to according to the Rasch approach. In general this means that an item is supposed to be answered correctly more often by examinees who perform well on the total test than by examinees who do badly on the total test and that all items do this to an equal extent. In this

---

[2] I am indebted to R. Robert Rentz, who kindly reviewed an early version of the Rasch test-equating discussion and offered a number of solid suggestions for its improvement.

regard, the Rasch approach is similar to traditional item-analysis operations.

All items that fit the model (and most of them typically do) are then *calibrated* on a new scale, that is, they are assigned values on a new difficulty scale, called the *logistic* scale. The unit of this scale is the *logit* (pronounced low-jit). The logistic scale has logit values that usually range from −3.0 to +3.0. This new scale is at the heart of the Rasch approach because the newly calibrated logit difficulty values will be subsequently employed to build equivalent tests. Let's see how this calibration business works.

First off, let's assume we have found that the first five items on our 55-item test do indeed fit the Rasch model. Their *p* values, based on administering the test to 500 examinees, are given below.

ITEM	p VALUES
1	0.73
2	0.91
3	0.44
4	0.51
5	0.76

After sending the items through a computer routine that coaxes, kicks, and cuddles them, we can also obtain each item's value on the logistic scale. Note that the more difficult an item is, the higher is its score on the logistic difficulty scale. This is the reverse of the traditional *p* value scheme where higher values indicate easier items.

ITEM	p VALUE	LOGIT VALUE
1	0.73	−0.2
2	0.91	−1.6
3	0.44	1.1
4	0.51	0.8
5	0.76	−0.4

Now what we want to do is to develop a new form of the test whose items will be equivalent *in logit value difficulty* to the original test. Here's how we do it.

We take some of the items that fit a Rasch model from the first test, say ten or so, then administer those ten items (which we call "linking items") plus all our new items to a new sample of examinees. Let's say we have seventy new items, so the test will be eighty items overall (the seventy new items plus the ten items from the first test). Because we know the logits of the ten linking items from the first analysis and because we know that the difficulties of those items ought to be the same in the second analysis, any observed difference in logit values for the ten items from the first to the second analysis simply reflects a different level of ability in the two samples. This observed difference (the difference between the mean item difficulties from the two analyses) can be used to adjust the item difficulties of all new items in the second test.

The resulting logit values can then be used in order to select 45 new items which, when added to the ten linking items from the earlier test form, give us a second form of the test whose average logit value is identical to that of the first form.

We can illustrate this process, showing how the Rasch approach can overcome disparities in the abilities of different samples, by imagining that our first sample was composed of individuals who were both less able or who had been given less on-target instruction (as is often the case in the early phases of new instructional programs). In addition to the *p* values and logit values of the same five items we saw before, we add five new items given to a group of more able (or better taught) students.

| | LESS ABLE STUDENTS | | | MORE ABLE STUDENTS | |
Item	p Value	Logit Value	Item	p Value	Logit Value
1	0.73	−0.2	56	0.83	−0.2
2	0.91	−1.6	57	0.97	−1.6
3	0.44	1.1	58	0.53	1.1
4	0.51	0.8	59	0.87	0.8
5	0.76	−0.4	60	0.84	−0.4

The fictitious data given here have been made simple for ease of explanation, but they could have arisen from real test items. Note that if we were using only *p* values, then the six new items (55-60) would have appeared much easier than the five original items (1-5). However because, on the basis of our linking items, we were able to determine that the second sample of examinees is substantially more able than the first group, we were able to compute logit values *as if the second sample had been identical in ability to the first sample.*

In comparing logits and *p* values, it should be noted that there is not a linear relationship between the two. Thus, a constant gain in *p* values is not accompanied by a constant gain on the logistic scale. The size of the gain in logits depends on the location on the *p*-value scale where the gain takes place.

As you can see, then, the logit values derived from the Rasch model's machinations tell us how difficult an item is. These logit values are based on an examinee's ability estimate tied to the original calibration of the items. It doesn't make all that much difference whether the original group was bright or dull, as long as there is some degree of variability in their ability levels (as indicated by their total scores on the test).

Let's try to describe the Rasch-equating approach again but somewhat differently. In attempting to equate a new form of the test with an old form, the process works like this: First we find out how *able* each new examinee is, based on their scores on some linking items from the earlier test. On the basis of this ability estimate, we then calculate logit values for the new test items. Let's say, for example, that we had a particularly able group of new examinees (based on their scores on the linking items). A Rasch computer program would then *adjust down* the logit difficulty values on the new items because the new examinees were more able than the original examinees. In essence, the Rasch program allows us to see how difficult the new items are *as if* the two groups of examinees had been identical in ability. All we need do, then, is select a group of new items whose logit values match those of the original test.

Here is an attempt to depict graphically what we have been talking about. In Figure 6–3 we can see that after Rasching the original 55 items (Step 1) and identifying ten linking items, we administered those along with 70 new items to a different sample of examinees (Step 2). The linking items are then used to calculate the ability levels of the new examinees and thereafter the logit values of the 70 new items (Step 3). From those 70 items, we select 55 (we could have also used the 10 linking items had we wished) that yield a mean logit value equivalent to that of the original test (Step 4).

Notice that the logit values of the original and subsequent items are based on the ability estimates of the examinees who took the test on the first occasion. Some Rasch specialists recommend recalibrating the test items

Step 1. Original 55-item test administered, Rasched, and suitable linking items identified	10 Items | 45 Items
Step 2. Ten linking items and 70 new items administered to new sample, then Rasched.	10 Linking Items | 70 New Items
Step 3. Linking items used to estimate new examinee's ability on difficulty scale of old test group, then determined logit values for few items.	10 Linking Items → Logit Values of the 70 New Items
Step 4. A new 55-item test is created with average logit value identical to that of original 55-item test.	Equivalent 55-Item Test Form

FIGURE 6–3 The Construction of a Rasch-equated test form.

every few tests or so to make sure they're basing logit values of subsequent test items on a representative, up-to-date sample.

As you can see, one of the real advantages of the Rasch approach to test equating is that we can add to item pools later, after our original administration of the test. Since we only need to have a handful of linking items, the test can also be administered in settings where scores truly count, thereby reducing the artificiality of situations in which examinees believe that they are taking the test only for "experimental" purposes.

Rasch Rapture

Recent converts to any religion are a dangerous lot. Some Rasch enthusiasts seem to believe they were anointed from beyond (Olympus, Heaven, or Princeton, New Jersey) to baptize the masses. We must be cautious with these zealots and require them to describe what they're about in sufficiently clear language so that we can really understand, at least on an intuitive level, what the Rasch model is up to.

Because the mathematics are so complex and the number crunching is usually consummated by a computer, it is all too tempting to say to the Rasch enthusiasts: "You take care of the analysis—I'll trust you." However, practicing educators should not abandon intellectual control of their endeavors, even to the quantitatively facile. Let's demand that the proponents of Rasch approaches describe their wares well enough so that we can decide whether they're worth buying. In the case of test equating, it looks like Rasch is a bargain.[3]

Even so, there are a number of assumptions regarding the Rasch model which must be satisfied by our data before we secure meaningful results. For instance, a set of items being calibrated by Rasch techniques are supposed to be *unidimensional,* that is, all be measuring a single attribute. Many hard-line Rasch specialists disagree about the meaning of unidimensionality, hence there is some uncertainty about the appropriateness of the Rasch for specific situations. In reality, of course, using the Rasch model does not actually make two test forms any more "equivalent," it merely aligns statistically the difficulty scales of the two forms.

INTERNAL CONSISTENCY

The final type of reliability we must consider represents a substantial departure from the three reliability strategies treated previously. In those three strategies, the basic task was to relate an examinee's scores on two

---

[3]The entire Summer 1977 issue (Vol. 14, No. 2) of the *Journal of Educational Measurement* is devoted to latent trait models (the Rasch model being the most visible of these). It is well worth reading.

tests (or two test forms) administered with or without a temporal delay. This final form of reliability is known as *internal consistency* and, as its title suggests, it focuses on the consistency of a test's internal elements, namely, its test items.

The previously treated methods of estimating reliability all require data from two testing sessions. Internal-consistency methods of calculating reliability can be used with data from only a single test administration. Internal-consistency estimates should be thought of as revealing the extent to which the items on the test are internally consistent with one another— that is, the extent to which the items are homogeneous. Such methods should not be used with *speeded* tests in which examinees only have a limited amount of time to complete the test.

The *split-half* technique consists of dividing a test into two equal halves, ordinarily by treating the odd, then the even, items as though they constituted separate tests. The entire test is administered to a group of individuals; then their two subscores (derived from the odd and the even items) are correlated. The resulting correlation coefficient is considered an estimate of the degree to which the two halves of the test are performing their functions consistently. Because longer tests are more reliable than shorter tests, it is possible to apply the Spearman-Brown prophecy formula which, using the correlation between the two half-tests, estimates what the reliability would be on the full-length test—that is, including both odd and even items. The procedure works as follows:

$$\text{Reliability on full test} = \frac{2 \times \text{reliability on half-test}}{1 + \text{reliability on half-test}}$$

The simplicity with which the Spearman-Brown formula can be used is illustrated in the following equation, where the half-test correlation coefficient is .60:

$$\text{Reliability on full test} = \frac{2 \times .60}{1 + .60} = \frac{1.20}{1.60} = .75$$

As we can see, use of the Spearman-Brown formula will increase the magnitude of the reliability estimate (unless the half-test $r = 0$).

A widely used index of the homogeneity of a set of binary-scored test items (that is, items which can be scored as right or wrong) is the *Kuder-Richardson* method, particulary formulae 20 (K - R20) and 21 (K-R21). The K-R21 formula is somewhat less accurate than the K-R20 formula, but it is so simple to compute that it is the most frequently employed estimate of internal consistency. One version of the K-R21 formula is the following:

$$\text{K-R21 reliability coefficient} = \frac{K}{K-1} \left(1 - \frac{M(K-M)}{Ks^2} \right)$$

where K = number of items in the test
       M = mean of the set of test scores
       s = standard deviation of the set of test scores

The K-R20 formula, for which K-R21 is a reasonable approximation in most situations, follows:

$$\text{K-R20 reliability coefficient} = \frac{K}{K-1} \left(1 - \frac{\Sigma pq}{s^2} \right)$$

where K = number of items in the test
     Σpq = sum of the variance of items scored dichotomously (right or wrong)
     s^2 = variance of the total test

Both of these formulae can be thought of as representing the average correlation obtained from all possible split-half reliability estimates. The K-R20 formula is used less frequently than K-R21 because it requires far more computation. Typically a computer is employed when one seeks a K-R20 estimate. The K-R21 formula is an algebraic derivation of K-R20 which assumes that the p values of all items (that is, the proportion of examinees who score correctly on an item) are identical. If that assumption is not satisfied, and it almost never is, then K-R21 will yield a slightly lower estimate of reliability than will K-R20. Although both formulae are used by large-scale test publishers (who have access to computers), classroom teachers must ordinarily rely on the K-R21 formula.

Formula fiddling.   If you want to gain a better intuitive insight into what's going on when people compute internal-consistency estimates, such as K-R21, take a few minutes and insert different numbers in the formula. Note, for example, that with any reasonably long test, the fraction to the left of the parentheses, that is, $\frac{K}{K-1}$, isn't going to make much difference because it will be approximately 1.0. For instance, $\frac{100}{99}$ is, for all practical purposes, the same as 1.0. With shorter tests we see that the effect of this $\frac{K}{K-1}$ fraction is to increase slightly the size of the K-R21 coefficient because with a ten-item test the fraction will be $\frac{10}{9}$ or 1.11.

However, the really influential components of the K-R21 formula are inside the parentheses. Since the expression is 1 minus a fraction, the *smaller the fraction is,* the bigger K-R21 will be. For instance, $1 - 1/4$ (or 0.75) is larger than $1 - 1/2$ (or 0.50). Now, recall that fractions which have smaller denominators represent larger quantities than those with larger denominators (for example 1/2 is larger than 1/10). Notice, then, that the larger the standard deviation of the test scores is, the smaller that the fraction in the parentheses will be. We see that smaller standard deviations decrease the size of K-R21 and larger standard deviations boost it.

Now, what about the expression in the numerator of that fraction? Well, first let's remember that if you want a big K-R21 (which would indicate the items on the test were quite internally consistent), you want a small fraction to be subtracted from the 1 within the parentheses. Assuming that the denominator of the fraction stays the same, we want the numerator to be *small* (for example, 1/3 is smaller than 2/3). Note that the closer the test mean is to the middle of the range of possible test scores, the larger will be the numerator of that fraction. For instance, imagine you have a ten-item test. If the mean of test scores is 5.0, then the numerator would be 5(10–5) or 25. If the mean was more toward the ends of the possible score range, for example, 9 or 1, then the numerator will be much smaller, for instance, 9(10–1) = 9 or 1(10–1) = 9. Because smaller numerators yield smaller fractions, hence larger K-R21 coefficients, how does this make any intuitive sense? Well, think of it this way: remember that the size of the standard deviation is most influential in this formula. Since as the mean of a distribution nears the extremes of the possible score points, the possibility of getting a large standard deviation is reduced because of the range restriction; the numerator of the fraction takes that range-restriction factor into account and compensates for the reduced possibility of getting a large standard deviation.

Now, the patient reader may ask, why did you take me down this treacherous trail into the mysteries of the K-R21 formula? The reason is that too many educators are intimidated by formulas of any sort, hence they fail to recognize that in most instances there is a commonsense rationale underlying most of these formulas—if only you can tease it out.

Well, what's the commonsense rationale of K-R21? Simply put, it is a formula which rests on the notion that if a test's items are relatively homogeneous, there will be lots of variance on the test because, for example, on a knowledge test, examinees who know the subject well will get very high scores since most of the items are measuring the same thing. Similarly, examinees who don't know much will do very badly because they'll fail across the board on similar sorts of items. Now the K-R21 formula incorporates this notion by stressing the impact of test-score variance although making a couple of adjustments for test length, $\frac{K}{K-1}$, and the possibility of getting a large standard deviation, M(K-M). If you've had any difficulty in comprehending the explanation of the past few paragraphs, it will be helpful to play number plugging for a bit. For instance, set up a few fictitious numbers in the formula, then juggle the size of the standard deviation, or the size of the mean, or the number of items in the test. See how these differences affect the size of K-R21.

The Kuder-Richardson method, as is the case with all internal consistency estimates, focuses on the degree to which the items in the test are functioning in a homogeneous fashion. Coefficient alpha, developed by Cronbach, is a more generalizable estimate of the internal-consistency form of reliability and can be used with test items that yield other than binarily scored responses.[4]

Coefficient alpha can be used, for instance, to compute the internal consistency of a set of test items (short-answer or essay) where each of the items could receive a range of points, not just be scored as correct or incorrect. The formula for coefficient alpha is

$$\alpha = \frac{K}{K-1} \left(1 - \Sigma \frac{s_i^2}{s_x^2} \right)$$

where K = number of items on the test
s_x^2 = variance of the total test
s_i^2 = the sum of the variances of individual items

Norm-Referenced Applications

As indicated earlier, internal consistency estimates are commonly computed by publishers of norm-referenced tests. Because, as we have seen, these estimates are heavily dependent on a test's variance, this is one reason that publishers of norm-referenced tests strive to produce tests with considerable score variance. After all, if a potential purchaser of two norm-referenced tests is choosing between two tests that are identical in all respects except that one has a K-R20 of 0.74 and the other has a K-R20 of 0.93, the latter test will typically be purchased.

It should be noted, however, that internal consistency of tests is sometimes, ever so subtly, proffered for more than it is. Internal consistency estimates tell us very little about a test's stability or the equivalence of different test forms. It is only what it says it is, a reflection of the extent to which items on the test are internally consistent.

Criterion-Referenced Applications

Since the thrust of criterion-referenced test developers is to produce a pool of homogeneous items that are congruent with a crisp description of a behavioral domain, the accumulation of internal consistency indices bears more directly on the *content validity* of the test than on its reliability, at least, its reliability in the sense of making consistent decisions with the test.

[4]Lee J. Cronbach, "Coefficient Alpha and the Internal Structure of Tests," *Psychometrika*, 16 (1951), 297–334.

"Mr. Huff, as a first year math teacher you have created tests with a perfect reliability — they yield scores that are consistently meaningless."

Although criterion-referenced test developers will undoubtedly continue to gather internal-consistency estimates on their measures and describe them under the heading of "reliability" information, the astute user of criterion-referenced tests will realize that these estimates bear most heavily on the accuracy with which the test describes and measures the behavior domain it sets out to measure.

It is apparent, given the different approaches to reliability that we have treated, some approaches will yield different size reliability coefficients than others. For instance, other things being equal, a test with a stability and equivalence coefficient of 0.90 would be preferred to a test with a K-R21 of 0.90. There are no hard and fast rules regarding how large a respectable reliability coefficient should be. Thus, since the required reliability of a test is situation-dependent, it is apparent that the skilled evaluator of tests will need to approach the issue of test reliability with great care.

THE STANDARD ERROR OF MEASUREMENT

The four methods of estimating a test's reliability have chiefly focused on the consistency of a group of examinees' scores on a test. What about the consistency of an *individual's* score? Suppose, for example, that you had determined that the stability r on a test was .82 and its K-R21 was 0.89, what would you be able to discern about the consistency (accuracy) of Larry Jones' score of 65 correct? Well, except in a general way, very little. To provide an index of the accuracy (or consistency) of an individual's test performance, we use an index referred to as the *standard error of measurement.*

The standard error of measurement can be thought of as a reflection of the variability of an individual's scores if the test were readministered again and again. However, because it is not practical to readminister tests interminably to an individual (the examinee becomes fatigued, annoyed, or senile), we estimate the variability of an individual's test scores based on data from a group. The formula for the standard error of estimate is the following:

$$s_e = s_x \sqrt{1 - r_{xx}}$$

where s_e = standard error of estimate
$\quad\quad s_x$ = standard deviation of the test scores
$\quad\quad r_{xx}$ = the reliability of the test

To illustrate the use of the formula, suppose we were working with a test that had a standard deviation of 7.5 and a reliability coefficient of .91. We would substitute in the formula and solve as follows:

$$
\begin{aligned}
S_e &= 7.5 \sqrt{1-.91} \\
&= 7.5 \sqrt{.09} \\
&= 7.5(.3) \\
&= 2.25
\end{aligned}
$$

Now, what does this 2.25 signify? Well, and this is based on some special properties of the normal curve that we'll investigate in the next chapter, we can use a value of ±2.25 to make some *confidence-band* assertions about the accuracy of an individual's test score. Suppose an examinee earned a score of 37 correct on a test. We could then say that our examinee's 37 lies plus or minus one standard error of measurement (2.25) of that individual's *true* score, that is, the individual's score if there were no errors of measurement whatsoever associated with the test score 68 percent of the time. Similarly, within plus or minus two standard errors of measurement of the observed score (37), we would know that the individual's true score fell 95 percent of the time.

Thus, we could build a 68 percent confidence band by adding 2.25 and subtracting 2.25 from the score of 37. In other words we could be 68 percent certain within the limits of 34.75 and 39.25.[5] A 95 percent confidence band would be ±2s_e or 32.50 to 41.50.

[5]Although this is not mathematically precise, it constitutes the usual way of interpreting confidence bands.

The authors of the APA-AERA-NCME *Standards* are particularly supportive of the standard error of measurement, as we can see from the following remarks:

> Reliability coefficients have limited practical value for test users. The standard error of measurement ordinarily is more useful; it has great stability across populations since it is relatively independent of range of talent, and it may be used to identify limits that have a defined probability of including the true score. Test users may use reliability coefficients in comparing tests, but they use standard errors of measurement in interpreting test scores. Information in a test manual about a standard error of measurement may often be more important than information about a reliability coefficient.[6]

ILLUSTRATIONS OF PUBLISHED RELIABILITY DATA

The chapter concludes with excerpts from three commercially published test manuals. The topics described are reliability of the internal-consistency and stability sort and, finally, the standard error of measurement.

Internal Consistency Estimates

The following is an excerpt from the technical manual of the *Cognitive Abilities Test* dealing with internal-consistency estimates secured for the test's three batteries (subscales) at various grade levels.[7]

> In considering the reliability of a test, we are concerned with estimating the precision with which one may generalize from one sample of behavior to other samples. The other samples may be obtained with other sets of test items drawn in the same way as in the present test from the universe of possible items. The other samples may be obtained at a different point in time. The other samples may involve both different items and a different time.
> From testing with a single test form one is limited to generalizing to a comparable set of test items given without a time interval. Kuder-Richardson Formula #20, or coefficient alpha, may be used to provide such an estimate. However, in a test made up of distinct subtests it is more appropriate to calculate KR #20 separately for each subtest and use the standard formula for the correlation of sums to estimate the correlation that would be obtained for the total test. This is due to the fact that items within a subtest may be expected to be qualitatively more uniform than items from different subtests.

[6] *Standards for Educational and Psychological Tests.* Prepared by a joint committee of the American Psychological Association, the American Educational Research Association, and the National Council on Measurement in Education (Washington, D.C.: American Psychological Association, 1974), p. 50.
   [7] R. L. Thorndike and E. Hagen, *Technical Manual, Cognitive Abilities Test,* Multilevel Edition (Boston: Houghton Mifflin, 1974), p. 15.

KR #20 reliability estimates by level and grade are shown in Table 4.1 [Table 6–1]. Typical values are about 0.94 for the Verbal Battery, 0.92 for the Quantitative Battery, and 0.93 for the Nonverbal Battery.

Stability Estimates

Presented next is information on the stability (as well as internal consistency) of a criterion-referenced reading test, the *IOX Basic Skill Test in Reading*. Note that the decision-consistency approach described earlier in the chapter has been employed.[8]

The forms of reliability analyses carried out were *stability* and *internal consistency*. Stability reliability was computed both via the customary test-retest correlation coefficient and also by considering the *consistency of decisions* which would result for an individual student on the two different testing occasions. In other words, students could pass (+) a given skill on the first occasion, but fail (−) it on the second occasion. This would result in an inconsistent decision (+ −). Another inconsistent decision would be an initial failure, but a pass on the second administration (− +). The person who was passed both times (+ +) or failed both (− −) was being measured (for decision purposes) consistently by the test.

To provide an index of the decision consistency for a particular test, all we need do is determine what percentage of the possible decisions are consistent, that is, + + or − −. For instance, if 40 of the 100 students were passed both times and 39 of the 100 students were failed both times, then the decision consistency would be 79%, that is, 40% plus 39%.

With the consistency-of-decision approach, however, it is necessary to establish passing standards for a skill so that a pass or no-pass decision can be made. In order to provide test users with the types of information they are apt to need for the following reliability analyses, four commonly used passing levels (60%, 70%, 80%, and 90%) were employed so that the consistency of decisions at each of these levels can be seen. Internal consistency was computed on the basis of a Kuder-Richardson 20 formula.

It should be noted that the subtests we are dealing with here are mainly *10-item* tests. Separate reliability analyses were carried out on a skill-by-skill basis (rather than on a total, aggregated score for the entire test) because of the IOX tests' pervasive emphasis on skill-by-skill diagnosis and instruction. Educators are familiar with the rather substantial reliability coefficients which often emerge from tests with upwards of 50–100 items. Such longer tests, quite naturally, will yield higher reliability coefficients than will 10-item tests. Thus, different expectations must be brought to a review of the reliability information presented in the following table.

It should also be noted that the less variant a set of test scores, the less likely that high reliability coefficients of the traditional types will be produced. Because the student performance levels on several of the IOX subtests were particularly high, thus resulting in lower variability because of a subtest's "ceiling effect," the reliability coefficients on such tests may have been de-

[8]*Test Manual, IOX Basic Skill Tests* (Los Angeles: Instructional Objectives Exchange, 1978), pp. 8–9.

TABLE 6-1   Kuder-Richardson Formula #20 Reliability Estimates by Test Level and by Grade (N = 500 for each grade)

TEST LEVEL	GRADE	VERBAL			QUANTITATIVE			NONVERBAL		
		Mean*	S D*	r_{11}	Mean*	S D*	r_{11}	Mean*	S D*	r_{11}
A	3	44.16	20.08	.957	31.76	11.60	.931	52.72	15.60	.949
B	4	53.48	18.77	.953	34.43	10.72	.916	57.10	14.35	.943
C	5	59.34	18.69	.952	36.88	10.92	.923	58.29	13.52	.933
D	6	65.79	16.34	.941	37.53	10.47	.916	59.13	12.96	.929
E	7	64.96	17.68	.949	35.96	10.51	.912	57.07	13.77	.937
F	8	63.75	16.80	.944	34.55	11.15	.912	56.00	13.42	.932
	9	68.68	15.71	.939	39.36	11.29	.918	58.51	12.63	.928
G	10	65.01	16.17	.940	37.17	12.09	.929	55.92	12.98	.928
	11	66.52	16.22	.942	37.53	12.21	.929	56.58	12.56	.923
H	12	60.87	16.38	.943	36.07	12.30	.927	53.09	12.06	.913

*Means and S Ds are reported in raw score units.

pressed. It is likely, for instance, that in districts where lower pupil performance would be found, resulting *higher* reliability indices would occur. In Table 6-2 the reliability data for the reading test are presented.

Standard Error of Measurement

Finally, an illustration is presented of how publishers of the *Cognitive Abilities Test* have provided information regarding the standard errors of measurement for various grade levels on that test's three batteries.[9]

> For interpreting the score of an individual, the standard error of measurement is a more useful statistic than a reliability coefficient. The standard error of measurement is an estimate of the standard deviation that would result for the scores of an individual if it were possible to measure him a number of times (without changing him either by practice or boredom). Thus, it indicates how large the fluctuations in scores may be expected to be or how often fluctuations of a given size may be expected to occur. Roughly:
>
> 2/3 of obtained scores will lie within ± 1 SE$_{Meas.}$ of the "true" score.
> 19/20 of obtained scores will lie within ± 2 SE$_{Meas.}$ of the "true" score.
> 997/1000 of obtained scores will lie within ± 3 SE$_{Meas.}$ of the "true" score.
>
> The standard error of measurement of a test may differ at different score levels. A test will often discriminate more accurately in certain score ranges than in others. To be really informed about the accuracy of a test, one needs to know its standard error of measurement at different score levels; then, one knows the range within which the test maintains its precision.
> The table showing standard errors of measurement by score level for

[9]Thorndike and Hagen, *Technical Manual,* pp. 16–17.

TABLE 6–2   Reliability Data for IOX Basic Skill Test in Reading Competency

RELIABILITY TYPE	SAFETY WARNINGS		FORMS AND APPLICATIONS		REFERENCE SOURCES		MAIN IDEAS		USING DOCUMENTS	
	Co-efficient	No. of examinees	Co-efficient	No. of examinees	Co-efficient	No. of examinees	Co-efficient	No. of examinees	Co-efficient	No. of examinees
Internal Consis-tency										
1st Admin.	.71	40	.87	32	.77	53	.70	52	.67	49
2nd Admin.	.44	35	.90	32	.72	51	.73	47	.75	46
Test-Retest	.48	32	.40	32	.62	46	.82	42	.69	39
DECISION CONSIS-TENCY	AGREEMENT PERCENTAGE N = 32		AGREEMENT PERCENTAGE N = 32		AGREEMENT PERCENTAGE N = 46		AGREEMENT PERCENTAGE N = 42		AGREEMENT PERCENTAGE N = 39	
90% level	78		75		72		86		87	
80% level	88		75		80		88		87	
70% level	94		81		87		90		90	
60% level	97		88		94		90		92	

the *Cognitive Abilities Test* is based on a split-half analysis of data from the norming administration of the tests. The values relate directly to single-form reliability estimates such as those reported in Table 4.2. If alternate forms administered at separate times had been used, standard errors would tend to be slightly larger, since correlations between two forms separated in time tend to be slightly lower than correlations derived from a single testing.

Actual computations were carried out in raw scores, but the values for $SE_{Meas.}$ have been converted to Standard Age Score equivalents, assuming an age that is typical for the level in question. The results are summarized by 10 point intervals in Table 4.3 [Table 6-3]. Notwithstanding the large N's for the total group, the $SE_{Meas.}$ at a specific score level is based on only a modest number of cases; therefore, the results tend to fluctuate somewhat in specific grade groups.

The $SE_{Meas.}$ values in Table 4.3 [Table 6-3] generally indicate somewhat greater precision for the *Cognitive Abilities Test* at the intermediate score levels than at the extremes. The tests were intentionally made with a large number of items of intermediate difficulty so that they would measure somewhat more accurately in the middle-score range. It must be anticipated that extreme scores will show somewhat greater shifts in SAS if an individual is retested.

Low scores should be interpreted with special caution. A very low score means that the test was too hard for the examinee. Since some of the few items that he did get right may have been a result of guessing, he was hardly measured by the test, and the results for him have limited meaning.

Having reviewed both reliability and validity, we turn in the next chapter to a consideration of how one employs comparative data to make interpretations about examinees' test performances.

However, before bidding adieu to reliability considerations, it should be noted that there are some exceedingly interesting developments in testing practice which may soon force us to do some serious rethinking about traditional notions of reliability and even validity. To illustrate, we are beginning to see the emergence of many *item banks,* some of which use computers to gain access to large pools of test items designed to measure particular skills, knowledge, or objectives. Proponents of these item banks often contend that many different equivalent forms of a test can be drawn from the bank simply by using a docile computer to assemble and print out the forms. We can safely predict substantial advancements in the sophistication with which items banking is used by test developers.[10]

PRACTICE EXERCISES

For the following five exercises, decide whether the reliability approach described is chiefly one of *stability, equivalence, equivalence and stability,* or *internal consistency.*

[10]See, for example, M. D. Hiscox, "Item Banks—Where Are They?" Northwest Regional Educational Laboratory, Portland, Oregon, June 14, 1979.

TABLE 6–3   Standard Error of Measurement in Standard Age Score Units As a Function of Raw Score Level

BATTERY AND SCORE LEVEL	GRADE LEVEL				
	Grade 3	Grade 5	Grade 7	Grade 10	Average
Verbal					
85	3.6	4.7	5.3	4.7	4.6
75	4.8	3.5	4.1	4.5	4.2
65	2.8	2.7	2.7	2.8	2.8
55	2.3	2.5	2.5	3.0	2.6
45	2.1	2.8	2.0	2.8	2.4
35	3.1	2.3	2.7	3.3	2.8
25	3.6	2.5	3.6	2.0	2.9
15	4.3	3.0	4.5	2.8	3.6
5	4.3	4.5	—	—	—
Wtd. Average	3.16	3.10	3.62	3.50	
Quantitative					
55	5.9	9.4	7.3	7.5	7.5
45	4.1	5.2	5.1	4.5	4.7
35	3.6	3.3	4.4	3.4	3.7
25	4.5	2.9	3.5	3.5	3.6
15	5.0	5.0	5.0	5.8	5.2
5	3.9	—	—	—	—
Wtd. Average	4.55	4.80	4.82	4.63	
Nonverbal					
75	7.0	6.7	7.4	7.0	7.0
65	3.3	4.1	4.4	5.3	4.3
55	2.5	3.0	3.1	3.6	3.0
45	3.2	3.0	2.4	5.6	3.6
35	3.4	4.0	2.8	2.8	3.2
25	3.5	3.5	5.1	4.5	4.2
15	2.2	—	3.0	—	—
Wtd. Average	3.74	4.41	4.37	4.84	

1. Clyde Collins builds a test for his history class, then computes a split-half coefficient which, because he recently completed "a top-drawer course in measurement" at a nearby college, he adjusts upward using a Spearman-Brown prophecy formula.

2. Julie Jones gives an end-of-unit sixty-item exam to her fourth-graders, then readministers the exam two weeks later, and correlates her pupils' scores on the two test administrations.

3. A commercial test publisher creates two forms of a test and readministers different forms to the same examinees after a one-month interval. The correlation between Forms A and B was .63.

4. A test development agency calculates K-R20 estimates on all of its norm-referenced tests as well as most of its criterion-referenced tests.

5. Developers of a new aptitude test create three forms of a new test, then determine the correlation coefficients among the three forms. Those r's were the following: A *vs.* B = .82, B *vs.* C = .79, A *vs.* C = .90.

ANSWERS TO PRACTICE EXERCISES

1. Internal Consistency
2. Stability
3. Equivalence and Stability
4. Internal Consistency
5. Equivalence

DISCUSSION QUESTIONS

1. What is your opinion of the respective merits of reliability coefficients versus the standard error of measurement?
2. If you were obliged to explain the meaning of the standard error of measurement to a group of lay citizens, how would you go about it in the most lucid fashion?
3. Can you describe different kinds of decision settings in which each of the four types of reliability estimates would be particularly helpful?
4. Assume that you were the president of a test-development firm which was attempting to compete for sales against major commercial test publishers. How much of your development resources would you spend on reliability as opposed to validity?

SUGGESTIONS FOR ADDITIONAL READING

BRENNAN, R. L. and M. T. KANE, "An Index of Dependability for Mastery Test," *Journal of Educational Measurement*, 14, no. 3 (Fall 1977), 277–289. This article describes an index of "reliability and dependability" which may be used with criterion-referenced tests. The Brennan-Kane index is beginning to find its way into psychometric analyses of criterion-referenced tests.

EBEL, ROBERT L., "How to Estimate, Interpret, and Improve Test Reliability," Chapter 14, *Essentials of Educational Measurement* (3rd ed.), pp. 274–295. Englewood Cliffs, N.J.: Prentice-Hall, Inc., 1979. Ebel provides his usual readable account of the ins and outs of reliability. He also considers the reliability of criterion-referenced tests and the reliability of essay test scores.

GRONLUND, NORMAN E., "Reliability and Other Desired Characteristics," Chapter 5, *Measurement and Evaluation in Teaching* (3rd ed.), pp. 105–131. New York: Macmillan, 1976. Gronlund offers a traditional, but particularly well-organized, treatment of test reliability. He devotes some attention to the reliability of criterion-referenced tests.

Standards for Educational and Psychological Tests. Prepared by a joint committee of the American Psychological Association, American Educational Research Association, National Council on Measurement in Education. Washington, D.C., The American Psychological Association, 1974. This is a "must" volume to be read by those who would be conversant with issues of test reliability.

STANLEY, JULIAN C., and KENNETH D. HOPKINS, "Test Reliability," Chapter 5, *Educational and Psychological Measurement and Evaluation* (5th ed.), pp. 114–

132. Englewood Cliffs, N.J.: Prentice-Hall, Inc., 1972. A comprehensive treatment of test reliability including illustrations from publishers' test manuals is presented here.

SWAMINATHAN, HARIHARAN, RONALD K. HAMBLETON, and JAMES ALGINA, "Reliability of Criterion-Referenced Tests: A Decision-Theoretic Formulation," *Journal of Educational Measurement,* 11, no. 4 (Winter 1974), 263–268. This article by Swaminathan and his colleagues describes a decision-based approach to the assessment of criterion-referenced test reliability.

TUCKMAN, BRUCE W., "Test Reliability," Chapter 10, *Measuring Educational Outcomes: Fundamentals of Testing,* pp. 252–310. San Francisco: Harcourt Brace Jovanovich, Inc., 1975. This is a highly practical account of considerations involved in testing reliability. Starting with the premise that "no measurement is perfect," Tuckman describes five specific procedures for assessing reliability.

We live in a society which, in many aspects, is remarkably competitive. People are constantly being compared with one another regarding appearance, wealth, intellectual prowess, and so on. This competitive orientation gets a substantial boost in the nation's schools where, in the earliest grades and ever after, educators are constantly striving to compare students with one another so that the best and worst students can be identified. Although most clinical psychologists decry this emphasis on competition because of its adverse impact on emerging self-concepts, there is little likelihood that our schools will soon be transformed into noncompetitive, idyllic gardens of cooperation.

While excessive emphasis on pupil-versus-pupil comparisons can obviously be harmful, there is a sense in which comparisons are indispensable if we are to make much sense out of an individual's performance. For instance, suppose you are a teacher who has just completed a brand new two-week instructional unit dealing with an aspect of ethics, and you want to find out whether your unit was a winner. Assuming you had developed a completely new (and as far as you know, unique) forty-item test measuring students' knowledge and attitudes about the ethical issue being studied,

Comparative data

how would you interpret the postinstruction performance of your class? Let's say the mean performance of your class on the test was 29.9. Is this good or bad? Was your unit a triumph or a disaster?

It's only when we are able to compare scores of individuals, or groups of individuals, that we begin to get a fix on answering the question "How good is this performance?" Getting back to the ethics example, you can see that if you had access to the performance of similar *but uninstructed* students on your forty-item test and discovered that their mean performances were all around 15.0 or so, your students' performance of nearly 30 looks pretty impressive. Let's say you also tried out your test on a group of philosophers specializing in ethics (a national philosophy conference fortuitously being held at a nearby hotel), and their mean score was 32.0, barely two points higher than your pupils. All of a sudden you'll get fairly ecstatic about your two-week ethics unit. You're apparently able to pick up where Aristotle left off. Ethics instruction appears to be your bag.

Please note in the foregoing example that insights regarding the meaning of a group's test performance arise as a consequence of comparing that group's performance with the performance of other groups. Similarly, the interpretation of an individual's test score can be appreciably enhanced by having data available regarding the performance of other individuals.

With a norm-referenced test, for example, if no normative data were available by which we could make comparisons, there would be little sense we could make out of a score, say, of 83 items correct. If we consult a normative table, however, and discover that a score of 83 items correct is higher than the scores earned by 97 percent of nearly 1,000 students who have previously taken the exam, then the score of 83 starts to take on some meaning. Even with criterion-referenced tests, where we have a far better idea of what an examinee's test performance signifies, comparative data can prove illuminating.

Now, although it is true that where comparisons are made, an invidious spirit of competitiveness often follows, this need not be the case. If educators can employ comparative data adroitly, in order to reach the sorts of conclusions about individuals and groups of individuals that *without such comparative data would be impossible,* yet resist the temptation to pin eternal "winner" and "loser" labels on students, we can pick up the dividends of comparative data while dodging the deficits of unbridled competitiveness.

As we saw in Chapter 3, the sorts of comparative data that are available with many educational tests constitute an important factor which can be used to evaluate a test. In this chapter we consider a variety of concepts associated with the use of comparative data for educational tests. For instance, we delve into the properties of the *normal curve,* since it is employed so frequently for comparison purposes. We also consider the various sorts of specially devised numerical schemes that are employed to represent an examinee's test performance in comparative terms. Finally, we take a hard look at the kinds of normative data that serve as the central comparative framework for test interpretation, that is, where normative data come from and how such data should be most effectively displayed. In order to evaluate a test on the basis of its comparative data, we obviously need to evaluate that comparative information itself. This chapter supplies the information you'll require in order to make these sorts of appraisals.

THE NORMAL CURVE

In Chapter 4 we saw that it was possible to represent distributions of test scores graphically. There is a statistically derived distribution, *the normal curve,* which is particularly useful in helping us as we compare an examinee's score to those of other examinees. Before describing how the normal curve can be used for such purposes, let's consider its chief characteristics.

As you may recall from Chapter 4, the normal distribution is a symmetrical, bell-shaped curve whose mean, median, and mode are identical. In addition, a normal curve has some other alluring qualities which make it useful. Consider, for example, Figure 7–1 where the normal curve is displayed. You will note that along the baseline of the curve, ordinates (vertical lines from the curve to the baseline) have been erected at distances of one standard deviation unit, plus and minus three standard deviations from the mean. Because of the properties of the normal curve, these ordinates always divide the distribution into predictable proportions. For instance, notice that between the mean and plus one standard deviation there is 34.13 percent of the distribution. Remember, that since the area under the curve line represents the proportion of scores in the distribution, if we had a set of test scores distributed in a perfectly normal fashion, then 34.13 percent of those scores would fall between the mean and plus one standard deviation. Similarly, the area between plus and minus one standard deviation of the mean would contain 68.26 percent of the scores.

In most statistics textbooks there are detailed tables which indicate precisely what proportion of the normal curve is bounded by ordinates erected at any point along the baseline in terms of standard deviation units.[1] To illustrate, by consulting one of these tables we would discover that a test score that was 1.30 standard deviation units above the mean would exceed 90.32 percent of the scores in a normal distribution. In other words, an ordinate erected at a point 1.30 standard deviation units above the mean of the normal curve would enclose an area (to its left) that was .9032 of the normal curve.

By becoming familiar with a table of the normal curve, you will be able to discover, for example, that the area plus and minus one-half standard deviation from the mean of a normal distribution includes nearly 40 percent of the distribution (19.15 percent of the distribution on either side of the mean). A table of the normal curve will also supply the precise height of any ordinate along the baseline in proportional relationship to the ordinate at the distribution's mean. For example, if we think of the ordinate at the norm's distribution's mean as being 1.0 in height, then the height of the ordinate at ± 1.0 standard deviation unit is 0.61 of that height.

As indicated earlier, the normal distribution is really a statistically

---

[1] It will most likely be of trivial passing interest to the reader to note that in this sentence I have used the expression *in terms of* in spite of my thoroughgoing disdain for this overused and typically misused three-word catch-all. (Analyze the phrase "in terms of" carefully, and you'll see how few times it strictly fills the verbal requirements of a situation.) This present instance of unadulterated tokenism is adopted to alert the reader that at no other point in the entire volume will a reiteration of that seemingly all-purpose phrase be encountered.

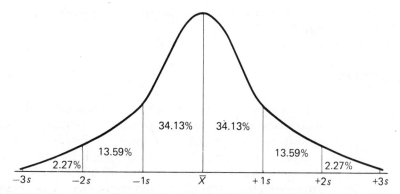

FIGURE 7-1 Percentages of the normal curve enclosed by ordinates erected at standard deviation points.

generated theoretical distribution. In the real world of education—a world filled with student-thrown chalkboard erasers, tardy pupils, and PTA meetings—do we ever encounter any variables (such as a particular kind of test score) which are distributed in a totally normal fashion? Probably not.

However, it is the belief of most educational specialists that a good many educational variables are distributed in an *approximately* normal manner. Now if you're dealing with an educational variable, such as one's measured aptitude to solve geometric problems, and you discern that the variable seems to be fairly normal in its distribution among individuals, then you can take advantage of the properties of the normal curve in interpreting examinees' performances. Even though your interpretations are approximations, you are to say that a person whose aptitude score turns out to be −1.0 standard deviation units from the mean has less aptitude than about 84 percent of all examinees (see Figure 7–1).

Later in the chapter we also see some interesting applications of the normal curve in transforming a set of raw scores from a nonnormal distribution to a fictitious normalized form.

In review, the normal distribution provides a convenient way to describe examinees' test performances if the data distributions we are working with turn out to be arranged in an approximately normal fashion. Since we can describe different examinees' performances according to this normal curve framework, we can thereby compare their performances. For instance, if John's score was 0.2 standard deviation units below the mean and Harry's score was 1.3 standard deviation units above the mean, we can compare their two performances by discovering the proportions of our normal curve bounded by ordinates erected at those two points on the baseline. The baseline of the normal curve, divided into whole and fractional standard deviation units, becomes a sort of interpretive yardstick for contrasting different examinees' test performances. A standard deviation's distance is the unit of measurement we use on that baseline to aid in our interpretations.

PERCENTILES

A particularly popular technique for comparing different individuals' test scores is to express them as *percentiles*. As this term is employed by most educators, a percentile is a point on a distribution below which a certain percent of the scores fall. For example, if we discover that Hortense has a test score that is equivalent to the 47th percentile, we thereby assert that Hortense's score topped 47 percent of other examinees. That's almost accurate.

A *percentile rank* gives an examinee's relative position on the percent of other scores falling below the examinee's obtained score. As Mehrens and Lehmann point out when distinguishing between *percentiles* and *percentile ranks:*

> Statisticians differ somewhat in the precise definition of these terms, but these differences are minor and need not concern us. Some use the terms *percentile* and *percentile rank* interchangeably.[2]

Although for most purposes this simple interpretation of a percentile as a point "below which a certain percent of scores fell" will prove sufficient, there are instances in which such an interpretation will get you in trouble. As a would-be measurement wizard, you should know that there are three similar but significantly different ways in which a percentile can be defined (*hence calculated*). A percentile can be defined as the percentage of scores in a distribution which

1. fall *below* the percent value given, or
2. fall *at or below* the percent value given, or
3. fall *below the midpoint of the* percent value given's *score interval.*

If you set out to compute your own set of percentile ranks for a group of test scores, it is obviously important for you to decide on which of these three definitions you'll be using. We can illustrate this difference by the following example. Suppose you were working with 200 test scores and started off your percentile computations by ranking the scores in order, from lowest to highest, then tried to calculate the percentile rank for a raw score of, say, 52 items correct. Assume that there were ten person who had

---

[2]W. A. Mehrens, and I. J. Lehmann, *Measurement and Evaluation in Education and Psychology* (New York: Holt, Rinehart & Winston, 1978), p. 143.

raw scores of 52. How do you treat those ten scores in your computations? This situation is presented graphically in Figure 7-2 where it can be seen that the theoretical limits of the 52 raw scores, that is, 52.5 and 51.5 can also be used in the computation of percentiles, depending on which of the three definitions you use. Although for most purposes the distinction in definition makes little practical difference in our interpretation of a score, it certainly does make a difference when we actually prepare a set of percentile ranks to represent raw score performances.

If we use definition (1), that is, where the percentage of the distribution falls *below* the 52 score, then none of the ten scores at 52 would be involved. Let's say these were half of the 200 scores below 52, then using definition (1), a raw score of 52 would be equal to the 50th percentile.

However, if we used definition (2), that is, where the percentage of the distribution falls *at or below* the 52 score, then all ten of the 52 scores would be tossed in our calculations and (since each score in a total of 200 scores equals half of 1 percent of the distribution) a score of 52 would then be equal to the 55th percentile.

If we instead opted for definition (3) where we use the *midpoint of the score interval* as our cut-off point, then we'd use half of the ten scores of 52, so a score of 52 would be equivalent to the 52.5th percentile.

Now these differences, the 50th, 52.5th, and 55th percentiles, may not seem enormous. They're not. However, it should be clear that when you set out to compute percentile ranks, you need to determine which approach you'll be taking. Most importantly, you must indicate to anyone using your percentile-equivalency tables just how you went about calculating the percentile values.

In general, definition (3) is preferred because it more equitably distributes the scores in a given raw score interval. In the example presented in Table 7-1, that definition has been employed in the calculation of the

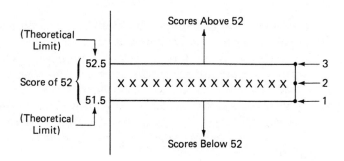

FIGURE 7-2   Options for computation of percentiles depending on whether the percentile value is defined as percentage of distribution (a) below, (b) at or below, or (c) below midpoint of value given.

percentile values. Note that the cumulative frequencies (column 3) are those frequencies *below the midpoint* of each score interval. Since we assume that half the scores in each interval fall above and half below the midpoint of the interval, we can think of the cumulative frequency for each interval as the sum of the frequencies below that interval plus half the frequencies within that interval. To convert the cumulative frequencies to percentages (column 4), we simply divide each score's cumulative frequency by the highest cumulative frequency. To illustrate, for the score 16 we divide the cumulative frequency of 2.0 by 8.0 to obtain 25.0 percent. These percentages are then rounded to obtain the percentile rank values (column 5).

In a percentile-equivalency table, typically only raw scores (column 1) and their equivalent percentile values (column 5) are supplied. Clearly, the small number of frequencies used in Table 7–1 would be insufficient to provide a stable and representative estimate of percentile equivalences. We shall delve into that issue later in the chapter.

Percentiles are sometimes referred to as *centiles.* The 25th percentile is often referred to as the *first quartile,* that is, the percentile below which 25 percent of the distribution's scores fall. The 50th percentile, which is also the median, is occasionally referred to as the *second quartile.* The 75th percentile is also called the *third quartile.*

A good many educators misuse the term *quartile* since they will say something such as the following: "Most of the students scoring in the first quartile were boys." This statement is in error because a quartile is a *point,* not a range of scores. It would be proper to say that most students who scored *below* the first quartile were boys. Those who misuse the term quartile mistakenly equate it with a *quarter* of the distribution. However, a quarter is not the same as a quartile.

STANDARD SCORES

Another useful technique for comparing examinees' test scores is referred to as a *standard score.* Whereas a percentile only tells us how an examinee's test score stacks up relative to test scores of other examinees (in percentage terms), a standard score tells us *in standard deviation units* where an examinee's score is with respect to the mean of the distribution. For a number of purposes, standard scores can prove most useful to measurement specialists. Like most vegetables these days, there are several varieties of standard scores.[3] We shall consider the most commonly used types of standard scores.

---

[3] It is now possible to grow purple tomatoes and blue carrots, although why one would wish to do so escapes me.

TABLE 7-1 Illustrative Computation of a Percentile Equivalency Table Using the "Midpoint of Score Interval" Definition of Percentile Ranks

RAW SCORE	SCORE FREQUENCY	CUMULATIVE FREQUENCY	PERCENT OF FREQUENCY	PERCENTILE RANK
20		8.0	100.0	100
19	1	7.5	93.7	94
18	3	5.5	68.7	69
17	1	3.5	43.7	44
16	2	2.0	25.0	25
15		1.0	12.5	13
14	1	0.5	6.2	6
13		0	0	0

Z Scores

If you recall our earlier discussion of the normal curve, you'll remember that by using the baseline of that curve as a sort of "standard deviation unit yardstick," we were able to make some useful statements about the proportion of scores exceeded by a score falling at a particular point on the baseline. The most fundamental of standard scores, the z score, relies on the same standard deviation unit yardstick. A z score tells us *in standard deviation units* how far a raw score is above or below the mean of its distribution. A z score of +1.5 would be one and one-half standard deviation units above the mean. A z score of −2.5 would be two and one-half standard deviations below the mean.

Careful consideration of the formula used to compute z scores will help you understand what a z score represents:

$$z = \frac{X - \overline{X}}{s}$$

where X = a raw score

$\overline{X}$ = the mean of the distribution

s = the standard deviation of the distribution

Let's use a simple example to show how this formula works. Suppose the mean of a distribution was 32.8 and the standard deviation of that distribution was 2.2. Now if a student gets a raw score of 35, we can see that the student scored one standard deviation above the mean. We can toss the necessary numbers in the formula and solve as follows:

$$z = \frac{35 - 32.8}{2.2}$$

$$= 1.0$$

We see that a z score of 1.0 let's us know that the raw score from which it was derived falls one standard deviation unit above the mean of its distribution.

In a normal curve, since plus and minus three standard deviation units account for most of the scores, z scores will range from -3.0 to $+3.0$ and account for all but a miniscule proportion of the distribution's scores. For any kind of distribution, normal or not, if all of the raw scores are converted into standard scores by our clever trick of subtracting the mean and then dividing by the standard deviation, the resulting distribution of z scores would have a mean of zero and a standard deviation of 1.0.

In Figure 7-3 we see what happens to a distribution when its raw scores have been zapped into z scores. Notice that the shape of the raw score distribution has not been altered one bit. It was negatively skewed going in and after all the raw scores have been converted to z scores, it is still negatively skewed. Only the means and standard deviation have been altered. Given a person's z score, along with the mean and standard deviation of the original raw score distribution, it is easy to reverse the process and find out what that individual's raw score is. For instance, if someone has a z score of -2.0 when the original mean and standard deviation were 78 and 6 respectively, then we can use the z score conversion formula and obtain the raw score as follows:

$$z = \frac{X - \bar{X}}{s}$$
$$-2.0 = \frac{X - 78}{6}$$
$$X = 66$$

A disadvantage of z scores is that they contain decimals and minus values. Most people, educators included, find decimals and minus values troublesome to work with, hence measurement specialists devised a scheme

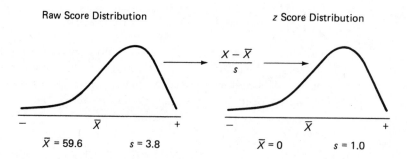

Raw Score Distribution   z Score Distribution

$$\frac{X - \bar{X}}{s}$$

$\bar{X} = 59.6$ $s = 3.8$ $\bar{X} = 0$ $s = 1.0$

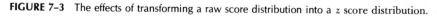

FIGURE 7-3   The effects of transforming a raw score distribution into a z score distribution.

to dodge decimals and unminus negative numbers. We refer to such standard scores as *transformed.*

T Scores

A *T score* is simply a z score that has been multiplied by 10 (to get rid of the decimals) and had 50 added to it (to get rid of minus values). The formula for the calculation of a *T* score, then, is

$$T = 50 + 10z \quad \text{or} \quad T = 50 + 10\frac{X - \bar{X}}{s}$$

As a consequence of these two operations, that is, adding by a constant and multiplying by a constant, the resulting distribution of *T* scores has a mean of 50 and a standard deviation of 10.

Let's see how a *T* score is computed. Suppose we have a distribution of test scores in which the mean is 64.6 and the standard deviation is 8.4. If a student earned a score of 60.4 on the test, we would calculate the *T* score for that raw score as follows:

$$
\begin{aligned}
T &= 50 + 10\frac{60.4 - 64.6}{8.4} \\
&= 50 + 10(-.5) \\
&= 45
\end{aligned}
$$

When encountering a *T* score of 45, we instantly know that the raw score it represents is one-half standard deviation below the mean of the raw score distribution in which it is located. Similarly, a *T* score of 60 would represent a raw score one standard deviation unit above its mean.

Some people refer to *T* scores as *transformed standard scores* because, of course, we do transform the original z scores. Other individuals use the expression *Z scores* instead of *T* scores. Because there is, as a consequence of so many different labels, the possibility of confusion when folks are talking about *T* scores, be sure that everyone is referring to the same entity when you're engaging in a discussion about standard scores.

That discussion can get even more confusing, indeed, when we discover that there are *normalized z* and *T* scores that are also used to describe an examinee's test performance. We turn now to a consideration of these normalized standard scores.

Normalized Standard Scores

Now let's put a pair of notions together that we've encountered so far and see how, in combination, they can provide us with yet another way to describe an examinee's performance in relationship to that of other examinees. We have seen that if scores are arranged in a perfectly normal fashion, we can state precisely what proportion of the distribution's scores are exceeded by a score at a particular point along the baseline of the curve. For example, a raw score which is plus one standard deviation above the mean in such a normal distribution of scores exceeds 84.13 percent of all the scores. To take maximum advantage of the normal curve's interpretive assistance, however, we must express a raw score in standard deviation units according to its distance and direction (above or below) from the mean of the distribution.

In addition, we've seen that z scores and T scores provide us, in a single number, with a raw score's location in relationship to the mean in standard deviation units. Now, *if* a distribution of scores were distributed normally, we could readily combine these two notions, since a z score of $+1.0$ or a T score of 60 would also tell us that the raw score being represented was one standard deviation above the mean, hence exceeded 84.13 percent of the distribution's scores. By coupling z or T scores with the normal curve's established proportions, easy and accurate interpretations of a raw score's relative position could be readily rendered. However, distressingly, not all distributions of test scores are arranged in a normal manner. Nature has, as usual, foiled a straightforward interpretive framework.

Unruffled by Mother Nature's capriciousness, measurement people have devised a scheme for using standard scores with nonnormal distributions. They merely act *as if* the distribution were perfectly normal. To illustrate, let's say you had gathered a set of test data for a new test and you discovered that the data were distributed in a markedly nonnormal fashion. Perhaps you really believe that the underlying attribute being measured was arrayed normally in the real world but that the test being used produced the nonnormal scores. Under these conditions, for ease of interpretation, you could convert the raw scores into *normalized standard scores*. A normalized standard score is a standard score (z or T) that would be equivalent to a raw score *if* the distribution had been perfectly normal.

There are two steps in calculating normalized z scores. First, convert each of the raw scores in the distribution to its percentile equivalent (as described earlier in the chapter). Second, consult a table of the normal curve (available in most statistical texts) to discover what the equivalent z score would be for each percentile. In Table 7–2 an abridged set of z values and percentile equivalents is presented for this purpose. A full-blown table of the normal curve would contain a more fine-grained breakdown of percentile equivalents than Table 7–2. To compute a normalized T score, simply multiply the tabled z score by 10, and add 50. As with nonnormalized standard scores, many people prefer to work with normalized T scores instead of normalized z scores because of the absence of decimals and minus values.

TABLE 7-2   Normalized z Scores and Percentile Equivalents

z SCORE	PERCENTILE	z SCORE	PERCENTILE
3.0	99.9	−0.1	46.0
2.9	99.8	−0.2	42.1
2.8	99.7	−0.3	38.2
2.7	99.6	−0.4	34.5
2.6	99.5	−0.5	30.9
2.5	99.4	−0.6	27.4
2.4	99.2	−0.7	24.2
2.3	98.9	−0.8	21.2
2.2	98.6	−0.9	18.4
2.1	98.2	−1.0	15.9
2.0	97.7	−1.1	13.6
1.9	97.1	−1.2	11.5
1.8	96.4	−1.3	9.7
1.7	95.5	−1.4	8.2
1.6	94.5	−1.5	6.7
1.5	93.3	−1.6	5.5
1.4	91.9	−1.7	4.5
1.3	90.3	−1.8	3.6
1.2	88.5	−1.9	2.9
1.1	86.4	−2.0	2.3
1.0	84.1	−2.1	1.8
0.9	81.6	−2.2	1.4
0.8	78.8	−2.3	1.1
0.7	75.8	−2.4	0.8
0.6	72.6	−2.5	0.6
0.5	69.1	−2.6	0.5
0.4	65.5	−2.7	0.4
0.3	61.8	−2.8	0.3
0.2	57.9	−2.9	0.2
0.1	54.0	−3.0	0.1
0.0	50.0		

Let's see how to obtain a normalized T score for a given score. Suppose you wanted to convert a raw score to a normalized T. You'd first find out, in its own raw score distribution, what percentile that raw score represented. We'll assume it turns out to be on the 92nd percentile. Then you'd go to Table 7–2 and look up a percentile of 92 in the percentile column, discovering that the closest percentile is 91.9 and that its equivalent z score is 1.4. We then multiply 1.4 by 10 and add 50 to obtain a normalized T score of 64.

Now even though you have learned how to compute normalized z and T scores, it may strike you that you've acquired a technical skill for generating fantasy. After all, a distribution is either normal or it isn't. If it isn't, then it just doesn't seem fair to massage it by means of number nudging so that it appears to be normal. After all, things ought to be represented the way they are.

Well, while your leanings toward verisimilitude are to be applauded, you will discover a few instances in which measurement people do have need of normalized standard scores. For instance, sometimes there are statistical analyses which need to be conducted on a set of data that require the scores to be in a normal shape. In such cases there may be an advantage in transforming a set of skewed raw scores into normalized standard scores. There are also techniques for comparing persons' scores on two different tests by using *normal curve equivalents* as the comparative device. In the late seventies the normal curve equivalent (NCE) received considerable attention because the U.S. Office of Education proposed a scheme to dispense federal education dollars which relied heavily on NCE conversions.

There are a number of solid technical reasons why the use of NCE conversions to compare scores from different tests constitutes an unsound procedure. There is substantial disagreement over the legitimacy of using NCEs in this fashion. If you find yourself faced with a decision to use or not use NCEs for comparative purposes, be sure to look further into this topic.[4]

From your perspective, however, it is more important to realize that there are normalized z and T scores floating around in measurement land and that some test publishers actually use these sorts of scores to describe data. You must be alert to the possibility that *normalized,* rather than routine, z and T scores are being employed. Be sure to find out which is which, since merely by looking superficially at a table of standard scores it is not all that apparent whether you're dealing with normalized or nonnormalized scores. Although it may seem a metaphysical impossibility, a z is not a z is not a z. For that matter, a T is not a T is not a T.

Stanines

A *stanine* is a normalized standard score based on dividing the normal curve into nine intervals along the baseline. Indeed, its very name, stanine, is formed by combining the *sta* of *sta*ndard and *nine*. Stanines are normalized in much the same fashion that we obtain normalized z and T scores, but because the stanine scale is a rather gross scale consisting of only nine values, it is more simple to determine the stanine values which correspond to given raw scores.

In Figure 7–4 the positions of the nine stanine values on the normal curve are represented. Note that with the exception of the first and ninth stanines, all of the stanines are of an identical size, namely, one-half standard deviation unit. The middle stanine, therefore, extends plus and minus one-fourth standard deviation unit from the mean. A distribution of

[4]See, for example, R. L. Linn, "Validity of Inferences Based on the Proposed Title I Evaluation Models," *Educational Evaluation and Policy Analysis,* I, 2 (March-April 1979), 23–32.

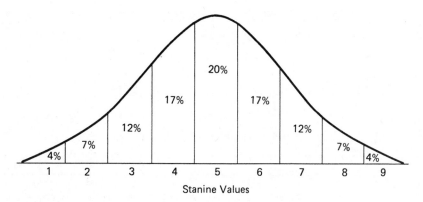

FIGURE 7-4 Stanine units represented in approximate percentages of the normal curve.

stanine scores has a mean of five and a standard deviation of approximately two stanine score units.

Stanines provide us with a rough approximation of an examinee's performance relative to that of others. Since we determine an individual's stanine by identifying the percentile to which a person's raw score would be equivalent, then using percentages given as in Figure 7–4 to locate the proper stanine, it is clear that stanines are *normalized*. Even if the original raw score distribution is decisively nonnormal, we follow our customary scheme for normalizing a score. To illustrate, if Rapunzel Jones earned a raw score that was (in her raw score distribution) equivalent to a 33rd percentile, then we would know that Rapunzel's score was in the middle of the fourth stanine, so we'd assign her a stanine score of four.

Because of the fact that we're losing a substantial degree of precision when we employ only nine values to represent a wide range of scores, some educators avoid the use of stanines. On the other hand, a good many educators rely heavily on stanine scores precisely *because* they constitute a more gross way of describing a student's score. Because of the imprecision of measurement, more than a few educators prefer to use gross descriptors in communicating test results and thus not misrepresent the precision of the data-gathering devices. Stanines, particularly in some geographic regions and for some test publishers, remain a popular way of describing an examinee's performance.

The relationship among stanines, percentiles, as well as the other standard scores we've been discussing, can be seen in Figure 7–5 where a widely used depiction of the normal curve, percentiles, and standard scores is presented. This figure, developed initially by the Psychological Corporation in 1947, has been used through the years in a host of measurement and statistical texts.

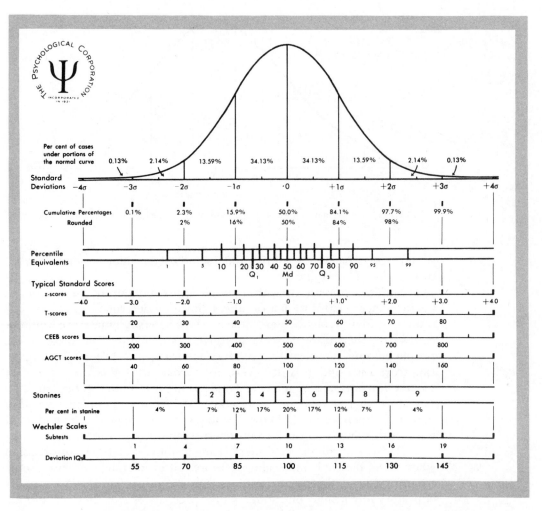

FIGURE 7–5 Relationship among normal curves, percentiles, and frequently used standard scores. (Reproduced and adapted by permission. All rights reserved, © 1947, 1952, © 1959, 1963, 1966, 1968 by the Psychological Corporation, New York, N.Y.)

Grade Equivalents

Another frequently used technique for describing an examinee's score is to express that score as a *grade equivalent* value. If a test has been administered to a large number of students so that it is possible to estimate what the median student will score upon entering the fourth grade in September, then whatever that raw score value is would be considered to be a grade equivalent score of 4.0. By dividing a school year into ten months, we can represent a student's score as, for example, 4.3 to indicate that the student's performance was equal to that of the median student three months into the fourth grade (December).

Grade equivalents are widely used for interpretive purposes because they seem so blessedly simple to understand. After all, if a youngster gets a test score on a nationally standardized achievement test that can be represented as 5.9 grade equivalent score, then it seems obvious that the child is functioning just below (by one month) the beginning of sixth-grade level. Unfortunately, there are some serious problems with grade equivalent scores that should be well understood by educators who are inclined to use them.

For one thing, no test publisher has the financial resources to do an across-the-board testing of youngsters, grades K through 12, on a month-by-month basis. Such an enterprise would be enormously costly to the test publisher, not to mention the intrusion it would make on students' instructional programs. As a consequence, test publishers usually test at a few grades, establish a relationship between test scores and grades, then use the relationship line to *estimate* the various grade-month points needed for all the rest of the scores that students at various ages will receive. However, these estimates are made by extrapolation and are often made on really shaky assumptions. For example, it is assumed that whatever is being tested is studied consistently from year to year. It is also assumed that a student's increase in competence is essentially constant over the years. It is further assumed that the test reasonably samples what is being taught at all of the grade levels for which scores are being reported. These assumptions are almost never satisfied.

A troublesome problem with grade equivalent scores is that they yield no clues as to an individual's percentile standing, a key comparative ingredient we've been able to snag from all of the previous score-representation schemes considered so far. To illustrate, a student might get a higher grade equivalent score on a reading test than on a mathematics test, yet have a substantially lower percentile rank on the reading test than on the math test.

A final problem with grade equivalent scores is that unsophisticated people automatically transform what *is* to what *should* be. For instance, a grade equivalent raw score for the medium, beginning eighth-grade student may be 112 items correct on a test. Since 112 equals an 8.0 grade equivalent score, many people may demand that all beginning eighth-graders should earn a score of 112 or higher. "After all," they assert, "isn't that what a beginning eighth-grade student should be doing?" They lose sight of the fact that it was the *median* eighth-grade performance that led to the grade equivalent score and that *by definition* 50 percent of the examinees will fall below this score. It's something like the school board president who remonstrated with the district superintendent because half of the district's pupils continued to fall below the median of their own examination performance.

For a number of reasons, therefore, grade equivalent scores should be used only with considerable caution and with plenty of accompanying disclaimers. It is often helpful, if grade equivalents must be employed, to accompany them with other descriptive schemes.

We have considered, now, a number of different techniques for representing an examinee's raw score performance. Many of them rely on the availability of comparative data before they can be used. If a teacher administers a norm-referenced achievement test and wants to secure percentile-equivalent performances for students, the teacher will typically want to base those percentiles on *national* normative data, rather than on the performance of the 33 students in that particular class. We can turn, now, to a consideration of the sorts of normative data which will lead to defensible use of the various comparative score descriptors we've been fussing over.

NORMS

In educational measurement we frequently encounter such expressions as *norms, norm groups,* and *normative tables.* In general, normative notions are based on the assembled performance summaries of a group of individuals who have been administered a particular examination. For instance, before developers of a new norm-referenced reading test publish their test, they will almost certainly administer that test to a large number of students (thereafter called the *norm group*), then summarize the results of those examinees' test scores in tables such as the one seen in Table 7–3. Note that the major contribution of the table is that it permits those using the test to identify the percentile equivalent for any examinee's raw score. In making sense out of an examinee's raw score, such *norm tables* are of immense assistance.

We must pause briefly in our explanation of normative data to draw attention to a frequent misuse of the term *norm* since there are some educators and far too many lay citizens who think of norms, just like grade equivalents, as representing what *should* be. In the sense that test developers gather normative information, they are merely assembling data regarding the current status of examinee performance. To equate what *is* with what *ought* to be is an instance of thoroughgoing wrongheadedness. People who are confused on this score assume that a *norm* is a synonym for *standard.* Such is not the case.

In Chapter 16 we delve at considerable length into the problem of

TABLE 7-3   A Typical Norm Table

%-ile Rank	Voc. V	Rdg. R	L-1	L-2	L-3	L-4	Total L	W-1	W-2	W-3	Total W	M-1	M-2	Total M	Comp. C	%-ile Rank	Stanine
99	55	59	60	59	61	60	58	57	58	55	54	54	53	51	53	99	
98	52	57	58	57	59	58	55	55	55	53	51	51	51	49	51	98	
97	51	55	57	55	58	57	54	53	54	51	50	50	49	47	50	97	9
96	49	53	56	54	56	56	53	51	52	49	48	49	48	46	49	96	
95	48	52	55	53	55	–	52	50	51	48	47	48	46	–	48	95	
94	47	51	54	52	54	55	51	49	49	47	–	46	45	45	47	94	
93	–	50	53	–	–	54	50	48	48	46	46	45	44	44	46	93	8
92	46	49	52	51	53	53	–	47	47	45	45	–	43	–	–	92	
91	45	48	–	50	52	52	49	–	–	44	44	44	42	43	45	91	
90	–	–	51	49	51	–	48	46	46	43	44	–	–	–	44	90	
89	44	47	50	–	50	51	–	45	45	–	–	43	41	42	–	89	
88	–	46	49	48	49	50	47	44	–	42	43	–	–	–	43	88	
87	43	–	–	47	–	–	46	–	44	–	–	–	40	41	–	87	
86	–	45	48	–	48	49	45	43	–	41	42	42	–	–	–	86	
85	42	–	47	46	47	48	–	42	43	–	41	–	39	40	42	85	
84	–	44	–	–	46	–	44	–	–	40	41	–	–	–	–	84	
83	–	–	46	45	–	47	–	41	42	–	–	41	–	39	41	83	7
82	41	43	–	–	45	–	43	–	–	39	40	–	38	–	–	82	
81	–	–	45	44	–	46	–	–	41	39	–	–	38	–	–	81	
80	40	42	44	43	44	–	42	40	–	–	–	40	–	–	40	80	
79	–	–	–	–	43	45	–	–	–	–	39	–	–	–	–	79	
78	–	41	43	42	–	–	41	39	40	38	–	–	–	38	39	78	
77	39	–	–	–	42	44	–	–	–	–	38	39	37	–	–	77	
76	–	40	42	41	–	–	40	–	–	–	–	–	–	–	–	76	
75	–	–	–	–	41	43	–	38	39	–	–	–	–	37	38	75	
74	38	–	41	40	–	–	39	–	–	37	37	38	–	–	–	74	
73	–	39	–	–	40	42	–	–	–	–	–	–	36	–	–	73	
72	–	–	40	–	–	–	38	37	38	–	–	–	–	–	37	72	
71	–	38	–	39	39	41	–	–	–	–	36	37	–	36	–	71	
70	37	–	39	–	–	–	–	–	–	36	–	–	–	–	–	70	
69	–	–	–	38	38	40	37	36	37	–	–	–	–	–	36	69	
68	36	37	38	–	–	–	–	–	–	35	35	36	35	35	–	68	6
67	–	–	–	–	–	39	36	–	–	35	–	–	–	–	–	67	
66	–	–	37	37	37	–	–	–	36	–	–	–	–	35	–	66	
65	–	36	–	–	–	38	35	35	–	–	–	35	–	–	–	65	
64	–	–	36	36	36	–	35	–	–	34	34	–	34	34	–	64	
63	35	–	–	–	–	37	–	–	–	–	–	–	–	–	34	63	
62	–	35	–	–	–	–	–	–	35	–	–	–	–	–	–	62	
61	–	–	35	35	35	36	34	–	–	–	33	34	–	–	–	61	
60	34	–	–	–	–	–	–	34	–	–	–	–	–	33	33	60	
59	–	34	34	–	–	35	–	–	34	–	–	–	–	–	–	59	
58	–	–	–	34	34	–	33	–	–	33	–	–	33	–	–	58	
57	–	–	–	–	–	34	–	33	–	–	32	33	–	–	–	57	
56	33	33	33	33	–	–	–	–	33	–	–	–	–	32	32	56	
55	–	–	–	–	33	–	32	–	–	32	–	–	–	–	–	55	
54	–	–	–	–	–	33	–	–	–	32	–	–	–	–	–	54	
53	32	–	32	32	–	–	–	32	32	–	31	32	32	31	31	53	
52	–	–	–	–	32	32	31	–	–	–	–	–	–	31	–	52	
51	–	31	31	31	–	31	–	–	–	31	–	31	–	–	–	51	
50	–	–	–	–	31	–	–	–	–	–	–	–	–	–	–	50	
49	31	–	–	–	31	–	–	31	31	–	30	–	31	30	30	49	5
48	–	–	–	–	–	–	30	–	–	–	–	–	–	30	–	48	
47	–	30	30	30	–	30	–	–	–	–	–	–	–	–	–	47	
46	30	–	–	–	30	–	–	–	30	30	–	30	30	–	–	46	
45	–	29	–	–	–	29	–	30	–	–	29	–	–	–	29	45	
44	–	–	29	29	–	–	29	–	–	–	29	–	–	29	–	44	
43	29	–	–	–	29	28	–	–	29	–	–	29	29	–	–	43	
42	–	28	28	28	–	–	–	29	–	29	–	–	–	–	28	42	
41	28	–	–	–	–	–	–	–	–	–	28	–	–	28	–	41	
40	–	–	–	–	–	–	–	–	28	–	28	–	–	–	–	40	
39	–	–	–	–	28	27	28	28	–	28	–	–	28	–	–	39	
38	–	27	–	–	–	26	–	–	27	–	–	28	–	–	–	38	
37	27	–	27	27	–	–	–	–	–	–	27	–	–	27	27	37	
36	–	26	–	–	27	–	–	27	–	–	–	–	27	–	–	36	
35	26	–	–	26	–	25	27	27	26	27	–	–	27	–	–	35	
34	–	–	–	–	–	–	–	–	26	27	–	27	–	–	–	34	
33	–	–	26	–	26	–	–	26	–	–	–	27	26	26	26	33	
32	25	25	–	–	26	–	–	26	–	–	–	–	26	26	26	32	
31	25	25	25	25	–	24	26	–	25	26	26	–	–	–	–	31	4
30	–	–	25	–	–	–	26	–	–	–	–	–	25	–	–	30	
29	24	–	–	24	25	23	–	25	24	–	–	26	25	–	–	29	
28	–	–	–	24	–	–	–	–	24	–	–	–	–	25	–	28	
27	–	24	24	–	24	22	25	24	–	25	25	–	24	25	25	27	
26	23	–	–	23	24	22	25	24	–	–	–	–	24	–	25	26	
25	–	23	–	23	–	–	–	–	23	–	–	25	23	–	–	25	
24	22	–	23	–	23	21	–	23	–	24	24	–	–	24	–	24	
23	22	–	23	–	23	21	–	23	–	24	24	–	–	24	–	23	
22	–	22	–	22	–	–	24	–	22	–	–	–	22	–	24	22	
21	21	–	22	–	22	20	–	22	21	23	–	–	22	–	–	21	
20	–	–	22	–	22	20	–	22	21	23	23	24	21	23	–	20	
19	–	–	–	–	–	–	–	–	–	–	23	–	–	–	–	19	
18	–	–	21	21	–	–	–	–	–	–	–	–	–	–	–	18	
17	20	21	–	–	21	19	23	21	–	22	–	–	–	–	23	17	3
16	–	–	–	–	–	–	–	–	20	–	22	23	20	22	–	16	
15	19	–	20	20	–	–	–	–	–	–	–	23	–	22	–	15	
14	–	20	–	–	20	18	22	20	–	21	–	–	19	–	–	14	
13	–	–	–	–	–	–	22	–	19	–	–	–	–	–	–	13	
12	18	–	19	19	–	17	–	19	–	–	21	22	–	21	22	12	
11	–	19	–	–	19	–	–	–	18	20	–	–	18	21	–	11	
10	17	–	18	18	–	16	21	–	–	–	–	21	17	–	–	10	
9	–	18	–	–	18	–	–	18	17	19	20	–	17	–	–	9	
8	16	–	17	17	–	15	–	–	–	–	–	20	–	20	21	8	
7	–	17	16	–	17	–	20	17	16	18	–	–	16	–	–	7	2
6	15	–	–	16	16	14	–	–	–	–	19	–	16	–	–	6	
5	14	16	15	15	–	–	19	16	15	17	–	19	15	19	20	5	
4	13	15	14	–	15	13	18	15	14	–	18	18	15	–	–	4	
3	12	14	13	14	14	–	17	14	13	16	17	–	14	18	19	3	
2	11	13	12	12	13	12	15	13	12	15	16	17	12	16	18	2	1
1	9	11	9	10	11	10	13	11	10	13	15	15	11	15	15	1	

standard setting. At this point, however, it should be recognized that while normative data may, and should, influence the standards we set, the two notions are certainly not identical. To illustrate, let's say you're a teacher who discovers that your pupils perform well below national norms on a test of U.S. history knowledge. Should you be concerned? Probably you should. Apparently, youngsters across the nation are learning more about history than your kids are, and you may want to spruce up your history instruction or simply spend more time on historical content. But what if your pupils are average or slightly above average on national norms? Can you now sit back compliantly and assume that your students know enough about history? Absolutely not.

The historical knowledge of the entire norm group may be well below what it *should* be. Maybe pupils throughout the country are learning less than they *should* about George Washington, Abraham Lincoln, and Sacajawea, Lewis and Clark's Indian guide. The point is that normative data merely let us know how examinees are currently performing. Although such information is very helpful, it should not be mixed up with notions about what a realistic expectation of examinee performance should be.

In Chapter 3 we saw that one of the evaluative factors by which we can evaluate an educational test was whether or not the test was accompanied by comparative data and, if so, what the quality of the comparative data was. We'll conclude the present chapter by highlighting some of the things you should be looking for when you appraise the quality of a set of normative data. If a test is not accompanied by comparative data, of course, you can instantly check it off as deficient on that score.

National and Local Norms

Most test publishers of instruments designed for nationwide use attempt to assemble a set of national norm data. They will administer the test to as large a sample of examinees as they can reasonably afford, attempting to cover, at least on a geographic sampling basis, the entire nation. If possible, they'll gather a sufficiently large set of test scores so that they can break down their normative tables according to sex, geographic region, type of school setting (for example, urban, suburban, rural), and so on. To create truly comprehensive normative data is a very, very costly business. For most test publishers, the accumulation of extensive normative data is reserved for those tests which seem apt to sell well enough to justify the major financial investment in the readying of first-rate normative information.

With tests less likely to sell in large volume, test publishers must apply realism in the gathering of normative information, and it is this sort of normative data, in particular, that should be rigorously evaluated when one considers such tests for possible adoption.

In the gathering of a decent set of national normative data, there are seemingly endless administrative details to be handled. School districts must be identified that will cooperate in the norming. Recalcitrant school officials must be persuaded that the testing's intrusion into the ongoing instructional program is worthwhile. (In passing, it should be noted that because of the recent upsurge in testing of all kinds, many school people are becoming justifiably resistant to testing of any sort. In such a setting, securing the necessary number of schools to cooperate in the norming is sometimes a minor miracle.)

There are numerous decisions to be made along the way during the assembly of normative data. For example, one of the factors that sells tests is the *size* of the normative sample. An educator choosing between two tests, which on other counts appear to be of equal quality, will often choose the test which has the larger (hence more "respectable") norm sample. Accordingly, there is a continuing temptation for supervisors of normative data gathering to go after the largest, most convenient sample at hand. Such *samples of convenience,* however, often fail to satisfy a number of other requirements needed in a good normative sample.

There are also subtle choices that must be made regarding *when* the normative testing should be done. It is in the commercial interest of test publishers *not* to have their tests be widely perceived by educators as "too tough." Since local school officials generally don't want their pupils to look like dullards on nationally standardized tests, such officials would certainly tend to avoid the adoption of tests which seemed certain to show that local students did not perform well according to national norms. Local school officials would tend, instead, to buy a test that gave their pupils a more reasonable chance to succeed.

Accordingly, if you are in charge of a norming operation and plan for a spring "end-of-academic-year" normative testing, would you want to test most of the youngsters in your norm group in April, May, or June? Well, since kids will have learned more by June than April, you might want to do your norm gathering earlier in the spring. Thus, if local educators subsequently contrasted their pupils' end-of-academic-year performance with that of pupils in your test's national norm group, the local youngsters would come out looking better than if you'd done your norm gathering later and thus allowed your test's norm group pupils to become as knowledgeable as possible. In reporting the time at which the normative tests were administered, therefore, it would be misleading if you indicated that "normative testing took place during April-June" when, in fact, the bulk of that normative testing took place in April.

The foregoing comment is not intended to suggest that test publishers are deceitful in their accumulation or presentation of normative data. No instances of deliberate data falsification by reputable test publishers have ever been recorded. It is just that educational testing in our nation is big business with a capital *B*. Since the financial stakes are high, the possibility of subtle, self-serving commercial decisions exists. As an evaluator of educational tests, you must be alert to the nuances as well as the major factors in appraising a set of national normative data.

Many educators believe that their test interpretations are markedly enhanced if they ready a set of local norms to be used, perhaps, in concert with national norms. Local norms can often prove highly helpful to local educators whose day-to-day decisions can be illuminated by comparing individual student performances to those of a more similar group than is typically true with nationally normed data. Sometimes, because national tests may not be accompanied by suitable normative data for the particular local group of students, it is imperative to prepare local norm tables.

To illustrate, suppose your school system is in the southwestern part of the U.S. and that your schools serve a dominantly Spanish-speaking student population. Let's say you discover, however, that in the sample of pupils who constituted the national norm group, few Spanish-speaking youngsters were represented. In such a case it may be requisite to garner local norms.

It is important, of course, if both local and national norms are available, not to confuse the two. To say that one of your students "score at the 59th percentile" would be insufficient. You'll have to add the phrase, "on local norms." You may discover that local and national norms are substantially different. Clarification regarding which norms are involved is, accordingly, requisite.

Criteria for Judging Normative Data

What sorts of factors should be considered when reviewing a set of comparative data? In the first place, of course, whether there is any comparative information or not can be readily answered. However, assuming that there are normative data at hand, what should we be looking for in deciding whether the data are adequate? Here are a few points to consider:

> *Sample size.* Is the sample in the norm group large enough to assure a reasonable degree of stability in the data base from which we must draw interpretations?
>
> *Representativeness.* Is the sample drawn in such a way as to represent the kinds of examinees for whom interpretations must be made?
>
> *Recency.* Were the normative data gathered in the last few years or is the information out of date because it was gathered too long ago?
>
> *Description of procedures.* Are the procedures associated with the gathering of the normative data sufficiently well described so that they can be properly evaluated?

Let's deal, briefly, with each of these four points. First off, we would prefer that test publishers employ as large a sample as possible because of the obvious resulting stability in the quality of the interpretations that we reach. Other factors being equal, if one normative sample has only 50 students per grade level and another has 1,000 students per grade level, the larger sample will be preferable.

However, size is not enough, and although this is not the place to engage in an extensive discussion regarding sampling procedures, it is apparent that a normative sample will be more useful if it can be stratified so that all relevant dimensions of interest have been included in it. For example, if there is reason to believe that boys perform differently than girls on a particular test, the normative data should be gathered so that we can split out separate norms for boys and girls.

The issue of whether to develop supplemental normative tables for particular minority groups is a vexing one. On the one hand, separate norms, for example, for Hispanic youngsters, would permit better interpretation of Hispanic children's test performance, particularly if there is a substantial difference between the Hispanic examinees' scores and those of the total population. On the other hand, the creation of separate racial norms tends to perpetuate the belief that certain minority groups are less able (even if their lower test performance arises because of previous instructional inferiorities). In general we are faced with a dilemma of risking long-term deficits (by having separate ethnic norms) or risking short-term deficits (by lumping all ethnic groups together). It is an issue to be considered most carefully, particularly by test developers, but also by those evaluating tests.

If all of the major factors that are related to test performance can be taken into account when the test norms are prepared, this would be ideal. Typically, limitations of resources preclude most test publishers from doing so to the extent that they would wish. Your job as a test evaluator will be to weigh the overall adequacy of the normative data's representativeness.

Typically, publishers of most widely used nationally standardized norm-referenced tests up-date their normative data every half-dozen years or so. For some kinds of tests this is more crucial than others. For instance, if the content of a field is shifting rapidly, as was the case some years ago in mathematics, then it is important to renorm the tests since it would be unfair to compare today's students to those who were taught with dissimilar curricular emphases. In other content or attitudinal areas, where there is more stability in the expectations we have of students, we can be a bit more relaxed with our requirements for test-norm recentness. You will have to decide whether you're working with a measured attribute that is apt to get out of date fairly rapidly. In any event, it obviously would be better to have norms assembled in recent, rather than medieval, times.

For all the foregoing reasons, it is necessary that explicit descriptions be provided of the procedures employed in assembling the normative data in the technical information that accompanies the test's norm tables. That description should leave little to the imagination, regarding the key details of how the tests were administered, to whom, when, under what conditions, and so on. When a test's technical information fails to provide a well-documented description of the various procedures used to secure normative data, a test evaluator should view such data with some suspicion and even a dash of disdain.

PRACTICE EXERCISES

Standard scores are really fun to work with, once you get the hang of them. For the ten questions in this chapter's self-test, you are free to use any of the tables or formulae in the chapter.

1. A student who scored at the 61st percentile would be in which of the following stanines?
   A. Fourth
   B. Fifth
   C. Sixth
   D. Seventh
2. What is the T score of an examinee whose raw score is 17 when the mean of the test score distribution is 20 and the standard deviation is 2.0?
   A. 55
   B. -1.5
   C. 35
   D. 20
3. What is the T score equivalent of a z score of 3.0?
4. A normalized T score of 30 is equivalent to which of the following percentiles?
   A. 2nd
   B. 30th
   C. 16th
   D. 40th
5. What is the z score equivalent of a T score of 40?
6. If a distribution of test scores is essentially normal, what approximate percentage of the scores would a person exceed whose T score was 60?
   A. 60%
   B. 84%
   C. 34%
   D. 16%

7. Given a fairly normal distribution of test scores, in which stanine would an examinee's score fall whose z score was −1.1?
   A. Fifth
   B. Fourth
   C. Third
   D. Second

8. If a distribution of test scores is decisively skewed, what percentile (approximately) will a *T* score of 60 be equivalent to?
   A. 84th
   B. 60th
   C. 98th
   D. Uncertain

9. A student scoring in the fifth stanine could have which of the following percentiles?
   A. 55th
   B. 50th
   C. 45th
   D. All of these

10. What is the normalized *T* score equivalent of an examinee's score at the 16th percentile?

ANSWERS TO PRACTICE EXERCISES

1. B	6. B
2. C	7. C
3. 80	8. D
4. A	9. D
5. −1.0	10. 40

DISCUSSION QUESTIONS

1. In the chapter, four criteria were given for judging the adequacy of normative data, namely, *sample size, representativeness, recentness,* and *description of procedures.* How would you rank these according to their importance? Why?

2. Do you believe that separate norms should be supplied for different ethnic groups? If so, why? If not, why not?

3. Do you think normative data should be used differently for interpreting the meaning of an examinee's performance than for evaluating the effectiveness of an educational program? Why?

4. Which of the standard scores treated in the chapter do you think is the most useful? Why?

5. Can you identify any reasonable characteristics in education which you would consider to be decisively normal and/or nonnormal in the manner in which they are distributed? If so, what are they?

SUGGESTIONS FOR ADDITIONAL READING

GRONLUND, NORMAN, E., "Interpreting Test Scores and Norms," Chapter 15, *Measurement and Evaluation in Teaching* (3rd ed.), pp. 387–424. New York: Macmillan, 1976. Gronlund examines with considerable care the varied interpretive techniques that can be used with test scores and test norms.

HOPKINS, CHARLES D., and RICHARD L. ANTES, *Classroom Testing: Administration, Scoring, and Score Interpretation,* Chapters 5–8, pp. 81–147. Itasca, Ill.: F. E. Peacock, 1979. The four chapters in this useful paperback book are relevant to the interpretation of test scores. Chapter 5 and 6 deal with standard score interpretations and other interpretive devices, such as percentiles. Chapters 7 and 8 focus on norm-referenced and criterion-referenced interpretations of test scores.

NOLL, VICTOR H., DALE P. SCANNEL, and ROBERT C. CRAIG, "Derived Scores and Norms," Chapter 3, *Introduction to Educational Measurement* (4th ed.), pp. 54–78. Boston: Houghton Mifflin, 1979. The authors of this measurement text, now in its fourth edition, describe a variety of derived scores of utility in interpreting examinees' performance.

POPHAM, W. JAMES, "Normative Data for Criterion-Referenced Tests?" *Phi Delta Kappan,* 58 (1976), 593–594. In this essay, your resolute author unresolutely commits a bit of backtracking and urges that norms be established for criterion-referenced tests.

8

Bias, as defined by *The American Heritage Dictionary,* describes a "preference or inclination that inhibits impartial judgment." That, of course, is why wise people will avoid bias. It interferes with judgment.

A Look at Test Bias

In connection with testing, bias exerts its typical nastiness. Tests that are biased yield results that are apt to be misinterpreted. It is interesting that although we have had many decades of educational testing in America, it is only during the past ten or fifteen years that educators have become somewhat sensitized to the possibility that our traditional testing procedures may be bursting with bias.

The kinds of bias that may be encountered in tests ranges wide. We can find instances of sex bias, religious bias, geographic bias, linguistic bias, and just about any other bias in the ball park. Perhaps the most insidious form of bias in educational testing is racial bias, since testing practices that are racially biased serve to stifle the attainments of individuals who have already been served up more than their share of social inequities. There

Test bias

are so many factors, economic, historical, and social, which operate to oppress people from minority groups that it constitutes a major educational tragedy when the progress of minority youngsters is stultified because of bias in testing.

Robert L. Williams, a black psychologist who created an intelligence test biased *in favor* of black people, the *Black Intelligence Test Counter-balanced for Honkies,* or the *Black Intelligence Test of Cultural Homogeneity,* makes the point eloquently as he points out how black-Americans have been systematically penalized by white-oriented tests:

> May I ask, "Is it more indicative of intelligence to know Malcolm X's last name or the author of Hamlet?" I ask you now, "When is Washington's birthday?" Perhaps 99% of you thought February 22. That answer presupposes a white

norm. I actually meant Booker T. Washington's birthday, not George Washington's. "What is the color of bananas?" Many of you would say, "Yellow." But by the time the banana has made it to my community, to the ghetto, it is brown with yellow spots. So I always thought bananas were brown. Again, I was penalized by the culture in which I live. "What is the thing to do if another child hits you, without meaning to do it?" The frequency of the response is determined by the neighborhood lived in. In my community, to walk away would mean suicide. For survival purposes, children in Black communities are taught to hit back; however, that response receives zero credit on current intelligence tests such as the Stanford-Binet (Form L–M). Thus, the test items are no more relevant to the Black experience than is much of the curriculum. Black children will naturally do worse on tests which draw items from outside their culture.[1]

Black-Americans, Hispanic-Americans, and most other minority groups have often suffered from educational testing practices that are unquestionably biased in favor of individuals from the majority culture. Educational tests have typically been written by white, middle-class Americans; tried out on white, middle-class examinees; and normed on white, middle-class students. Is it any wonder that youngsters from other racial groups or lower socioeconomic strata would fare more poorly on such tests than children of the white, middle-class types who spawned them?

It should be noted, however, that no allegation is made here of malevolence on the part of test developers or test users. No, it has been less a case of maliciousness than a case of freewheeling *ignorance*. Test developers have ignorantly assumed that a white, middle-class item writer could generate items that would provide minority examinees with an equal chance to get a correct answer. All too often that assumption has been woefully unwarranted.

At an obvious level, let's say test items contain words or phrases that are common to the white, middle-class experience but foreign to, for example, Chicano children from the barrios of East Los Angeles. Those barrio children, unable to understand the vocabulary of the test items, will perform less well on the test than they would have if they had comprehended the vocabulary.

At a less obvious level, think about the subcultural value evidenced in the previous quotation from Williams. If a black ghetto child has been forced to embrace a "fight-when-attacked" value, that child should not be penalized on a Stanford-Binet test by test items that are looking for a "turn-the-other-cheek" response. Ghetto and barrio children must often avoid cheek turning if they are to survive.

Test bias is operative whenever there are (1) qualities in a test itself,

---

[1]Robert L. Williams, "Black Pride, Academic Relevance, and Individual Achievement," in *Crucial Issues in Testing*, eds. R. W. Tyler and R. M. Wolf (Berkeley, Calif.: McCutchan, 1974). Reprinted with permission of the publisher.

(2) the way in which it is administered, or (3) the manner in which its results are interpreted that unfairly penalize or advantage members of a subgroup because of their membership in that subgroup. This sort of definition of test bias has been bouncing around in measurement circles for a decade or so, but it's more complicated to define test bias than it appears at first blush.

First off, note that the test-bias sword chops in both directions. If members of a subgroup are penalized by a test because of their membership in that subgroup, the test is obviously biased. Most of the examples that come to mind when we think of test bias are of such a negative sort. However, a test is equally biased if it *advantages* members of a subgroup, thus penalizing all other subgroups. Let's say we whipped up a new aptitude test that drew so heavily on notions derived from the Orient that Asian-Americans would do wonderfully, while all others would flop. Such a test, though not penalizing a particular group, would also be unfair.

Test Bias versus Instructional Shortcomings

Every time that members of a minority group score lower on a test item than members of the majority group, does that mean the test item is biased? Think hard about that question before you answer. Now, if you qualify to continue reading by having devoted hard thinking to your answer, here's the correct response: absolutely not! Although such a test item *may* be biased, it may also be totally unbiased and may be detecting deficits in the instruction received by minority children.

In the late seventies and early eighties, a number of states established minimum competency testing programs which called for high school students to pass certain competency tests, usually in reading, writing, and arithmetic, prior to being awarded a high school diploma. When these tests were administered on a statewide basis, it was sometimes discovered that a sizably larger proportion of minority pupils failed the tests than was the case with white pupils. However, that fact *does not automatically indicate that the competency tests were biased.* What it may indicate is that the instructional program in that state has failed to provide the state's minority children with the kinds of competencies they should have in order to pass the prescribed tests.

In some states, for example, the state department of education staff members computed separate p values, that is, the proportion of students answering an item correctly, for majority and for minority students. Any item for which there was a substantial disparity in p values was considered biased, hence excised from the test. No effort was made to see if, indeed, there was something in the test item which might have rendered it biased. The mere fact that more minority youngsters answered an item incorrectly was considered proof that the item was biased.

However, subsequent analyses of some of the discarded items revealed no ingredients whatsoever that could be considered to penalize unfairly any minority group. The alternative hypothesis, therefore, appears far more tenable, namely, that the minority youngsters did poorly on those items because they had been badly taught. By tossing out such items merely on the basis of differential p values, the very items were eliminated that could reveal the skills and knowledge which the minority youngsters lacked.

While it is perfectly sensible to employ empirical schemes, such as looking for disparate p values between, for example, the scores of children from high versus low socioeconomic strata, any items thus identified *should then be judged* to see whether they possess features that constitute bias against low socioeconomic status youngsters. If the items do indeed possess such elements, then the items should obviously be modified or jettisoned. If no biasing elements can be identified, however, the alternative hypothesis seems likely, that is, that the low socioeconomic status youngsters were not well taught with respect to these items.

If, for instance, you asked children to come up with the result of adding two plus two and a group of minority students happened to answer the item incorrectly more often than majority students, you obviously wouldn't toss out the item. Everybody ought to know what two plus two is. (After all, our entire mathematics edifice is predicated on the fundamental truth that two plus two equals approximately four.) However, when the test item deals with a less obvious skill or bit of knowledge, some measurement folks let differences in p values take the place of sensible judgment.

CULTURE-FAIR TESTS

In an effort to circumvent the problems associated with tests that yield different scores for different subgroups, efforts have been made to create *culture-fair* testing instruments. Typically, these tests have been largely nonverbal in nature. Some of the more widely known of these instruments are Cattell's *Culture-Fair Intelligence Tests, Raven's Progressive Matrices,* the *Leiter International Performance Scale,* and the *Davis-Eells Test of General Intelligence.*

The Davis-Eells test, often referred to as the prototype of culture-fair tests (even though insufficient sales failed to warrant its continued publication), was predicated on the general strategy of trying out items and eliminating those on which children from lower socioeconomic or different cultural backgrounds scored significantly worse than others. The test consists of problems thought to be common to the experience of all urban children and is entirely pictorial, except for the directions which are read aloud by the test administrator. The test was designed for children in grades one through six.

The following are sample items from the test.[2] One type of problem is referred to as "probabilities." A picture is presented showing a situation, and the examinee is given (read aloud by the test administrator) three possible explanations. The test taker's task is to pick the most likely explanation.

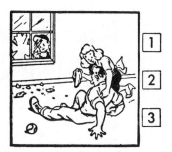

No. 1   The man *fell down* and hit his head.

No. 2   A ball *came through the window* and hit the man's head.

No. 3   The picture *does not show how* the man got the bump on his head. Nobody can tell because the picture doesn't show how the man got the bump.

Which number was true?

Another type of item in the *Davis-Eells Test of General Intelligence* is called "analogies." These items present a pictured relationship between two objects in an example, then a new object and three pictorial options. In

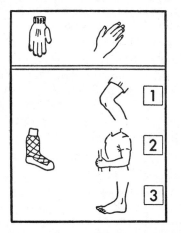

[2]Sample items from the *Davis-Eells Tests of General Intelligence,* copyright © 1952, 1953 by Harcourt Brace Jovanovich, Inc. Reproduced by special permission from the publisher.

each case, the relationship between elements in the example is suggested or made clear by the test administrator before the examinee is required to choose the appropriate analog for the new object from the three options.

Another part of the test is called "best ways" and presents pictorial problems with three possible solutions depicted. The examinee's task is to select the picture which shows the best way to solve the problem.

The Davis-Eells test has received a great deal of research attention, and some evidence has been gathered which indicates that it possesses a degree of validity. For instance, Davis-Eells test scores correlate around .50 with the *Otis Quick-Scoring Mental Ability Tests* and approximately .40 with standardized achievement tests in reading, language, and arithmetic. On the whole, however, the Davis-Eells test has failed to fulfill its promise as a genuinely culture-fair test.[3]

Cattell's *Culture-Fair Intelligence Tests* employ a somewhat different approach to the creation of unbiased testing instruments. Four different types of items are found in the tests. Series items oblige the student to select a choice that completes a series. Classification items require examinees to choose something that does not belong in a set. Matrices items require examinees to find a choice that completes a pattern. In the conditions items, a dot must be placed in one of the choices that coincides with the conditions present in a boxed figure.[4]

Three levels of this test are available, aimed at ages four to eight, eight to thirteen, and ten to sixteen. As seen in the sample items, the tests are essentially perceptual and nonverbal, since directions are read aloud to examinees so that they understand the task. Several studies have been reported which indicate that economically disadvantaged children, both whites and blacks, score slightly higher on the Cattell tests than they do on

[3]For example, see Victor H. Noll, "Relation of Scores on Davis-Eells Games to Socioeconomic Status, Intelligence Test Results, and School Achievements," *Educational and Psychological Measurement*, 20 (Spring 1960), 119–129.

[4]Sample items from the Cattell *Culture-Fair Intelligence Test*, copyright © 1949, 1957 by the Institute for Personality and Ability Testing, Champaign, Ill. Reproduced with permission.

An Introduction to IPAT CULTURE FAIR INTELLIGENCE TESTING

NOTE: The present notice is intended only as a brief first exposure to IPAT Culture Fair Intelligence Tests, from which, it is hoped, the reader will go on to study much more complete evidence and information in the Manuals and Technical Handbooks for the scales. They cannot effectively be evaluated or used without this fuller study.

Do the following sample problems:

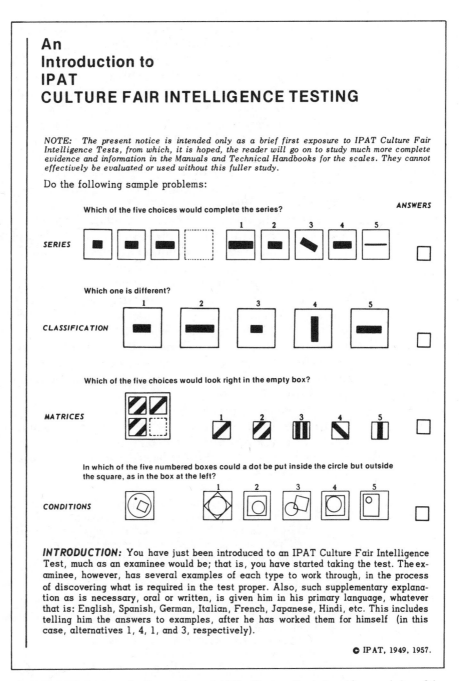

INTRODUCTION: You have just been introduced to an IPAT Culture Fair Intelligence Test, much as an examinee would be; that is, you have started taking the test. The examinee, however, has several examples of each type to work through, in the process of discovering what is required in the test proper. Also, such supplementary explanation as is necessary, oral or written, is given him in his primary language, whatever that is: English, Spanish, German, Italian, French, Japanese, Hindi, etc. This includes telling him the answers to examples, after he has worked them for himself (in this case, alternatives 1, 4, 1, and 3, respectively).

© IPAT, 1949, 1957.

more traditional aptitude tests.[5] These results have been used to demonstrate the greater fairness of the Cattell approach, in contrast to the more heavily verbal orientation of typical aptitude and achievement tests. Nevertheless, when one considers the entire array of available evidence regarding the validity of the *Culture-Fair Intelligence Tests,* a negative conclusion must be drawn regarding their utility.[6] Although the tests do not appear to be intrinsically unfair to any culture, it is not true that groups from one culture or subculture score as well on the tests as groups from another culture or subculture. Indeed, even nonverbal tests may be biased against (or in favor of) certain subgroups since there is research evidence to suggest that certain subcultures include more pictures, puzzles, and other nonverbal stimuli than do other subcultures.

In general, interest in developing culture-fair tests is definitely declining. In part this reduction of interest is due to the lack of success among those who pioneered the creation of culture-fair tests. In part it has also been recognized that if human development is viewed as a process dependent upon an interaction between inherited qualities and environmental factors, assessment instruments must tap the effects of those environmental forces. Only by focusing on dimensions of lesser significance can test developers, therefore, create assessment devices that will be fair to those from substantially different environments. Oakland and Matuszek conclude that "psychologists generally agree that one test cannot be universally applicable and fair to persons from all cultures and still assess important psychological characteristics."[7]

The general strategy employed in most so-called culture-fair tests involves the avoidance of heavy dependence on verbal material. Most attempts to develop culture-fair intelligence tests, therefore, have yielded nonverbal instruments. Ebel dismisses the utility of these instruments as follows:

> But there is no good reason to believe that these nonverbal tests get any closer to basic nature intelligence than do the verbal test. Ability to do well on them can also be learned. And since verbal facility is so important an element in school learning, and in most areas of human achievement, what the nonverbal tests succeed in measuring seems to have little practical usefulness.[8]

---

[5]For example, see Keith Barton, *Recent Data on the Culture-fair Scales,* Information Bulletin 16 (Champaign, Ill.: Institute for Personality and Ability Testing, 1973).

[6]See, for instance, the reviews of these tests in O. K. Buros, ed., *Fifth* and *Sixth Mental Measurements Yearbooks* (Highland Park, N.J.: Gryphon Press, 1959 and 1965).

[7]Thomas Oakland and Paula Matuszek, "Using Tests in Nondiscriminatory Assessment," in *Psychological and Educational Assessment of Minority Children,* ed. T. Oakland (New York: Brunner/Mazel, 1977), p. 62.

[8]Robert L. Ebel, *Essentials of Educational Measurement,* 3rd ed. (Englewood Cliffs, N.J.: Prentice-Hall, Inc., 1979), p. 350.

DELIVERY ROOM

"Congratulations on your new son, Mr. Hill. I'm here to test his aptitude before the environment mucks him up."

WAITING RM.

CULTURE FREE TESTING ASSOC.

A rather distinctive approach to developing a culturally fair assessment scheme has been developed by Mercer and is described as the *System of Multicultural Pluralistic Assessment (SOMPA).*[9] Essentially, Mercer's strategy depends on the use of a battery of instruments and compares a child's score, not only against a national norm group, but also against children from comparable backgrounds. Designed for use with children who are five to eleven years of age, information is drawn from administration of several tests to the child and also from an interview with the child's principal caretaker. The score on one of the intelligence tests administered to the child is then "corrected" by use of multiple regression techniques on the basis of the total array of information.

Mercer compares the correction to a golf or bowling handicap. She believes that the *uncorrected* scores can be used to isolate immediate educational needs and thus, to make instructional decisions. She contends that the *corrected* score can be employed to gauge a child's "latent scholastic potential."

Mercer argues that by using the corrected score, fewer children would

[9]Jane Mercer, *SOMPA, System of Multicultural Pluralistic Assessment* (New York: The Psychological Corporation, 1977).

be labeled as mentally retarded. There is some debate over this proposal, since funds for special education are often distributed on the basis of whether or not a child has been labeled as retarded. It is unclear whether the funds needed for special instructional programs can be maintained if the "retarded" label is eliminated.

SOMPA has already attracted considerable attention. It is apparent that this strategy will be the subject of some controversy and, hopefully, much research in future years.

EVALUATING FOR TEST BIAS

From the preceding discussion, it should be evident that eliminating test bias constitutes a nontrivial measurement problem. Perhaps the best approach that we can currently employ is to exercise the best evaluative judgments that we can muster in reviewing the test itself, the procedures used to administer it, and the interpretations made from the test's results.

Reliance on a judgmental approach to detecting and, once detected, eliminating test bias forces us immediately to a consideration of "who will render the judgments?" Suppose, for example, that we're trying to see whether Puerto Rican youngsters in New York City are being unfairly penalized by items on a test of reading achievement. Should we have the test items reviewed by a panel of white, middle-class school teachers? Obviously not. But how about a panel of Spanish-speaking teachers? Well, maybe yes or maybe no. What if the Spanish-speaking judges were middle-class Chicanos from San Diego? Is the ability to speak Spanish sufficient to qualify one to judge the suitability of test items for any Spanish-speaking group? Of course not. Similarly, the experience of black people in the rural South may not coincide at all with that of blacks who were raised in the urban North.

The implication of all this question-and-answer business in the previous paragraph is that those who will be doing the judging must be truly conversant with the examinee population for whom the tests are designed. If tests for Puerto Rican youngsters are involved, then Puerto Rican judges should be used to review the test items. If tests are to be used for large groups of examinees, say for a national test, then the use of a judgmental approach to the detection of test bias starts to get really difficult.

Testing, as indicated earlier, is big business. Businesses must sell their wares if they're going to stay in business. This means that they must set their prices at a competitive level if they are going to be successful in selling their merchandise. If you were going to buy a battery-powered electric bagel slicer and were choosing between two models, one of which cost twice as much as the other, you'd probably opt for the less expensive choice. On the other hand, anyone who is kinky enough to want a battery-powered electric bagel slicer might go for the more costly model.

Bagel slicers aside, it is apparent that if publishers of national tests wanted to do a really super job in having their instruments reviewed by panels representing all minority groups with whom the test might be used, the costs (of paying the reviewers and revising the test based on their comments) could be substantial. These substantial costs would in many cases boost the price of the test beyond what was commercially competitive. Thus, even well-intentioned test publishers find themselves in a financial bind when it comes to the elimination of test bias. What is morally justifiable may be economically suicidal.

Some test publishers deal with this dilemma by adopting a flagrantly tokenistic strategy. For instance, one recently published reading test had all of its test items reviewed by one white, one black, and one Spanish-speaking reviewer. Any item which was judged to be biased *by all three judges* was removed from the test. Surprise of surprises, not too many items were tossed out.

However, it's easier to snipe at questionable practices than it is to propose constructive solution strategies. If users of educational tests become so sensitized to the perils of biased tests that they *demand* full-scale bias-reduction operations prior to purchasing a test, all test publishers would soon comply with these demands. Moreover, since this would result in an across-the-board increase in the price of tests, no one test publisher would need to forsake that necessary competitive edge. To reiterate a point which has and will be made often in this volume, the production of high quality educational tests is not inexpensive. Decisions made on the basis of inexpensively produced tests, however, will typically result in errors that are both humanely and socially more expensive than one realizes.

Detecting Bias in Test Items

Whether are not there is evidence of the test publisher's bias-reduction efforts, but particularly if there is no evidence of such operations, what does one look for in the test items themselves? For example, if you wished to set up your own panel of judges and screen the items in a test you were considering for possible adoption, what sorts of things should you consider?

Tidwell has assembled an excellent series of practical suggestions for developing unbiased test items.[10] We can transform these item-construction

---

[10]Romeria Tidwell, *Guidelines for Reducing Bias in Testing* (Los Angeles: Instructional Objectives Exchange, May 1979).

guidelines into a series of questions which could constitute the basis of a test bias item-review operation.

Inoffensiveness.   Is the language used in test items, as well as the activities reflected in the items, apt to be offensive to members of any group? Items must be reviewed to see whether on racial, sexual, cultural, religious, or socioeconomic grounds, there are elements that would offend examinees. Suppose a test item described "Mr. Gonzalez picking up his weekly welfare check," it is certain that some Hispanics would be offended because of the implication that Spanish-surname individuals are unemployed and on the government dole.

Alternatively, let's say a test item incorporated some of those classic sexual stereotypes in which women are depicted as homemakers and men as breadwinners. Only insensitive item writers would employ such sexually offensive images these days. However, ample evidence exists that there are plenty of insensitive people wandering the world. Some of them end up as writers of test items.

Relevancy.   Are the activities reflected in test items relevant to the life experiences of the persons responding to the items? For examinees to respond sensibly to test items, they ought to know what the test item is talking about. Suppose you were trying to answer a test item in which a key word was "mulgat." You clearly don't know the meaning of mulgat, because I just made it up. You'd have the same difficulty in responding to the mulgat item that a ghetto child might when an item asserts that "those at the dinner party partook of caviar prior to the entree." It's just as easy to say that "people at dinner had chicken as the main course." The former phrasing may be irrelevant to the experiences of many examinees; the latter phrasing is more apt to be consonant with the life experiences of most examinees. Even upper-class children have had chicken for dinner.

Similar connotations.   Are the connotations of key words and phrases in the test items essentially the same for all examinees? If a test item asserts that a musical "record was really bad," does that mean the record was a loser? Well, some people would certainly say yes. However, for black teen-agers in the seventies, to say something was "bad" was really to indicate that it was good. Terms or expressions in test items that carry mixed signals for different audiences must be spotted, then modified or excised.

Avoidance of wordiness.   Are test items written in a straightforward, uncomplicated, easily read manner? Some writers of test items are really frustrated Faulkners who seize upon the test items they're writing to author snippets of the "great American novel." Yet, excessive wordiness can obviously interfere with an examinee's ability to respond appropriately to a test item. Often, because of their more limited opportunities to interact with complex verbal stimuli, minority youngsters or those from lower socioeconomic strata will find convoluted and wordy items to be particularly confusing.

Moderate stimulation.   *Is the context of test items so interesting to examinees that they will be distracted from the task at hand?* Let's say you're a teen-ager and you encounter a mathematics test item in which your favorite rock group is being compared unfavorably to several other, blatantly inferior, rock groups. Perhaps you'd become so annoyed at the "obviously unfair" evaluation that you'd concentrate on the rock groups instead of the mathematics problem you are supposed to solve.

Sometimes, in an effort to make their materials relevant, item writers toss in content so provocative in nature that the examinees actually get distracted by this excessively stimulating material. For instance, if a test is to be taken by adolescents, then items should not contain statements such as, "American teen-agers spend millions of dollars a year in fruitless attempts to treat pimples and blackheads." Acne-ridden students who read this item will automatically assume that every other student will be thinking about them after reading this item. Be sure to appraise test items with respect to their probable stimulus value for the examinees who'll be completing the items.

Try to blend these five questions, and perhaps others, into a systematic checklist which is routinely employed as you appraise the extent which a test's items are potentially biased. The five questions can also prove useful when considering items that, on the basis of empirical data, appear to favor or penalize certain subgroups.

One might think that test developers will become excessively sensitive as they try to create bias-free items. However, in the case of item construction, there's almost no such thing as hypersensitivity to potential biasing elements. If there's any, even remote, likelihood that one or more examinees will be adversely affected by an item's construction, why not strive to reduce even that remote bias potential.

Detecting Bias in Test Administration

Besides the test items themselves, another likely source of bias is associated with the procedures employed in the administration of the test. The actual administration of a test constitutes a complex interaction among examiner variables, examinee variables, and situational variables. Supposing, for example, that a large group of black adolescents were being tested in a stuffy, poorly lit cafeteria by a white examiner whose surly manner would arouse hostility in white saints, much less black teen-agers. Suppose also that these black youngsters had previously performed rather badly on tests similar to the one being administered in an uncomfortable room by a borderline bully. Is it any wonder that these examinees might perform less well than they might in other test-administration settings?

Examiners. Without question, the behavior displayed by an examiner during the test's administration can be influential in determining the way that examinees will perform on the test. While research assembled thus far does not indicate that examiners need to be of the same race as examinees,[11] there is some tendency for adult and older adolescent blacks to prefer working with black psychologists and counselors, rather than whites with comparable training.[12]

More important than racial match is the demeanor of the examiner as perceived by the examinees. If the examiner is a cold, aloof individual who is convinced that the examinees being tested will perform badly on the test, those sentiments will often be sensed by examinees. Test administrators should systematically sort out any stereotypic expectations they have regarding particular types of examinees. Either they should get these expectations under control or replace themselves with less offensive test administrators.

So much for the negatives. Now, on the positive side, it is desirable to use examiners who understand the verbal and nonverbal behavior of the individuals being examined. Examiners who are attentive to examinee reactions will be able to sense when certain actions may be warranted, such as restructuring a situation where examinees appear to be displaying less than satisfactory motivation to do well on the test.

In the same vein, Tidwell recommends that "tangible actions should be taken to motivate examinees to perform at their optimal achievement levels."[13] She argues that many minority youngsters, having experienced previous failures in such examinations, may be anxious to "check out" psychologically from the exam as soon as they encounter a question or two they can't answer. To heighten the attending behavior of minority youngsters, Tidwell recommends that such examinees should be urged often to do their very best work when being tested. Minority examinees should also be informed that they will be confronted with difficult test items and *just like other groups of students,* they are not expected to answer all or even most of the items correctly. This kind of proactive stance is advocated in order to counter a minority child's response which, upon stumbling over a few items, might be, "I can't do well on this test like all those white kids." The

[11]Oakland and Matuszek, "Using Tests in Nondiscriminatory Assessment," p. 60.
[12]J. Sattler, *Assessment of Children's Intelligence* (Philadelphia: Saunders, 1974).
[13]Tidwell, *Guidelines,* pp. 15–16.

child would then cease to expend the necessary energy on subsequent items. To head off such defeatist dispositions, test administrators will obviously have to be on their toes.

Examinees.   All examinees should be equally familiar with the nature of the test being taken. Some youngsters, particularly those who come from other nations, are less familiar with typical American testing situations than they need to be in order to perform well on tests. Such youngsters (indeed, any youngsters who are intimidated by the nature of the test itself) should be given ample practice opportunities to become accustomed to the *form* of tests being used.

In a way we should be attempting to make sure that minority examinees acquire the same degree of "test wiseness" that we often encounter in white, middle-class examinees who may answer an item correctly because of their familiarity with testing practices, not their knowledge of the content being tested (for example, "always choose the longest answer in a multiple-choice test—it's more likely to be correct than the shorter options").

In particular, considerable attention should be directed to reshaping the expectations of minority children who have a history of unsuccessful performance on examinations. Such youngsters should be given successful test experiences in less threatening situations, then encouraged to bring heightened motivation and aspirations to the "big stakes" testing situations.

The setting.   For any examinee it is important to provide a comfortable test administration setting that is conducive to promoting the examinee's best efforts. For a minority examinee such settings may be *imperative*. For example, suppose that you are a seasoned, white test taker. You could probably do well on a test if it was administered in an outhouse during a hurricane. However, suppose, instead, that you're a minority test taker who has often flopped on tests. If the setting is less than comfortable, that might be just the straw that snaps the camel's back.

Detecting Bias in Interpretations

To the extent that we employ criterion-referenced tests, rather than norm-referenced tests, there is somewhat less concern about biased interpretations, since the focus is on whether or not the examiner can (does) display a behavior of interest. With norm-referenced tests, however, the strong possibility exists that we will reach a biased interpretation of an examinee's score because we use an inappropriate set of normative data on which to base our inference regarding what that score signifies. This possibility leads to an interesting and important issue regarding whether we should advocate the gathering and utilization of separate normative data for particular subgroups of minorities, for example, black-Americans or Hispanic-Americans.

In the first place, it is necessary for any large-scale normative samples to be *drawn* on a stratified basis so that, for instance, with national norms, a representative proportion of blacks, Hispanics, native Americans, and Asians will be included. Obviously, if the normative sample percentages of minority examinees are at variance with those in the population at large, it would be misleading to employ those normative data in interpreting an (underrepresented) examinee's test results.

However, even if the national norms are sufficiently representative, in some cases minority examinees will still be disadvantaged. For instance, if we're using the *Graduate Record Examination (GRE)* as a screening test to select students for graduate school, it may turn out that minority applicants may systematically be excluded if we merely select applicants on the basis of the highest *GRE* scores.

This has led some educators to propose that separate norms for minorities be created in addition to national norms. Oakland and Matuszek, for example, contend that "the availability of both national and localized norms, particularly when reported by various social class and racial-ethnic groups, provides for greater accuracy and clarity in interpreting test scores."[14] A number of those who have addressed themselves to the test-bias issue share this point of view.

On the other side of the argument, however, there is the danger that by establishing separate normative tables for minority subgroups, we thereby authenticate the notion that these groups are essentially different from the majority, that is, less able than the majority, and that those differences are unalterable. There is a strong spirit of second-classism that surrounds the advocacy of separate norms for minorities. Although there is little doubt that, at the present, greater "accuracy and clarity in interpreting test scores" might be gained, there is the long-run danger that we shall never promote an educational system where race is not a dominant factor if we continue to employ racial variables in our test interpretations.

Some believe that whenever the use of national normative data results in the selection of students in such a way that racial composition of those selected is markedly different from the total population, a quota system should be employed. This sort of quota scheme would work as follows: If there are 22 percent black students in a given age group, then the 22 highest-scoring black children should be selected. Such quota schemes have been the subject of considerable controversy, both educational and legal, with claims of "reverse racism" being leveled by white applicants who have been excluded because of such procedures. Others, advocating a term of

[14]Oakland and Matuszek, "Using Tests in Nondiscriminatory Assessment," p. 56.

"compensatory justice," argue that such quota schemes are requisite in order to correct for prior social inequities.

It is clear from the foregoing discussion that many issues relative to test bias are far from resolved. We do not yet possess a tidy tool kit by which we can unbias any potentially biased testing device. However, perhaps most importantly, modern educators are far more cognizant of the possibility of test bias than were their predecessors. Vigilance against test bias can help us isolate and then excise biased testing practices. Even with our best efforts, some test bias will surely slip by. Without our best efforts, minority and low socioeconomic youngsters are certain to be unfairly treated. That is intolerable.

PRACTICE EXERCISES

In the following excerpts from test items there are instances of the five types of item-writing errors described in the chapter, that is, *offensiveness, irrelevancy, dissimilar connotations, wordiness,* and *excessive stimulation.* If you need to review the nature of these notions, refer to pages 191–93. Then decide which one of the five is primarily present in each of the following statements that might be found in test items for a high school level achievement test.

1. Mary held her chair as first cellist in the symphony for four years.
2. The poor residents of the neighborhood, as usual, didn't vote in the election.
3. Most of the black students were bused across town for remedial classes.
4. Over 47 percent of teen-agers report that they have had vivid sexual fantasies involving their teachers.
5. What is the cumulative summation of the integer two when appended to a quantity of an identical nature?

ANSWERS TO PRACTICE EXERCISES

1. This appears to violate the *relevancy* dimension, since many youngsters would not be familiar with the fact that in symphony orchestras the strongest performers are designated as "first chairs." Beyond that, they may be unfamiliar with the fact that a cellist plays a cello (whatever that is).
2. This statement would most likely be *offensive* to those from poverty backgrounds. The implication that poor people are not good citizens would offend.
3. This, too, would be an example of a statement *offensive* to black people. There's no reason to toss in such gratuitous slurs regarding the abilities of any racial group.

4. This statement reflects *excessive stimulation,* since it's more than possible some examinees would pause to decide if they were in the 47 percent who *had* experienced such fantasies or the 53 percent who *hadn't.*

5. This is a pretty clear case of *wordiness.* The statement might have said "what's two plus two?"

DISCUSSION QUESTIONS

1. Suppose you were hired to head up the test-discrimination subgroup of a major test publishing house. What sort of procedures would you install to reduce the presence of bias in your firm's operations?

2. Do you believe that there should be separate racial group norms for tests? Why?

3. In what ways can test bias be present for criterion-referenced tests?

4. How would you propose that the competing demands of "low sales price" and "unbiased tests" be dealt with by commercial test publishers?

5. Do you think it is possible, in spite of previously unsuccessful efforts, to build a culture-fair test? If so, what would it be like?

SUGGESTIONS FOR ADDITIONAL READING

GARDNER, WILLIAM E., and DOROTHY J. GARDNER, "Achievement Test Construction and Selection for Black Children," *Journal of Non-White Concerns,* 6, no. 3 (April 1978), 148–156. The authors analyze ten factors which, they believe, account for most of the inaccuracies associated with the use of tests for educational selection of black children.

IRONSON, G. H., and M. J. SUBKOVIAK, "A Comparison of Several Methods of Assessing Item Bias," *Journal of Educational Measurement,* 16, no. 4 (Winter 1979), 209–225. Test data from 1,691 blacks and 1,794 whites were analyzed to determine the agreement among four methods of empirically detecting item bias. For the 150 items analyzed, the investigators reported that three of the methods exhibited agreement and some evidence of validity. This research report dealing with empirical techniques for spotting potentially biased items is highly illuminating.

LINDEN, KATHRYN W., JAMES D. LINDEN, and ROBERT L. BODINE, "Test Bias: Fuss n' Facts," *Measurement and Evaluation in Guidance,* 7, no. 3 (October 1974), 148–156. The authors present a readable description of their views regarding sex bias and minority group bias in testing. Six specific suggestions for nonbiased testing conclude the article.

OAKLAND, THOMAS, ed., *Psychological and Educational Assessment of Minority Children.* New York: Brunner/Mazel, 1977. This volume contains five excellent chapters plus a useful collection of appendices, all of which deal with varied perspectives on nondiscriminatory assessment.

PHILIPS, BERMAN, N., ed., "Assessing Minority Group Children," New York: Behavioral Publications, 1973. This book is a special issue of *Journal of School Psychology* devoted to the assessment of minority group youngsters. An interesting appraisal of the differences between norm-referenced and criterion-referenced assessment of minority-youth children is included, along with an appraisal of white assessment procedures as they apply to minority children.

PINE, S., and S. WATTAWA, "A Computer Program for Evaluating Items Bias," *Educational and Psychological Measurement,* 38, no. 1 (Spring 1978), 147–151. The authors briefly describe a computer program for comparative evaluation of the degree of item bias associated with items used for two subgroups in a population. The program provides statistics that are useful in assessing item bias.

TIDWELL, ROMERIA, *Guidelines for Reducing Bias in Testing.* Los Angeles: The Instructional Objectives Exchange, May 1979. This practical monograph provides a series of specific guidelines for counteracting test bias in connection with the development of test items, the administration of tests, and the interpretation of test scores.

TOLOR, ALEXANDER, "Assessment Myths and Current Fads: (A Rejoinder to a Position to a Position Paper) on Nonbiased Assessment," *Psychology in the Schools,* 15, no. 2 (April 1978), 205–208. This provocative analysis describes a number of fallacies which the author believes have been made in connection with the issue of test bias. For example, the author focuses on fallacies (1) that the use of norms is detrimental to a child's well-being, and (2) that tests lack value because they fail to help teachers improve teaching.

part

CREATING EDUCATIONAL TESTS

If, as some anthropologists contend, a distinguishing feature of human society is that we use tools, it follows that humanity's toolmakers are pretty important folks. This analysis holds true for the field of educational measurement, where the *users* of educational tests must often employ instruments *developed* by others. Accordingly, a key skill to be acquired by educators is the ability to construct a high-quality test. In Part Three there are six chapters aimed at providing you with the skills needed to be a developer of useful educational measuring devices.

We undertake this task very step-by-stepishly, starting off with the initial task of the test developer, namely, specifying the rules for constructing test items. Then we consider the ins and outs of devising and improving the most common types of paper-and-pencil tests, as well as several less typically employed measurement ploys. Finally, we look hard at a special class of assessment problems associated with measuring affective sorts of student behaviors. Hopefully, at the close of Part Three the reader will be able to go forth and actually turn out a defensible test or two.

9

Those who must create an educational test should obviously devote plenty of attention to planning what the test will contain. We can think of a continuum that describes the care and intensity of planning needed for test development. For the creation of tests to be used with many examinees, such as a nationally standardized test of academic aptitude, a highly detailed, full-blown planning effort is required. On the other hand, if a fourth-grade teacher is whipping up an end-of-unit test in geography covering three-weeks' worth of instruction on South America, an elaborate approach to planning the test is not warranted.

It is not that classroom teachers should be cavalier about planning what a test will be like. However, a realistic appraisal of the classroom teacher's responsibilities—and in particular the intellectual fatigue that accompanies a full day's struggle with recalcitrant learners, suggests that few classroom teachers will have sufficient time or energy to do more than a modest job in planning most of their tests.

However, tests *should* be planned. The more important the stakes, the more systematic that planning should be. Thus, as we describe aspects of the test-planning process in this chapter, the reader will recognize that the

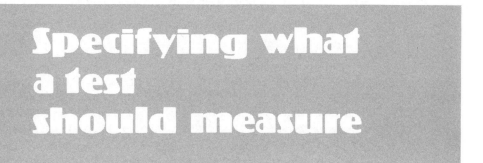

Specifying what a test should measure

use to which the test will be put plays the major role in determining how much planning is necessary. Too many instructors, from the undergraduate to the postgraduate level, attempt to spin out an educational test with little or no advanced planning. That is an error.

Lest elementary or high school teachers think that here is another instance where a college professor is smearing the practices of lower-grade instructors, let me assure you that some of the very worst instances of test planning I have ever witnessed have taken place in graduate programs at universities. I have seen professors, even those who have previously taught measurement courses, and they ought to know better, crank out questions for doctoral- or masters-degree qualifying examinations without any genuine effort to plan what the test questions ought to cover. No thought was given to how the various questions on the exams related to each other or to the graduate training which students had previously received. For many of my colleagues, the test-development strategy employed is clearly a "whatever-pops-into-your-head" approach to item generation.

We all realize that every conscientious teacher would like to devote more time to planning a high-quality exam. It's just that sufficient time for such planning is often not at hand. Therefore, as we wander through various schemes for test planning in the remainder of this chapter, readers must recognize that the zeal with which their schemes should be implemented will depend heavily on the resources, that is, time and money, available to the test developer.

While harassed teachers can be excused, or at least forgiven, for unsystematic test planning, such is not the case with commercial test publishers or the numerous school districts and state departments of education that have in recent years engaged in large-scale test development. Since the tests produced by these major development efforts are characteristically used with numerous individuals and are often employed to make important decisions, no half-hearted planning efforts can be countenanced. Developers of such high-stakes tests should play the planning game, as described in succeeding paragraphs, as though it were a World Series or Superbowl.

Practical Constraints

The most difficult phase of test planning occurs when we must specify the nature of the test items that constitute the test. The bulk of this chapter deals with that specification enterprise. However before fussing with the exotics of test specifications, test developers need to give some attention to such prosaic questions as "How long can the test be?"

Let's say, for instance, that you were heading up the development of a high school basic-skills test in mathematics for a commercial publisher and had polished and repolished the test until it simply glistened with psychometric niceties. Alas, it took most youngsters 120 minutes to complete the test, and some youngsters took almost 200 minutes to complete the test. Since most high school class periods are 45 to 55 minutes in length, you have created a test which would require at least three, and maybe even four, class periods for its administration. Because school people are usually reluctant to toss a four-period exam at their students, you would have produced a test whose likelihood of use would be most limited. More careful advance planning could have headed off such a calamity.

Besides the length of time available for testing, there are other rather routine concerns of a practical nature. For instance, will the form of the test be such that hand or machine scoring is possible? In some large school districts it is a necessity that the test yield student responses which can be optically scanned (by electronic scanning machines or an unemployed Cyclops). If this is so, it would be a serious error to create a test consisting of short-answer items that would have to be hand scored.

Then there is the problem of test security. Will it be necessary to develop an entirely new form of the test in subsequent years, or can this year's test be reused? The extent to which new forms of the test will be needed and the degree to which equivalent difficulties on these tests are required will dictate how many items must be developed and field tested.

Is the test to be a timed test (speed test) in which examinees are given a finite amount of time to complete the test? Will the examinees require any special resources during the completion of the exam, such as dictionaries or electronic calculators?

These kinds of considerations may result in the recognition that there are practical requirements associated with the test's administration and scoring that constrain the nature of the test itself. Such constraints should be recognized and accommodated in subsequent planning for the test.

A RANGE OF ASSESSMENT OPTIONS

All right, let's say that in planning the test you've given reasonable attention to the sorts of practical constraints just described. How should you go about figuring out what will actually be on the test? Well, there's a high probability that inexperienced test planners will gravitate too quickly toward the sorts of tests with which they are most familiar. Since most of us grew up by taking endless numbers of multiple-choice tests, there is a high probability that test developers will initiate—and conclude—their planning of the test without seriously considering other assessment options.

In the next several chapters we review many different types of test schemes. Some of them are of a paper-and-pencil sort. Others involve observations of examinees in action. Still others focus on the appraisal of examinee-created products, such as an art student's ceramic creation or a home economics student's banana cream pie.

Now, in a very real sense, each of these diverse assessment strategies consists of its own "test items." The necessity to produce a yummy banana cream pie is a test item in a homemaking class. However, of course, it is not a multiple-choice test item, hence many educators do not think of such approaches when they set out to plan their tests.

Even if the decision is made to create a paper-and-pencil test, there are all sorts of options open to the creative test planner. For example, in addition to the omnipresent multiple-choice item, we can use short-answer items; matching exercises; binary-choice items, such as true-false items; essay items; or variations and combinations of these categories.

What you'll need to do is get a reasonably good idea of what sort of attribute you wish to measure, for example, what skill or attitude you have in mind. To illustrate, let's say I'm a speech teacher and I want to see how well my students can "organize their prespeech plans." With this general idea in mind, I should then review *all reasonable contenders* for the task of finding out how well my students can plan their speeches. I should think of paper-and-pencil approaches, such as whether students can, under examination circumstances, write out a respectable organizational outline on a speech topic that I supply. Perhaps, as a variant of that approach, I could construct test items which would require examinees to choose among alternative outlines for speeches, some of which were more defensible than others. I should also consider oral-assessment schemes, such as having students describe aloud their plans for a speech on a preassigned topic. Ingenious test planners could come up with still other assessment options. The important principle here is that *premature closure* on particular test strategies, particularly of the traditional multiple-choice variety, is to be eschewed.

Whatever decision has been made regarding the type, or types, of test items to employ in the test, the next task is to create a set of *test specifications*, that is, the blueprint for the generation of test items. The remainder of this chapter is devoted to a description of how test developers should go about creating test specifications, first for norm-referenced measures and then for criterion-referenced measures.

TEST SPECIFICATIONS FOR NORM-REFERENCED TESTS

Developers of norm-referenced tests, just as developers of criterion-referenced tests, want to create good measuring instruments. Because they do, the developers of norm-referenced tests will spend considerable time in planning their test. However, there is a substantial difference between norm- and criterion-referenced tests with respect to the specificity with which the measured behaviors on the test need to be described. Unlike criterion-referenced tests, in which a thorough and complete description of the measured behavior is imperative, for norm-referenced tests we can afford the luxury of more general descriptive information. Since, in a norm-referenced test, we are chiefly concerned with *relative* contrasts among examinees (as opposed to a criterion-referenced test's focus on *what it is* that examinees can or can't do), the degree of descriptive rigor required for norm-referenced tests can be more relaxed.

Although most published norm-referenced tests have been created according to some sort of specifications, it is usually the case that these specifications are not terribly explicit. Indeed, even the traditional textbooks on educational measurement, focusing as they usually do on norm-referenced assessment strategies, typically fail to provide more than a page or two on the topic of test specifications or, as they are sometimes called, *test blueprints.*

Two-Way Grids

How, then, do creators of norm-referenced tests set forth their plans to govern the creation of items? Well, the most common way is to create a two-way grid in which one dimension reflects the *content* to be covered in the test and the other dimension describes the kinds of examinee *behavior* to be assessed on the test. In its most typical form the two-grid consists of content categories at the left and behavior categories across the top, such as the two-way grid presented in Table 9–1, where the numerals in the center of the grid reflect the number of items dealing with each of the topics at one of the four levels of examinee behavior (in this instance drawn from the first four levels of the widely used Bloom *Taxonomy of Educational Objectives*).[1] In the illustration in Table 9–1 we can readily see how the fifty items in this examination are allocated to both content-and cognitive-behavior levels.

If the developers of the test are distressed that there are only about half as many items calling for student analysis as opposed to the items calling for knowledge or comprehension, then this situation can be altered by replacing knowledge or comprehension items with analysis items. If the test developers are distressed that topic 4 has too few items, then this deficiency can also be rectified. Clearly, two-way grids, such as this, can be helpful in apportioning items on tests so that those constructing a test can avoid inadvertent overemphases or underemphases.

The rows and columns on such grids can be made more or less fine grained than those in Table 9–1. For example, one could describe examinee cognitive behavior on test items as only "recall" or "beyond recall," as seen in Table 9–2, where there is also a more detailed breakdown of content than is seen in the previous two-way grid.

In Table 9–2 we see an evenly distributed allocation of 100 items across both content and cognitive level categories. Again, if any substantial disproportionalities are revealed, these can be modified.

It is possible, of course, to add additional dimensions to a table of

[1]Benjamin S. Bloom, and others, *Taxonomy of Educational Objectives, Handbook I: The Cognitive Domain* (New York: D. McKay, 1956).

TABLE 9–1   A Typical Two-Way Grid Used as Norm-Referenced Test Specifications

| | NUMBER OF TEST ITEMS FOR EACH COGNITIVE LEVEL | | | | |
	Knowledge	Comprehension	Application	Analysis	Total
Topic 1	3	2	2	4	11
Topic 2	4	3	3	2	12
Topic 3	3	5	5		13
Topic 4	2	3		0	5
Topic 5	3	2	2	2	9
Total	15	15	12	8	50

specifications so that we really have three-way or four-way grid. To illustrate, suppose you were developing a norm-referenced achievement test in which you not only were attentive to content and behavior (as in the previous two examples), but also wanted to make sure that the test items were equally balanced on dimensions such as sex (of those individuals described in the items) or item type (multiple-choice or true-false). These features would be added as third or fourth dimensions to a grid that would, of course, be more difficult to depict in a simple table. You could use parentheses, brackets, or some other scheme to represent the additional dimensions.

TABLE 9–2   A Two-Way Grid With Detailed Content Categories and Only Two Levels of Cognitive Behavior

| | ITEMS PER COGNITIVE LEVEL | | |
CONTENT OF ITEMS	Recall	Beyond Recall	Total
Topic A	12	14	26
Subtopic A_1	4	5	(9)
Subtopic A_2	5	3	(8)
Subtopic A_3	3	6	(9)
Topic B	10	11	21
Subtopic B_1	5	6	(11)
Subtopic B_2	5	5	(10)
Topic C	14	11	25
Subtopic C_1	7	3	(10)
Subtopic C_2	7	8	(15)
Subtopic C_{2a}	3	4	(7)
Subtopic C_{2b}	4	4	(8)
Topic C	14	14	28
Subtopic D_1	6	7	(13)
Subtopic D_2	8	7	(15)
Total	50	50	100

The key question is *when* should a set of specifications be created for a norm-referenced test, before or after the test is written? The answer, without question, is *before* the test is put together. Two-way grids, as we have seen, can be useful in-process checks of whether there are too few or too many items of a particular kind. However, if the specifications are really going to guide the creation of a test (and if they aren't, then the test might be developed mindlessly), they should be permitted to influence the item-generation process.

A review of the item-grids presented in the technical manuals of many norm-referenced tests, because of the almost incoherent pattern of item allocations found there, suggests that such grids are often after-the-fact appendages which exercise little influence over the production or selection of test items.

Content or Skill Listings

Another technique used in test specifications for norm-referenced measures is to list only the content categories in the test, along with the number of items per category. Perhaps, the objectives (or skills) covered by the test are listed along with the number of test items per objective (or skill). We see such a scheme depicted in Table 9–3 where the 1977–78 *Functional Literacy Test* used by the State of Florida is broken down according to items per skill.

By inspecting a table, such as 9–3, we can see that the test developers apparently set a minimum number of items per skill, namely, four. The reason that certain skills are assessed by five, six, or seven items is not clear, although in some instances these minor anomolies arise merely because of the form of the item itself (such as an item structure which really requires two, rather than one, answer from examinees).

We can also note that the level of skill descriptions in such tables is often insufficient to really tie down the explicit nature of the items themselves. For example, note the many mathematics skills cited in Table 9–3 which read somewhat as follows, "solve problems involving comparison shopping." Well, that leaves a whale of a lot of latitude in what might be in the actual items. The items could include very subtle comparison-shopping problems in which two jars of peanut butter must be contrasted according to weight, cost, and crunchiness. Alternatively, the problems could be so obvious that even a mathematical incompetent could solve them: "If two cans of candied okra are equal in quantity and quality, but Can A costs 50 percent more than Can B, which should you buy?"

However, the specificity level of the content descriptors in test specifications for most norm-referenced tests is such that the item writer is constrained only generally in the creation of items. Moreover, since norm-referenced tests are chiefly intended to permit relative comparisons among

TABLE 9-3 Number of Skills and Items in Florida's 1977–78 Eleventh-Grade Functional Literacy Test

SKILL NO.	BRIEF DESCRIPTION OF FUNCTIONAL LITERACY SKILL	NO. OF ITEMS
	Mathematics	
17	Determine elapsed time between two events.	4
24	Determine equivalent amounts of money.	4
30	Solve problems involving whole numbers.	5
32	Solve problems involving decimal numbers and percents.	4
33	Solve problems involving comparison shopping.	5
34	Solve problems involving a rate of interest.	5
35	Solve purchase problems involving sales tax.	5
36	Solve purchase problems involving discounts.	4
37	Solve problems involving measurement.	4
38	Solve problems involving the area of a rectangle.	4
39	Solve problems involving capacity.	4
40	Solve problems involving weight.	4
41	Find information in graphs and tables.	7
	Mathematics Total	59
	Communication Skills-Reading	
11	Infer main idea of a selection.	6
12	Find specific information in a selection.	5
16	Infer cause or effect of an action.	5
20	Identify facts and opinions.	4
21	Identify an unstated opinion.	5
26	Identify source to obtain information on a topic.	5
28	Use index cross-references to find information.	5
29	Use highway and city maps.	6
	Reading Total	41
	Communication Skills-Writing	
32	Include necessary information in letters.	7
33	Complete a check and its stub.	5
34	Complete common application forms accurately.	5
	Writing Total	17
	Functional Literacy Test Total	117

examinees with respect to rather loosely defined attributes, for instance, "knowledge of algebra," then the level of descriptive rigor employed in the test specifications for most norm-referenced tests may be sufficient.

I believe that developers of norm-referenced tests need to be far more explicit in their test specifications than has historically been the case. Whereas there is no necessity to create elaborate and circumscribing specifications, such as those needed with criterion-referenced tests, the creators of norm-referenced tests have often been too cavalier in their use of test specifications. By moving more *toward* the descriptive stringency associated with criterion-referenced test specifications (but not going all the way), the resulting norm-referenced measures are bound to be improved.

Let's turn now to a consideration of the more constraining specifications we need for criterion-referenced measures. Remember, since the thrust of criterion-referenced testing is to supply a lucid description of the examinee's measured behavior, it is only natural that we will (should) encounter more exacting test specifications with criterion-referenced tests.

TEST SPECIFICATIONS FOR CRITERION-REFERENCED TESTS[2]

In generating a set of criterion-referenced test specifications, the initial step is to get a general idea of what it is that the test is going to measure. Without exception a test will be designed to measure some behavioral capability or tendency on the part of the examinee. For tests of a cognitive and psychomotor sort, we are interested in seeing what the examinee is able to do. For tests in the affective arena, we usually want to see what the examinee's dispositions are. It is only logical, therefore, that the first step in creating a set of test specifications is to isolate, at least in very general terms, the examinee behavior that one wishes to measure.

Level of Generality

Perhaps the most crucial decision to be made concerns the *level of generality* that will be reflected in the behavior being measured. For example, we could try to build a criterion-referenced test that assessed a child's ability to do rather discrete things, such as *spell words,* or rather complex things, such as *write essays.* How big a chunk of behavior will we try to have our test measure?

An argument in favor of tackling tiny segments of examinee behavior is that with such finite kinds of examinee behaviors one can more satisfactorily isolate and describe the key dimensions of the behaviors to be measured. Larger, more complex examinee behaviors are much tougher to define with sufficient specificity.

There are limits, however, in the utility of numerous criterion-referenced tests. People can tolerate only so much information. If we generate many tests, each measuring a miniscule examinee behavior, there is little likelihood that anyone is going to pay much attention to the results. There'll be too much data to process. Besides, if our tests were all built to tap small chunks of behavior, the amount of examinee testing time required would be enormous.

It is, therefore, more sensible to adopt a *limited-focus* measurement

[2]The following treatment of criterion-referenced test specifications in an updated adaptation of exposition of that topic as found in W. James Popham, *Criterion-Referenced Measurement* (Englewood Cliffs, N.J.: Prentice-Hall, Inc., 1978), pp. 115–135.

strategy in which we attempt to isolate a small number of high-import behaviors to be measured, even though such behaviors turn out to be quite complex. This means we must think of truly significant examinee behaviors that subsume more elementary behaviors. As we shall see, whether or not we adopt a limited-focus strategy has considerable implications for the degree of detail that we build into our test specifications, hence the accuracy with which we describe examinee performance.

If we must work with many tests, our specifications will have to be sparse, because otherwise those using the tests would not have the patience to wade through them. However, if we isolate only a small number of behaviors to measure, our specifications may become more detailed, since test users can attend more conscientiously to a smaller number of assessment targets.

There are situations, of course, in which one would strive to measure less complicated kinds of examinee behaviors. If we were trying to develop diagnostic tests that allowed us to pinpoint the *en-route* skills a learner had mastered or failed to master, then clearly we would have to devise tests that measure smaller chunks of behavior.

Having considered the level-of-generality question, a developer of criterion-referenced tests should spend a good deal of time trying to get a fix on the appropriate kinds of examinee behaviors to assess. Moving prematurely to closure here represents a major error since the amount of specifying that must be done (in order to create a good set of criterion-referenced test specifications) should never be directed toward the delimitation of indefensible behaviors.

Alternative Assessment Schemes

Having determined the level of generality to be sought, the next step in creating a set of test specifications involves the actual selection of the behavior to be measured. This is a really difficult task.

For almost any generally described kind of human attribute—for instance, a certain type of intellectual skill—we can conjure up a number of legitimate ways to assess its attainment. For example, if we are attempting to measure a student's ability to subtract, there are numerous approaches we could employ to find out whether the youngster can display subtraction skills. For instance, we might present the student with routine subtraction problems, such as $30 - 8 = ?$, or perhaps in equation form, such as $26 - 8 = X$, or possibly in a story problem form such as, "Sue had 34 worms and gave 14 away. How many worms does she have left?" There are many more options, of course, even with this rather simple task. When the behavior to be measured becomes more complex, such as when we try to measure an individual's problem-solving ability, then the alternatives become truly myriad.

The test specifier should try to think of all the reasonable contenders—that is, measurement approaches—that might be employed to assess the attribute under consideration. Each of these approaches should be analyzed with respect to whether it (1) truly measures the attribute to be assessed and (2) measures that attribute better than the other, alternative measuring tactics.

Having surveyed several alternative measurement tactics, it may be appealing to try to build a test that draws items from each of these alternatives and thereby yields a more representative assessment of the attribute being measured. However, the defect in that approach is that unless we want an interminably long test, we will only be able to include an item, or at most a few items, reflecting the alternative measurement tactics. Only a few items per measured behavior fail to provide us with a reliable estimate for that behavior. What we end up with is a miscellaneous hodgepodge of almost impossible-to-interpret test results, rather than a meaningful representation of the behavior we're trying to measure. No, even though it may seem a bit risky, we have to select a *single* alternative.

Generalizability as a selection factor.

Generalizability as a selection factor.   It is a significant decision, of course, to constitute a criterion-referenced test by including only items congruent with *one* type of measured behavior, as opposed to including items representing diverse indicators of the attribute being measured. If we choose the latter course of action, we end up with a potentially more representative, but less satisfactorily described, set of results. If we choose the former, our results are more readily interpretable. Moreover, if we can only select the *one* form of measured behavior that is the most generalizable, then we get the best of both worlds—that is, an adequate reflection of the attribute being assessed plus an understandable set of test results.

This problem has been depicted in Figure 9–1, where four different measurement alternatives, each designed to assess the same attribute, are presented. Notice that each of the four alternatives overlaps the others to some extent, but that alternative four takes in the largest components of the other three. If students could master the form of behavior being tapped by alternative four, they would be more apt to master the forms of behavior being measured in the other three approaches. In such an instance alternative four should be selected. Ideally, of course, we'd prefer an even larger overlap so that alternative four literally blanketed the other options.

It is possible to employ empirically based procedures in order to select among contending measurement alternatives. To do so we would be re-

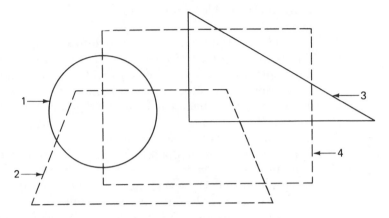

FIGURE 9-1 Alternative measurement tactics designed to measure the same attributes.

quired to create full-blown test specifications for each of the possible measurement alternatives, develop item pools based on each set of specifications, then actually try out these pools of items with suitable examinees. If we could represent an ideal set of data for selecting one of several competing measurement alternatives for a particular criterion-referenced test, it would turn out something like the fictitious data represented in Table 9-4 in which the percentage of students mastering each of five different measuring tactics is presented. As you examine the table, imagine that a large group of examinees has completed five different sets of test items, each representing a different approach to measuring the same general attribute. First those examinees who master a particular alternative are identified. (We could set any level of mastery we desired, but since this is a fictitious example, and we can thus afford to set high standards, let's say the mastery is reflected only by a perfect performance.) Now notice that the examinees mastering alternatives two and four don't do all that well on the other options. Indeed, they do rather badly. Those mastering alternatives one and five fare better on the other forms of the behavior. However, the hands-down winner is alternative three, in which we see that those who display mastery of this form of measurement display, almost as consistently, mastery of the other contending behaviors. In this instance, obviously, the test specifier would want to select alternative three.

When selecting the form of behavior to be measured, we usually don't go to the trouble of actually creating sets of alternative test items and sending hoards of examinees through them. For practicality's sake, test specifiers usually have to make their best guess as to the generalizability of competing measurement tactics. Perhaps, in some happy future, we'll have time enough, money enough, and examinees enough (we'd need loads) to

TABLE 9-4   Fictitious Percentages of Examinees' Mastery of Five
             Measurement Alternatives

EXAMINEES MASTERING TEST	PERCENTAGE WHO ALSO MASTERED TEST				
	1	2	3	4	5
1		65	52	74	61
2	38		27	26	49
3	89	98		100	94
4	48	26	38		48
5	75	69	58	81	

corroborate empirically the analytically derived estimates. But for now, it seems that test-specification folks are going to have to engage in some pretty shrewd estimating of a potential measurement tactic's generalizability.

Teachability as a selection factor.   When I first became serious about criterion-referenced measurement, in the late sixties, I spent a good many hours thinking about the problem of how one should go about isolating the attribute to be assessed. After a fair amount of stumbling, I finally concluded that *generalizability* was the single, most important factor to use in selecting criterion-referenced test strategy from the many options typically available. If you could select the assessment option which, if mastered, would reflect examinee mastery of alternative assessment schemes, you definitely had made the proper choice.

However, in the past few years I have come across a second factor of almost equal import. This second condition in the selection of *most,* not all, criterion-referenced tests is the *teachability* of the designated behavior. As we shall see in subsequent paragraphs, it is possible to carve out a set of specifications in various ways. Some of these ways will lend themselves more directly to effective instructional design than others.

For any criterion-referenced tests that are to be used in connection with instructional enterprises, it is imperative to select the assessment strategy and fashion the specifications in such a way that effective instructional design can be based on those specifications. Some assessment approaches, though they might be generalizable, would not describe learner behavior that was particularly amenable to instruction. Other assessment approaches would. In selecting an assessment strategy with a built-in likelihood that it can be taught, care must be exercised not to distort the thing you're trying to measure. If, for example, you want to tap a student's ability to write essays, then even though we could devise a readily teachable multiple-choice test that dealt with initial capitalization and terminal punctuation (sounds like a disease), the readily teachable test would not reflect with fidelity what we were really trying to measure, that is, the ability to whomp up a fine essay.

We treat the topic of teachability more thoroughly in Chapter 17. At this point it will suffice to recognize that two factors are often involved in the selection of an assessment strategy for criterion-referenced tests. The first of these is the generalizability of the behavior being measured across other assessment strategies that might be chosen. The second factor, to be employed in settings where criterion-referenced tests are being used in an instructional context, is the amenability to instruction of the assessment strategy chosen.

All right, let's assume that after setting out the measurement alternatives and engaging in a fair amount of comparative shopping among them, a decision has been made. A particular assessment tactic has been isolated. Incidentally, the use of collegial review at this point in the test-specification enterprise is particularly helpful in weighing the respective merits of different testing tactics. The next thing we have to do is actually generate the test specifications.

Ingredients of Criterion-Referenced Test Specifications

There are many ways in which one could specify the critical facets of a set of test specifications. However, the scheme to be presented here has the advantage of having been used under supervision for a substantial amount of time in the criterion-referenced test-development activities of the Instructional Objectives Exchange. Initial attempts to employ precursors of this specification scheme have led to a series of modifications that are incorporated in the currently recommended approach.

Before going into detail regarding each of the five test specification components, a brief description of each may prove useful:

1. *General description:* A brief depiction, in general terms, of the behavior being assessed by the test.
2. *Sample item:* An illustrative item that reflects the test-item attributes to be delimited in the following two components.
3. *Stimulus attributes:* A series of statements that attempt to delimit the class of stimulus material that will be encountered by the examinee.
4. *Response attributes:* A series of statements that attempt either to (a) delimit the classes of response options from which the student makes *selected responses* or (b) explicate the standards by which an examinee's *constructed responses* will be judged.
5. *Specification supplement:* In certain cases it may be necessary to add an appendix or supplement to the preceding four components. This supplement typically provides a more detailed listing or explanation of eligible content.

Now, we consider each of these test specification components in greater detail.

General description. The first ingredient in a set of criterion-referenced test specifications should be a one- or two-sentence general description of what it is that the test measures. The purpose of the general description is to provide a succinct overview of the set of behaviors to be described more fully later in the specifications.

In some criterion-referenced test specifications this component is referred to as an "objective." Yet, because many criterion-referenced tests will be used as preinstruction status-determiners, not necessarily as measures of instructional intentions, the phrase "general description" appears to be more defensible.

Here is an example of a general description taken from a criterion-referenced test dealing with the scientific method.

> *General description.* When given brief, previously unseen fictitious accounts of the research activities of natural and physical scientists, students will answer questions (keyed to the accounts) calling for the identification of particular phases of the scientific method being illustrated.

Because of the general description's brevity, users of a criterion-referenced test can quickly discern whether or not the test it represents is potentially the kind of test they wish to employ. If so, of course, they will have to read further regarding the complete details of the test, particularly as specified in the stimulus-attributes and response-attributes sections.

Recalling an earlier step in the test-specification process, that is, the choice among competing ways of measuring a given attribute, we can typically make these comparative judgments on the basis of the kinds of statements employed in a general description. In considering possible measurement tactics, it is usually necessary to describe such alternatives at least at the level of detail seen in the one- or two-sentence general description.

It should be apparent that a test specifier would have to possess the gift of prophecy in order to anticipate early in the game what a complete set of test specifications, particularly the stimulus-attributes and response-attributes sections, will look like. Accordingly, the general description statement is often phrased tentatively when one commences a set of test specifications. Indeed, it usually ends up looking quite different as a consequence of the more detailed analysis that occurs when the remaining components of the test specification are explicated.

Sometimes, particularly when the test is designed to measure an examinee behavior supposedly linked to an affective attribute, for example, a person's attitude toward a particular institution or group of people, it is not apparent what affective variable the examinee's behavior is supposed to be reflecting. In such instances, it is often wise to build a brief explanatory or rationale statement into the general description in order to clarify the significance of the behavior being assessed.

Sample item.   The second component in a test specification should be a sample item, complete with directions to the student, which might be used in the test itself. Such illustrative items are usually easy to supply since the test frequently consists of a number of relatively short items. Therefore, it is a simple matter to select one of these items for illustrative purposes. Sometimes, when the test is more complicated and the items more lengthy, it becomes difficult to supply a sample item. Nevertheless, an illustrative item should always be provided as the second component of each set of test specifications.

There are two reasons for providing a sample item. First, some people using the specifications, particularly busy individuals, may find their need for test description satisfied with the general-description statement and the illustrative item alone. Such people, if forced to read the entire specifications, might avoid test specification completely. However, they can be abetted by the communication, albeit incomplete, provided by the specifications' general description plus a sample item.

The second purpose of the sample item is to provide format cues for those who must generate the items for the test. Of course, it often makes little difference what the format of a given type of test is. For instance, is it really important whether a true-false item presents the examinee with T-F or F-T options? Undoubtedly not. Yet, there are instances when format variations do seem to be important. In such cases an illustrative item can go a long way toward setting forth the preferred form in which items are to be constructed.

Stimulus attributes.   Examinees, in any test, will be presented with some sorts of stimuli which, in general, are designed to yield a response. In the third component of criterion-referenced test specifications, the attributes of this stimulus material are set forth. It is at this point that the test specifier may yearn for the less-taxing intellectual challenges of advanced forms of the Graduate Record Examination. Here is where work gets unbelievably cerebral.

In the stimulus-attributes section of the test specifications we must set down all the really influential factors that constrain the composition of a set of test items. This means that we must first think through exactly what those factors are and how they can be most accurately and succinctly described. We have to decide how to cope with content considerations. Just how should a range of eligible content be most effectively circumscribed?

Sloppy thinking here by the test specifier will yield a meaningless set of specifications. Anything less than the most rigorous standards of intellectual scrutiny will result in specifications that are imprecise or, worse, misleading.

Are there any general rules that test specifiers should always adhere to, regardless of the nature of the attribute being measured by the test? Well, to be completely definitive—yes and no. The general rule is that the test specifier has to spell out all of the critical or controlling dimensions that will allow someone to create a set of test items that will, without exception, be viewed as congruent with the constraints set forth in the specifications. Yet, because of the vast range of criterion-referenced tests that might be created, it is impossible to set forth in advance what those controlling dimensions might be.

We can take the matter of *content* as an example of this difficulty. In some tests the role of content will be rather minimal. For example, if we were creating a test to assess children's prowess in performing particular sorts of psychomotor skills, content considerations might be totally absent. In certain mathematics and science tests we might find it rather easy to set out the class of content that should be used in test items. In other fields— for example, history or literature—we might be hard pressed to define the nature of the content we wished our tests to treat. Hence, although content characteristics will usually be important in a set of test specifications, it is difficult to provide a universally applicable scheme for isolating them.

One technique for treating content is to spell out the rules (algorithms) that are to be used in generating or delimiting the content. For instance, in an English test "only sonnets may be employed that possess the following characteristics: (then the requisite qualities of an eligible sonnet could be cited)." Another scheme for isolating content is to actually cite all the eligible content that might be included. For example, if a criterion-referenced spelling test is to deal with 500 hard-to-spell words, then all 500 such words would undoubtedly have to be listed in the test specifications, typically as a supplement. If a geometry test is going to deal with a finite set of geometric shapes, then we might actually list all of the eligible shapes. As always, the test specifier has to be clear and concise.

The ideal way of dealing with content is to isolate and describe the defining attributes of all eligible content that might be employed in the test. If the test specifier believes this to be an impossible task, a better-than-nothing alternative would be to include a few examples of acceptable *and* unacceptable sorts of content. Indeed, as a general rule in the creating of test specifications, when it is impossible to explicate any ingredients with satisfactory rigor (perhaps because we just can't clarify their constituent elements), it is often helpful to provide actual exemplars and nonexemplars.

Having asserted that there are no certain rules that will apply across the board in generating the stimulus attributes of a set of test specifications, how does a test specifier go about the task of isolating significant stimulus attributes? The first thing to recognize is that the stimulus-attributes section of the specifications usually accounts for most of the important variability in a criterion-referenced test. The stimulus-attributes section of the specifications sets out the limits about what the examinee will encounter before making a response on a test. It is here that the test specifier will lay out the major rules for generating the key kinds of items which constitute the test. Therefore, it is the most critical component of most criterion-referenced test specifications.

For example, suppose we were creating a series of criterion-referenced tests dealing with the U.S. government and wished to construct test specifications defining a competency having to do with the functioning of the three branches of government—that is, the executive, the legislative, and the judicial. In the stimulus-attributes section of the specifications we would have to set forth any genuinely important rules to be followed by item writers in creating the test items that would reflect the kind of competency we are trying to assess. What kinds of discriminations does the examinee have to be able to make in order to display mastery of the test's competency? Will there only be discriminations involving the three main branches of government? If so, what sorts of situations would lead to a choice of the executive branch, rather than the legislative or judicial? What kinds of rules can be generated that reflect these important factors so that a test developer (or someone interpreting an exam) can make sense of the factors that are involved in these discriminations?

In attempting to isolate the genuinely pivotal dimensions of test items to include in a set of specifications, it often helps to ask, "What are the *absolutely indispensable elements* that item writers must consider in producing test items?" Such absolutely indispensable elements of test items can often be contrasted with less critical, "nice-to-take-account-of" dimensions. Characteristically, we should rank our delimiting statements from imperative to desirable and decide on the number of such statements largely on the basis of each statement's significance but bounded by the permissible length of the specifications.

In deciding what rules to include in a test specification, it is particularly helpful to try to prepare several *trial test items,* then analyze what kinds of choice points were encountered as the items were being prepared. Such analyses often prove useful in revealing the significant dimensions of the test items that must be delimited in the specifications. While it is sometimes possible to isolate all the important stimulus attributes of a set of test items deductively, in the absence of such trial test items, the inductive strategy has much to commend it.

The form of the statements to be incorporated in the stimulus-attributes section, as well as the response-attributes section, is worthy of consideration. Quite often the specifier will isolate a particular dimension of the test items that could be treated with several separate, though related, statements. For example, we might be able to cite the following limitations for a set of sentences to be included in a test dealing with English usage: (1) Only simple or compound sentences should be used. (2) No sentence should exceed 25 words in length. (3) No more than three internal punctuation marks will be permitted. For economy's sake it is sometimes preferable to combine such separate statements into a single, clause-laden sentence, such as the following: (1) Only simple or compound sentences, 25 words or less in length, and containing no more than three internal punctuation marks will be used. This approach typically results in a less lengthy, more readily used set of specifications. To list the three factors separately would sometimes produce an excessively lengthy set of statements, so lengthy as to discourage one from employing the set of specifications.

Response attributes. The final component of a set of specifications focuses on the examinee's response to the elements generated according to the stimulus-attributes section. Only two types of responses on the part of the examinee exist. The examinee can either *select* from response options presented in the test, for example, as in true-false or multiple-choice questions, or the examinee can *construct* a response, for example, as in essay, short-answer, or oral presentations. Thus, only *selected responses* or *constructed responses* will be encountered, and in the response-attributes section of the specifications the rules regarding these two response possibilities will be treated.

If the test involves a selected response, rules must be provided for determining, not only the nature of the correct response, but also the nature of the wrong-answer options. For instance, in a multiple-choice test it would be imperative to first state the guidelines for creating the correct answer. Next, the test specifier must spell out the various classes of wrong-answer options that might constitute any item's distractors. It is not appropriate merely to indicate that such distractors will be "incorrect." Instead the precise nature of these wrong answers must be carefully explicated. Characteristically, consideration of the kinds of wrong answers used in trial test items will provide clues regarding the sorts of distractor classes to isolate. Having spelled out such right- and wrong-answer options in the specifications, the resulting test items must cleave faithfully to these rules. *Only* such distractors can be used. There can be no last minute addition of selected-response options that are "almost correct" but fail to satisfy the stipulations set forth in the specifications.

One helpful way of identifying what kinds of wrong-answer options to include in a set of test items for cognitive tests is to think through the various ways that an examinee usually "goes wrong." The typical sources of confusion or the factors interfering with the student's understanding of the concept often show the classes of eligible wrong answers that should be incorporated in the specifications.

As we see in Chaper 17, it is most helpful for instructional designers to have the wrong-answer options spelled out with clarity. Frequently, for certain types of cognitive skills, by focusing on the most likely ways that students can make mistakes, teachers can eliminate those proclivities to err.

Although the difficulties of delineating the response-possibilities section for selected-response sorts of tests are considerable, they become almost trivial when a test specifier attempts to spell out the response-attributes section of specifications for tests involving constructed responses. Here the task is to explain the criteria that permit reliable judgment of the adequacy of examinees' constructed responses. Ideally, these criteria would be so well formulated that to determine the acceptability of any constructed response would be child's play. Realistically, however, criteria possessing such precision can rarely be created. The test specifier will have to think as lucidly as possible about such criteria, and even then, there may be more slack in this section of the specifications than we would like. It is again useful to create some *trial responses* and much as we did with trial test items, attempt to learn more about possible judgmental criteria by actually trying to appraise the acceptability of examinee responses. Precisely what is it that inclines us to say one response is acceptable and another response unacceptable? What makes them different? When we get at these distinctions, we are beginning to isolate the crucial criteria whereby response acceptability may be judged.

If the test specifier has tussled with this problem and produced a response-attributes section that still leaves some clarity to be desired, it sometimes helps to add an actual example or two of acceptable, as well as unacceptable, responses.

In coping with constructed responses, it is particularly important to avoid the inclusion of hedging phrases, such as, "responses must be appropriate to the context of the stimulus" or "answers should be plausible outgrowths of the materials provided." Obviously, the test specifier is dodging the issue by using words such as *appropriate* and *plausible*. If those kinds of terms are employed, it is imperative to clarify in more detail precisely what it is that constitutes plausibility or appropriateness—that is, what it is that renders one response appropriate and another inappropriate. If the test specifier can't resolve the question of how to identify acceptability of responses without resorting to hedging tactics, then it is preferable not to have a test dealing with that topic or skill. A false illusion of clarity will be created when, in fact, none exists. We can't really do much with an examinee's constructed-response test performance when we really don't know rather well what constitutes an acceptable or unacceptable performance.

Specification Supplement

There are instances in which our specifications deal with sets of content— for example, a series of rules or a list of important historical figures. If we included this content information in either the stimulus-attributes or response-attributes section, we would have created a set of specifications too voluminous for the typical reader. Beyond that, by being obliged to wade through such lengthy content citations, a reader of the specifications might actually be distracted from some of the important noncontent specifications. In such cases it is often convenient to include a supplement at the close of the specifications that sets forth such information. Such a supplement is obviously optional.

An example of criterion-referenced test specifications follows. It presents an illustrative set of specifications for a criterion-referenced test in reading.

AN ILLUSTRATIVE SET OF CRITERION-REFERENCED TEST SPECIFICATIONS FOR A HIGH SCHOOL LEVEL COMPETENCY TEST IN READING[3]

Determining Main Ideas

General Description

The student will be presented with a factual selection such as a newspaper or magazine article or a passage from a consumer guide or general-interest book. After reading that selection, the student will determine which one of four choices contains the best statement of the main idea of the selection. This statement will be entirely accurate as well as the most comprehensive of the choices given.

Sample Item

Direction: Read the selections in the boxes below. Answer the questions about their main ideas.

The Cold Facts

Had you lived in ancient Rome you might have relieved the symptoms of a common cold by sipping a broth made from soaking an onion in warm water. In Colonial America you might have relied on an herbal

---

[3]Test specifications for the *IOX Basic Skill Test in Reading* (Los Angeles: Instructional Objectives Exchange, 1978, with permission).

concoction made from sage, buckthorn, goldenseal, or bloodroot plants. In Grandma's time, lemon and honey was a favorite cold remedy, or in extreme cases, a hot toddy laced with rum.

Today, if you don't have an old reliable remedy to fall back on, you might take one of thousands of drug preparations available without prescription. Some contain ingredients much like the folk medicines of the past; others are made with complex chemical creations. Old or new, simple or complex, many of these products will relieve some cold symptoms, such as a stopped up nose or a hacking cough. But not a single one of them will prevent, cure, or even shorten the course of the common cold.

---

1. Which one of the following is the best statement of the main idea of the article you just read?
   a. Old-fashioned herbal remedies are more effective than modern medicines.
   b. There are many kinds of relief, but no real cures, for the common cold.
   c. Some of today's cold preparations contain ingredients much like those found in folk remedies of the past.
   d. Americans spend millions of dollars a year on cold remedies.

Stimulus Attributes

1. Each item will consist of a reading selection followed by the question, "Which one of the following is the best statement of the main idea of the (article/selection) you just read?" Eligible reading selections include adaptations of passages from factual texts such as general interest books and consumer guides and pamphlets. Care should be taken to pick selections of particular interest to young adults and to avoid selections which may in the near future appear dated. Each reading selection will be titled, will be at least one paragraph long, and will contain from 125–250 words. Not more than 1,000 words of reading material can be tested in any set of five items. At least two of the five items in any set of five items must contain reading selections that are more than one paragraph long.

2. If necessary, the following modifications may be made to a selection used for testing:
   a. A title may be added if the selection does not have one, or if the selection represents a section of a longer piece whose title would not be applicable to the excerpt. If a title is added, it should be composed of a brief, interest-getting and/or summarizing group of words.
   b. A selection may be shortened, but only if the segment which is to be used for testing makes sense and stands as a complete unit of thought without the parts which have been omitted. If necessary, minor editing can be done to a reading selection which represents a shortening of a longer piece, but this editing should be for the purposes of clarity and continuity only, and not for the purposes of increasing or decreasing the difficulty level, or changing the content, of the text.

3. Reading selections used for testing should not exceed a 9th grade reading level, as judged by the Fry readability formula.

Response Attributes

1. A set of four single-sentence response alternatives will follow each reading selection and its accompanying question. All of these statements must plausibly relate to the content of the reading selection, either by reiterating or paraphrasing portions of that selection, or by building upon a word or idea contained in the selection.
2. The three incorrect response alternatives will each be based upon a lack of one of the two characteristics needed by a correct main idea statement: *accuracy* and *appropriate scope*. A correct main idea statement must be accurate in that everything it states can be verified in the text it describes. It must have appropriate scope in that it encompasses all of the most important points discussed in the text that it describes.
3. A distractor exemplifies a *lack of accuracy* when it does any one or more of three things:
   a. Makes a statement contradicted by information in the text.
   b. Makes a statement unsupported by information in the text. (Such a statement would be capable of verification or contradiction if the appropriate information were available.)
   c. Makes a statement incapable of verification or contradiction; that is, a statement of opinion. (Such statements include value judgments on the importance or worth of anything mentioned in the text.)
4. A distractor exemplifies a *lack of appropriate scope* when it does one of two things:
   a. Makes a statement that is too narrow in its scope. That is, the statement does not account for all of the important details contained in the text.
   b. Makes a statement that is too broad in its scope. That is, the statement is more general than it needs to be in order to account for all of the important details contained in the text.
5. The important points which must be included in a main idea statement are those details which are emphasized in the text by structural, semantical, and rhetorical means such as placement in a position of emphasis, repetition, synonymous rephrasing, and elaboration. Whether any given main idea statement contains all of the important points that it should is always debatable rather than indisputable. The nature of the question asked on this test; i.e., select the *best* main idea statement from among those given, attempt to account for this quality of relative rather than absolute correctness.
6. The distractors for any one item must include at least one statement that lacks accuracy and one statement that lacks appropriate scope. On a given test, between 10 and 20 percent of the distractors should be sentences taken directly from the text.
7. The correct answer for an item will be that statement which is both entirely accurate and of the most appropriate scope in relation to the

other statements given. If a sentence in the text itself qualifies as the best main idea statement which can be formulated about the selection, that sentence may be reiterated as a response option. No more than 20 percent of the items on a given test may have as their correct answer a main idea statement which is a direct restatement of a sentence in the text.

AN ILLUSTRATIVE SET OF CRITERION-REFERENCED TEST SPECIFICATIONS FOR A HIGH SCHOOL LEVEL COMPETENCY TEST IN WRITING[4]

Expressing Ideas In Writing

General Description

Students will be given an issue with which they are likely to be familiar, then asked to write a paragraph in which they (1) take a position on either side of the issue and (2) support the position taken. The paragraph will be judged either (a) according to the extent to which the writing sample satisfies separate criteria dealing with organization and mechanics or (b) holistically, that is, through an overall appraisal of the writing sample's acceptability.

Sample Item

Directions: In this part of the test you will be writing an original paragraph on an assigned topic. You will be given scratch paper on which to compose a first draft of your paragraph, and lined paper on which to write the final version of your paragraph.

Four different topics appear below. You will be told which one you are to write about. For each topic, background information on a familiar issue is provided along with a specific writing assignment. You are to write a paragraph in which you choose one side of the issue and then give reasons to support your choice.

When you write your paragraph, be sure to:

1. Use a topic sentence to state your choice of a side on the assigned issue.
2. Have all the sentences in your paragraph support your topic sentence.
3. Use correct grammar, spelling, and punctuation.
4. Pay special attention to clear handwriting.

Background: Some people believe that vending machines selling candy should be allowed at elementary schools. Other people believe there should be no candy machines permitted at elementary schools. *Assignment:* Write a paragraph in which you explain why you are in favor of, or opposed to, permitting candy machines at elementary schools. Be sure to support the side of the issue you have chosen.

[4]Ibid (with permission).

Stimulus Attributes

1. The topic presented to the students must be one with which almost all high school students would be familiar, e.g., a topic dealing with a situation commonly encountered in daily living.
2. The topic must embody an issue which permits the students to take at least two sides, e.g., in favor of or opposed to the issue described. Eligible topics would be, for example:
   a. Prohibiting young people's attendance at a movie because they have not reached a particular age.
   b. Teachers' use of physical punishment in public schools.
   c. Allowing girls and boys to participate in the same school sports programs (such as football).
   d. Having parents restrict the number of hours each day that their children can view television.
3. Two sentences will provide a brief background regarding the issue with both the pro and con positions expressed. This section will be labeled: *Background.*
4. The *Background* will be followed by the Assignment which states: "Write a paragraph in which you explain why you are in favor of, or opposed to (*Insert a brief description of one side of the issue*). Be sure to support the side of the issue you have chosen."

Grading Procedures

1. Two judgment strategies can be used for grading students' writing samples. The first is a *separate* criteria approach, wherein the paragraphs are given points according to their satisfaction of distinctive criteria (such as those to be set forth below). The second is a holistic approach, wherein a *single* overall assessment is made of each paragraph's acceptability. While it is true that even in the holistic approach one employs judgmental criteria, such as the extent to which a paragraph displays acceptable organization, these criteria are applied in a composite sense rather than in a criterion-by-criterion manner.
2. Irrespective of which judgmental procedure is selected, it is imperative that those individuals who will be judging the paragraphs engage in a number of training/clarification sessions prior to their actual judging of the paragraphs. Judges should read a random selection of paragraphs, render their judgments independently, then share these judgments and discuss any differences with other judges. Disagreements regarding the meanings of certain criteria should be resolved. This process should be continued until a high degree of inter-judge agreement is achieved.
3. During the actual scoring of the paragraphs, it is desirable to have each paragraph judged independently by two judges, with a third judge being called on to resolve disagreements.
4. The Basic Skill *Test Manual* contains more detailed instructions on how to organize the scoring of student writing samples.

Criteria

1. The following criteria are offered as potentially useful in judging students' paragraphs. Additions or deletions to these criteria can be made by the group judging the paragraphs. Clearly, the integrity of each criterion would have to be explicated by the judges reading the paragraphs. For example, the criterion dealing with appropriate punctuation might be interpreted to refer only to end-of-sentence punctuation, rather than to internal punctuation.

2. The criteria are organized under the two general headings of organization and mechanics.

Organization

(1) The student has written about the assigned topic. (A minimum number of sentences would need to be established.)

(2) The paragraph includes a topic sentence which embodies a position regarding the assigned topic.

(3) All other sentences in the paragraph support the topic sentence.

Mechanics

(1) The paragraph is written legibly. (This is usually considered a prerequisite to the application of other criteria.)

(2) Complete sentences are used, rather than fragments or run-on sentences. (How many, if any, fragments or run-ons are permitted would need to be established.)

(3) Words are spelled correctly. (The ratio of misspelled to correctly spelled words to be considered acceptable would need to be established.)

(4) Punctuation is appropriate. (The punctuation to be considered and the number of permissible errors would need to be established.)

(5) Grammar is acceptable. (The grammatical conventions to be judged and the ratio of errors to total words or sentences to be allowed would have to be established.)

3. In applying criteria according to the separate criteria approach a predetermined number of points per criterion would be given to the paragraph. For example, a 1-2-3-4-5 scale or a 1-2-3 scale might be used to indicate the extent to which the paragraph displayed acceptable spelling, punctuation, etc. Points would be added to yield a total score for the paragraph.

4. Judges might incorporate such criteria in a holistic grading approach, but they would be applied in an overall, rather than separate fashion. It might be possible, of course, to employ two sets of criteria, one for organization and one for mechanics, thus yielding two distinct scores for each paragraph.

When we attempt to assess human behavior, we are obviously tackling one of the more formidable challenges in the neighborhood. A criterion-referenced test purports to describe an examinee's status with respect to a well-explicated class of behaviors. It would seem to follow, therefore, that if the test specifier produces a satisfactory set of delimiting statements, we would be able to describe with complete clarity how someone performed regarding the kinds of test items circumscribed by the specifications. Yet, there are at least two limitations that restrict us from attaining the ultimate degree of descriptive rigor we might wish for in our specifications.

In the first place, our understanding of the attribute being measured is often less than perfect. This is certainly apparent in the case of elusive attributes, such as those in the affective realm. It is also the case with a good many higher-level cognitive behaviors, where the nuances of acceptable versus unacceptable examinee performance almost defy delimitation. For example, it is probably possible to isolate and describe the criteria needed to judge a student's essay if all we are trying to do is discern whether it contains flagrant stylistic errors. However, if our attempt is to assess a student's ability to create genuinely high-quality prose, the possibility of reducing our scoring format to a reliable and all-inclusive scheme quickly evaporates. Such uncharted terrains will typically prevent the test specifier from achieving the desired degree of precision.

A second factor that prevents us from removing all sources of ambiguity in our test specifications, even when dealing with examinee behaviors we understand better, is the rather pedestrian consideration of a person's willingness to read through and assimilate extensive sets of delimiting statements. Recalling our earlier discussion of attributes in the stimulus and response sections of the test specifications, we tried to sort out those that were absolutely imperative from those that were relevant but not crucial. If we worked to remove *all* ambiguity from our specifications, we could literally go on and on in our delimiting statements, moving all the way from pivotal dimensions to the least important aspects of the test items. However, by that time we would have created a tract long enough to rival a master's thesis. No one would have the patience to read the thing.

Thus, for both of these reasons, we have to be realistic regarding the likelihood that a given set of test specifications will eliminate ambiguity as well as we might wish. Figure 9–2 depicts a theoretical continuum of descriptive clarity for educational tests.

At the left of the continuum we can think of educational tests that are totally ambiguous—that is, tests which leave the user completely confused about what it is they measure. At the right of the continuum we can picture

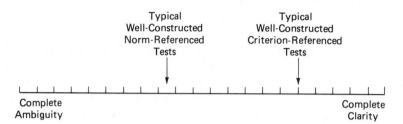

Typical
Well-Constructed
Norm-Referenced
Tests

Typical
Well-Constructed
Criterion-Referenced
Tests

Complete
Ambiguity

Complete
Clarity

FIGURE 9–2 A theoretical continuum of descriptive clarity for educational measurement devices.

a situation, theoretical to be sure, in which there was absolutely no doubt about what a given test performance signifies. Now, although criterion-referenced test specifiers will probably never attain the ultimate unambiguous end of the continuum, they should strive to be as clear as they can reasonably be. As the figure suggests, a well-constructed criterion-referenced test should be far more descriptive than a norm-referenced test, even a well-constructed norm-referenced test.

Of course, the clarity that criterion-referenced tests possess will depend almost exclusively on the quality of the test specifications used to generate the test items and to describe subsequent examinee performance. Unfortunately, perhaps because of the recentness of our work with such specifications or perhaps because of the nature of the task itself, we do not yet possess a refined and tested set of rules to guide those who must create criterion-referenced test specifications. Measurement folks have been thrashing around, trying to get a fix on the kinds of test descriptors that will prove most effective. For example, I previously endorsed the notion of *amplified objectives* which were, as the expression indicates, elaborated statements of an instructional objective. However, I have abandoned that approach (which represents a midlevel in descriptive detail) in favor of the more detailed test specifications, coupled with some sort of more brief descriptive summary of those specifications.

Unlike a sharply honed technology, the job of creating decent criterion-referenced test specifications is still an art form. However, the art form is moving toward the status of an early-stage technology. Hopefully, the remarks in this chapter have isolated some of the issues to be considered as one creates truly laudable sets of criterion-referenced specifications.

TWO FUNCTIONS OF TEST SPECIFICATIONS

There are two principal functions that a set of test specifications can fulfill. The first of these is to communicate to *test users* what it is that the test is measuring. In the field of education, for example, we quickly think of teachers and administrators who must get a fix on what their students' test scores really mean for instructional purposes. Similarly, one thinks of the numerous individuals who must understand the nature of pupils' test performance in order to evaluate the effectiveness of an educational program. For example, the quality of public schooling is of considerable interest to school board members, state and federal legislators, and a host of everyday citizens (as opposed to alternate-day citizens).

Thus, a major purpose of a set of test specifications is to communicate to test users so that those users more accurately comprehend the nature of the behavior being measured. Anyone who is charged with creating a set of test specifications must remember to develop the specifications that do a good job of communicating with those who will have occasion to use the test's results.

The second mission of a set of test specifications is to lay out the details of the behaviors being measured so that *item writers* can generate pools of appropriate items. Such items are those that measure the examinee's status with respect to the behavior defined in the test specifications. In other words, the purpose of the test specifications is to communicate, but this time the communication is aimed at item writers, instead of test users.

Clearly, there are differences in the kinds of specifications one might devise for item writers, as opposed to test users. Sometimes, for example, the item writers will be subject-matter experts who can tolerate a much bigger dose of technical terminology and lengthy detail than can test users. Ideally, we might like to have one set of explicit specifications for item writers and another less detailed set for test users. In that situation there would really be only one set of specifications (the one for item writers) plus an abridged version for the test users. The genuinely defining details of the behavioral domain being measured would be present in the more elaborate set of specifications.

This is not to suggest that such a two-layered specification approach is unwise. Indeed, it may be needed, particularly when the users of a test are not technically knowledgeable. However, for purposes of this discussion, we'll be considering test specifications that can simultaneously serve both audiences—test users and item writers.

Recently, I have been experimenting with the notion that a two-tiered level of test specification may prove most useful, particularly for a criterion-referenced test's descriptive scheme. At one level would be the full-blown set of specifications, replete with all the necessary verbal constraints so that upon reading the specifications, one would have a really good grasp of what the test measured. Having produced such a set of specifications, it would be possible to isolate those elements that have important implications for instructional design, and to place these in a one- to two-page summary. Such a summary could be profitably employed by busy teachers who typically are most interested in the instructionally relevant components of the test specifications. If they wish, the teachers can consult the more elaborate specifications. Time will tell whether this two-tiered descriptive strategy is a viable one.

In review, even though one would think that with so many years of test development behind us, we would have really resolved the more perplexing uncertainties associated with the care and feeding of test specifications, significant uncertainties still abound. Hopefully, the push toward more stringent descriptive schemes that has been spurred by activity involving criterion-referenced tests will yield uncertainty reduction for those employed in test specification for both norm- and criterion-referenced measures.

PRACTICE EXERCISES

Presented below are five vignettes describing a test specifier at work. Read each vignette, then decide whether it is likely that the specifications are being proposed for (a) a *norm-referenced test* or (b) a *criterion-referenced test.*

1. *Measure Treasure Unlimited* (MTU) is a commercial test development agency specializing in customized test creation. A team of MTU test developers have recently prepared a set of test specifications in which (a) the content of the test is listed by category and subcategory and (b) the item types are described as multiple-choice, matching, or true-false. MTU item writers are given these specifications with the admonition that they create items "consonant with the specifications and with MTU's awe-inducing image."

2. A set of specifications for a multiple-choice test has been produced by a state department of education staff. The specifications emphasize detailed delineations of the *stems* of all items, that is, the stimulus material in each item, plus the varieties of eligible response alternatives, that is, the correct answer and the distractors or as the specifications describe them, the "foils."

3. A set of specifications has been created after the initial generation of the test items to use as a "content-coverage check" by the test-development section of a commercial test development company.

4. The test-development staff of Metropolis School District has churned out a set of test specifications in which topics to be covered and levels of cognitive skill required for each item are arranged. At least five items of each type (content and cognitive skill level) are to be prepared.

5. Three classroom teachers collaborate to create a set of test specifications for a geography test. The characteristics of each eligible test item are set forth with considerable detail, approximately two pages of descriptive prose per item-type. There are to be ten items of each type on the test.

ANSWERS TO PRACTICE EXERCISES

1. This seems to be a test-specification strategy more suitable for a norm-referenced test.
2. These specifications sound, because of their considerable detail, most likely to have been created to guide the development of a criterion-referenced test.
3. Although for both norm- and criterion-referenced tests it is preferable to have the specifications prior to item generation, it is almost impossible to build a sensible criterion-referenced test without specifications. Hence, this sounds like the test specifications are apt to be used in an after-the-fact fashion with a norm-referenced test.
4. This sounds like a set of superspecifications for a norm-referenced test.
5. These three geography teachers are clearly bent on banging out a criterion-referenced test, at least if we can infer that from the detailed specifications they have prepared.

DISCUSSION QUESTIONS

1. What do you suspect are the time and cost differentials needed to prepare norm- and criterion-referenced test specifications along the lines described in the chapter?
2. Why have norm-referenced test specifications historically been on the sketchy side?
3. Would it be possible to develop a first-rate criterion-referenced test from typical norm-referenced test specifications? Why?
4. Would it be possible to develop a first-rate norm-referenced test from typical criterion-referenced test specifications? Why?
5. What do you think are the most significant problems that would be encountered when creating a set of norm-referenced test specifications? How about a set of criterion-referenced test specifications?

SUGGESTIONS FOR ADDITIONAL READING

BERK, RONALD A., "A Critical Review of Content Domain Specification/Item Generation Strategies for Criterion-Referenced Tests." Paper presented at Annual Meeting of the American Educational Research Association, San Francisco, April 1979. Berk describes six strategies for specifying content domains used during the sixties and seventies. The effectiveness of each strategy is assessed in relationship to its guidance in the production of test items consonant with the defined domain.

CHASE, CLINTON I., "Teacher-Made Tests: Preliminary Considerations," Chapter 5, *Measurement for Educational Evaluation,* pp. 95–114. Reading, Mass.: Addison-Wesley, 1978. General approaches to the planning of teacher-made tests are described, including the development of a table of specifications.

GRONLUND, NORMAN E., "Planning of the Classroom Test," Chapter 6, *Measurement and Evaluation in Teaching* (3rd ed.), pp. 135–163. New York: Macmillan, 1976. This chapter deals with the planning stage in the preparation of classroom tests. Considerable treatment is given to the preparation of tables of specifications for norm-referenced tests as well as criterion-referenced tests.

MEHRENS, WILLIAM A., and IRVIN J. LEHMANN, "Classroom Testing: The Planning Stage," Chapter 7, *Measurement and Evaluation in Education and Psychology* (2nd ed.), pp. 159–203. New York: Holt, Rinehart & Winston, 1975. Attention is devoted here to the use of objectives as a vehicle for isolating the appropriate content in educational tests. Treatment is also given to tables of specification.

POPHAM, W. JAMES, "Domain Specification Strategies," in *Criterion-Referenced Measurement: State of the Art,* ed. Ronald A. Berk. Baltimore: The Johns Hopkins University Press, 1980. The author describes his personal experiences in constructing test specifications during a decade of work at the Instructional Objectives Exchange. Earlier strategies are described, along with reasons for their rejection. More recent approaches to the specification of test items are described.

TUCKMAN, BRUCE W., "Constructing Objectives," Chapter 2, "Basing Test Items on Objectives," Chapter 3, pp. 20–73. *Measuring Educational Outcomes: Fundamentals of Testing.* San Francisco: Harcourt Brace Jovanovich, Inc., 1975. The role of objectives in planning a test and building items based on those objectives, particularly the manner in which the test items can be based on the objectives, is discussed in Chapters 2 and 3 of this introductory measurement text.

AND FOR THOSE WHO TIRE OF READING

Writing Tests Which Measure Objectives. Distributed by Vimcet Associates, Inc., P.O. Box 24714, Los Angeles, Calif. 90024. In this thirty-minute filmstrip-tape program, Eva Baker describes procedures for employing the *item-form* strategy in the development of criterion-referenced test.

10

There is something intrinsically heartwarming in being able to categorize anything into two tidy categories. For example, objects are either animate or inanimate; it is either day or night; and people are either men or women. Yes, two-way classifications restore our confidence that the world, at least some parts of it, isn't all that complex.

In the field of educational measurement, at least as we've been treating it so far, we seem to be answering most questions with an altogether equivocal, "It depends." Such a wishy-washy response, for instance, is wholly suitable when responding to such queries as: "How many test items per skill should a test contain?" or "How high does a reliability coefficient *really* have to be?" or, finally, "What is the maximum permissible size of a standard error of measurement?"

With so much indeterminacy abounding in measurement land, it may be comforting to encounter one solid, honest-to-goodness, two-way split that does a decent classification job. Fortunately, it's a fundamental one. *All of the test items employed in educational assessment devices call for examinees to make either a selected response or a constructed response.* Examinees make selected responses when they choose among the options on a multiple-choice test or

Selected-response tests

when they opt for true, rather than false, in a true-false test. Examinees make constructed responses when they whip out a series of essay answers or when they respond to short-answer test items.

However, our happy little two-category scheme holds up even when we're dealing with more exotic types of examinee responses. For instance, when students present an extemporaneous speech in a public-speaking class, the speech constitutes a constructed response. When a student creates a ceramic bowl in a pottery class or a pair of bookends in a wood-working class, those are also constructed responses. When student choices of magazines are monitored during a free-reading period (that is, to see which types of magazines the students choose) as an indication of the students' interests in certain types of literature, this is an instance of a selected response.

It is impossible to find examinee responses that don't fit the *selected-versus constructed-response* classification scheme. It is an *exhaustive* classification scheme. However, as any lover of classification schemes might ask, is it also *mutually exclusive?* Well, fortunately, the selected- versus constructed-response category scheme is also mutually exclusive. A given examinee response is always either selected (as from among options) *or* constructed (as in oral, written, or manual production activities).

Now one could, of course, combine both sorts of responses into a single item. The most common instance of this occurs when teachers ask students to first answer a true-false item (a selected response) and then correct any false items by writing out a modified statement which is true (a constructed response). What we have in such items is a two-part test item; one part of which demands a constructed response, and one part of which demands a selected response. The two types of examinee responses are not merged (thus casting doubt on our delightful two-category system); they are only juxtaposed.

In this and the next chapter, we consider the most common kinds of paper-and-pencil test items. Later chapters deal with such procedures as the rating and systematic observation of examinee behaviors. However, since the bulk of educational testing consists of paper-and-pencil assessment instruments, it's only natural to lavish more attention on how to construct winning test items of a paper-and-pencil variety.

Each chapter includes a discussion of the advantages and disadvantages of relying on its particular item-type, that is, selected- or constructed-response items. Each of the two chapters then treats the most common paper-and-pencil test items of its category. In this, the selected-response chapter, we look at *binary-choice items, multiple-choice items,* and *matching items.* In Chapter 11, the constructed-response chapter, we consider *short-answer items* and *essay items.* For each type of item, the dividends and deficits of that item-type are described. In addition, a set of explicit item-writing guidelines is presented for each type of item. Most of the item-writing guidelines are accompanied by illustrative test items which violate or adhere to the guidelines.

The Necessity of Practicality

The alert reader may have noted in the previous paragraph that this and the next chapter are apt to be terribly applied. The reader will learn all sorts of details about how to prepare decent test items. We have, indeed, moved from the somewhat theoretical thrills of Part Two ("Evaluating Educational Tests") to the practical task of constructing educational tests.

However, theory unimplemented is theory in a vacuum. We now need to consider how one takes all those lovely ideas of reliability, validity, and so on, then blends them into first-rate tests. And there's the rub. If you're a test developer, whether a classroom teacher or a staff member in a commercial testing agency, you can have mastered all the psychometric niceties we treated earlier, yet turn out actual tests that are terrible disasters.

If we're going to go to the trouble of gauging a test's validity and reliability, or of developing a set of norm-tables for it, let's be sure that the items themselves are as good as we can make them. That's the purpose of this and the next chapter, namely, to provide the sort of guidance to item writers that will permit them to avoid obvious errors in the construction of test items.

If you're a classroom teacher, for example, and never plan to compute a Spearman-Brown Prophecy Formula as long as you live, you'll still find much of value in this chapter and the one following it. Too many classroom teachers (kindergarten through college) have never considered carefully the rules for writing test items. As a consequence, their tests are often rife with the kinds of errors that you, upon completion of these two chapters, would never think of making.

Any individual who prepares tests that serve as the basis for making meaningful decisions about examinees has a *moral* responsibility to learn how to develop decent test items. In the remaining pages of this and the next chapter you encounter a host of experience-based guidelines which, if followed, allow you to generate test items that while perhaps not perfect, as least avoid the obvious and so readily correctable flaws that permeate most teacher-made tests.

Obstacles to Good Item Writing

Irrespective of whether test developers have decided on a selected- or constructed-response item format, there are still a number of dumb mistakes that can be made as test items are written. Because dumbness, once isolated, is a bit easier to avoid, let's consider five common impediments to good item writing:

1. Unclear direction
2. Ambiguous statements
3. Unintended clues
4. Complicated syntax
5. Difficult vocabulary

Unclear directions.   In the foregoing list of impediments, all are particularly pertinent to test developers. For openers, take the matter of writing directions to the examinee that explain how to go about responding to the items. All too often such directions are added belatedly, just before the test is put together in its final form. After all, the person who has been grinding out all of the test items will surely have a clear idea of how an examinee is supposed to respond. Unfortunately, that kind of knowledge-able item writer sometimes ascribes too much insight to the examinee and thus writes test directions that are far too sketchy. Item writers must assume that test takers are a truly primitive lot; hence, writers should develop the directions with consummate care.

For instance, sometimes the directions for a set of matching items does not make it clear whether the examinee can use a response for more than one "match." If the examinee thinks you can, but the test's developer thought you couldn't, an obvious problem will result, not to mention a lower-than-warranted test score for the examinee. Directions should really be tried out in advance on a few examinees to make certain that these directions accurately communicate the intent of the test developer. Writing test directions for very young children, say first-graders, is particularly difficult for test developers who are unfamiliar with the numerous ways in which little tots can evade our best efforts to constrain them. Ideally, the directions for a set of test items should be written prior to or at least during the preparation of the items. Last-minutery in the creation of test directions is a definite no-no.

Ambiguous statements.   Ambiguous writing is almost always to be avoided, unless one is a politician or member of the diplomatics corps. In test items an ambiguous statement is particularly reprehensible since examinees may, because of that ambiguity, come up with an incorrect response even when, in reality, they know the answer. For example, consider the following true-false item, and note how the *faulty reference* of the relative pronoun renders the statement ambiguous.

An Ambiguous True-False Item

There is substantial research evidence that many teachers become hostile toward certain students because of their low self-concepts.

Suppose you were a student who had to come up with a true or false response to this question. Your dilemma would stem from the fact that the "their" can refer to the teachers' low self-concepts or the students' low self-concepts. Given the present form of the statement, there's no way to tell whose low self-concepts are referred to by the "because." If, as a student, you get a continual stream of such ambiguous items, you can be pretty sure than your own self-concept will sink a little.

The difficulty with the sort of faulty references commonly seen when writers employ relative pronouns, such as *his, her,* and *their,* is that the writers themselves have an abundantly clear idea *in their own heads* who the pronoun's referent is. Unfortunately, the examinee is not privy to that information. However, an item writer will often fail to recognize such problems because to the item writer, the pronoun's referent is obvious. Good item writers will, however, remove *any* possibility of ambiguity from their items.

Unintended clues.   A third obstacle to the creation of stellar test items arises when item writers inadvertently toss in clues which permit examinees to come up with correct answers to items that they couldn't answer correctly without those unintended clues. If there are many of these unintended clues in a test, the test's validity will surely be impaired.

To illustrate, many inexperienced item writers of multiple-choice tests will make the correct answer twice as long as the other response alternatives. The test-wise student will often opt for the longer answer in such a situation and, of course, will often be right. Writers of true-false items often give away the correct response by adding a qualifier, such as *never* or *always,* to an item. Since most examinees realize there are very few absolutes in the world, the astute answer to such items is invariably "false."

Still other writers provide unintended grammatical clues to the correct answer. A common item-writing error of this sort is seen in the following where the correct answer to a multiple-choice question is given away by the article *a,* which is the concluding word in the item's initial phrase.

A Gramatically Cued Multiple-Choice Test Item

The annual award received by a musical recording artist for outstandingly successful recordings is called a

   a. Oscar
   b. Emmy
   c. Obie
   d. Grammy

Since three of the response options are words which start with vowels, and should use the article *an* (not *a*) immediately before such words, the choice *Grammy* stands out like a sore grandparent.

Because item writers themselves will often be unable to spot unintended clues that they might leave in items, it is particularly helpful to have a colleague review one's items with the charge to look for fairly blatant give-away elements in the items.

Complicated syntax.   A fourth obstacle to effective item writing occurs when items are written which incorporate convoluted syntax. Use of many clauses is to be avoided. Writers such as James Joyce or Thomas Hardy are known for their labyrinthine sentence structures. Some of their clause-laden meanderings extend almost forever. Joyce and Hardy would probably have made poor item writers. Note the following item, and you'll see how the use of introductory clauses, appositive clauses, and gratuitiously tossed-in clauses can make the task of the examinee unbelievably difficult.

A True-False Item with Snarled Syntax

Having slain Hector, the feared Trojan warrior, Achilles, who was considered by all to be the most valiant of the Greeks, was destined to perish because of a flaw which, incurred while he was being immersed in the River Styx as an infant, he possessed.

If you find yourself writing items such as the preceding (the item happens to be *true*), try to take a workshop in "lean sentence structure." If your sentences contain so many "whos" and "whichs" that they resemble an Annual Pronoun Convention, then strike a blow for simplicity. Many examinees won't be able to wade through such syntactical gyrations.

Difficult vocabulary.   Anyone, given the inclination and a copy of the *Oxford English Dictionary,* can write sentences with words that others can't understand. Whereas such a writing style may enhance a neurotic writer's self-esteem, it has no place in the preparation test items.

The use of polysyllabic terminology in test items is particularly reprehensible because it does not penalize examinees evenhandedly. For example, students get a break who come from highly verbal families in which dinner-time conversations seem sustained by a thesaurus. Students from less verbal environments will surely stumble over exotic terms. The use of hypersophisticated vocabulary, then, isn't merely confusing; it's also unfair.

In review, we have briefly considered five obstacles to good item writing which, distressingly, pop up in educational tests all too frequently.

Whether the items are of a selected-response or constructed-response sort, these five flaws should be avoided.

Let's turn now to the first of the three types of selected-response items to be treated in the chapter, that is, the *binary-choice item*.

BINARY-CHOICE ITEMS

A *binary-choice item* provides only two responses and directs the examinee to select one. The most common form of binary-choice item is the true-false test, but this item category also includes any kind of item where the examinee is given a statement or question, then asked to respond yes-no, right-wrong, agree-disagree, and so on. When we are working with subject matter that breaks down into two discrete categories, we can also employ binary-choice items by presenting several examples of two categories, then asking the examinee to go through each example and decide whether it is logical or illogical, animate or inanimate, and so on.

Without a doubt, the most common use of binary-choice items is to measure an examinee's ability to identify the correctness of factual statements or term definitions. The following are some examples of typical binary-choice items.

Directions. Read each of the following statements and, if the statement is true, place a T before it; if the statement is false, place an F before it.

_____ 1. During the 1980s we saw a decline in U.S. space exploration activity.

_____ 2. A peace treaty between Egypt and Israel was ratified by both nations in 1979.

_____ 3. President Jimmy Carter was often referred to as *Peanuts* because of his unusual body structure.

Directions. Circle the Y (for *Yes*) or the N (for *No*) to indicate whether the following statements accurately describe you.

Y   N   1. I would rather play with my friends than go to school.

Y   N   2. I never try to be tardy to class.

Y   N   3. I become restless as the school day wears on.

Due to the typical brevity of binary-choice items, many people believe that such items, particularly of the true-false variety, can be cranked out almost mindlessly. There are thousands of true-false items being used this very minute which support that contention. To create a good true-false item is not a simple task, and the most widespread weakness in this type of item is that insufficient attention is given to its development.

Because binary-choice items can be written so tersely, it is possible to cover a wide content range with them. Typically, this is the most frequently cited advantage for such items. Well, perhaps it is simple to generate any old kind of binary-choice item, but to create a good item of this type takes a considerable amount of effort and time.

Perhaps the overriding weakness of the binary-choice item is the ease with which examinees can guess the correct answer. By chance alone, an examinee who knows nothing about an exam ought to be able to get a 50 percent correct score. Given the inadvertent clues that sometimes are found in most sets of test items, the correct-by-chance score rises even higher. There really isn't a good way of circumventing this deficiency, so the user of binary-choice items will have to recognize that even a middle-ability gorilla who is able to choose between two options ought to get about half the items right.

It should be pointed out, however, that even if "blind guessing," as opposed to "informed guessing," is taking place, its influence on test scores diminishes as the length of the test increases. Whereas the blind guesser has a 50 percent chance of getting a single true-false item correct, the chance of getting a perfect score on a five-item test shrinks to 3 percent and on a ten-item test to one-tenth of one percent. Reasonably long true-false tests of, say, 100 items are capable of securing reliability coefficients in the .85 to .95 range, thus suggesting that there's something being measured more consistently than the examinee's skill in guessing.

When true-false items are used, they often encourage students to engage in verbatim memorization of statements from the text or teacher's remarks. Most teachers, of course, do not wish to promote such memorization behavior. Even so, by lifting statements from the text or by adroitly inserting a *not* into a textbook's positive statement, teachers obviously set conditions so that rote memory pays off.

Another difficulty with the true-false item is that it presents as its options two extremes that rarely match up with the real world. In the real world we usually find that things are *relatively* true or *relatively* false. In the true-false item there is no place for gradations of truth or falsity. How many times, for example, have sophisticated test takers yearned for response options such as "somewhat true" or "pretty largely false."

Some item writers have tried to salvage the true-false item by modifying it so that, for instance, an examinee is supposed to correct a false statement. Of course, such modifications move this item partially into the constructed-response category and thus create the problems of objectivity in scoring that accompany such items. Frankly, most of these makeshift remedies fail to ameliorate the overall weaknesses of the true-false item.

However, lest you think that the measurement community in its entirety finds true-false items repugnant, it should be noted that Robert L. Ebel, one of educational measurement's recognized leaders, is a stalwart proponent of the true-false item. In his measurement text Ebel mounts a powerful argument supporting the virtues of the true-false test item.[1]

The basis of Ebel's advocacy of true-false items is summarized in the following four propositions which he defends with verve in his text:

1. The essence of educational achievement is the command of useful verbal knowledge.
2. All verbal knowledge can be expressed in propositions.
3. A proposition is any sentence that can be said to be true or false.
4. The extent of students' command of a particular area of knowledge is indicated by their success in judging the truth or falsity of propositions related to it.

There is little doubt that if item writers are truly attentive to the potential deficits of binary-choice items, such as those mentioned in the preceding paragraphs, reasonably decent items of this sort can be generated. One place where the astute test maker should employ them is in situations in which the subject-matter content being tested breaks down naturally into two categories. For instance, if a chemistry teacher is testing whether students can distinguish between organic and inorganic compounds, a binary-choice test format may be the only sensible one to employ. If so, however, the test writer should be particularly careful not to provide unintended clues to the correct answer, since coping with student guessing already presents a serious problem.

Item-Writing Guidelines

The chief problems in creating binary-choice items are to avoid ambiguity and to formulate items that don't contain inadvertent clues. Adhering to the following guidelines will be of considerable value in dodging these deficiencies.[2] These and other guidelines, incidentally, refer exclusively to

[1]Robert L. Ebel, *Essentials of Educational Measurement*, 3rd ed. (Englewood Cliffs, N.J.: Prentice-Hall, Inc. 1979), Chap. 7.

[2]Several of the guidelines to be offered here and in the subsequent chapter were drawn, with adaptation, from a similar effort to isolate the commandments of item writing. W. James Popham, *Criterion-Referenced Measurement*, Chapter 3 (Englewood Cliffs, N.J.: Prentice-Hall, Inc., 1978).

items for *cognitive,* not *affective,* tests. We deal with affective tests in Chapter 14.

1. *Conceptualize binary-choice items in pairs, not singly.* If we recall that binary-choice items work best when two discrete categories are being sampled (such as *true* and *false*), it should become apparent that if there is a good statement to reflect one of the two categories, there usually is an opposite version of that statement which reflects the other category. For example, relying on some concepts treated in earlier chapters, the following pair of true-false items is presented.

True Version

As a test's reliability increases, the likelihood of the test's being valid increases.

False Version

As a test's reliability increases, the likelihood of the test's being valid decreases.

Unless a parallel but opposite version of a statement can be produced, the statement is usually not a good contender for a true-false item. Although only one of the two statements will actually be used on the test, the practice of conjuring up both versions, at least mentally, often helps item writers identify potential shortcomings in binary-choice items, particularly of the true-false variety.

2. *Phrase the item so that a superficial analysis by the examinee suggests a wrong answer.* If the test items are designed to test examinees, and not merely be give-away items, then one way to heighten the difficulty of the test is to phrase items in such a way that a casual reading of the statement will lead the examinee to the wrong answer. Note, for example, the following right-wrong item which, at first glance, sounds pretty commendable.

Right-Wrong:

Because of the inherent diversity of human beings, most classroom teachers and instructional psychologists recommend an individually designed instructional sequence for each learner. (Wrong)

This statement really reeks of goodness, because of such heart-warming phrases as "the inherent diversity of human beings;" thus examinees might be willing to bestow a hasty *right* on such an item. More careful analysis, however, suggests that most classroom teachers, particularly those who have been teaching for more than one week, would recognize the considerable impracticality of whipping up a truly individualized instructional sequence for each student. A more careful consideration of the statement, therefore, should indicate to an examinee that the correct answer is "wrong."

3. *Rarely use negative statements, and never use double negatives.* It is often difficult for students, particularly with true-false items, to agree that a negative depiction of a phenomenon is accurate. However, when a true-false statement contains a double negative, then matters really get perplexing. For instance, consider how you would respond to the two statements below if you were to encounter them as part of a true-false test on the history of South America:

Too Many Negatives

T   F   In 1911 Hiram Bingham, who became a U.S. senator and governor of Connecticut, did not discover the lost Inca city, Machu Picchu, because of his considerable disinterest in antiquity.

Better

T   F   In 1911 Hiram Bingham, who became a U.S. senator and governor of Connecticut, discovered the lost Inca city, Machu Picchu, because of his considerable interest in antiquity.

The initial phrasing of the question about Machu Picchu contains two negatives which, of course, cancel out each other. Some people like to pepper their tests with such double negatives. Well, although we can allow writers a bit of literary license now and then, we should permit writers of true-false items no such liberties when it comes to double negatives. Moreover, triple negatives, obviously, are an abomination. For example, try this one:

True-False

None of Britain's recent prime ministers was unaware of the absence of sufficient energy resources in the British Isles themselves.

---

4. *Don't include two concepts in one statement.* When an item writer treats two ideas in a single statement, it is possible that the first idea is false, the second idea is false, or the relationship between the two ideas is false. Clearly, some students will have a tough time sorting out which of these situations is present. The previous Machu Picchu item illustrated this point. In the following statement, what should guide the student in coming up with an overall judgment about the statement's truth or falsity?

Weak

   T   F   Tournament badminton players use feathered shuttlecocks because goose feathers are more bulky than hummingbird feathers.

While both of the main ideas in the sentence are correct—that is, tournament badminton players do, indeed, use feathered shuttlecocks, and goose feathers are surely heftier than hummingbird feathers—it is the *because* that renders the statement false. The best idea is to avoid these kinds of complexities by sticking with a single idea per statement.

5. *Have an approximately equal number of items representing the two categories being tested.* If you're working with right-wrong, true-false, or animate-inanimate, try to provide items so that roughly half will represent one category. Some students have what we call a *response set* such that they tend to guess *true* more often than *false* or *wrong* more often than *right*. So that such students will not be unduly penalized, avoid having a heavy proportion of items reflecting only one of the two categories being used. It is, incidentally, unwise to create *exactly* half the items of one sort and *exactly* half of another, because some test-wise students will then be aided as they try to guess their way through the unknown items in the test.

If you are anxious to get your test items to discriminate among examinees, as would be the case with a norm-referenced test, then it is wise to employ more false than true statements in the test. A few researchers have identified what they call an *acquiescent response set* among examinees. The way the response set works is that if examinees have no certain knowledge of a statement's falsity, they are more willing to accept such an assertion as true. In practice this means that in cases of doubt they'll tend to mark more false statements as true than true statements as false.

6. *Keep similar the length of items representing both categories being tested.* Item writers tend to make true statements longer, particularly in true-false tests, because of all the qualifiers that must be inserted to make such items indisputably true. Cunning students can, therefore, guess at *true* for a long

item and *false* for a terse one. Similarly, no matter what the two categories are, for example, acceptable-unacceptable, there should be no systematic length bias in favor of either of the two types of answers.

MATCHING ITEMS

A *matching item* consists of two parallel lists of words or phrases that require the examinee to match items in one list with the appropriate items in the second list. Items in the list for which a match is sought are referred to as *premises,* and items in the list from which selections are made are called *responses.* Typically, the student is directed to match items from the two lists according to a particular kind of association indicated in the test's directions. For example

---

Directions. On the line to the left of each military conflict listed in *Column A* write the letter of the U.S. president in *Column B* who was in office when that military conflict was concluded. Each name in Column B may be used no more than once.

Column A

_____ 1. World War I
_____ 2. World War II
_____ 3. The Vietnam Involvement

Column B

a. Johnson
b. Kennedy
c. Nixon
d. Roosevelt
e. Truman

Because matching items, such as these, invariably call for the examinee to relate two things that have some factual or logical basis for association, this type of item can be applied in only a small number of situations.

The preceding example illustrates a common feature of well-constructed matching items. Note that the lists in each column are *homogeneous,* that is, all of the items at the left deal with different military conflicts, whereas all of the items on the right consist of names of U.S. chief executives. This type of homogeneity is desirable in such items because it contributes to the plausibility of all matching possibilities, hence minimizes the extent to which unknowledgeable examinees can guess correctly.

In addition, observe that there are more items in Column B than in Column A. This illustrates an *imperfect match,* a quality that increases the effectiveness of matching items since examinees who know most (but not all) of the pairs in the item cannot easily guess the last few on the basis of elimination.

Matching items are typically used for detecting the examinee's knowledge of simple associations, such as the relationships between (a) famous people and (b) their accomplishments, (a) definitions and (b) terms, or (a) historical events and (b) dates. Because of its brevity, the matching item is an efficient way of measuring one's knowledge of such simple associations.

Dividends and Deficits

The major advantage of a matching item is its compact form, thus making it possible to tap a good deal of information while taking up little testing space on a printed page. Such items can also be efficiently scored. As with true-false items, however, this kind of item can often promote a student's memorization of low-level factual information at the expense of higher-level intellectual skills. An additional advantage of such items is that they are relatively easy to construct (although not as simple as most people think). The main trick in generating a good matching item is to come up with two homogeneous sets of things to be associated. Since we most often crank out extra ingredients to list in the response column, it is sometimes difficult to generate enough plausible response options.

Matching items, if well written, encourage examinees to cross-reference and thus integrate their knowledge because of the necessity to refer to the relationships among members of the responses and premises. On the other hand, matching items do not work well if we are trying to test unique ideas, since we need pools of related ideas to insert in the matching format.

The main weakness of the matching item is that it is restricted to assessment of mere associations, typically of a very factual sort. Such items are particularly susceptible to the inclusion of unintended cues which enhance the examinee's chances of guessing correctly.

It is typically impossible to devise an *entire* test of matching items. Usually, therefore, we find only a part of an exam consists of such items. As indicated, the potential applications of matching items are few, but even so there are several rules which we should follow when employing this sort of exercise.

Item-Writing Guidelines

The major considerations when creating matching items should be to set them up so the examinee can respond quickly, without confusion, and unabetted by clues that lead to correct guesses.

1. *Use relatively brief lists, and place the shorter words or phrases at the right.* For the examinee, brief sets of premises and responses are much easier to work with than lengthy, apparently interminable lists. By the time that

students have sorted through a lengthy list of responses, for instance, they may have forgotten the premise for which they were seeking a match. From the item writer's point of view, shorter lists make it easier to develop homogeneous sets of premises or responses.

By placing the shorter words or phrases on the right, the examinee is encouraged to complete the matching item efficiently by reading the lengthier premises first and then scanning the response column until the correct answer is, hopefully, detected.

2. *Employ homogeneous lists in a matching item.* As mentioned earlier, in any single matching item it is important to make sure that the set of premises is composed of similar sorts of elements. In the same way, the set of responses for any matching item should be homogeneous. For example, if we're matching famous women and their accomplishments, then the list of accomplishments (because each accomplishment's description is sure to be lengthier) will be on the left and the list of women's names on the right. All statements in the premise list should be descriptive of a particular woman's accomplishments. For example, none should simply list the birthdate of a woman in the response list. Similarly, only women's names should appear in the response list.

The following is an example of a matching item which violates this guideline. Neither the set of premises nor responses is homogeneous. Note that it is impossible to come up with a cohesive description for either the list at the left or the one at the right. They are heterogeneous, not homogeneous, clusters.

Heterogeneous Lists

Directions. Match the letters of items in the list at the right with the phrases in the list at the left. Each letter may be used once, more than once, or not at all.

_____1.	Formerly ruled by czars	a. The Great Wall
_____2.	Site of the Valley of the Kings	b. America is discovered.
_____3.	The People's Republic of China	c. U.S.S.R.
_____4.	1776	d. Great Britain
		e. Egypt
		f. A nation is created.

Next is an example of a matching exercise that adheres to this guideline. Note that the list of premises consists exclusively of descriptions of professional basketball players, whereas the list of responses includes only the names of basketball players.

Homogeneous Lists

Directions. On the line at the left of each description, place the letter of the name of the professional basketball player who fits the description. Each player in the list at the right may be used only once.

Description	Player
____1. A Los Angeles Laker guard from West Virginia known as "Mr. Clutch" and "Zeke from Cabin Creek."	A. Bill Russell
	B. Elgin Baylor
	C. Bob Cousy
____2. A towering center who played college basketball at the U. of Kansas and once scored 100 points in a pro game.	D. Wilt Chamberlain
	E. Oscar Robertson
	F. Kareem Abdul Jabbar
____3. Having led the University of San Francisco to the NCAA championship, this 6'10" center dominated pro basketball for many years with the Boston Celtics.	
____4. As one of Indiana's most famed high school players, this 6'5" all-star played for the University of Cincinnati before becoming what many consider to be the finest guard ever to play pro basketball.	

---

3. *Include more responses than premises.* To eliminate the likelihood that the student who knows most of the answers will be able to guess correctly at the last few responses, be sure to toss in a few extra response options. In the previous examples about U.S. presidents and basketball players, note that there are more responses than premises.

4. *List the responses in a logical order.* To avoid unconsciously giving the student extra clues, such as when some item writers unthinkingly list all the correct responses first and only toss in a few wrong answers at the end of the response list, be sure to list the responses alphabetically or in some logical, for example, chronological, order. The U.S. presidents in the previous example were listed alphabetically.

5. *Describe the basis for matching and the number of times a response may be used.* In the directions at the beginning of a matching item, be sure to set forth in clear language just what the examinee should use as the basis for attempting to match responses to premises. Also, be sure to indicate whether a response can be used once, more than once, or not at all. The phrase: "Each name on the list at the right may be used once, more than once, or never" is commonly employed. Such directions, as with several of our other guidelines, reduce the likelihood that the wily student will be able to outguess the cunning test maker.

6. If possible, *place all premises and responses for a matching item on a single page.* Merely to make examinee's responses to an item more efficient and to avoid the noisy flap of oft-flipped pages, it is more sensible to put all of the premises and responses for a matching item on the page.

MULTIPLE-CHOICE ITEMS

Without question, the most popular form of test item is the *multiple-choice item.* As the most widely used selected-response type of item, it is applicable to a number of different types of testing situations. It can be used to test mere recall of factual knowledge, really powerful sorts of intellectual skills, or significant attitudinal dispositions. The most common kind of multiple-choice item presents the examinee with a question along with four or five possible answers, from which one is to be selected. Nevertheless, the stimuli to which the student makes responses need not be merely verbal nor for that matter, simple. We can measure truly sophisticated sorts of examinee responses if we're clever enough to devise the kinds of multiple-choice items that assess those sorts of behaviors.

The initial part of a multiple-choice item will typically be a question or an incomplete statement. This section of the item is known as the *stem.* The stem could, of course, be a map, an illustration, graph, or some other sort of presentation. In essence, it is the stimulus to which the examinee makes a response. The possible answers are referred to as *alternatives.* In the set there are several wrong answers and at least one correct answer. The wrong answers are called *distractors* since it is their mission in life to distract the unknowledgeable or unskilled examinee from too readily guessing the right answer. Distractors are also referred to as *foils.*

We also have a choice between the *direct-question* and the *incomplete-statement* format. Usually the direct question is preferable when used with younger examinees, but the incomplete-statement form is more concise. It is best to employ the direct-question format unless the item writer can maintain the stem's clarity while effecting a substantial shortening of the stem. Both of these formats are illustrated next, and at the same time, an example is given of the *best-answer* and *correct-answer* type of multiple-choice item.

Direct-Question Form (best-answer approach)

Which state is generally thought to have the most effective state-operated environmental protection agency?
   a.   Wyoming
   b.   Pennsylvania
   c.   Ohio
   d.   Montana

Incomplete-Statement Form (correct-answer approach)

The capital of Florida is
   a.   Miami
   b.   Tallahassee
   c.   Tampa
   d.   Fort Lauderdale

Observe that the top example calls for the examinee to select the best of the four alternatives, whereas the bottom example asks for the one correct answer. There are many kinds of situations for which there exists more than a single correct answer. There may be several correct answers, but one of them is the best—that is, *most* correct—answer. The alternatives for a multiple-choice test item can be built so as to incorporate these relative degrees of correctness. Of course, this is one of the most appealing features of the multiple-choice item since it can call for the examinee to make subtle gradations among contending alternatives.

There is another reason to favor the *best-answer* approach over the *correct-answer* model. It is often difficult for the item writer to come up with a correct-answer alternative so precisely phrased that all authorities will concur with its correctness. It is much easier to build distractors, one of which will, in the view of all acknowledged experts, be better than the other alternatives.

Dividends and Deficits

One virtue of the multiple-choice item is its considerable flexibility. It can be applied to the assessment of so many different sorts of cognitive and affective outcomes. As a selected-response type of item, it can be objectively scored, thus leading to tests with greater reliability and ease of scoring. For instance, when we compare a multiple-choice item with even a short-answer type of constructed-response item, we see that the multiple-choice form leads to far more simple and more consistent scoring. Since examinees can't figure out what the item writer is searching for in the short-answer item, they may come up with all sorts of exotic responses. In the multiple-choice item, response options are circumscribed.

Ambiguous Short-Answer Item

Recent research suggests that political success is most often due to _____.

Unambiguous Multiple-Choice Item

Recent research suggests that political success is most often due to
   a. the candidate's charisma
   b. financial resources of the candidate
   c. the parental training of the candidate
   d. the whims of the electorate

Another advantage of multiple-choice items, particularly over binary-choice items, is that the increased alternatives make it more difficult for examinees to guess the correct answer, thereby increasing the reliability of each item.

From an instructional perspective, there is yet another plus for multiple-choice items. Since there are several alternatives, it is also possible to build in distractors that reflect particular kinds of wrong answers, thereby allowing an educator to use students' item responses diagnostically by spotting the *classes* of incorrect responses that examinees make. Teachers can then follow up with additional instruction based on the most common sorts of errors that an individual student or a class of students make.

Multiple-choice items are also relatively unaffected by examinee *response sets*—that is, tendencies on the part of examinees to respond in particular ways such as when students favor "true" responses in true-false tests. It is possible, of course, that certain somewhat peculiar students may display response sets toward the choice of certain letters (choice *b*, for instance). Fortunately, few of these folks exist.

A major weakness of multiple-choice items is that when a series of alternatives is presented to examinees they can often *recognize* a correct answer that, without assistance, they could never *construct*.

An additional weakness, one shared by all selected-response items, is that the examinee has no opportunity to synthesize thoughts, write out creative solutions, and so on. Another weakness, encountered particularly by novice item writers, is that it is sometimes difficult to generate a sufficiently large set of plausible distractors. Thus, a beginner's multiple-choice item sometimes looks as obvious as the following example.

Undemanding Distractors:

Mickey Mouse's two nephews are

    a. Huey, Dewey, and Louie
    b. Clarabelle Cow
    c. Morty and Ferdy
    d. Abbott and Costello

Any genuine devotee of Mickey Mouse would know that Morty and Ferdy are, although among the least honored of the Disney mice-people, Mickey's legitimate nephews. The other distractors, on all sorts of counts, are obviously wrong.

Item-Writing Guidelines

Perhaps because of its popularity, there are more guidelines for the creation of the multiple-choice item than for any other type of selected- or constructed-response item. We treat the most important of these rules now, illustrating them when necessary.

    1. *The stem should present a self-contained question or problem.* The examinee should be able to read the stem, discern what the question or problem is, then go about selecting the correct answer from the alternatives. A badly constructed multiple-choice item sometimes presents only a word or phrase in the stem, forcing the examinee to read through all of the alternatives before figuring out what the item is really about. To avoid this weakness, the item writer ought to be confident that the item's stem, framed either as a direct question or as an incomplete statement, is meaningful in itself. Some item writers check to see if an item stem is self-contained by attempting to read it without any of its alternatives, then seeing if it is complete enough to serve as a short-answer item. If so, the stem is usually sufficiently complete. Consider the following two examples, and note that the first item does, in fact, include a self-contained stem, whereas the second item's stem

is essentially meaningless. Observe also that both items are *best-answer* rather than *correct-answer* items.

Reprehensible

President Franklin Roosevelt
   a.   lived for some years after the death of his wife, Eleanor.
   b.   was originally governor of California before becoming president.
   c.   was a swimmer in the Olympic Games prior to becoming a politician.
   d.   died in office during World War II.

Praiseworthy

President Franklin Roosevelt's most significant domestic accomplishment during his presidential years was
   a.   terminating the Great Depression.
   b.   creating the CCC.
   c.   unifying the Democratic Party.
   d.   rotating his vice-presidents.

---

2. *The stem should contain as much of the item's content as possible.* Multiple-choice items should be written so that the examinee can quickly scan the alternatives after considering the stem. If, however, we load the alternatives with many words, rapid scanning is obviously impossible. Now this rule cannot always be followed, since in order to test certain kinds of learning outcomes we may have to set up a series of lengthy alternatives. However, if it is not imperative to create lengthy alternatives, the item writers should stuff the stem with most of the relevant content.

3. *If possible, avoid negatively stated stems.* The problem with negatively formulated stems is that such phrasing can confuse examinees who, if the stem were phrased positively, would readily choose the correct alternative. Most of the time, with a little brain bending, a writer can come up with a way to transform a negatively stated item into its positive counterpart. In the following example we see two items that get at the same knowledge. The top item will surely confuse those examinees who fail to note the *not* in the item. The bottom item would only be confusing to examinees who think the Mississippi River is in New Jersey.

Crummy

Which one of the following cities is not located in a state west of the Mississippi River?

a. Los Angeles
b. Cleveland
c. Denver
d. Reno

Yummy

Which one of the following cities is located in a state east of the Mississippi River?
a. Los Angeles
b. Cleveland
c. Denver
d. Reno

Incidentally, notice that both of the items in the example are *correct-answer* multiple-choice items.

However, there are some situations in which we might be interested in having the examinee spot something that should not be done. For example, suppose we were constructing a test of an examinee's ability to supply first-aid assistance to heart attack victims. Perhaps we want to be sure that the examinees would *not* make any serious error that would jeopardize the victim's survival until more competent medical assistance arrived. In such cases we might wish to list sets of alternative actions, some of which should never be taken. For these kinds of structures it is quite acceptable to use negatively framed stems, but the item writer should call the examinee's attention to the negative formulation by capitalizing, underscoring, or otherwise dramatizing the *not* or *never*.

4. *Be sure that only one alternative represents the correct or best answer.* Item writers will sometimes erroneously write an item that contains two or even more correct answers. Most experienced teachers who write their own multiple-choice tests have experienced numerous postexam confrontations as their more able students do battle over whether the teacher's scoring key is correct. Care must be taken, perhaps by having colleagues or a supersmart student review all alternatives carefully, not to include more than one right answer.

Dismal

Which of the following U.S. presidents is regarded as the Democrat who introduced the greatest number of domestic *social improvement* programs?
a. Kennedy
b. Johnson

c. F. Roosevelt
d. Hoover

Delightful

Which of the following U.S. presidents is regarded as the Democrat who introduced the greatest number of domestic *social improvement* programs?
a. Johnson
b. Nixon
c. Kennedy
d. Hoover

In the preceding two items we see that one could reasonably argue whether Lyndon Johnson or Franklin Roosevelt had introduced the greatest number of domestic social improvement programs. By replacing Roosevelt with Nixon in the bottom version of the item, the choice of Johnson becomes far less debatable.

Sometimes an item writer, vexed with the fact that more than two alternatives to a multiple-choice item seem plausible, will alter the directions to the items so that more than one alternative may be chosen. The following is an example.

A Modified Binary-Choice Format:

Which, if any, of the following geometric figures necessarily contains at least one right angle? You may choose one, more than one, or none of the alternatives.
a. Parallelogram
b. Square
c. Rhomboid
d. Rectangle

There is nothing wrong with using such items, but the item writer should recognize that a multiple-choice item is no longer being employed. What we now have is a series of four binary-choice items. The examinee is obliged to make an on-off decision for each alternative since there may be one, more than one, or no correct answers. As we have seen previously, there are some limitations associated with binary-choice items, particularly with respect to their guessability.

5. *Each alternative should be grammatically consistent with the item's stem.* If you will recall our earlier discussion of inadvertent clue giving, you'll remember the poor item that had a stem ending in *a* and only one alternative

that commenced with a consonant instead of a vowel (Grammy). Clearly, such item-writing mistakes give away the correct answer to one and all. There are similar kinds of grammatical oversights, such as seen in the following example in which the item writer unconsciously points to the first item's answer.

Laughable

In the commercial publishing of a book, *galley proofs* are most often used
a. page proofs precede galley proofs for minor editing.
b. to help isolate minor defects prior to printing of page proofs.
c. they can be useful for major editing or rewriting.
d. publishers decide whether the book is worth publishing.

Laudable

In publishing a book, *galley proofs* are most often used to
a. aid in minor editing after page proofs.
b. isolate minor defects prior to page proofs.
c. assist in major editing or rewriting.
d. validate menus on large ships.

Notice that in the first stem the only alternative that meshes grammatically with the stem is choice *b*. Only a grammatical goon, therefore, would choose choices *a, c,* or *d*. In the second item we see that all alternatives are grammatically consonant with the stem, hence are eligible contenders to be the correct answer, at least on syntactical grounds.

6. *Avoid creating alternatives whose relative length provides an unintended clue.* We want to write items that find out what examinees know, can do, or believe. A multiple-choice item in which most of the alternatives are terse, but one resembles an epistle from St. Paul to the Romans, may incline the unknowledgeable examinee to go for the epistle-length alternative. After all, one gets so much more for one's choice. To counter this error, of course, all we need to do is write alternatives that are relatively similar in length. In the following examples, to shape up the out-of-balance alternative *d* in the top item, the item writer merely shortened it to coincide with the length of the other choices.

Reprehensible

Epistemology is that branch of philosophy which deals with
a. the nature of existence
b. morality

    c. beauty
    d. the nature and origin of knowledge, that is, the manner in which human beings sense and process external stimuli in the form of knowledge.

Virtuous

Epistemology is that branch of philosophy which deals with
    a. the nature of existence
    b. morality
    c. beauty
    d. the nature of knowledge

Another type of inadvertent clue, sometimes seen in weak multiple-choice items, involves using some type of distinctive word in the item's stem, then using a different form of that word in one of the alternatives. For example, suppose we employed the word *appellation* in the stem, and then used the word *appellate* in one of the alternatives. Some examinees might opt for that alternative merely because of the verbal association. Try to avoid such verbal associations unless there is an important reason for using them.

    7. *Make all alternatives plausible.* Even an item's distractors should appear alluring to the unknowledgeable examinee. Don't write items so that there is only one obviously correct alternative and several *idiot choices.* Each distractor's plausibility should be carefully gauged. If any appear to be ludicrously wrong, they should be replaced.

    In some instances this rule is easier to dispense than to follow. It's often devilishly tough to come up with a large enough number of reasonable contenders as distractors. Sometimes this takes more time than creating a genuinely super stem. In the previous example about Mickey Mouse's nephews, we saw an extreme example of one reasonable alternative and *three* idiot choices. With just a bit of massaging, the Morty and Ferdy choice could have been surrounded by more plausible foils. Even "Forty and Merdy" would have been better than "Abbott and Costello."

    Incidentally, although we haven't talked previously about the *number of alternatives,* now might be a good time. You'll notice that all of the multiple-choice examples used so far in the chapter have had four alternatives. Generally speaking, most measurement people recommend four or five alternatives, because that number cuts down sufficiently on examinee guessing. If you go with only three alternatives, for instance, the examinee has a 33 percent chance of coming up a winner on chance alone. If you start having up to six or seven alternatives, the reading requirements for each item begin to bulge. Consequently, if there are no compelling reasons to the contrary, a set of four or five alternatives per item would seem appropriate. We have used only four choices here in order to conserve trees.

8. *Randomly use each alternative position for correct answers in approximately equal numbers.* We have learned about examinees' response sets, such as tending to mark all doubtful true-false items as true. Well, item writers have their response sets also. If all the four-alternative, multiple-choice items ever written on earth were assembled into a gigantic examination, what alternative do you suppose whould be used most often for the correct answer, that is, *a, b, c,* or *d?* You'd go to the head of the test-construction class if you chose *c.*

Item writers, particularly nonprofessional ones, being for the most part a fairly normal lot, are loath to give away the right answer too soon, hence avoid choices *a* or *b.* Yet, they fear making the last answer—that is, *d*—the correct choice too often. Consequently, if you're ever faced with a multiple-choice test and must guess wildly, go with choice *c.*

To avoid this weakness, of course, merely set up the correct answers so that they will bounce around among the alternative positions roughly the same number of times. Any scheme for systematically randomizing, such as relying on a table of random numbers, will prove serviceable for the purpose.

9. *Unless important, avoid alternatives such as "none-of-the-above" or "all-of-the-above."* In many instances multiple-choice item writers employ phrases such as "none of the above" because they've run out of ideas for plausible distractors and want to create a final option. Although there are limited numbers of cases in which a "none-of-the-above" response works suitably, *the "all-of-the-above" option is rarely appropriate.*

A major problem with the "all-of-the-above" alternative is that an examinee may read alternative *a,* recognize that it is correct, mark the answer sheet, and never consider choices *b, c,* or *d.* Other examinees who spot that two of the alternatives are correct will, even without knowing anything about the third alternative, naturally choose the "all-of-the-above" alternative. Both sorts of problems can be avoided by eliminating the "all-of-the-above" response as an option.

When we rely on "none-of-the-above" as an alternative, we are forcing the item into a correct-answer rather than best-answer form, since if we ask the examinee to identify a best answer of several rather poor alternatives, it's still possible to pick the best among poor choices. Consider the voter's dilemma in many elections!

A correct-answer rather than best-answer structure, of course, robs us of the possibility of creating alternatives with gradations of correctness, one of the most appealing features of the multiple-choice item.

Nevertheless, there may be significant sorts of outcomes that can be conceptualized in such a way that the "none-of-the-above" response forces the student to consider the item's other alternatives more carefully. Use of the "none-of-the-above" alternative ordinarily makes a test more difficult than when it is not used. This occurs because the "none-of-the-above" option creates the possibility that there may be no correct answer among the other alternatives. In such cases it would seem more suitable to use the "none-of-the-above" response as a fifth choice in a five-alternative, multiple-choice item. Be sure to call the examinee's attention to the possibility that none of the initial alternatives may be correct and that in such instances the "none-of-the-above" option should be selected.

A Really Rotten Item

A cure for tension headaches is
 a. aspirin
 b. relaxation
 c. codeine
 d. none of the above
 e. all of the above

This item is a genuine loser on several counts. First off, it violates our ninth guideline by using *both* a "none-of-the-above" and an "all-of-the-above" response. Second, although the item writer apparently wanted choice *e* to be the correct answer, since *a, b,* and *c* can all reduce tension headaches, when you choose choice *e,* that also includes choice *d.* Since choice *d* (none of the above) negates the correctness of *a, b,* and *c,* the examinee is in trouble city. It is, as indicated, a genuinely ineffective item.

The Allure of Multiple-Choice Items

Since multiple-choice items are employed so prevalently in teacher-made and commercially developed tests, many fledgling test writers gravitate immediately to this form of testing. As indicated before, the multiple-choice test is loaded with advantages. It's versatile, objectively scoreable, and not too subject to guessing. Besides that, since it has its separate alternatives, we can try out an item, gather empirical data regarding how each of its components work, and spruce it up until it's an object for adoration.

However, there are other legitimate forms of testing, some involving selected responses and some involving constructed responses. We shouldn't forget these other approaches. Besides that, depending on what we're trying to measure, we can remold the classical multiple-choice format so that it better suits our purposes. For instance, we can create two-stage items involving both selected and constructed responses (where examinees must, for example, choose an answer, then improve it). In other words, beware of the multiple-choice item's seductive appeal. Test developers need other weapons to do battle effectively with the numerous assessment problems they face.

There is no doubt, of course, that of the selected-response options we've been considering, the multiple-choice item has some particularly appealing features and few of the drawbacks associated with binary-choice and matching items. In Chapter 12 we see how to shape up selected-response test items once they have been born. However, even though there are dandy empirical schemes for improving the quality of selected-response test items, by adhering to the guidelines given here, item writers will be more apt to produce test items that need only a band-aid or two, not major surgery.

PRACTICE EXERCISES

Items of the type we have been discussing throughout the chapter are presented here. Each item will contain at least one, and sometimes more, deliberate violations of the item writer's guidelines associated with that type of item. The items may also display one of the five general obstacles to good item writing presented early in the chapter.

Before undertaking these practice exercises, spend a moment or two reviewing all of the item-writing guidelines and the five obstacles. Then see if you can spot the most salient flaws in the following items:

1. *True or False:* America's literary circles became preoccupied with Adolf Hitler in the 1960s as a direct result of the 1960 publication of *The Rise and Fall of the Third Reich* by Robert Payne.
2. *Right or Wrong:* Current rules of etiquette suggest that it is not considered improper for a man to avoid helping a woman into an automobile.
3. *Matching:* Match the inventions on the left with the inventor on the right.

	Inventions		*Inventor*
_____	1. Telephone	a.	Bell
_____	2. Electric light bulb	b.	Edison
_____	3. Phonograph	c.	Franklin
_____	4. Waxed paper	d.	Marconi

4. *Multiple Choice:* Good writing is
   a. predicated on the eschewing of obfuscatory verbiage
   b. the culmination of a euphoric and ethereal procreation
   c. the residue of relentless, of onerous, effort
   d. all of the above

5. *Multiple choice:* One of the chief ingredients in the Greek dish, moussaka, is an
   a. eggplant
   b. carrot
   c. melon
   d. brussels sprout

A major practice exercise: If you're reading this text in connection with some kind of course or workshop (as opposed to reading it because of its enthralling storyline), why not try to play the same game you've just completed with these five practice items. Prepare items, as many as your energy and time permit, which incorporate one or more flaws. Then get a classmate to try to identify those flaws. By creating exercises of this sort, you'll become much more familiar with the practicalities of generating the various types of items we've been treating.

ANSWER TO PRACTICE EXERCISES

1. This binary-choice item violates guideline four, "Don't include two concepts in one statement." Not only are there two ideas and a statement of causality present, but the volume referred to was authored by William L. Shirer. Robert Payne wrote *The Life and Death of Adolf Hitler* in 1975. It is this sort of trivial deviation from facts and details that often spurs criticisms of true-false items.

2. This binary-choice item violates guideline three about the inclusion of double negatives. There are so many negatives in the practice item that an examinee's head would swim. Phrasing it negatively, it is unlikely that the examinee's head would remain in a nonswimming state.

3. This matching item has two chief problems. First off, it violates guideline three because there are not more responses than premises. Secondly, it fails to describe the basis for matching (guideline five), so that the unsuspecting examinee will fail to realize that Edison invented everything listed except the telephone.

4. There are several problems with this multiple-choice item. For one thing, one of the five obstacles to good item writing seems to be present, namely, the use of a difficult vocabulary. Many of the terms employed are far too obscure and could have been replaced with simpler and more comprehensible words. A second defect of the item is that it violates guideline one, which calls for the stem to be a self-contained question or problem. This stem isn't. The stem should also contain as much of the item's content as possible (guideline two). This stem doesn't. Besides that, there's a violation of guideline nine since we find an "all-of-the-above" option. In sum, it's a pretty putrid item.

5. This multiple-choice item violates guideline five which calls for each alternative to be grammatically consistent with the item's stem. Of the four alternatives, only eggplant meshes with the article *an*.

DISCUSSION QUESTIONS

1. If you were trying to present the *relative* advantages of binary-choice, multiple-choice, and matching items to a group of elementary school teachers, how would you go about it? What would the major points of your presentation be?
2. How would you contrast the merits of selected- versus constructed-response test items?
3. Which of the three types of selected-response test items treated in the chapter would take the most time and effort to produce?
4. Are any of the three types of selected-response items more appropriate for the needs of classroom teachers? Why?
5. Based on your own experience with tests, can you think of any additional item-writer guidelines for these sorts of items? If so, what are they?

SUGGESTIONS FOR ADDITIONAL READING

EBEL, ROBERT L., "True-False Test Items," Chapter 7, *Essentials of Educational Measurement* (3rd ed.), pp. 111–134. Englewood Cliffs, N.J.: Prentice-Hall, Inc., 1972. This chapter constitutes a classic in support of the virtues of true-false test items. Ebel mounts an effective defense of true-false items in the face of criticisms from most measurement specialists. He supplies a series of practical suggestions for the preparation and improvement of true-false items.

KARMEL, LOUIS J., and MARYLIN O. KARMEL, "The Objective Test," Chapter 16, *Measurement and Evaluation in the Schools* (2nd ed.), pp. 420–437. New York: Macmillan, 1978. A discussion of the ways in which teachers should prepare true-false items, matching-items, and multiple-choice items is provided in this chapter.

MARTUZA, VICTOR R., "The Traditional Approach to Test Construction," Chapter 14, *Applying Norm-Referenced and Criterion-Referenced Measurement in Education*, pp. 198–244. Boston: Allyn and Bacon, 1977. The author provides an extensive series of rules for the preparation of multiple-choice items.

MEHRENS, WILLIAM A., and IRVIN J. LEHMANN, "Writing the Objective Test Item: Short Answer, Matching, and True False," Chapter 9, "Writing the Objective Test Item: Multiple-Choice and Context-Dependent," Chapter 10, *Measurement and Evaluation in Education and Psychology* (2nd ed.), pp. 239–272. New York: Holt, Rinehart & Winston, 1975. In Chapter 9 Mehrens and Lehmann describe approaches to the preparation of matching and true-false items. In Chapter 10 a discussion is offered of how to prepare multiple-choice and "context-dependent" test items.

STANLEY, JULIAN C., and KENNETH D. HOPKINS, "Constructing Specific Types of Objective Tests," Chapter 10, *Educational and Psychological Measurement and Evaluation* (5th ed.), pp. 217–266. Englewood Cliffs, N.J.: Prentice-Hall, Inc., 1972. This chapter features an analysis of true-false items, multiple-choice items, matching exercises, and rearrangement exercises.

11

Constructed-response tests are those that call for the examinee to *produce* something instead of merely choosing between two or more alternatives. There are many settings in which we wish to know whether individuals can produce satisfactorily. In some of those settings it makes no sense to rely on anything other than a constructed-response testing strategy.

In the most commonly cited instance of this sort, English teachers typically want their students to be able to prepare satisfactory written compositions, for instance, essays, personal letters, or business letters. In order to get a solid fix on whether a student can whip out an acceptable paragraph or two, the only truly valid way of gauging that skill is to have the student actually author some paragraphs. Even if we discovered by means of selected-response test items that the student knew all the rules of spelling, punctuation, and usage, there is no assurance, *on the basis of the selected-response test alone,* that the student could actually produce an acceptable paragraph.

Generally, a particular measurement strategy is recommended when it is believed that for some practical reason (such as cost) a constructed-response approach to assessment is not feasible. That strategy is to employ

Constructed-response tests

a selected-response test as a *proxy* for the constructed-response behavior of interest, hoping that the examinee's performance on the selected-response test will serve as an acceptable *surrogate* for the constructed response. There are many instances in which this strategy works beautifully. Indeed, in some studies in which efforts have been made to verify the legitimacy of a proxy selected-response test, the correlation between individuals' scores on a constructed-response test and their scores on a proxy selected-response test are as high as .95.

This is understandable, of course, because in many situations both a selected- and constructed-response test are really tapping a fundamental skill or knowledge that manifests itself equally well under the two conditions. For example, in a graduate class that I teach on the subject of educational evaluation, students must complete a final examination which has two major sections, one consisting of 30 multiple-choice questions. A second, longer section of the exam consists exclusively of constructed-response items. Over the years it has become apparent to me that students who score well on the multiple-choice items will usually score well on the essay sections of the test, and those who score low on one section are apt to score low on the other section. Just for kicks a few years ago, I went back over my grade books for the last few years and discovered that correlation between student's scores on the two sections was almost .90. In view of the fact that for each exam paper it takes me about ten minutes to score the essay section and only twenty to thirty seconds to score the multiple-choice section, I am sorely tempted (in classes of thirty or so) to skip the essay responses completely. I could save myself about five hours of test scoring. Besides that, since my exams are similar from year to year, I get tired of reading essentially the same kinds of responses. But, of course, I resist the temptation. After all, if graduate students devote four hours to completing an exam, they expect the professor to at least browse through their efforts.

However, there are situations in which we do not have much confidence that a selected-response test will serve as a proper proxy for the constructed-response behavior in which we are interested. For example, suppose you are a speech teacher and you want to assess the end-of-year skill of your would-be Demosthenes. There is just no way that a selected-response test, even a genuinely exotic one, can tell you whether your students can deliver an effective impromptu or extemporaneous speech. To see if they can give effective speeches, you must let them speak.

Products and Behavior

If you think about it for just a moment or two, you will realize that all of the examples we have been using for constructed-response behaviors fall nicely into one of two types. Either the examinee is constructing some sort of *product,* as in the case of an essay exam, or some sort of *behavior,* as in the case of an impromptu speech. This two-part classification scheme takes care of all examinee responses, and it is particularly useful when thinking about constructed-response tests.

For instance, how would you classify the following sorts of examinee responses? Are these instances of tests in which a *product* or *behavior* is yielded?

Well, *A* and *C* represent examinee products, and *B* and *D* constitute examinee behaviors. One of the interesting aspects of this distinction between products and behaviors is that when we employ behaviors in an educational measurement situation, we must make certain that the behavior is *recorded.* Unlike student products, such as the oil painting and the

Examinee Response	*Product or Behavior?*
A. Builds an end-table in woodshop class	_____
B. Runs the 100 meter dash in a P.E. class	_____
C. Creates an oil painting in art	_____
D. Dances the *bossa nova* in a ballroom dancing class	_____

end-table, which can be subsequently appraised with respect to their quality, student behaviors disappear once they occur. Suppose, for instance, that a female pole vaulter was practicing by herself at the college track stadium. Let's say that she put together an incredible vault and soared over the bar at 22 feet! However, sadly, if nobody recorded that spectacular pole vault, there is no way to verify that it ever occurred. Thus, whether we employ videotape, film, audiotape, or rely on a judge's recording (such as when a speech teacher assigns a grade for a student's speech), we must make certain that for measurement purposes there is a recording made of constructed responses that constitute behaviors, as opposed to those yielding products.

In Chapters 13 and 14, we look more closely at the schemes one employs in observing and rating examinee behaviors. We also look at methods for dealing with ways of appraising examinee products, other than the types of exam responses to be treated in this chapter, namely, short-answer and essay responses. Student answers to short-answer and essay items constitute a special class of examinee products which, because of their frequency of occurrence, we treat here in some detail.

RELATIVE MERITS OF SELECTED- AND CONSTRUCTED-RESPONSE ITEMS

There are, of course, other ways of dividing the test-item world than according to whether the items require the examinee to select or construct answers. For instance, some writers distinguish between *recognition* and *production* types of test items. Other writers classify test items according to whether they are *subjectively* or *objectively scoreable*. Others talk about *short-answer* or *long-answer* sorts of items. However, in most of these systems there is a certain degree of confusion about short-answer items. Such tests—for example, a fill-in-the-blank kind of measure—are surely not as easy to score objectively as a true-false test; yet they are not as subjective as essay exams. Similarly, how *long* can a short-answer item be before it becomes a *long-answer* item? With the selected-response versus constructed-response scheme, no such overlap exists.

The most crucial attribute of any well-developed test is that it validly assesses what it sets out to measure. However, beyond that fundamental consideration, there are additional factors to which test developers should attend. Among these are the pros and cons of using various kinds of test items. To illustrate, it is possible to contrast selected- and constructed-response items according to their merits on several dimensions. Let's examine a few of these, indicating whether selected-response or constructed-response items come out ahead.

Types of outcomes measured.   To assess the examinee's knowledge of factual information, the selected-response test item is clearly the winner. Many selected-response items represent a far more efficient way of assessing such knowledge than, for example, one or two essay-type constructed-response items. Selected-response items, however, can be used for many more purposes than merely to gauge one's factual knowledge. Such items can also be used to measure examinees' possession of complex intellectual skills, not to mention their attitudes, interests, and so on. The most important ingredient in a selected-response item is the stimulus material that provides the setting for which the examinee selects a response. If the stimulus material merely calls for the examinee to choose among alternatives reflecting factual knowledge, the item is obviously focused only on the assessment of such knowledge. On the other hand, if the stimulus material presents a complex situation in which the examinee must make choices that require the use of fine-grained and sophisticated discriminations, the item is clearly destined for a more ambitious measurement mission.

Selected-response items are not appropriate for measuring examinees' abilities to synthesize ideas, to write effectively, or to perform certain types of problem-solving operations. Although not efficient for measuring an examinee's factual knowledge, constructed-response items constitute the only reasonable way of assessing students' abilities to write, to synthesize ideas, or to perform certain kinds of complex intellectual operations which call for originality. If you want to find out how well a student can write an original essay, for instance, you'll be unable to find any kind of a selected-response item that even comes close to assessing such a skill.

Item preparation.   Even though it usually takes longer to prepare constructed-response items than is thought, less time is typically required to turn out a few essay items than is needed to develop a large number of selected-response items. This time requirement is reversed, however, when it comes to scoring the tests.

Item scoring.   When an exam is over and the last students have turned in their test papers, test administrators have to face that arduous task of scoring the tests. For the educator who uses selected-response items, a job is in store. For the educator who uses constructed-response items, a tough job is in store. Anyone who has speedily scored a series of student responses to multiple-choice items will report that the task can be completed pretty quickly. For lengthy, constructed-response items, however, the task sometimes seems to go on interminably.

Besides the time required to score the tests, there is another substantial scoring difference between these two testing approaches. Selected responses can be scored with impersonal objectivity. Constructed responses— even short-answer items, but particularly long essay answers—are subjectively scored. Subjective scoring typically results in inconsistency which, in turn, yields unreliable test results. We shall treat this problem more carefully later in the chapter.

Form of examinee's response.   With a selected-response item, the examinee is forced to deal with the kinds of responses made available. Examinees can recognize or even guess the correct answers to selected-response items. Constructed-response items, on the other hand, provide less structure for the examinee, thus permitting (encouraging?) frequent flights of verbal fancy. Crafty students, particularly those with writing ability and a fair amount of intelligence, can overwhelm the inattentive test scorer with reams of irrelevant rhetoric. Such baloney, of course, cannot be employed in responding to selected-response items.

Instructional impact.   The structure of tests tends to shape the nature of students' learning. Thus, if constructed-response tests are typically employed by a teacher, that teacher's students will tend to be concerned with broader kinds of subject-matter considerations and with the ability to organize and present ideas carefully that such tests typically entail. Selected-response tests, on the other hand, tend to encourage students to master a more comprehensive collection of factual information or to acquire the kinds of intellectual skills measured by the particular items employed.

Item-types to use.   In reviewing the various advantages and disadvantages of selected- and constructed-response items, it is apparent that there is no simple victor. Although we pick up certain advantages by choosing a constructed-response format, we also acquire a number of liabilities, and vice versa. Because the practical problems of scoring many students' exams is an important one and because of the subjective scoring problems associated with constructed-response tests, selected-response items have been used with greater frequency. Often, by employing creative forms of a multiple-choice test, for example, one can measure really high-level student competencies. If either selected- or constructed-response items will do the assessment job to be accomplished, the selected-response form should usually be chosen on practical grounds alone.

Yet, there are instances when only a constructed-response test format will really get at the student skill to be measured. There is no other way to determine how well a child can write cursively than by having the youngster write cursively. To use a selected-response item as a substitute would surely be invalid. There are times when our first thought is to use a constructed-response format, but further consideration might allow us to identify a selected-response scheme that would serve as a suitable surrogate. Clearly, the initial decision we make about which of these two testing approaches to employ will influence the remainder of our test-development activities.

SHORT-ANSWER ITEMS

Short-answer items oblige an examinee to supply a word or phrase in response either to a direct question or in order to complete an incomplete statement. A short-answer can be contrasted with the essay examination chiefly because of the brevity of the response that the short-answer item solicits. When short-answer items call for very extensive responses on the part of the examinee, they should be considered essay items and treated as such. The following are examples of short-answer items.

Completion. The name of the individual who invented fudge brownies is:

_____

Direct Question. What was the name of the individual who invented fudge brownies?

_____

Short-answer test items are particularly suitable for measuring relatively simple types of learning outcomes, such as an examinee's knowledge of factual information. For example, we might present a complex geometric figure for the examinee's consideration, then ask a series of short-answer questions about various of the figure's features and how they are related. Although short-answer items are typically used for the assessment of simple kinds of learning outcomes, it is conceivable to present very complex questions so that the examinee's brief response reflects a high-level intellectual operation.

Dividends and Deficits Since it often deals with relatively unsophisticated sorts of learning outcomes, the short-answer test item is considered to be one of the easiest to construct. However, as we have seen with other apparently simple sorts of items, the short-answer item also requires considerable care on the part of the item writer to make sure that a satisfactory item is produced.

A key advantage of short-answer items is that they require the student to create an answer rather than merely to recognize it. With any sort of selected-response items, alert students have access to the correct answer. Their task is to spot it. With constructed-response items, however, it is necessary to *produce* the correct answer, not merely to choose it. Thus, the kind of partial knowledge that might enable a student to snag a correct answer in a selected-response test is insufficient for responding correctly to a short-answer test item.

The principal weakness of short-answer items is the difficulty we have in scoring them satisfactorily. Because it is possible that the student will construct a variety of responses, such as using synonyms for the answer intended by the item writer, it is sometimes troublesome to know whether a given answer is correct. Furthermore, there is the problem of legibility. Some students may produce a correct answer which is literally undecipherable by even the most astute cryptographer. Beyond that, how should a test scorer respond to grammatical foul-ups or misspelled words? Should full or partial credit be given?

It is also much more time consuming to score short-answer items than it is to score selected-response items. If a large number of selected-response answer sheets are involved, they can usually be transferred to computer punch cards or can be scored by means of some of the more advanced types of optical scanning equipment where the test papers are "read" and scored by machines. Short-answer items, however, require a human scorer to render a judgment on each of the responses. This takes time, plenty of time.

Item-Writing Guidelines.   Although it is thought that the short-answer item is one of the easiest kinds of item to construct, there are still potential deficiencies in the way that individuals prepare such items. We will examine some of the more salient of these pitfalls.

1. *A direct question is generally preferable to an incomplete statement.* Particularly when an examination is designed for young children, but even for older examinees, the direct-question format should be preferred. This is a more familiar form to youngsters and therefore is less apt to induce confusion. In addition, the direct question usually forces the item writer to phrase the item in such a way that less ambiguity is present. It is astonishing how many times an item writer will create an incomplete-statement type of short-answer item that turns out to be ambiguous. Because the item writer had clearly in mind what should complete the sentence, it is assumed that the examinee will think along those same lines. This assumption usually is unwarranted. Item writers must strive to come up with questions on incomplete statements for which there is one, and only one, answer. It is

sometimes helpful for the item writer to think first of the intended answer, then build a question for which that answer is the *unique* appropriate response.

2. *Structure an item so that the required response should be concise.* Responses to short-answer items, whether they consist of direct questions or incomplete statements, should be brief phrases, words, numbers, or symbols. By providing clear directions at the beginning of the test and by phrasing questions carefully, it will be clear that the examinee's response should be brief.

However, the quest for brevity in a response should not supersede the phrasing of the item so that the kind of response called for is clear. Note, for instance, in the following examples that both item writers wanted the response "biped." Yet, the first item will surely produce a galaxy of reasonable responses. The second item, by the addition of the phrase, "is technically classified as a," reduces the item's ambiguity.

Dismal.   An animal that walks on two feet is _____.

Defensible.   An animal that walks on two feet is technically classified as a _____.

Incidentally, for computational problems in mathematics it is wise to specify (perhaps in parentheses) the degree of accuracy, such as how many places beyond the decimal point are required.

3. *Place the blank near the end of an incomplete sentence or in the margin for a direct question.* If blanks are placed at the beginning of an incomplete sentence, the examinee may have forgotten what is sought by the time that the sentence has been read.

Troublesome

The _____ is the legislative body which constitutionally must ratify all treaties with foreign nations signed by the president of the United States.

Terrific

What is the legislative body which constitutionally must ratify all treaties with foreign nations signed by the president of the United States? _____

In these examples we see that even the examinee who knows that the U.S. Senate must ratify foreign treaties might get a bit lost with the item in which the blank occurs near the beginning of the sentence. The second item, in addition to the fact that it is a direct question, permits much more efficient scoring than if the test scorer must dip in and out of sentences to check answers. With answers lined up in a list, one needs only scan the answers to see whether they're correct or incorrect.

4. *For incomplete-statement types of items, restrict the number of blanks to one or, at most, two.* When the item writer employs too many blanks in an incomplete statement, the ambiguity index of the item rises dramatically. Note, for instance, the following example, and try to decide how you would respond to it. When items have so many blanks as the following, they are sometimes referred to as *Swiss cheese items.*

Swiss Cheese Item

After heroic struggles, in the year _____, _____ and _____ discovered _____.

---

5. *Blanks for answers should be equal in length.* Novice item writers often vary the length of the blanks for short-answer items consistent with the length of the expected answer. This practice, of course, results in providing unintended clues as to what answer is sought. The length of item blanks should be identical throughout the test so as to avoid this problem.

6. *Provide sufficient answer space.* Though it is true we are talking about the short-answer item, we need not make them skimpy-answer items. In the following example, we see that the examinee would be in trouble by trying to write out "the Gettysburg Address" in the space available. A little more generosity on the test developer's part is warranted.

An Excessively Frugal Answer Space

What is the name of the famous address by Abraham Lincoln which commences with the phrase "Fourscore and seven years ago?"   _____

THE ESSAY ITEM

By all odds, the most common type of constructed-response test item is the essay question. Essay questions can be used to measure complex as well as simple types of learning outcomes, but since its primary application involves the examinee's ability to write, synthesize, and create, we will focus on the item as a vehicle for assessing these more elaborate types of outcomes.

Restricted and Extended Responses

It is often thought that the item writer exercises no control over the examinee's freedom of response in essay items. To the contrary, however, such test items can be structured so that the examinee is obliged to produce a very short answer, almost resembling a short-answer response, or an elaborate, lengthy answer. The two types of test items that reflect this distinction are referred to as *restricted-response questions* and *extended-response questions.*

A restricted-response question decisively limits the form and content of the examinee's response. Content is typically restricted by limiting the scope of the topic to be treated in the response. The form of the response, such as its length, is restricted in the way the question is phrased. Some examples are presented.

Restricted-Response Questions

Describe, in a paragraph of no more than fifty words, the three most common causes of indigestion.

List, in brief statements, three similarities between the United States' involvement in the Korean and Vietnam conflicts.

Another technique for restricting the examinee's response is to provide a certain amount of space on the test paper and require that the response be made within the confines of that space. The problem with this tactic, however, is that some examinees typically employ a tiny handwriting style, whereas others use large, bold handwriting. The former writers might be able to squeeze a small novella into the provided space; the large-penmanship people might be able to scrawl out only a few sentences or a lengthy clause.

Limiting examinees' responses to restricted-response essay items makes the scoring of those items more straightforward and reliable. Such items, however, are characteristically less valuable as measures of learning outcomes that require the student to display organization and originality.

Extended-response questions provide the examinee with far more latitude. The student typically produces a longer answer and is less constrained regarding the nature of that answer. Some examples of extended-response items follow.

Extended-Response Questions

Explain the meaning of the two phrases *formative evaluation* and *summative evaluation,* then describe the relationship between these two concepts.

Critically evaluate the impact upon American life of the energy crises of the seventies, particularly with respect to the alteration in Americans' expectations regarding the role of government.

There is general agreement that extended-response questions call for more sophisticated responses on the part of the examinee, but there is considerable doubt as to whether these complex responses can be satisfactorily scored. In a few paragraphs we shall examine some of the guidelines that can be employed to score more accurately such extended-response questions. However, you should recognize that, generally, the more extended the response called for in the question, the less reliably it can be scored.

Dividends and Deficits

As a tactic to assess certain kinds of complex learning outcomes, the essay item is indisputably the best approach. Since this kind of item sometimes requires a student to put together ideas and express them in original ways, there is no way of simulating that kind of requirement in a selected-response item or, for that matter, even in a short-answer item. Moreover, a constructed-response item, such as the essay question, requires the student to *produce,* rather than merely recognize, a correct answer, thus rendering the essay question a far more taxing kind of test item.

Essay items are also popular because they provide an opportunity for students to improve their writing skills. In recent years an increasing amount of criticism has been leveled against public schools because of the poor quality of student writing. Essay questions provide an additional opportunity for students to practice their writing skills.

It is often believed that essay items are easy to create, yet we shall see that this advantage is more apparent than real. Although most teachers can, while strolling toward class, dash off a series of essay questions, those questions characteristically will be rather abysmal. To create essay questions that do a decent assessment job, far more test-construction time is required.

The deficits of the essay test are sufficiently significant that were it not for the fact that the essay gets at really worthwhile kinds of learning outcomes, it might never be used. Without a doubt, its most serious deficiency is the unreliability of scoring. Many investigations have shown that essay questions are scored differently by different judges and that this variability in scoring markedly reduces reliability. If you will recall our earlier discussion of reliability, a test that is unreliable cannot be valid for any purpose. Unreliable scoring yields an unreliable test, hence, an invalid one.

There are procedures that can be employed to increase the reliability of scoring, and these will be considered shortly. It should be pointed out that when essay examinations are used for *program evaluation* purposes, rather than making decisions about individual learners, reliability and validity considerations are conceptualized differently. These points are considered later in Chapter 14 when we discuss procedures for assessing affective types of learner responses.

Another problem with the essay item is the amount of time necessary to score examinees' answers. If the scoring is done conscientiously, an enormous number of hours will have to be spent in scoring the tests. Faced with the prospect of spending an endless number of hours in scoring, many test scorers restrict their judgments to superficialities, thus reducing the validity of the entire testing operation.

Any experienced teacher can tell you that the essay question also provides a marvelous opportunity for the wily student who knows little to dazzle the teacher with clever writing and a compelling vocabulary. Many students bluff their way effectively through essay questions without knowing much about the subject matter treated in the question. Too many people who score essay tests are impressed with the student's general verbal ability or writing style, rather than focus on the examinee's responsiveness to the question.

A final deficit flows from the fact that relatively few essay questions can be answered (since they require so much examinee response time). As a consequence, subject-matter content cannot be sampled very efficiently. Only a few questions can be employed in a single test, and this often leaves lacunae in the content coverage of the examination.

Item-Writing and Item-Scoring Guidelines

Since, with essay questions, the pivotal problems are associated both with the writing of items as well as with the scoring of the tests, we will consider rules for writing essay items and for scoring essay responses.

1. *Frame questions so that the examinee's task is explicitly defined.* At a silly extreme, we might think of an unlucky student who encounters a nebulous essay question, such as, "Insightfully, discuss truth." Obviously, the examinee's task is ill defined, and different examinees would interpret the question quite divergently. Try to add a sufficient amount of detail to the question so that the focus of the intended response is really clear. In the

following examples, one of the questions clearly supplies insufficient guidance to the examinee.

Outlandish. Discuss democracy in America.

Outstanding. Describe how the system of "checks and balances" built into the U.S. Constitution was designed to preserve the democratic system envisioned by the Constitution's architects.

As limitations to the questions are added, we obviously move toward the restricted-response form of an essay question. Even with extended-response kinds of items, however, it is necessary to add sufficient guidance for the examinee so that the general thrust of the question is apparent.

2. *Specify the value and an approximate time limit for each question.* Although the item writer usually knows how much time should be used for each question's response, examinees will be less certain. It is helpful, therefore, to provide some rough estimates of how long the examinee should spend on each question.

If the examination is to be used for classroom-grading purposes, it is also desirable to supply the examinee with an idea of the weighting—for example, number of points—to be given to each item. Sometimes item weightings appear to be identical as far as the examinee is concerned, yet a teacher will have in mind that the last two questions are the really pivotal ones and will be weighted more heavily. The student, unaware of this well-kept secret, may emphasize the early part of the examination and give the last few questions inadequate attention, thereby coming up with an unsatisfactory examination performance.

3. *Employ a larger number of questions that require relatively short answers rather than only a few questions that require long answers.* This guideline suggests that by using many restricted-response essay questions one can do a better job of content sampling. With only a few questions on an essay exam, there is so much emphasis on a limited number of content areas that if, in a three-question essay test, for example, a student has overlooked one of the three topics, there goes one-third of the exam down the drain. Thus, it is preferable to have a good many items requiring responses of a half a page than to have two or three responses that demand responses of several pages in length.

4. *Do not employ optional questions.* Even though it is a routine practice to provide several essay questions, then allow the examinees to choose questions that suit them, this is an unwise procedure. An examination, for example, may include five essay questions and require the examinee to

respond to only three of them. The students, of course, enjoy this procedure because they can select questions where their knowledge is most strong. Yet, except for its beneficial effects in inducing student euphoria, the use of optional questions has little to recommend it.

When examinees respond to different questions, they are actually taking different tests. Therefore, the possibility of evaluating their achievement on a common basis disappears. It is also possible that if students are aware that the optional question procedure will be employed, they can prepare several answers in advance and attempt to plug them into certain questions on the examination.

In most instances, the use of optional questions on an examination reflects the examiner's uncertainty about what it is that the examination should really be measuring. The more equivocal the examiner is about the importance of the examination's contents, the more likely that optional questions are to be employed. They should be avoided.

5. *Verify a question's quality by writing a trial response to the question.* Anyone who is fashioning an essay question ought to be able to conjure up a pretty good answer for the question. If the item writer can't produce a fine answer, then it is more than likely the question has some problems. These problems, certain to be encountered by the examinees later on, can be spotted and rectified on the basis of the item writer's trial response.

Too many times essay questions are drummed up in a hustle by teachers who assume that there are no substantial problems with the question. Only during the exam itself, with all sorts of pressures on students, are the fatal flaws in the item discovered. That's too late. A trial response can help item writers detect defects in their essay questions.

6. *Prepare a tentative scoring key in advance of considering examinee responses.* Any kind of scoring key prepared in advance will usually need to be modified to some extent as the actual papers are scored. Sometimes examinees will interpret questions a bit differently than the examiner had in mind or may come up with different insights than were anticipated. Yet, it is extremely helpful to prepare a scoring key in advance of scoring essay exams. The advance scoring key should list the major considerations that would be looked for in an acceptable response or, on the contrary, the major defects that might appear in an unsatisfactory response.

Without advanced scoring guides or criteria for judging responses, the grading of student papers becomes a gigantic guessing game. Different professors bring their own criteria to bear in judging students' responses. More often than not, professors pass students who write smoothly and employ a sufficiently rich vocabulary to convey a sense of verbal acuity. Under such circumstances many students win. Some lose. Some of the winners should be losers, and vice versa. Advanced scoring keys, communicated among different essay graders, would help reduce this anarchic situation. Moreover, even though the creation of such scoring keys may oblige teachers to lavish more effort on the exam process than has been their custom, the ensuing validity and *justice* of the examination process should make it well worth the effort.

7. *Score all answers to one question before scoring the next question.* Too many scorers of essay examinations try to score an entire examination at one time, one question after another, then turn to the next examinee's paper. This is a particularly unsound practice since the examinee's response to one question can influence the scorer, adversely or positively, regarding the scoring of the next question. A far more consistent evaluation occurs if all of the answers to the first question are graded together, then all of the answers to the second question, and so on. In scoring the responses to different questions, the order of the papers should also be altered.

8. *Make prior decisions regarding treatment of such factors as spelling, penmanship, and punctuation.* Since factors that are irrelevant to the major learning outcomes being measured can sometimes influence test scorers, it is important to decide in advance how to treat them and not leave this decision to the exigencies of the moment as a particular examinee's test paper is graded. In some cases, of course, these very considerations will form a major focus of the essay examination, as in instances when an English teacher is having students produce essays to reflect their essay-writing skill. In such instances, the teacher may be legitimately concerned about spelling or punctuation. Often, however, the essay will focus on different factors than spelling and syntax. The scorer should give careful *advance* consideration to the extent to which sloppy syntax and stumbling spelling should influence the score. There are no hard-and-fast rules regarding such matters, so the examiner will have to decide whether these kinds of extraneous factors are sufficiently relevant to the examinee's general learning prowess that they should be included in the scoring scheme.

9. *Evaluate essay responses anonymously.* Since our knowledge of a particular student will sometimes becloud our appraisal of that student's response, it is particularly important not to look at the student's name prior to grading the paper. A classroom teacher, for example, can have students place their names on the reverse side of the last page of the examination, thereby permitting the examinations to be graded anonymously.

10. *Score essay responses holistically or analytically.* Essay answers can be scored in two ways. Both of these may induce the use of a scoring key, such as was described in guideline six. The first of these scoring approaches is referred to as an *analytic* scoring strategy. In an analytic scoring approach, an examinee's response is assigned (or not assigned) a given number of points on a criterion-by-criterion basis. For example, suppose in a U.S.

government class, the teacher had created an essay question for which the ideal response would have focused on four distinct problems in a current political crisis. The teacher develops a scoring guide which gives students up to five points for each of these four problems, that is, twenty points for a perfect response. For each of the four problems, the teacher assigns one point if the student's response mentions the problem, one or two additional points if the problem is well described, and one or two more points if the problem's possible solution is described. Thus, an analytic scoring guide something like the illustrative guide in Figure 11–1 is employed.

A scoring guide, such as the one illustrated in Figure 11–1, can be completed by the teacher, then returned to the student. This is one of the more significant advantages of an analytic scoring approach, because a low-scoring student can be informed in a relatively detailed manner just what deficiencies need to be corrected.

In contrast to an analytic scoring approach, we can grade essays on a *holistic* basis. As its name implies, the holistic approach views the essay response as a whole, and the test scorer renders a single, overall score or grade. Now holistic scoring should not be thought of as a necessarily crude, judgmental scheme where the essay grader plucks a global judgment from the air. A scoring guide, not unlike the previously seen analytic guide, can be used to help structure the expectations of the essay scorers. However, unlike the analytic method, where point-by-point allocations are made, the holistic scorer renders judgment in one big blob.

Holistic scoring schemes can be quite cavalier or amazingly careful. In particular, holistic scoring of student essays, paragraphs, and other sorts of written compositions, has been refined over the years.[1] By employing some of these refinements, holistic scores have been able to come up with amazingly high interjudge agreements, that is, where different judges scoring the same essays produce remarkably consistent scores.

The advantage of the holistic approach to scoring student compositions on responses to essay exams is, of course, that it really saves time. The disadvantage, however, particularly if the examination is being used in connection with an instructional program, is that the student gets only global, not particularized, feedback.

If there is to be additional instruction for the student, then it seems clear that an analytic scheme is preferable. For instance, if a student has prepared an inferior composition in an English class, it does that student little good to know that the composition was "flawed." What the student

---

[1]Educational Testing Service (ETS) in Princeton, New Jersey 08540, has played a leadership role in creating improved procedures for the holistic scoring of essays. Excellent guidelines for the holistic scoring of essays can be obtained from ETS.

SCORING GUIDE

Problem Area	Identified (1 point)	Described (1–2 points)	Solution (1–2 points)
Local Control	1	2	1
Federal Support	1	1	
Legal Constraints	1	2	2
The Media	1		

Student's Name Joe Hill

Total Points 12

FIGURE 11–1 An Illustrative Analytic Scoring Guide for an Essay Examination in a Government Class.

really needs to know is the detailed reasons that the composition was a loser. The particulars having been isolated, the student can then get cracking to eliminate those sorts of deficiencies.

Clearly, then, the choice between analytic and holistic scoring approaches is sometimes a difficult one. It depends on the purpose of the examination, the scoring resources available, the permissible turn-around time (that is, how much time can be allowed for scoring), and a host of similar factors. In some cases, both a holistic and analytic scoring scheme can be adopted.

In the Detroit Public Schools, for example, student compositions are scored holistically in connection with a high school proficiency examination. Those compositions which are considered failures on the basis of the holistic scoring are then rescored analytically. Because only a fraction of the papers are failures on the basis of the holistic scoring, this two-step scheme saves scorers considerable time and money for test scoring.

A Final Admonition

Most of us grew up in educational settings in which constructed-response tests were churned out almost unthinkingly by teachers. Because we have been the victims of such instant assessment schemes, we may be inclined to think that constructed-response tests, although time consuming to score, can be tossed out in the twinkling of an eye.

However, as this chapter has attempted to stress, creation of constructed-response tests is not fool's play. Great pains should be taken to create the items. No less attention should be given to the scoring procedures. Of course, if you have developed a truly defensible set of test specifications for the test (as seen in Chapter 9), most of these matters will have been addressed at that time. However, many classroom teachers will not have the luxury of spinning out splendid sets of test specifications. Particularly for such teachers it is hoped that the foregoing guidelines will prove serviceable.

PRACTICE EXERCISES

Before tackling these practice exercises, please review the guidelines for short-answer and essay items provided in the chapter. *Then* go through each of the following items, and see if you can spot which guideline is violated. We will start off with three short-answer items, then close out with a pair of essay items.

1. *A short-answer item.* What were the underlying causes of World War I?

   _____
   _____
   _____
   _____
   _____

2. *A short-answer item.* _____ was the vocation of nine of the 56 original signers of the U.S. Declaration of Independence.

3. *A short-answer item.* _____ _____, one of Canada's greatest _____, created _____ during the _____ century.

4. *An essay item.* In whatever depth you consider suitable, discuss the evolution of humankind.

5. *Directions for an essay test:* Directions to students: Choose two of the following three items, each of which will be worth fifty points. Then write for approximately sixty minutes on the two items chosen.

A more elaborate practice exercise: Because many of the guidelines for essay tests are associated with the scoring of these sorts of items, it would be excellent practice for you to create an entire set of step-by-step procedures to be used in the scoring of an important essay exam. If possible, give your scoring procedures to someone else who can critique their merits.

ANSWERS TO PRACTICE QUESTIONS

1. This item violates guideline two which calls for the item to be phrased so that the required response should be *concise.* The question, as currently phrased, could reasonably be answered by students for at least a week or two. It stimulates an essay-type response, not a short answer.

2. This short-answer item runs counter to guideline three which dictates that blanks be placed near the end of an incomplete sentence. We could have flipped the statement around or turned it into a direct question.

Incidentally, the vocation of nine of the 56 original signers of the U.S. Declaration of Independence was farming (or agriculture). There's just no telling when you'll next be asked to supply this tidbit of truth.

3. This is a classic Swiss cheese item and, as such, violates guideline four. Even Canadians would have a tough time answering the item.

4. This item is clearly not a restricted-response type of essay item. On the contrary, it supplies no restrictions at all. It violates guideline one, since the examinee's task is not explicitly defined. It also is inconsistent with guideline two, because no value or time limit has been cited. Not only has no time limit been set, the examinee is told to write on "whatever depth you consider suitable."

5. This test violates guidelines three and four. First, as optional selection of items is permitted, this is clearly contrary to guideline four. Then only two long-response items are used, rather than more short-response items; this is a violation of guideline three.

DISCUSSION QUESTIONS

1. After having reviewed the pro and con sides of both selected- and constructed-response items, what factor would induce you to personally select one or the other item-types?
2. Try to think of at least a half dozen types of constructed-response kinds of test items including (a) examinee behaviors, then (b) examinee products. Are there any similarities in the kinds of items you have identified?
3. Although it is clear that for constructed-response items one can isolate instances of examinee behavior versus examinee products, could this also be said for selected-response items? If so, how?
4. What is your own view regarding the relative virtues of holistic versus analytic scoring of student compositions? How about the scoring of responses to any essay examination in a U.S. history course; would your opinion change?
5. Why do you think that essay exams, in spite of considerable criticism of those exams during the forties and fifties, remained relatively popular among teachers?

SUGGESTIONS FOR ADDITIONAL READING

CHASE, CLINTON I., "Essay Examinations," Chapter 7, *Measurement for Educational Evaluation*, pp. 144–155. Reading, Mass.: Addison-Wesley, Inc., 1978. Chase discusses the strength and limitations of essay tests along with ways to improve essay examinations and to score essays more reliably.

GRONLUND, NORMAN E., "Measuring Complex Achievement: The Essay Test," Chapter 10, *Measurement and Evaluation in Teaching* (3rd ed.), pp. 232–248.

New York: Macmillan, 1976. In this chapter Gronlund probes the advantages and disadvantages of essay questions, then offers a series of suggestions for constructing essay questions and for scoring essay responses.

HOPKINS, CHARLES D., and RICHARD L. ANTES, "Scoring," *Classroom Testing: Administration, Scoring, and Score Interpretation,* pp. 19–40. Itasca, Ill.: F. E. Peacock, 1979. In this booklet an analysis is given of how to score "supply-type" items, including completion items, short-answer items, and essay items. Contrasts between the analytical and global methods of scoring are provided.

STANLEY, JULIAN, C., and KENNETH D. HOPKINS, "Constructing and Using Essay Tests," Chapter 9, *Educational and Psychological Measurement and Evaluation* (5th ed.), pp. 197–216. Englewood Cliffs, N.J.: Prentice-Hall, Inc., 1972. In appraising essay tests in relationship to their reliability and validity, Stanley and Hopkins describe the role of essay testing for college admission as well as computer scoring of essay tests.

12

Neophyte authors suffer from the common misconception that really seasoned writers can instantly dash off prose or poetry which rarely needs revision. Inexperienced writers of educational tests also tend to believe that their first-draft items should equal their last-draft items.

A useful pilgrimage for such novices would be a visit to the British Museum. In the authors' room of that fabulous museum, the manuscripts of writers such as Keats, Wordsworth, and Byron are on display. It is initially surprising, but then highly comforting, to see that even these literary giants revised, and revised, and revised their efforts. Visitors to the museum can see the often lengthy chain of drafts that precede the final poem or essay as these revered writers fussed over their work.

Well, if Keats and Milton were willing to shape up their writing, item revision should not be considered beneath the dignity of any item writer, whether a veteran or beginner. This chapter describes ways of transforming early-version test items into a form which, though a bit less lustrous than a Shakespearian sonnet, are markedly superior to an item writer's initial efforts.

Improving test items

Empirical and Judgmental Techniques

In considering the possible approaches to salvaging a flawed test item, it is helpful to isolate two fairly distinctive improvement strategies. The first of these are *judgmental* schemes in which the dominant reliance is on the human judgment that individuals render when they inspect, then weigh the merits of particular test items. Such judgmental strategies (*a priori* strategies, if you're feeling in the mood for a little ritzy Latin) can range in rigor and sophistication from a rather casual review of items, to a highly sophisticated review. We often see classroom teachers relying on their own instincts as they endeavor to sharpen up their tests. These efforts would be a good example of an unsystematic use of judgmental item-improvement schemes.

A second approach to item-improvement can be characterized as *em-*

pirical (or, if you're still in the need of a little dead-language polish, *a posteriori*) methods. In contrast to judgmental methods of item-improvement, which rely only on someone's judging the quality of test items, empirical schemes for item-improvement require us to try the items out on honest-to-goodness examinees, gather data regarding how the examinees performed on the items, then analyze these data in various ways to help us isolate possibly defective items.

It is important to note that when we employ empirical item-improvement techniques, we are focusing on *examinee* response data, that is, examinees' actual responses to the test items. We are not looking at just any old data. For instance, in the use of judgmental approaches to item improvement we might secure judges' ratings of particular test items, then analyze the very devil out of these judgmental data. Merely because we're playing around with data, however, does not render our approach empirical instead of judgmental. The data are not examinee-response date, but only data derived from judges.

Incidentally, although in practice we often find more frequent application of empirical item-improvement methods to selected-response items can be improved by judgmental, as well as empirical, techniques.

Although these two item-improvement strategies will be considered separately here, almost no respectable measurement specialist would recommend that we rely exclusively on either judgmental or empirical approaches. More often than not, if resources permit, both strategies should be employed. typically, the use of empirical item-improvement schemes precedes the application of judgmental strategies. Test items are tried out, the results of the tryout are subjected to one or more analyses, and these analyses are made available to individuals who then judge the items. Those judgments, however, are thus abetted by the results of the empirical item analysis.

Even busy classroom teachers, if they can somehow snag an extra hour or two every month or so, can employ both empirical and judgmental schemes to improve their tests. However, if time pressures or financial resources preclude the use of a combined empirical-judgmental approach to item improvement, it is better to use only one of the approaches than to avoid item improvement altogether. Educational test items usually need revision.

It is interesting to realize that in the past several decades the choice between judgmental and empirical item-improvement strategies has been almost perfectly correlated with the *size* of the test-development effort. In large-scale test-development projects, such as those involving nationally standardized achievement or aptitude tests, the major emphasis has been on empirical item-improvement procedures. Test items have been tried out, often with thousands of examinees. Results of these tryouts have then been subjected to all the exotic machinations that today's high speed computers permit. Analyses of these empirical results have then guided the revision of the test items.

On the other hand, the sorts of small-scale test-refinement efforts that go on in a teacher's classroom have almost always emphasized a judgmental strategy. Classroom teachers, either because they are already too busy or because they aren't familiar with empirical item-improvement methods, have relied on judgmental techniques to revise their tests. In the typical case, Mrs. Jones will review the final exam she used in last year's algebra class in order to judge which items are in need of revision or replacement. Although there are a few cases in which classroom teachers have employed empirical test-improvement schemes, these are certainly exceptions.

Norm- and Criterion-Referenced Applications

Throughout the text it has been emphasized that although there are instances when it doesn't make any substantial difference whether we are using norm-referenced tests or criterion-referenced tests, in some cases the distinction between norm- and criterion-referenced measures is quite significant. Such is the case with respect to item improvement, where we find that with norm-referenced tests we tend to rely more on empirical methods and with criterion-referenced tests we more frequently opt for judgmental methods. Why is this so?

Well, if you'll recall the earlier discussion of criterion-referenced tests, you'll realize that the chief stress in a criterion-referenced test is to come up with a clear description of the behavioral domain being measured and then to make sure that the test's items are congruent with that description. These are tasks which must be performed *judgmentally*. Indeed, in determining the rigor with which a criterion-referenced test's behavioral domain is described, there is no sensible alternative to human judgment (although we might dress it up with all sorts of numerical ratings and exotic quantitative analyses). Since the descriptive enterprise by test developers involves the spinning of a sophisticated verbal net that aptly captures a class of examinee behaviors, there's just no way we could toss such descriptions into a computer, even a big computer, and find out how adequate our description was.

Moreover, since the determination of a criterion-referenced test's (1) descriptive rigor and (2) congruence of items with the test's description (or specifications) are activities which *precede* the administration of tests to examinees, it is apparent that with criterion-referenced tests, at least in the early stages of the item-improvement game, we'll be emphasizing judgmental approaches.

For norm-referenced tests, however, we need to focus on the efficiency of the instrument in detecting legitimate differences among examinees so that we can defensibly contrast their performances against one another. This being the case, it is evident that we pick up our best insights regarding the refinement of items in a norm-referenced test by actually trying out the test with examinees, then seeing how well the items contribute to the detection of differences in examinees. Thus, for norm-referenced tests there is a greater reliance on empirical methods in the improvement of test items.

Naturally enough, since the last half century of educational measurement saw measurement buffs stressing norm-referenced testing applications, it is not surprising that our technical tool kit of empirical item-improvement techniques is far better stocked than is the case with judgmentally based techniques.

However, as will become apparent later in the chapter, there are certainly instances when both norm- and criterion-referenced test items would be substantially benefited from the application of judgmental- *and* empirical-improvement procedures. We should not be surprised, however, given the central thrusts of norm- and criterion-referenced measures, that in general the refiners of norm-referenced tests will lean toward empirical schemes while their criterion-referenced cohorts will tilt toward judgmental techniques.

JUDGMENTAL IMPROVEMENT OF TEST ITEMS

There are several sources of judgmental data by which we can improve test items. First off, of course, we can secure judgmental data from the item writers themselves. A person who writes a test item can subsequently review that item according to all sorts of standards. If item writers themselves are to be used in supplying such judgments, then just as authors frequently find it helpful to set aside manuscripts for a time prior to revision, it is often beneficial for item writers to wait a week or so before reviewing their own items. After the immediacy of creation has worn off, it is often more likely that parents can discern flaws in their progeny. Item writers are no different.

In addition to those who actually authored the items, it is possible to assemble independent judges who, though conversant with the subject matter, have no proprietary interests in particular items. Because of their lack of partisanship, independent reviewers are most valuable in the implementation of an effective judgmental item-improvement operation. External reviewers can do more than merely spot defective items; they can proffer remedies for those items.

Finally, examinees themselves can judge item quality. For example, students can be asked to comment if they find items ambiguous, misleading, too hard, too easy, and so on. If students are employed in this capacity, one should be wary of viewing their actual item-response data as typical. It is difficult for a student simultaneously to play the role of test taker and test critic. Care should be taken, therefore, to use examinees as reviewers only in those situations where the effects of a possibly distorted performance will not penalize an examinee.

Review Foci for Nonexaminee Reviewers

Well, now that we know *who* might be doing the judging, *what* should they be looking for in their reviews? Let's look first at the sorts of review foci that might be employed by item writers themselves or external reviewers. Later on we consider a different approach for examinees themselves.

The actual dimensions which serve as the basis for the review vary, of course, depending on the purposes of the examination. However, generally speaking, the following sorts of considerations serve as the emphases of most item-review judgment schemes:

1. Is the item congruent with its specifications?
2. Are there violations of standard item-writing guidelines?
3. Is the content of the item accurate?
4. Is the item culturally or otherwise biased?

Each of these questions, perhaps rephrased more specifically in accord with the particular purposes of the test, could serve as a bit of general guidance for judges. Alternatively, if one prefers something a bit more systematic, an item-review form could be devised in which the item judges would need to respond to such questions. If a defect was noted in any item, the judge might be asked to supply suggestions regarding possible improvements. Let's briefly consider each of the four questions just cited.

Item-specifications congruence.   To judge whether an item is congruent with the set of specifications from whence it supposedly sprang, judges obviously have to consider both the specifications and the items themselves. In the case of norm-referenced tests, as we saw in Chapter 8, these specifications are often less detailed than is true with criterion-referenced specifications. As a consequence, judges will more likely discover that items on a norm-referenced test coincide with that test's somewhat less explicit specifications.

Reviewers of criterion-referenced items will have to be highly attentive to the ingredients of test specifications, since these specifications will be far more detailed, hence, far more circumscribing. In the case of criterion-referenced tests, as Berk has noted, such tests must be consonant with the specifications or objective which it is supposedly measuring:

> It cannot be overemphasized how crucial this characteristic is to the effectiveness of the total test and the usefulness of the results. Irrespective of all other characteristics, *an item that is not congruent with its objective should not be included on the test.* (italics in original)[1]

One scheme for checking on the rigor (attentiveness?) of the item judges is to toss in a few deliberately incongruent items to detect whether judges are at least spotting such clearly incongruent items. Judges who fail to spot such "lemon" items should have their judgments disregarded.

Adherence to item-writing guidelines.   With respect to the violation of the sorts of item-writing rules that we described in the last two chapters, a reviewer of items obviously needs to be familiar with a wide range of such rules. For example, if an item reviewer runs across a multiple-choice item in which the wrong-answer distractors are all short, while the correct answer is long, then that shortcoming needs to be noted. There can, of course, be deficiencies in test items other than violations of the customary item-writing guidelines. Reviewers of test items will have to keep their wits about them in order to detect such flaws.

Content accuracy.   If test items deal at all with academic content, such as achievement tests in history, language arts, or biology, then it is obviously important to have the content in those items be accurate. For example, if a test item in a grammar exam incorrectly indicates that "relative pronouns which modify gerunds should be in the objective, not possessive case," then a skillful item reviewer should spot that content error. It is true, of course, that not too many people realize (or care about) the appropriate case of relative pronouns which modify gerunds, but think what terrific item reviewers you have if they can see that the "him" in the following math item should be "his."

A grammatically flawed arithmetic item

Jill always admired John's speed in going to the store. Each week he went to the store three times and took only twenty minutes each time. How much *total time* was involved in him going to the store?

---

[1]Ronald A. Berk, "Criterion-Referenced Test Item Analysis and Validation" (Paper presented at the first annual Johns Hopkins University National Symposium on Educational Research, Washington, D.C., October 1978), p. 18.

If your item reviewers can detect such nuances, then think how well they ought to weed out more flagrant flaws.

Item bias.   In Chapter 8 we spent considerable time discussing the ways in which tests can be biased. Item reviewers should be even alert for blatant and subtle biases in items, whether racist, sexist, religious, or socioeconomic, If, for example, a test item describes "Mrs. Gomez, a servant," then some Hispanic-Americans may, with justification, be offended if it appears that Spanish-speaking people are destined to occupy positions of servitude. To remedy such an item, either transform Mrs. Gomez to Mrs. Green or, more aggressively, elevate Mrs. Gomez to the status of a corporate executive. When using judges to review test items, be sure to alert them to the necessity of monitoring items for possible bias.

To recapitulate, the use of judges to review test items, whether those judges are the item writers themselves or outside reviewers, can definitely improve test items. Judgmental review of items can be carried out informally or rather systematically. Informal reviews are doubtlessly better than no reviews at all. Formal, systematic reviews are even better. Devising a scheme where both item writers *and* external reviewers judge items would be particularly effective.

As indicated previously, judgmental item-refinement procedures can be used to augment the quality of both selected-response and constructed-response sorts of items. All too often we see measurement specialists giving item-improvement attention to selected-response test items (particularly of the multiple-choice species), yet spending no time on the improvement of, for instance, essay items. Well, essay items need attention too. Judgmental techniques can be particularly effective in improving constructed-response items.

Examinee Judgment

When setting out to improve test items, a rich source of data is often overlooked because we typically fail to secure advice from examinees. Yet, since examinees have experienced test items in a most meaningful context, more or less like an executionee experiences a firing squad, examinee judgments can provide useful insights regarding particular items and, for that matter, such other features as the test's directions and the time allowed for completing the test.

As noted before, the kinds of data secured from examinees will vary, depending on the type of test being used, but questions such as the following, can usually be addressed with profit to examinees after they have completed an examination:

Item-Improvement Questionnaire for Examinees

1. If any of the items seemed confusing, which ones were they?
2. Were there any items that had more than one correct answer? If so, which ones?
3. Were there any items that had *no* correct answers? If so, which ones?
4. Were there words in any items that confused you? If so, which ones?
5. Were the directions for the test, or for particular subsections, unclear? If so, which ones?

It is important to let examinees finish a test prior to their engaging in such judgmental exercise. (Note the use of the possessive pronoun modifying the gerund *engaging*. You are, obviously, reading some grammatically top-drawer stuff here.) If examinees are asked to *simultaneously* play the roles of test takers and test improvers, they'll probably botch up both. No examinee should be expected to serve two functions, at least at the same time.

Simply give examinees the test as usual, collect their answer sheets or test booklets, and provide them with new, blank booklets. *Then,* distribute a questionnaire, such as the one seen earlier. In other words, ask people to play examiners and item reviewers, but to play these roles consecutively, not simultaneously.

Now, how do you treat examinees' reactions to test items? Let's say you're a classroom teacher and a few students come up with a violent castigation of one of your favorite items. Do you automatically buckle by scrapping or revising the item? Of course not; teachers are made of sterner stuff. Perhaps the students were miffed about the item because they didn't know how to answer it. One of the best ways for students to escape responsibility for a dismal test performance is to knock the test itself. One should anticipate a certain amount of carping from low-scoring examinees.

However, after allowing for a reasonable degree of complaining, student reactions can sometimes provide useful insights for teachers and even test developers from high-powered testing agencies. To overlook examinees as a source of judgmental test-improvement information, for both selected-response and constructed-response items, would be a serious error.

EMPIRICAL IMPROVEMENT OF TEST ITEMS

We turn now to the use of examinee-response data on the improvement of test items. A range of empirical item-improvement techniques has been well honed over the years, particularly for purposes of norm-referenced measurement. We consider these more traditional item-analysis procedures first, turning later to a few more recent wrinkles for improving items on criterion-referenced tests.

Difficulty Indices

For both norm- or criterion-referenced tests, one useful index of an item's quality is its difficulty. The most commonly employed item-difficulty index, often referred to these days simply as a *p value,* is calculated as follows:

$$\text{Difficulty } p = \frac{R}{T}$$

Where R = the number of examinees responding correctly (right) to an item.
Where T = the total number of examinees responding to the item.

To illustrate, if 50 students answered an item, and only 37 of them answered it correctly, then the p value for that item's difficulty would be

$$\text{Difficulty } p = \tfrac{37}{50} = .74$$

It should be clear that such p values can range from 0 to 1.00, with higher p values indicating items that more examinees answer correctly. For example, an item with a p value of .98 would be one which was answered correctly by almost all examinees. Similarly, an item with a p value of .15 would be one which most examinees missed.

The p value of an item should be viewed in relationship to the examinee's chance probability of getting the correct response. For example, if a binary-choice item is involved, then on the basis of chance alone examinees should be able to produce a p value of .50. On a four-option multiple-choice test, a .25 p by chance alone would be expected.

Sometimes slight variations of the basic item-difficulty formula are applied so that, for example, we find a difficulty index where

$$\text{Difficulty} = \frac{\text{right}}{\text{total}} \times 100$$

In this instance, of course, multiplying by 100 the ratio between correct and total item responses gets rid of the decimal point so that difficulty indices range from 0 to 100. Other folks may prefer to use percentages, so that an item's difficulty value can range from zero percent to 100 percent. However, in all of these indices, what we are isolating is the proportion of total examinee responses that are correct. As we shall see, item p values can prove most serviceable in empirically shaping up the items.

A note of caution should be registered at this point, because measurement people sometimes err by referring to items with high p values, say .80 and above, as "easy" items, while items with low p values, say .20 and below, are described as "difficult" items. Those assertions may or may not be accurate. Even though we typically refer to an item's p value as its *difficulty* index, the actual ease or difficulty of an item is tied to the instructional program surrounding it.

Let's say you are whipping up a new test of verbal aptitude, and you administer your test to a host of examinees who are unfamiliar with its contents. In such instances it undoubtedly makes sense to think of high p value items as easy and low p value items as tough. However, there are other situations.

Suppose you are teaching a course in physiology at a medical school and have produced a test which, if taken by the typical person off the street, would prove a terror. On all items, those who were not medical students would almost always miss an item asking for "the location of the oblagatum." However, if you're a skillful teacher, let's say the end-of-course p value for that item is .95. Does such a p value really indicate that the item is intrinsically "easy," or does it mean that a well-taught group of examinees will answer it correctly?

Suppose that down the hall, a colleague of yours is teaching the same course to another group of students. Because your colleague is a dull-witted person, only 48 percent of the students in this class answer the oblagatum item correctly. Isn't that even more reason to believe that the item isn't easy at all? Thus, when considering high p values, be a bit reluctant to characterize those items automatically as easy.

Item Discrimination Indices

For norm-referenced tests one of the most powerful indicators of an item's quality is the *item discrimination index*. In brief, an item discrimination index typically tells us how frequently an item is answered correctly by those who perform well on the total test. In principle, an item discrimination index reflects the relationship between examinees' responses on the total test and their responses on a particular test item. Indeed, one approach to computing an item-analysis statistic is to calculate a point biserial correlation coefficient between (1) the *continuous variable* of total test score and (2) the *dichotomous variable* of performance on a particular item, that is, correct or incorrect.

When I was a graduate student many years ago, and encountering the topic of item discrimination indices, I thought that there was only *one* way to tell how well an item discriminated. Since that time, I've discovered that there is no single, sanctified approach to the detection of an item's discrimination efficiency. There are many different indicators that can serve us well since, in all instances, an item discrimination index is nothing more than a "red flag" which indicates that there *may* be a flaw in an item.

In essence, a *positively discriminating item* indicates that an item is answered correctly more often by those who score well on the total test than by those who score poorly on the total test. A *negatively discriminating item* is answered correctly more often by those who score poorly on the total test than by those who score well. A *nondiscriminating item* is one for which there's no appreciable difference in the correct response proportions of those who score well or poorly on the total test. This set of relationships is summarized in the following chart (remember that the *caret* signs, < and >, signify *less than* and *more than*.)

TYPE OF ITEM	PROPORTION OF CORRECT RESPONSES ON TOTAL TEST
Positive Discriminator	High Scorers > Low Scorers
Negative Discriminator	High Scorers < Low Scorers
Nondiscriminator	High Scorers = Low Scorers

Now, how do we go about computing an item's discrimination index? Well, the following procedure can be employed for both the analysis of classroom tests as well as the analysis of more elaborate examinations. When there are differences between the procedures that one might use for classroom or other exams, these will be noted.

1. *Order the test papers from high to low by total score.* Place the paper having the highest total score on top, and continue with the next highest total score sequentially until the paper with the lowest score is placed on the bottom.

2. *Divide the papers into a high group and low group with an equal number of papers in each group.* For classroom tests it is common to split the groups into upper and lower halves. If there is an odd number of papers, then simply set aside one of the middle papers so that the number of papers in the high and low groups will be the same. If there are several papers with identical scores at the middle of the distribution, then randomly assign them to the high or low distributions so that the number of papers in the two groups is identical.

For more substantial item analyses, it is recommended that the high and low groups be determined by selecting the upper and lower 27 percent of the papers. Over four decades ago, Kelley demonstrated that these percentages maximized the discrimination efficiency of the analysis while still providing high and low groups of sufficient size to be reliable.[2]

[2]T. L. Kelley, "The Selection of Upper and Lower Groups for the Validation of Test Items," *Journal of Educational Psychology,* 1939, 17–24.

"Here's how we shape up our multiple choice items. We call it 'pin the distractors on the item stem.'"

For the analysis of classroom tests, it makes little difference whether teachers employ high and low groups of 25 or 33 percent. The use of 50 percent groups has the advantage of providing enough papers to permit reliable estimates of upper and lower group performances.

3. *Calculate a* p *value for each of the high and low groups.* Determine the number of examinees in the high group who answered the item correctly, then divide this number by the number of examinees in the high group. This provides us with p_h. Repeat the process for the low group to obtain p_l.

4. *Subtract* p_l *from* p_h *to obtain each item's discrimination index (D).* In essence, then

$$D = p_h - p_l$$

Remember, the size of D will vary somewhat depending on which percentages of the group papers are used in the high and low groups.

Suppose you are a classroom teacher and are in the midst of conducting an item analysis of your midterm exam items. Let's say you split your class of thirty youngsters' papers into two equal upper- and lower-half papers. All 15 students in the high group answered the item 31 correctly, but only five of the 15 students in the low group answered it correctly. The item discrimination index for item 31 would be $1.00 - .33 = .67$.

Now, how large should an item's discrimination index be in order for one to consider the item acceptable? Using the upper and lower 27 percentages to calculate the discrimination index, Ebel offers the following experience-based guidelines for indicating the quality of norm-referenced test items:[3]

DISCRIMINATION INDEX	ITEM EVALUATION
.40 and above	Very good items
.30-.39	Reasonably good but possibly subject to improvement
.20 .29	Marginal items, usually needing and being subject to improvement
.19 and below	Poor items, to be rejected or improved by revision

The influence of difficulty levels.   A review of the procedures for determining an item's discrimination index will suggest that an item's ability to discriminate is highly related to its overall difficulty index. For example, an item which is answered correctly by all examinees has a total p value of 1.00. Similarly, for that item the p_h and p_l are also 1.00. Hence, the item's discrimination index is zero ($1.00 - 1.00 = 0$). A similar result would ensue for items in which the overall p value was zero, that is, items which no examinee answered correctly.

With items which have very high or very low p values, it is thus less likely that substantial discrimination indices can be secured. Later in the chapter we see that this situation has prompted proponents of criterion-referenced tests (who often hope that almost all postinstruction responses will be correct) to search for alternative ways to calculate indices of item quality.

Internal and external criteria.   Thus far we have been describing an item-analysis operation which involves the use of an internal criterion, that is, the examinee's score on the total test. It is also possible to conduct item analyses with the use of an external criterion. In some cases, for the situation at hand, the use of an external criterion makes more sense.

To illustrate, suppose we were developing a new aptitude test which was designed to help admit applicants to medical school. Suppose, further, that we had administered a trial version of this new test to the first-year class at a local medical school and twelve months later had obtained a first

---

[3]Robert L. Ebel, *Essentials of Educational Measurement*, 3rd ed. (Englewood Cliffs, N.J.: Prentice-Hall, Inc., 1979), p. 267.

year's grade point average (GPA) for each student. Now, since we are really attempting to predict the GPAs with our new aptitude test, it makes sense to use the GPA as an external criterion and compute item discrimination indices much as before. In other words, instead of ordering the test papers according to total test scores, the papers would now be ordered, from highest to lowest, according to GPA. All other steps in the item-analysis procedure are identical to those described previously.

However, whether internal or external criteria are applied, item discrimination indices are merely that, *indicators*. They should not be regarded as Holy Writ. A low or a particularly negative item discrimination index should alert us to the *possibility* that an item is defective and either needs corrective surgery or mercy killing. However, it is only a possibility. After reviewing the item carefully, it may be decided to retain the item in its present form.

For norm-referenced tests, however, items that fail to discriminate properly are not doing their share. They are not doing their share in detecting the variability among examinees that is so crucial if we are going to make the necessary kinds of fine-grained comparative contrasts among examinees. Thus, refiners of norm-referenced tests would do well to follow Ebel's previously presented guidelines regarding discrimination indices and modify or delete those which fail to approach his .30 to .40 minimum standard.

Distractor Analysis

For an item which, perhaps on the basis of its p value or its discrimination index, appears to be in need of revision, it is necessary to look much deeper. In the case of multiple-choice items, we can gain further insights by carrying out a *distractor analysis* in which we see how the high and low groups are responding to the item's distractors.

Described next is a typical setup for conducting a distractor analysis. Note that the asterisk indicates that choice B is the correct answer to this item. For this item the difficulty index (p) was .50, and the discrimination index was a $-.33$. An inspection of the distractors reveals that there appears to be something in alternative D that is tempting the students in the high group. Indeed, while over half of the high group opts for choice D, not a single student in the low group went for choice D. Alternative D needs to be reviewed carefully.

ITEM NO. 7		ALTERNATIVES			
(p = .50 D = −.33)	A	B*	C	D	Omit
Upper 15 students	2	5	0	8	1
Lower 15 students	4	10	0	0	1

Note also that alternative C is doing nothing at all for the item. No student selected choice C. In addition to reviewing choice D, therefore, choice C should be made a bit more appealing. It is possible, of course, particularly if this is a best-answer type of multiple-choice item, that alternative B, the correct answer, needs a bit of massaging as well.

For multiple-choice items, in particular, but also for matching items, a more intensive analysis of examinee responses to individual distractors can frequently be illuminating. In the same vein, careful scrutiny of examinees' responses to essay and short-answer items can typically supply useful insights for revision purposes.

Item Analysis for Criterion-Referenced Tests

As indicated earlier, when using criterion-referenced tests there are situations where we hope that most students will score well on tests. In such instances, since the p values of both high and low students would approach 1.0, traditional item-analysis approaches are destined to yield low discrimination indices. Accordingly, some alternative approaches to item analysis for criterion-referenced tests have been devised in recent years.

There are two general approaches which have been employed thus far, depending on the kinds of criterion groups available. The first scheme involves the administration of the criterion-referenced test to *the same group of examinees* both prior to and following instruction. The disadvantages of this approach is that one must wait for instruction to be completed before securing the item-analysis data. Another problem is that the pretest may be *reactive,* in the sense that its administration sensitizes students to certain items so that the students' posttest performance is actually a function of the instruction *plus* the pretest's administration.

The second approach is to locate two *different groups of examinees,* one of which has been already instructed and one of which hasn't. By comparing the performance on items of instructed and uninstructed students, we can pick up some useful cues regarding item quality. This approach has the advantage of avoiding the delay associated with pretesting and posttesting the same group of students and also of avoiding the possibility of a reactive pretest. Its drawback, however, is that we must rely on human judgment in the selection of the "instructed" and "uninstructed" groups. The two groups should be identical in all other relevant respects, for example, in intellectual ability, but different with respect to whether or not they have been instructed. The isolation of two such groups sounds easier than it usually is.

Pretest-posttest differences.   Adopting the initial strategy of testing the same groups of students prior to and after instruction, we can use an item discrimination index derived by Cox and Vargas.[4] This index is calculated as follows:

$$D_{ppd} = p_{post} - p_{pre}$$

where p_{post} = proportion of examinees answering the item correctly on posttest.

p_{pre} = proportion of examinees answering the item correctly on pretest.

The value of D_{ppd} (discrimination based on the pretest-posttest difference) can range from -1.00 to $+1.00$, with high positive values indicating that an item is apparently sensitive to instruction.

For example, if 41 percent of the examinees answered item 27 correctly in the pretest and 84 percent answered it correctly on the posttest, then item 27's D_{ppd} would be .84 − .41 = .43. A high positive value would indicate that the item is apparently sensitive to the instructional treatment. Items with low or negative D_{ppd} values would be earmarked for further analysis since they are not behaving the way one would expect them to behave.

Uninstructed versus instructed group differences. If we use two groups, that is, an instructed and an uninstructed group, one of the more straightforward item discrimination indices is D_{uigd} (discrimination based on uninstructed versus instructed group differences).[5] This index is calculated as follows:

$$D_{uigd} = p_i - p_u$$

where p_i = proportion of instructed examinees answering an item correctly.

p_u = proportion of uninstructed examinees answering an item correctly.

This index can also range in value from -1.00 to $+1.00$. To illustrate its computation, if an instructed group of examinees scored 91 percent correct on a particular item, while that same item was answered correctly by only 55 percent of an uninstructed group, then D_{uigd} would be .91 − .55 = .36. Interpretations of D_{uigd} are similar to those used with D_{ppd}.

Berk has provided an excellent discussion of the pros and cons of these two items discrimination indices, as well as several other indices for use with criterion-referenced tests.[6]

---

[4]R. C. Cox and J. S. Vargas, "A Comparison of Item Selection Techniques for Norm-Referenced and Criterion-Referenced Tests" (Paper presented at the annual meeting of the National Council on Measurement in Education, Chicago, Ill., February 1966).

[5]L. Levin and F. Marton, *Provteori och provkonstruktuon* (Stockholm: Almquist and Wiksell, 1971).

[6]Berk, "Criterion-Referenced Test Item Analysis and Validation."

Item homogeneity.   Several writers have argued that since the items on a criterion-referenced test are supposed to assess a single behavioral domain, one way of reviewing a criterion-referenced test item is to discern the extent to which it functions in a manner similar to the rest of the items in the test.

One rather straightforward procedure for discovering whether the items on a criterion-referenced test are functioning similarly is to compare the p values on all items. For instance, let's say that on a 25-item test of competency x we found that 20 of the items had p values of between .70 and .90, but that three items had p values of only .45, and two others had p values of 1.00. The fact that the p values on the few items were different would suggest that we might give those items special scrutiny when we were judging their congruence with the test's specifications. The dissimilar p values may also suggest that the test specifications themselves are in need of revision.

The question arises, however, whether the items on a criterion-referenced test need to be homogeneous in their difficulty levels. The answer to that question is *no*. Although with rather small-scope behavioral domains one might anticipate fairly comparable items to be produced in accord with test specifications, when the behavior domain expands, the probable homogeneity of the items decreases. Since, as recommended earlier, for instructional purposes the size of domains should be relatively large, this means that in many instances one would expect a fairly wide range of p values.

Another approach to the determination of item homogeneity for criterion-referenced tests is to see whether responses to the items are affected similarly by instruction. Well over a decade ago I experimented with this approach as a way of spotting potentially flawed items on a criterion-referenced test.[7] The general strategy I chose was to compare items based on whether examinees answered the items correctly (1) or incorrectly (0), before and after instruction. The possible combinations for an examinee's responses to items on a pretest-posttest basis are, of course, correct-correct (11), incorrect-incorrect (00), incorrect-correct (01), and correct-incorrect (10). By considering all the items on a criterion-referenced test to determine the median, that is, *prototypic* item, I was able to use a chi-square statistical analysis to see if the responses to particular items were deviating significantly from what one might expect by chance alone.

Pettie and Oosterhof modified this chi-square procedure so that it could be used with a single test administration (pretest only) by contrasting

---

[7]W. J. Popham, "Indices of Adequacy for Criterion-Referenced Test Items (Paper presented at the 1970 meeting of the American Educational Research Association) and included in W. J. Popham, ed., *Criterion-Referenced Measurement: An Introduction* (Englewood Cliffs, N.J., Educational Technology Publications, 1971), pp. 79–98.

the difficulty index of each item with the median difficulty of a set of items.[8] One of the problems with both of these chi-square schemes is that no critical values have yet been established for identifying sufficiently aberrant items. In other words, how significant must a chi-square value for an item be before we castigate that item for its atypicality? Even more importantly, as indicated a few paragraphs earlier, how large must a behavioral domain be before we get uneasy about substantial item heterogeneity? These issues are as yet unresolved.

Once Improved, The Number of Items

As one inspects the various indices of item quality that are being developed for use with criterion-referenced tests, it becomes apparent that at this point there is still a great deal of fluidity in the measurement field regarding what sorts of item-analysis procedures are most appropriate for these sorts of tests. Given the fact that it took a number of decades for developers of norm-referenced item-analysis schemes to reach closure on preferable procedures, this is not surprising. However, for the near future, we had best anticipate a certain amount of scrambling and indeterminancy with respect to item analysis for criterion-referenced measures.

Suppose we have tried on a set of preliminary items for purposes of improving them. After employing all of these delightful empirical and judgmental techniques to the improvement of these test items, we might hopefully have produced a pretty defensible batch of items. The next question is, "How many test items should we actually use in creating the final version of our test?"

This is obviously an important question for devotees of norm-referenced or criterion-referenced tests, because if we use too few items in the test, we don't get a reliable fix on the examinee's status with respect to the behavior we're measuring. If we use too many items, there is lost economy on two counts—the unnecessary items we've produced and the unnecessary time we take from examinees as they wade through superfluous items.

For one thing, there are situations in which we may set very stringent minimum levels of required learner proficiency—for example, demanding that the learner score 95 percent or better on a test. There are other situations in which we set very relaxed standards of requisite minimum proficiency, such as 50 percent. The level of proficiency we establish can influence the number of items needed in a test.

There is also the problem of making the wrong decision on the basis

[8]A. A. Pettie and A. C. Oosterhof, "Indices of Item Adequacy for Individually Administered Mastery Tests" (Paper presented at the Annual Meeting of the American Educational Research Association, San Francisco, April 1976).

of the test results. Let's say we're using criterion-referenced tests in an instructional setting to monitor the progress of students as they move through a course. At various points in the course, each student must complete a test in order to establish whether the student has mastered the skills taught during that part of the course. If we make an error in judging the student's mastery, which kind of error is more serious? In other words, is it worse to advance students who have not mastered material to the next course unit (known as *false-positives*), or is it worse to hold back students (*false-negatives*) who have actually mastered necessary skills? Of course, there may be no difference in real life consequences associated with these two kinds of mistakes, but quite often there is. The relative gravity of making either kind of decision error is usually referred to as *loss ratio*. Not surprisingly, the relative gravity of these two kinds of decision errors can influence the number of items needed in a test.

In addition, there is the matter of examinees' actual level of functioning. If we are testing a group of examinees whose average competency with respect to the test is about 95 percent, we can use a different number of test items than if we are testing a group of examinees whose average competency is about 20 percent.

All three of these factors unfortunately operate to confuse the situation so that no one can spin out a simple answer to the question of how many items. As always, we find that the world is more complex than it really has a right to be.

Several writers have tussled strenuously with the test-length problem. Novick and Lewis offer a sophisticated Bayesian statistical strategy for dealing with test length.[9] Using their approach requires that we make estimates regarding the factors just described—that is, desired level of examinee proficiency, loss ratio, and examinees' actual level of functioning. These three values are then used with previously prepared tables to obtain general recommendations regarding how many items per behavioral domain are needed.

Other procedures for dealing with the test-length problem have been discussed by Harris[10] and have been provided in the binomial model devised by Millman.[11] Millman's scheme has received considerable attention,

[9]M. R. Novick and C. Lewis, "Prescribing Test Length for Criterion-Referenced Measurement," in *Problems in Criterion-Referenced Measurement*, eds., C. W. Harris, M. C. Alkin, and W. J. Popham, CSE Monograph Series in Evaluation, no. 3 (Los Angeles: UCLA Center for the Study of Evaluation, 1974).

[10]C. W. Harris, "Some Technical Characteristics of Mastery Tests," in *Problems in Criterion-Referenced Measurement*, eds., C. W. Harris, M. C. Alkin, and W. J. Popham, CSE monograph series in evaluation, no. 3 (Los Angeles: UCLA Center for the Study of Evaluation, 1974).

[11]J. Millman, "Criterion-Referenced Measurement," in *Evaluation in Education: Current Applications*, ed., W. J. Popham (Berkeley, Calif.: McCutchan, 1974).

primarily because of its simplicity. Essentially his approach involves the use of binomial model based on the examinee's ability to pass or fail each item in a behavior domain. For specified passing score percentages—for example, 80 percent correct—Millman's tables permit us to identify, for tests of different length, how many students would be misclassified according to their true level of functioning—that is, their true or accurately measured skill level.

The Bayesian approach generally permits the use of shorter tests than does the binomial approach because the Bayesian model requires more assumptions than does the less restrictive binomial model. To oversimplify a bit, for many educational settings in which criterion-referenced tests will be used, either the binomial or Bayesian approaches dictate that tests should consist of somewhere between ten and twenty items per behavioral domain. For norm-referenced tests covering broader ranges and different categories of behavior, many more items are requisite.

Now whether a test developer wants to go to the trouble of employing either technique will depend, of course, on the importance of the test being devised. If the stakes are really high, as might be the case when an exam is being used to license health practitioners, we don't want to create tests too short to do a good job in isolating incompetents. If, on the other hand, the test is only one of several used as part of a first-year algebra course, a more relaxed approach to the test-length question may be in order. As you can see, reaching a decision about an acceptable minimum for test length is a long way from being simple. The test-length issue is one of the more serious technical issues currently being tackled by measurement specialists.

PRACTICE EXERCISES

Part A

Decide whether each of the item-improvement procedures sketched in the following five items is dominantly an *empirical* or a *judgmental* item-improvement strategy.

1. The test items on a criterion-referenced test are improved on the basis of the D_{ppd} item-analysis statistic.
2. Items on a norm-referenced test are analyzed using the upper and lower 27 percents of the score distribution in order to detect negatively discriminating and nondiscriminating items.
3. English teachers in Washington High School routinely share their end-of-year examinations so that the exams can be critiqued by colleagues.
4. Using a costly and sophisticated item-refinement approach, a commercial testing firm hires a minimum of ten item reviewers to rate (1) the congruence of each item with its specifications and (2) the content accuracy

of each item. The mean ratings of reviewers (on a 5-point scale) are calculated. Items failing to achieve a near rating on each criterion of 2.5 or higher are revised.

5. A group of item analysts judge the quality of items based on the extent to which an item's p value from a field trial is within the general range of p values for the total set of items.

Part B

Assume that you are in the process of revising a series of items and secured the following sets of information. Review each solution, and decide first *whether* you would revise the item and, if so, *how* you should revise the item.

6. Item 17 on a criterion-referenced test of mathematics skill has an after-instruction p value of .93 and an item discrimination index based on a point biserial correlation coefficient (of item scores with total test scores) of .12. Should this item be revised?

7. An item on a norm-referenced aptitude test has a p value of .26 and a discrimination index of .10. Is it likely that the item should be revised?

8. Although judged incongruent with its test specifications by three independent reviewers, item 47 on a norm-referenced test of history has a p value of .52 and a discrimination index of .49. Is it likely that item 47 should be altered?

9. Here is the distractor analysis for a multiple-choice item on a norm-referenced test of secondary school pupils' reading abilities. Review the data, then suggest what sort of changes, if any, you would urge for the item.

ITEM 14	A	B	C*	D	E	OMIT
(p = .69) Upper 27%	1	0	15	0	4	0
(D = .15) Lower 27%	3	0	12	3	1	1

10. An item on a twenty-item criterion-referenced test of a physical competency has a p value fully .30 lower than the p values on all other items. Should this item most likely be revised?

ANSWERS TO PRACTICE EXERCISES

1. Empirical
2. Empirical
3. Judgmental

4. Even though there are some data involved in this example, even data for which one can compute honest-to-goodness means, this is still a judgmental approach to item improvement.

5. Empirical, although the item analysts *judged* the empirically derived p values. Even with empirical item-analysis schemes someone ultimately has to judge "how good is good enough." However, in empirical schemes these judgments are imposed by the availability of examinee-response data, such as we see in this example.

6. Well, this information certainly doesn't indicate that the item *must* be revised. It is perfectly acceptable for items on a criterion-referenced test, particularly those on which the p values are high, to display low discriminating efficiency. While the item might warrant a bit closer look, there's nothing in the statistical data to cause alarm.

7. For a norm-referenced test, items of this sort should most likely be revised.

8. Absolutely. Although item specification is often stressed most with criterion-referenced tests, even for norm-referenced tests we must make certain that an item is relatively consistent with its specifications (usually stated somewhat generally) for the test. All the empirical indicators notwithstanding, item 47 needs some reworking.

9. Since the value of D is only .15, and this is a norm-referenced test, the item certainly seems to be in need of revision. As one reviews the distractor analysis, it appears that choice E is attracting too many of the students in the high group and too few of the students in the low group. Hence, choice E should be scrutinized further. In addition, choice B is snagging no one. It, too, should be reviewed carefully. As always, these item statistics should be guides, not Gods. An inspection of the nature of the other alternatives will determine whether, and how, alterations should be made.

10. It's difficult to tell. If the behavioral domain being measured is a fairly broad one, then the presence of a deviant p value does not indicate automatically that the item needs to be revised.

DISCUSSION QUESTIONS

1. If you were *obliged* to choose between empirical or judgmental approaches to item improvement, which would you choose and why?

2. How do you think an item's p value should be most effectively used in item analyses?

3. Should all tests be subjected to item analysis of an empirical sort? Why?

4. Can you think of an explicit procedure for reviewing essay items that is analogous to the distractor-analysis schemes used with multiple-choice tests?

5. Under what circumstances, if any, might a nondiscriminating test item be considered an acceptable item?

6. Are there circumstances under which a negatively discriminating item might be acceptable? If so, what are these circumstances?

SUGGESTIONS FOR ADDITIONAL READING

BERK, RONALD A., "A Consumer's Guide to Criterion-Referenced Test Item Statistics," *National Council on Measurement in Education*, 9, no. 1 (Winter 1978), 8 pp. This is a highly readable account by Berk of various schemes which specialists have proposed for use in appraising the quality of criterion-referenced test items. It is recommended reading for anyone interested in improving item quality for criterion-referenced tests.

BERK, RONALD A., "Item Analysis," in *Criterion-Referenced Testing: State of the Art*, ed. Ronald Berk. Baltimore: The Johns Hopkins University Press, 1980. Berk provides an extensive treatment of item-analysis procedures in this chapter. The pros and cons of various types of item-analysis procedures for criterion-referenced measures are presented.

EBEL, ROBERT L., "How to Improve Test Quality Through Item Analysis," Chapter 13, *Essentials of Educational Measurement* (3rd ed.), pp. 258–273. Englewood Cliffs, N.J.: Prentice-Hall, Inc., 1979. Ebel offers a lucid description of how to employ item-analysis procedures to improve test quality.

NOLL, VICTOR H., DALE P. SCANNEL, and ROBERT C. CRAIG, "Trying Out and Evaluating the Teacher-Made Test," Chapter 7, *Introduction to Educational Measurement*, pp. 195–220. Boston: Houghton Mifflin, 1979. In this chapter the authors provide schemes for analyzing test results, particularly in relationship to the use of item-analysis improvement schemes.

STANLEY, JULIAN C., and KENNETH D. HOPKINS, "Item Analysis for Classroom Tests," Chapter 11, *Educational and Psychological Measurement and Evaluation* (5th ed.) pp. 267–281. Englewood Cliffs: Prentice-Hall, Inc., 1972. In this chapter the authors include a description of item-analysis procedures for classroom tests. A simplified test-analysis procedure is described, along with a step-by-step scheme for carrying out such an analysis.

13

If all the educational assessment devices were stacked on top of each other, it would make quite a pile. If we removed from that pile all of the paper-and-pencil tests, then the remaining pile would be quite small.

Yes, there's little doubt that the vast majority of educational tests are traditional paper-and-pencil instruments which attempt to measure an individual's potential, as in the case of aptitude measures, or an individual's skill and knowledge, as in the case of an achievement test. However, there are many significant aspects of learner behavior for which paper-and-pencil tests prove either inefficient or downright inappropriate. For example, can you think of a sensible paper-and-pencil test that could be used to assess a student's ability to deliver an impromptu speech in a public speaking class?

There are times, therefore, when educators must bid farewell to their handy collection of paper-and-pencil measures, turning instead to alternative assessment techniques. The two most prominent of these are *observations* and *ratings*. In this chapter we consider these two data-gathering approaches, attempting to note ways in which high-quality observations and ratings can be carried out. Incidentally, in the next chapter we deal with the

Observations and ratings

assessment of such affective dimensions as learner attitudes and interests. Observations and ratings are particularly effective ways of securing data from which we can draw inferences about an examinee's affective status.

Behavior and Products

When educators attempt to observe or rate learners, as we saw in Chapter 11, it turns out that they end up focusing on learner *products* or learner *behaviors*. Typical learner products, for instance, would include a charcoal sketch by a student in an art class or an ashtray created by a student in a ceramics class. Typical learner behaviors, for instance, would include an extemporaneous speech in a public speaking class or a tumbling routine in a gymnastics class.

Sometimes we will wish to concentrate on the behaviors used by a student during the early stages of the student's creation of a product. For example, an art teacher might observe the way that a beginning art student holds a paint brush, attempting to correct students who, for instance, dip the wrong end of the brush into the paint. Later on the art teacher will evaluate only the final product, that is, the student's painting.

Ratings and Observations

Although some educators use the terms *ratings* and *observations* interchangeably, this is an error. The two operations are different. When we *rate* individuals' behaviors or products, we typically attempt to render qualitatively different judgments. For instance, suppose judges at a swimming meet are rating the efforts of the springboard divers. The ratings are made along a continuum of quality ranging from least to most skilled. Similarly, if we attempt to rate the quality of a first-grade pupil's handwriting, then once more we try to render ratings which reflect subtle gradations of quality, usually on a scale that ranges from the deftness of a medieval monastery copyist to the awkward scrawl of a clumsy beginner.

Thus, *ratings* oblige someone to render a *qualitative judgment* along one or more continua. These judgments may be applied either to learner behavior ("She earned a 7.8 rating on the parallel bars.") or to learner products ("I rated her original sonnet as 'above average' based on its poetic structure.").

Whereas ratings oblige judges to draw qualitative distinctions between learners' behaviors or products, observations merely oblige someone to indicate whether specified behaviors are *present* or *absent*. For instance, whole truckloads of classroom observation schedules have been devised over the years for use in the study of teaching. These observation schedules are used as follows: Observers are first trained in the use of the schedules (forms), then they observe classrooms to detect whether or not teachers and students display certain behaviors. In most cases, the observers also record the frequency with which a certain behavior is displayed. The observers are not supposed to render judgments regarding whether the observed behaviors are good or bad, skillful or sloppy, since such judgments would transform the operation into a rating process.

Observations are applied only to learner behaviors, not products. We can *observe* or *rate* a team of debaters as it tears into its opponents. We *rate* the quality of the written resource materials that the debate team has prepared. We can't *observe* the written resource materials.

Observations, particularly those that are systematically conducted, tend to deal with much more precise behaviors than is often the case with ratings. School administrators, for instance, are sometimes asked to supply a rating of a teacher's "overall effectiveness." It would be meaningless to attempt to *observe* such a large and nebulous dimension. Thus, although one sometimes encounters extremely detailed rating forms, observations tend to be ever more find grained than ratings are. One difference between after-the-event ratings and during-the-event observations is that ratings are often based on a more or less haphazard composite of recollected observations, because the rater has not seen an individual in all pertinent situations and, even if so, selectively recalls such situations when the rating is made. Systematic observations, on the other hand, are based on more careful planning and scrutiny of ongoing behavior. Characteristically, the objectivity of systematic observations will be higher than the objectivity of ratings. That is, interobserver agreement tends to exceed interjudge agreement. In addition, ratings can be used with both learner behavior and learner products. Observations are used only with behaviors.

SYSTEMATIC OBSERVATIONS

There are two distinctive types of systematic-observation situations. In one case we observe a representative sample of behavior in situations that really occur in life. Such actual situations vary considerably for different individuals. In the second case we make observations in a standardized situation that is, insofar as possible, identical for all individuals. There are advantages and disadvantages in each of these approaches, of course. For instance, the standardized-observation system controls for the possibility that (unaccounted for) situational variables will contaminate the nature of the observed behavior. On the other side of the case, an individual's behavior is typically less natural in a contrived situation than in a routine one.

In the 1960s and 1970s we witnessed the birth of innumerable observation scales for use in observing teachers, students, supervisors, and so on. Many of these scales have been developed with the proprietary care of the gold prospector who is certain that "this time I'll hit the mother lode." Although the literature abounds with observation scales, it seems every recent arrival on a particular educational scene is compelled to fashion a new observation scale that is "just right" for the perceived problem. Of course, a good many of these scales are next to worthless, conceptually unclear, and conducive to unreliable observations. Even so, the educator in need of observation scales would be wise to examine available scales prior to engaging in a scale-development escapade. It is often easier to modify existing scales than to create a fresh measurement monster.

One effective way of sampling the behavior of interest is to engage in *time-sampling* observation. In other words, the observer can select specific samples of time, perhaps selected randomly, to carry out observations. Another scheme, often used during classroom observations, is to set up discrete, short observation segments, such as five minutes, one minute, or thirty seconds. During each of these consecutive segments the observation scale is used anew. Such techniques usually result in more carefully recorded data—not to mention more exhausted observers.

The observers themselves are the pivotal people in our observation extravaganza. Careless observers produce worthless data. Conscientious observers, *with proper training*, can yield excellent evidence. Proper training of observers, complete with specific directions, practice sessions, and interobserver disagreement resolution, is imperative. Carrying out one or more shakedown observation tryouts, with subsequent correction sessions anticipated, is the way to initiate a systematic observation effort.

Tools and Techniques

Mehrens and Lehmann draw a useful distinction between observation *tools* and observation *techniques*.[1] They point out that "an observation technique generally implies the use of a particular observation tool such as a checklist. . . . However, the process of observing and recording an individual's behavior is what is meant by the term observational technique."

Thus, even if educators select or create an outstanding observation tool, they can set up such flawed observation techniques that meaningless data would result. For instance, failure to train observers properly in the use of the observation tool would typically produce questionable outcomes. Similarly, failure to employ an appropriate time-sampling observation plan would further discredit the observational technique.

To illustrate, let's say you were carrying out an investigation in which you had allocated observers two hours of observation per child as they performed routine classroom activities. Should you have the observers spend all of their time in one two-hour lump, or should you space out the observations so that smaller snippets of children's behavior can be observed?

There is some evidence that spacing out the observations into 24 five-minute segments will give you a much better sample than will longer, less frequent observations. Furthermore, if at all possible, these five-minute observations should be made at systematically selected different times of the day so that the observers don't always scrutinize Tommy's behavior immediately after lunch recess when he has interacted meaningfully with his peanut butter and jelly sandwiches.

[1]W. A. Mehrens and I. J. Lehmann, *Measurement and Evaluation in Education and Psychology* (New York: Holt, Rinehart & Winston, 1975), p. 346.

The issue of how to decide on an appropriate time-sampling plan should illustrate that the selection of a defensible observation tool is only half the battle. Effective observations oblige us to devise and implement a defensible observational technique.

Checklists

Perhaps the most commonly employed observation tool is the *checklist*. A checklist, as its name implies, simply presents a list of behaviors which an observer is to look for. If a particular behavior is present, the observer checks that behavior on the list. In Figure 13-1 we see a checklist devised over half a century ago by Ralph W. Tyler, one of the true giants of educational thought in the 1900s.

Note that some of the items on the checklist, as a well-constructed checklist should, call for the observer only to make the judgment of whether or not a behavior was present (and with this checklist, in what sequence that behavior took place). Note also, however, that some of the items on Tyler's list call for qualitative judgments on the part of the observer, for instance, the items in the lower left-hand corner of the checklist that oblige the observer to determine the skills in which the student needs further training. These items call for the sorts of judgments that should be restricted to ratings. However, let's allow Ralph an error or two. After all, we've had over fifty years to *rate* his checklist.

Checklists can be modified to some extent so that the presence or absence of specified behaviors can be observed within certain time periods, for example, two minutes. However, a checklist should really be restricted to determining whether or not behaviors have occurred, not whether these behaviors were good or bad, polished or putrid.

Even with "present versus absent" behaviors, the designer of a checklist will still have a choice regarding the *specificity* of the behaviors to be observed. For example, we could create a checklist in which we asked an observer to check whether the teacher displayed "positive verbal behaviors toward pupils." Such a dimension would be a fairly general descriptor of teacher behavior. We could also set forth five more specific types of teacher verbal behavior which we consider positive, such as "praises student's work" or "greets students in a friendly fashion." The more general the elements on a checklist are, the more latitude observers have to make errors. In general it is wiser to go for more specific observable behaviors.

Anecdotal Records

A departure from the customary observation operations, with their time samples and multidimensional checklists, is the *anecdotal record*. Anecdotal records are descriptions of observed events, in a classroom discussion, for

STUDENT'S ACTIONS	Sequence of Actions	STUDENT'S ACTIONS (Continued)	Sequence of Actions
a. Takes slide	1	ah. Turns up fine adjustment screw a great distance	
b. Wipes slide with lens paper	2	ai. Turns fine adjustment screw a few turns	
c. Wipes slide with cloth		aj. Removes slide from stage	16
d. Wipes slide with finger		ak. Wipes objective with lens paper	
e. Moves bottle of culture along the table		al. Wipes objective with cloth	
f. Places drop or two of culture on slide	3	am. Wipes objective with finger	17
g. Adds more culture		an. Wipes eyepiece with lens paper	
h. Adds few drops of water		ao. Wipes eyepiece with cloth	
i. Hunts for cover glasses	4	ap. Wipes eyepiece with finger	18
j. Wipes cover glass with lens paper	5	aq. Makes another mount	
k. Wipes cover glass with cloth		ar. Takes another microscope	
l. Wipes cover with finger		as. Finds object	
m. Adjusts cover with finger		at. Pauses for an interval	
n. Wipes off surplus fluid		au. Asks, "What do you want me to do?"	
o. Places slide on stage	6	av. Asks whether to use high power	
p. Looks thru eyepiece with right eye		aw. Says, "I'm satisfied"	
q. Looks thru eyepiece with left eye	7	ax. Says that the mount is all right for his eye	
r. Turns to objective of lowest power	9	ay. Says he cannot do it	19, 24
s. Turns to low-power objective	21	az. Told to start a new mount	
t. Turns to high-power objective		aaa. Directed to find object under low power	20
u. Holds one eye closed	8	aab. Directed to find object under high power	
v. Looks for light			
w. Adjusts concave mirror			
x. Adjusts plane mirror			
y. Adjusts diaphragm		**NOTICEABLE CHARACTERISTICS OF STUDENT'S BEHAVIOR**	
z. Does not touch diaphragm	10	a. Awkward in movements	
aa. With eye at eyepiece turns down coarse adjustment	11	b. Obviously dexterous in movements	
ab. Breaks cover glass	12	c. Slow and deliberate	✓
ac. Breaks slide		d. Very rapid	
ad. With eye away from eyepiece turns down coarse adjustment		e. Fingers tremble	
ae. Turns up coarse adjustment a great distance	13, 22	f. Obviously perturbed	
af. With eye at eyepiece turns down fine adjustment a great distance	14, 23	g. Obviously angry	
ag. With eye away from eyepiece turns down fine adjustment a great distance	15	h. Does not take work seriously	
		i. Unable to work without specific directions	✓
		j. Obviously satisfied with his unsuccessful efforts	✓

SKILLS IN WHICH STUDENT NEEDS FURTHER TRAINING	Sequence of Actions	CHARACTERIZATION OF THE STUDENT'S MOUNT	Sequence of Actions
a. In cleaning objective	✓	a Poor light	✓
b. In cleaning eyepiece	✓	b. Poor focus	
c. In focusing low power	✓	c. Excellent mount	
d. In focusing high power	✓	d. Good mount	
e. In adjusting mirror	✓	e. Fair mount	
f. In using diaphragm	✓	f. Poor mount	
g. In keeping both eyes open	✓	g. Very poor mount	
h. In protecting slide and objective from breaking by careless focusing	✓	h. Nothing in view but a thread in his eyepiece	
		i. Something on objective	
		j. Smeared lens	✓
		k. Unable to find object	✓

FIGURE 13-1 Check list for evaluating skill in the use of the microscope. (From Ralph W. Tyler, "A Test of Skill in Using a Microscope," *Educational Research Bulletin*, 9:493–496. Bureau of Educational Research and Service, Ohio State University. Used by permission.)

example. The observer is free to note any behavior that appears important and is not required to focus on the same traits for all subjects. The observer records in a few paragraphs exactly what was observed and attempts to keep facts and interpretations separate. Records are usually made as soon after an incident as possible in order to reduce errors of recollection. When gathered periodically over some segment of time, such accumulated observations sometimes offer a more striking depiction of behavior than would have been yielded by other more routine techniques. Used judiciously, anecdotal records can provide a rich and welcome change of pace from the bland quantitative orientation of most observation procedures.

A major advantage of anecdotal records is that they provide us with a depiction of actual behavior in a natural setting. Anecdotal records also offer us the possibility of describing events that are perhaps exceptional, but potentially significant.

A chief disadvantage of anecdotal records, particularly for classroom teachers, is that they take an enormous amount of time to write up and organize. Whereas anecdotal records might constitute a useful data-gathering tool if one had enough money to hire special anecdotal recorders, to ask busy teachers to record these possibly insightful, but time-consuming, vignettes is pure folly.

In addition, it is difficult for teachers to maintain their objectivity when dealing with their own students. Teachers may fail to "see" a favorite pupil engage in a reprehensible act, while being unable to overlook even minor transgressions by the class clown.

Anecdotal records, in spite of several appealing features, are written about more often in measurement textbooks than they are used in the real educational world. As an observational technique, this writer wouldn't rate them all that high. Speaking of ratings, let's turn to that topic.

RATINGS

Ratings, as indicated earlier, are qualitative judgments regarding something. In education these judgments are typically rendered regarding student behaviors or student products.

Behavior Ratings

The kinds of learner behaviors usually rated include students' abilities to sing, play musical instruments, and perform various physical skills. An example of a sample rating form for judging the quality of a student's speech-making ability is presented in Figure 13–2.

In the rating form seen in Figure 13–2 we can observe that only two

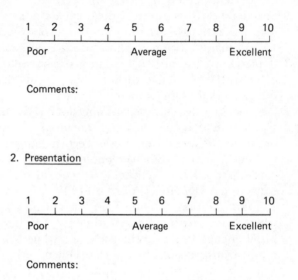

SPEECH RATING FORM

Directions to Rater. Judge a pupil's speech by rating the student's organization and presentation on a 1 to 10 scale. Circle the number for each dimension that best reflects the quality of that dimension.

1. Organization

```
1   2   3   4   5   6   7   8   9   10
└───┴───┴───┴───┴───┴───┴───┴───┴───┘
Poor            Average         Excellent
```

Comments:

2. Presentation

```
1   2   3   4   5   6   7   8   9   10
└───┴───┴───┴───┴───┴───┴───┴───┴───┘
Poor            Average         Excellent
```

Comments:

FIGURE 13-2 A two-dimensional rating form for judging student speeches.

rather global dimensions are used (speech organization and speech presentation). Some rating forms (often called rating scales) provide much more detailed breakdowns of attributes to be rated. In a former life as a high school speech teacher, I found myself at speech tournaments using rating forms that contained as many as thirty separate rating dimensions for use in judging a single speech!

Ratings of behaviors can be supplied at the same time as the behavior is occurring (such as when gymnasts are rated during the course of their routines), soon after the behavior has occurred (such as when a principal rates a teacher's performance after leaving the teacher's classroom), or a long time after the behavior has occurred (such as when teachers are asked by potential employers to rate students who completed the teacher's class some years earlier).

The closer the rating is to the behavior's occurrence, the more confidence we can place in the ratings. In some instances, however, since rating students *while* they are performing would induce unnecessary anxiety, it makes sense to supply ratings immediately after the conclusion of the performance.

Product Ratings

In addition to rating student behaviors, we can also rate student products, such as the creative accomplishments of pupils in art or homemaking classes. Other, more frequently encountered student products that need to be rated include book reports, graphs, maps, and various sorts of term projects. An example of a rating scale that is used to evaluate a student's handwriting is presented in Figure 13-3.

The product rating scale in Figure 13-3 is used by moving an actual sample of the student's handwriting along the scale until the quality of the student's handwriting best coincides with the examples on the scale. The pupil's handwriting is then scored with the grade-placement or age-equivalent values provided on the scale.

Whereas raters of student behaviors usually try to render their ratings during or immediately following the behavior's occurrence (since, in essence, the behavior evaporates following its occurrence), raters of products have the convenience of getting around to the rating operation when the spirit moves them. If we wished, we could rate the workmanship of the furniture found in Tutankhamun's tomb centuries after those treasures were created. Such ratings, of course, would be of limited utility to the folks who created the furniture. As they say, immediate knowledge of results is preferable to delays of any substantial magnitude.

However, it is clear that one of the considerable advantages of the rating of products stems from the leisure with which those products can be rated. Instead of being obliged to rate a series of student book reports within seconds after they have been turned in, a teacher can pack them off home and spend a fun-filled weekend rating the book reports.

Common Rating Scales

The three most commonly used types of rating scales are *numerical* rating scales, *graphic* rating scales, and *rankings*. We briefly consider each of these types of rating forms.

Numerical rating scales. Perhaps because of the simplicity with which they can be constructed, we often encounter numerical rating scales in education. A numerical rating scale presents a series of numbers, each tied to a particular rating, then asks the rater to assign numerical values to each of the attributes being rated. For instance, an excerpt from a typical

GRADE PLACEMENT	HANDWRITING SCALE	AGE EQUIV. (IN MONTHS)
3.0	*The quick brown fox just came*	99
3.5	*over to greet the lazy poodle.*	105
4.0	*The quick brown fox just came*	111
4.5	*over to greet the lazy poodle*	117
5.0	*The quick brown fox just came*	123
5.5	*over to greet the lazy poodle*	129
6.0	*The quick brown fox just came*	136
6.5	*over to greet the lazy poodle*	142
7.0	*The quick brown fox just came*	148
7.5	*over to greet the lazy poodle*	154
8.0	*The quick brown fox just came*	160
8.5	*over to greet the lazy poodle*	166
9.0	*The quick brown fox just came*	172
	over to greet the lazy poodle.	

FIGURE 13–3 Handwriting scale used in the *California Achievement Tests,* Form W. Reproduced by permission of the publisher, CTB/McGraw-Hill, Del Monte Research Park, Monterey, CA 93940. Copyright © 1957 by McGraw-Hill, Inc. All rights reserved. Printed in the U.S.A.

sort of numerical rating form is seen below where teachers are being rated according to various qualities.

Excerpt from a Teacher Rating Form

Directions. For each behavior cited below, circle the appropriate number by using the following scheme:

5 = *Excellent*, 4 = *Above Average*, 3 = *Average*,
2 = *Below Average*, and 1 = *Poor*

A.   Establishes good rapport with students
    1 2 3 4 5

B.   Presents subject matter clearly
    1 2 3 4 5

C.   Maintains proper discipline in classroom
    1 2 3 4 5

In some rating forms great care is taken to provide verbal descriptors for each of the numerical ratings. In other rating forms there is far less clarity regarding what a given numerical rating really signifies. For instance, if you were given a 1 to 10 numerical rating scale to judge the quality of paragraphs, where 1 = Inferior and 10 = Superior, how would you rate the paragraph you're now reading? Moreover, assuming you were generous and gave it a seven, would that seven mean the same thing to other raters as it means to you? Vaguely described numerical rating scales can lead to ratings that are quite unreliable.

Graphic rating scales.   Graphic rating scales take advantage of the fact that many people can use visual images to help them make qualitative gradations in their ratings. A graphic rating scale presents each characteristic to be rated along with a horizontal line on which the rater is to place a check. The following is an excerpt from a graphic rating scale for judging the frequency of student participation in extracurricular activities.

Excerpt from an Extracurricular Participation Form

Directions. Indicate the degree to which a student participates in the various aspects of extracurricular activities cited below by placing an X mark on the line beneath each item.

1. Takes part in club activities

Always	Frequently	Occasionally	Seldom	Never

2. Participates in team athletics

Always	Frequently	Occasionally	Seldom	Never

3. Participates in some aspects of student government

Always	Frequently	Occasionally	Seldom	Never

Graphic rating scales can be designed so that the rating options are identical for all characteristics to be rated, such as we see in the rating-form excerpt for extracurricular activities. Such unchanging rating-form options constitute a *constant-alternatives* scale. A *changing-alternatives* scale permits the descriptors associated with each horizontal line to be altered.

At its leanest variation a graphic rating form simply provides one-word descriptors, such as "seldom" or "frequently." Because such terse descriptors fail to communicate all that well to most raters, more elaborate phrases are sometimes employed on the rating form, leading to what we might refer to as a *descriptive-graphic rating scale*. For instance, taking the first characteristic on the extracurricular participation rating form, we might modify it as follows:

A Descriptive-Graphic Rating Dimension

1. Takes part in club activities

Is highly active; participates much more than most	Occasionally plays a role in club activities	Never participates; is indifferent to club activities

Comments:

Since descriptive-graphic rating scales frequently are changing-alternatives scales, it is common to provide raters with a "comments" space so that they can clarify certain of their ratings. A number of measurement people believe that descriptive-graphic rating scales are the most suitable for use in schools because of their greater specificity than the typical numerical or graphic rating forms. Descriptive-graphic rating forms oblige the designer of the rating form to come up with some clarifying descriptive information.

Ranking. Although technically different than rating, ranking approaches are usually thought of along with rating methods. Using this approach, student behaviors on products are ranked from highest to lowest, best to worst, most effective to least effective, and so on. If a ranking procedure is employed, it is usually recommended that ranks are initially assigned at both ends of the continuum toward the middle. In other words, first rank the top few products and the bottom few products, then gradually work toward the midranks.

When many objects or pupils must be ranked, the ranking method becomes most onerous. Even with a handful of pupils to rank, if there are many dimensions on which students must be ranked, ranking can become most cumbersome. Even more time consuming is a special application of ranking known as the *paired-comparison method* in which each pupil is compared with every other pupil so that the rater can indicate which of the two pupils is superior on the characteristic being rated. Although more reliable than typical ranking procedures, the paired-comparison method takes so much time that most raters are genuinely enervated by the enterprise. The paired-comparison ranking method is best left to applications in well-financed research and evaluation studies. It is not a procedure that classroom teachers will find enthralling.

Sources of Error in the Rating Process

There are three common sources of error in the rating operation which can contribute to unsatisfactory data. First off, there is the *rating scale*. Secondly, there are the *raters* themselves who may bring a number of nasty error tendencies to the enterprise. Finally, there are errors in the rating *procedure*, that is, the process by which the raters employ the rating scale.

Rating-instrument flaws. The major defect with most rating instruments is the lack of descriptive rigor with which the characteristics to be rated are described. Given this lack of rigor, ambiguity exists in the interpretation of judges. The result is a set of unreliable ratings. For example, if judges are to rate teachers on the extent to which they are "controlling," some judges may view this as a positive quality, and some may view it as a negative quality. Clearly, an inadequately clarified rating form can lead to all sorts of "noise" in the data provided by raters.

Procedural flaws. Among the problems with the rating operation, we usually encounter demands on raters to rate too many qualities. Overwhelmed raters are raters rendered ineffectual. A currently fashionable oxymoron[2] in education is that "less is more." This is certainly the case with

---

[2]An oxymoron is a literary device in which the desired effect is achieved by means of juxtaposing inherently contradictory notions, such as "mournful optimist" or "Army Intelligence."

respect to the number of characteristics that we should thrust under a rater's nose. Care should be taken that no more than a half dozen or so characteristics are to be rated.

Another procedural error, often seen in the accumulation of ratings, is the failure to combine, or average, ratings from independent raters. The use of many raters is an excellent way to secure decent data because individual errors tend to cancel each other out and a more accurate average rating emerges.

Rater personal-bias errors.   If you recall Chapter 8's consideration of bias, you'll remember that bias is clearly an undesirable commodity. Raters, albeit unintentionally, are frequently biased. Three kinds of *personal-bias* errors are usually encountered.

The first of these, known as *generosity error*, occurs when a rater's bias leads to higher ratings than are warranted. Raters with a proclivity toward generosity errors see good even where no good exists.

On the other extreme, some raters display *severity errors*. A severity error, of course, is a tendency to underrate phenomena. When a pupil's products deserve a *good*, a rater suffering from this personal-bias error will award it only an *average* or even a *below average*.

A final sort of personal bias error is known as *central-tendency error* and describes a tendency for raters to view everything as "in the middle of the scale." Very high or very low ratings are avoided by such folks. They prefer the mean or the median.

It is sometimes possible to fashion a rating form so that such errors can be minimized. As a graduate student, I participated in such an effort in connection with a federally sponsored research project. The highlights of that effort might be instructive to the reader.

I was a research assistant, anxious to do a creditable job on the research project to which I had been assigned. One aspect of the study called for us to secure administrator ratings of teacher effectiveness from almost 1,000 school administrators. I had been reading about administrator ratings of teacher effectiveness, hence was aware that many administrators are biased toward generosity errors. Thus, instead of a normal distribution of effectiveness ratings, what one characteristically obtained when administrators rated teachers was something like the negatively skewed distribution seen in Figure 13–4. As the solid curved line indicates, most administrators rate teachers well above average. Indeed, if an administrator gives an "average" rating to a teacher, that generally can be interpreted as "below average."

Well, because statistical techniques work better with data which are distributed in a normal fashion, the project director was worried about the probably nonnormal distribution that we would get from our 1,000 school

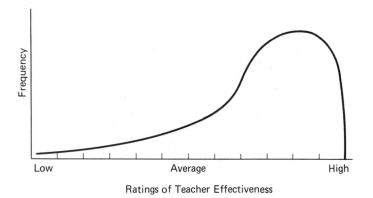

FIGURE 13–4 Typical administrative ratings of teacher effectiveness.

administrators. He directed me to, "try to come up with a wrinkle in our rating procedure which will dodge the generosity error of school administrators." Clearly, it was a challenge.

For well over a week I thrashed around, trying to devise a solution to the problem. No luck. Then, by chance, I was watching a televised motion picture awards ceremony where the master of ceremonies suspensefully opened the ever-present "sealed envelope" to see who had won the award. At last I began to form an idea for solving the rating problem. I took my plan to the project director. He bought it completely, and we set out to implement the scheme. Here's how it worked.

A school administrator (usually a principal) received mailed instructions to "mentally rank in order of decreasing effectiveness all teachers in the school," assigning 10 percent of the teachers to the top 10 percentage of overall effectiveness, 10 percent of the teachers to the next 10 percentage of effectiveness, and so on. Administrators were informed that, *of necessity*, their teachers would be distributed evenly across the entire range of effectiveness. *Then*, and only then, the administrator was to open a sealed envelope which was enclosed with the mailing. In that envelope was the name of one of the teachers in the school. The administrator was to assign that teacher the previously determined rating based on the prior 10 percentage rating operation. By using my ingenious scheme, we were able to alter the typical distribution of administrative ratings, as seen in Figure 13–5 in which the broken line reflects the distribution of ratings we received. Turn now to Figure 13–5 to discover the effects of my creativity.

As you can see, my idea did not exactly constitute a major methodological breakthrough in the ratings of teachers. Apparently, sealed envelopes notwithstanding, administrator tendencies toward generosity errors are tough to eliminate.

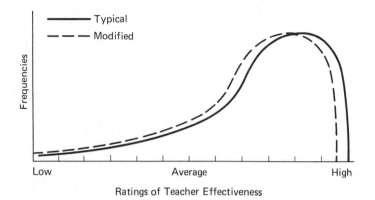

FIGURE 13-5 Typical (solid line) and modified (broken line) administrative ratings of teacher effectiveness.

Halo effect. A particularly frequent error arises when a judge's overall impression of a person influences how the judge rates the person on individual characteristics. This error is known as *halo effect*. If a rater has a favorable attitude toward an individual, that individual will get a host of favorable ratings (deserved or not) on a number of individual characteristics. Similarly, if a rater has an unfavorable attitude toward an individual, the individual will get a pile of unfavorable ratings on all sorts of separate characteristics.

One way to minimize halo effect to some extent is to reverse the order of the high and low positions on the rating scale occasionally so that the rather cannot *unthinkingly* toss out a whole string of positives (or negatives).

Training Raters

When we employ a complex and sophisticated observation form, it is generally recognized that observers will have to be trained to use it properly. Often, because rating scales are sometimes more general and *apparently* easier to use, the training of raters is underemphasized or overlooked completely.

However, a well-organized training session for raters can do wonders for the quality of the data we secure from ratings. In the training session the value of accurate and honest ratings should be stressed. The typical errors made by raters should be discussed and castigated. Discussions of such rater mistakes as severity errors and halo effect can minimize them.

Give raters plenty of practice opportunities, and discuss any atypical ratings so that the raters can recognize probable sources of deviation. Try to motivate the raters to supply on-target and unflawed ratings.

In conclusion, we have explored observations and ratings in this chapter. For the most part, we dealt with the application of these two procedures to the kinds of learner products and behaviors that represent cognitive and, less often, psychomotor behaviors. In the next chapter we take a good look at affective measures. As that chapter makes clear, observations and ratings are particularly useful in the tapping of examinees' affective dispositions.

PRACTICE EXERCISES

Part A

Decide whether the following five operations are best described as *ratings* or *observations*.

1. The behavior of pupils is viewed by researchers through a one-way mirror to discern the frequency with which they display five specific behaviors which have been previously identified as reflecting boredom.
2. The quality of a singer's ability to display a range of tones is noted by trained research assistants.
3. Students are watched by the teacher to see whether or not they voluntarily participate in class discussions.
4. The significance of students' final essays in a political science course is evaluated by a team of former congressmen and congresswomen.
5. A team of individuals from a private consulting group known as *Observations Unlimited* spend a month in various teachers' classrooms, then rank the caliber of class atmosphere, from high to low.

Part B

Consider the following descriptions of rating schemes, then decide whether each one represents a *numerical scale*, a *graphic scale*, a *descriptive-graphic scale*, a set of *rankings*, or a *paired-comparison* method.

6. Raters order the quality of all 14 contestants in a singing competition, from least to most effective, assigning a 1 to the best, a 2 to the second best, and so on.
7. Ratings are supplied on a horizontal line (scale) which provides a few one-word indications of what the scale represents.
8. Each student is contrasted by raters with all other students in deciding which students have made reasonable progress in social growth during the academic year.
9. Using a 10 = Outstanding and a 1 = Inferior, raters assign numbers to book reports prepared by the school's gifted class.

10. Raters use a form consisting of a series of changing-alternative dimensions, represented by horizontal lines, with a fair amount of verbal descriptive information to clarify each dimension.

ANSWERS TO PRACTICE EXERCISES

Part A

1. Observation
2. Ratings (A qualitative judgment is involved.)
3. Observation
4. Ratings
5. Ratings (the name of the consulting group notwithstanding)

Part B

6. Rankings
7. Graphic Scale
8. Paired-Comparison Method
9. Numerical Scale
10. Descriptive-Graphic Scale

DISCUSSION QUESTIONS

1. If you were asked by members of a school advisory council to describe the fundamental differences between observations and ratings, how would you approach the task?
2. Can you think of any fairly defensible guidelines which would help one decide when observations should be employed, rather than ratings, and vice versa? If so, what are they?
3. How would you design an optimal training program for observers? Would it be identical to or different from a training program for raters?
4. What kinds of attitudinal variables might be effectively assessed by means of observations or ratings?
5. How are the "value-free" data from an observation ultimately transferred into a useful form for educational decision making?

SUGGESTIONS FOR ADDITIONAL READING

CHASE, CLINTON I., "Observational Techniques for Evaluating Processes and Products," Chapter 8, *Measurement for Educational Evaluation*, pp. 156–173. Reading, Mass.: Addison-Wesley, 1978. A thorough discussion is provided in this chapter of observational techniques for evaluating processes and products.

GOODSTADT, MICHAEL, and SIMMIE MAGID, "When Thurstone and Likert Agree—A Confounding of Methodologies," *Educational and Psychological Mea-*

surement, 37, no. 4 (Winter 1977), 811–818. An examination of the similarities and differences in methodologies and tasks in Liker′ Method of Summated Ratings and Thurstone's Method of Equal-Appearing Intervals is presented.

GRONLUND, NORMAN E., "Evaluating Learning and Development Observational Techniques," *Measurement and Evaluation in Teaching* (3rd ed.), pp. 427–451. New York: Macmillan, Inc., 1976. An extensive discussion of rating scales is found in this chapter, including numerical, graphic, descriptive-graphic, and ranking methods. Gronlund provides an excellent discussion on anectodal records as observational techniques, along with a series of practical suggestions for improving the effectiveness of anecdotal records.

MEHRENS, WILLIAM A., and IRVIN J. LEHMANN, "Other Teacher-Made Evaluation Procedures," Chapter 12, *Measurement and Evaluation in Teaching* (3rd ed.), pp. 336–385. New York: Holt, Rinehart & Winston, 1975. In this chapter a distinction is drawn between procedures and products. Based on this distinction, a series of tools for use in observation are proferred. The authors describe various types of rating scales and offer ways to improve the quality of the data secured from rating scales.

MORGAN, MARGARET K., and DAVID M. IRBY, *Evaluating Clinical Competence in the Health Professions*. St. Louis: C. V. Mosby, 1978. In this collection of 23 papers, attention is given to assessment techniques in the health professions, particularly those involving the evaluation of one's clinical competency. A number of excellent insights regarding how to assess clinical competency pepper this intriguing volume.

NOLL, VICTOR H., DALE P. SCANNEL, and ROBERT C. CRAIG, "The Measurement of Personality and Affect: Observational Techniques," Chapter 12, *Introduction to Educational Measurement*, pp. 373–401. Boston: Houghton Mifflin, 1979. Observational techniques are treated in this chapter with respect to the measurement of personality and affect.

TUCKMAN, BRUCE W., "Checklists and Scales to Measure Performance and Behavior," Chapter 7, *Measuring Educational Outcomes: Fundamentals of Testing*, pp. 170–203. San Francisco: Harcourt Brace Jovanovich, Inc., 1975. An excellent description of performance tests is provided in this chapter.

WEBB, E. J., and others, *Unobtrusive Measures: Nonreactive Research in the Sciences*, Skokie, Ill.: Rand McNally, 1966. This delightful volume describes a series of exotic observational procedures. Of particular value in the assessment of affect, the book is laden with clever schemes for observing student behavior.

AND FOR THOSE WHO TIRE OF READING

How to Prepare Teaching Performance Tests. Distributed by Vimcet Associates, Inc., P.O. Box 24174, Los Angeles, Calif. 90024. This thirty-minute filmstrip-tape program describes the rationale and the development of procedures for preparing teaching performance tests, that is, a test to assess the skill of a teacher in promoting learner-mastery of prespecified instructional objectives.

Using Teaching Performance Tests for Instructional Improvement and Skill Assessment. Distributed by Vimcet Associates, Inc., P.O. Box 24174, Los Angeles, Calif. 90024. The role of the teacher-performance test in instructional improvement which assesses the skill of teachers is described in this thirty-minute filmstrip-tape program.

14

If all possible situations were listed for which educators need measurement devices, most of them could be handled quite conveniently by cognitive tests. Tests of cognitive aptitude or tests of cognitive achievement pretty well satisfy the chief assessment needs of most teachers and administrators. However, of course, there are other specialists roaming the educational landscape. Counselors and school psychologists, for example, have assessment requirements which extend well beyond the confines of the cognitive domain. Most often these assessment needs extend into the affective realm. In this chapter we're going to investigate how one should go about developing affective assessment devices.

The Cognitive, Affective and Psychomotor Domains

Before turning to a discussion of affective measures, however, we need to do a bit of term defining. A *cognitive* measure is one which deals principally with the examinee's mental abilities or achievements. A test of one's intellectual aptitude, for example, would constitute a commonly encountered cognitive measure.

Creating affective measures

A *pyschomotor* measure deals chiefly with the examinee's small-muscle or large-muscle physical skills or aptitudes. For instance, tests of one's typing ability or one's skill in skiing would be examples of psychomotor tests.

Affective measures focus on the examinee's attitudes, values, interests, and feelings. For example, a measure of children's self-concepts as learners, that is, the manner in which the children viewed themselves as students, would be an example of an affective measure.

It is important to qualify such assertions by saying, for instance, that a psychomotor assessment device deals *primarily* (not exclusively) with physical skills. For most testing devices, an examinee responds to some extent with all three types of behavior. For instance, a student fills out an attitude inventory (*affective*) by using a pencil to make marks on an answer sheet (*psychomotor*) which requires the intellectual skill (*cognitive*) to place responses for item one alongside answer space one on the answer sheet. Yet, because the responses focus on an attitudinal dimension, the instrument is classified as affective.

Educators have, for centuries, attended to these three domains of learner behavior. Moreover, many educators, for example, teachers in medieval church schools or in synagogue schools, have probably focused on a *spiritual* domain as well. The point is, of course, that for analytic purposes educators can slice up learner behavior in many different ways.

However, those who do the best slicing job typically get their way of carving up the world accepted. Thus, when in 1956 Benjamin S. Bloom and his colleagues published the widely known *Taxonomy of Educational Objectives, Handbook I: The Cognitive Domain*, no further slicing was requisite.[1] In that important volume, Bloom and his coworkers set forth the main elements of the cognitive, affective, and psychomotor domains. In addition, a hierarchical division of learner behaviors in the cognitive domain was provided, which started off with low-level, memory behavior (*knowledge*) and ended up with high-level, cognitive skills such as synthesis and evaluation.

Because the various levels of the cognitive domain might sometimes be needed in connection with the creation of tests, they will be briefly described. It should be noted, however, that whereas the three major divisions of the taxonomies have been widely accepted (cognitive, affective, and psychomotor), the particular levels within each domain have never been used to any appreciable extent by educators. Nevertheless, because you surely want to be a superinformed educator, here are the cognitive domain's six levels.

> KNOWLEDGE. Knowledge involves the recall of specifics or universals, the recall of methods and processes, or the recall of a pattern, structure, or setting. It will be noted that the essential attribute at this level is recall. For assessment purposes, a recall situation involves little more than "bringing to mind" appropriate material.
>
> COMPREHENSION. This level represents the lowest form of understanding and refers to a kind of apprehension that indicates that a student knows what is being communicated and can make use of the material or idea without necessarily relating it to other material or seeing it in its fullest implications.
>
> APPLICATION. Application involves the use of abstractions in particular or concrete situations. The abstractions used may be in the form of procedures, general ideas, or generalized methods. They may also be ideas, technical principles, or theories that must be remembered and applied.

[1]B. S. Bloom, ed., and others, *Taxonomy of Educational Objectives, Handbook I: The Cognitive Domain* (New York: D. McKay, 1956).

ANALYSIS. Analysis involves the breakdown of a communication into its constituent parts such that the relative hierarchy within that communication is made clear, that the relations between the expressed ideas are made explicit, or both. Such analyses are intended to clarify the communication, to indicate how it is organized, and the way in which the communication manages to convey its effects, as well as its basis and arrangement.

SYNTHESIS. Synthesis represents the combining of elements and parts so that they form a whole. This operation involves the process of working with pieces, parts, elements, and so on and arranging them so as to constitute a pattern or structure not clearly present before.

EVALUATION. Evaluation requires judgments about the value of material and methods for given purposes. Quantitative and qualitative judgments are made about the extent to which material and methods satisfy criteria. The criteria employed may be those determined by learners or those given to them.

Most of these levels have been broken down into various subcategories. For example, under evaluation there are two categories that deal with "judgments in terms of internal evidence" and "judgments in terms of external criteria." The knowledge category has twelve separate subdivisions.

The 1956 *Taxonomy* languished almost unnoticed for several years after its initial publication. However, in the early sixties the nation's intense interest in instructional objectives altered that situation dramatically. Sales of the *Taxonomy* started to soar, and educators nationwide started spouting phrases such as "affective objectives" and "cognitive objectives" with ease. The cognitive, affective, and psychomotor domains became household notions for most school people during the sixties.

In 1964 David R. Krathwohl and his colleagues extended Bloom's pioneering efforts by publishing a second taxonomy of objectives, but this time one which concentrated on the affective domain.[2] As with the cognitive taxonomy, Krathwohl and his collaborators attempted to subdivide the affective realm into relatively distinct divisions. Five different levels of affective objectives were described in the affective taxonomy:

RECEIVING (Attending). The first level of the affective domain is concerned with the learner's sensitivity to the existence of certain phenomena and stimuli, that is, with his or her willingness to receive or to attend to them. This category is divided into three subdivisions that indicate three different levels of attending to phenomena—namely, awareness of the phenomena, willingness to receive phenomena, and controlled or selected attention to phenomena.

RESPONDING. At this level one is concerned with responses that go beyond merely attending to phenomena. Students are sufficiently motivated that they are not just "willing to attend" but are actively attending.

[2]D. R. Krathwohl, B. S. Bloom, and B. B. Masia, *Taxonomy of Educational Objectives, Handbook II: The Affective Domain* (New York: D. McKay, 1964).

VALUING. This category reflects the learner's holding of a particular value. Learners display behavior with sufficient consistency in appropriate situations that they actually are perceived as holding this value.

ORGANIZATION. As learners successively internalize values, they encounter situations in which more than one value is relevant. This requires the necessity of organizing their values into a system such that certain values exercise greater control.

CHARACTERIZATION BY A VALUE OR VALUE COMPLEX. At this highest level of the affective taxonomy internalization has taken place in an individual's value hierarchy to the extent that we can actually characterize him or her as holding a particular value or set of values.

Arriving as it did on the heels of increased educator interest in instructional objectives, the affective taxonomy stimulated a fair amount of interest among educators. But, sadly, although there was a fair amount of rhetoric tossed about regarding "the fundamental importance of the affective realm," we saw the emergence of few actual assessment devices that attempted to tap affective behavior.

In part, the dearth of measures to assess an examinee's affective status is due to the considerable difficulty in devising genuinely valid affective instruments. As we see in this chapter, it is awfully hard to create a reliable and valid instrument which assesses the elusive kinds of quarries we must pursue in the affective domain.

A Closer Look at Affect

When individuals are asked to define what they mean by the term, "affective," they offer examples instead of definitions. They'll say something like, "Affective variables are nonintellectual attributes, such as one's attitudes, interests, and values." In a sense, they define affect by saying what it *isn't*, namely, that it isn't intellectual behavior. However, it is possible to define affective variables more precisely by noting how we actually use affective measures. If you think about it just a bit, you'll realize that we assess an individual's affective state—for example, with some kind of attitudinal inventory—not directly to find out how the person scores on the inventory. No, instead we want to use that score on the inventory to get a fix on how the examinee will respond in the future to similar, but typically more realistic, stimulus situations. In other words, since we use responses to our affective measure as predictors of the examinee's future acts, we can conceive of affective measures as an attempt to assess the examinee's future dispositions.

If we try to measure an adolescent's interests in certain vocations, for example, we're really trying to get a fix on the kinds of jobs that will be interesting to that youngster in later life. When we try to measure children's attitudes toward the democratic process, we really are trying to find out how they will be likely to act toward our democratic system when they grow up. We see whether children currently enjoy art and music to help us predict whether they'll derive pleasure from art and music later in life.

Many psychologists have spent their entire professional lives trying to draw subtle and defensible distinctions among such constructs as attitudes and values. Some specialists believe, for instance, that an attitude consists of an individual's *set* (or tendency to behave) toward a fairly limited class of objects, such as when certain people are annoyed by small, nervous, and fidgety dogs. In contrast, a value consists of a person's set toward a much broader class of objects, such as when a person holds the value of human life in such high esteem that all nonhuman life is expendable—including small, fidgety dogs as well as big, docile ones.

There are several exceptions to the general rule that affective measures are future oriented, such as when we want to assess students' current attitudes toward school because we want to alter any situation contributing to negative attitudes. However, most of the time we are trying to isolate some current behavior that will be predictive of examinees' future behaviors. The affective disposition itself can never be captured. We must infer the examinee's status with respect to that attitude by devising a current situation in which the examinee's affective state will be revealed, allowing us to predict the examinee's future behaviors in situations governed by the affective disposition with which we're dealing.

Although measures in the cognitive domain attempt to find out what the examinee can do intellectually, and measures in the psychomotor domain attempt to find out what the examinee can do physically, measures in the affective domain attempt to find out what the examinee will do in the future. Cognitive and psychomotor tests generally deal with competency assessment. Affective tests generally deal with dispositional assessment.

With cognitive measures there is a handy "number correct" that we can use as a reflection of an examinee's performance. Affective measuring devices, unfortunately, often don't lend themselves to readily discernible scoring schemes. On occasions the test developer must engage in a good deal of exotic analytic work in order to come up with a defensible scoring key. Sometimes the scoring approaches are apparent from the nature of the items employed. For instance, suppose we're asking children to register the extent of their agreement on a five-point scale—strongly agree to strongly disagree—with statements about school, some of which are positive and some of which are negative. If the youngsters agree with a positive item, then they get a plus score. If they agree with a negative item, then they get a minus score. Similarly, if they disagree with a negative statement, they get a plus; whereas if they disagree with a positive statement, they get a minus.

The real task, in this example, is to decide what constitutes a reasonably positive attitude toward school. Very frequently, educators are looking for shifts in affective responses, such as promoting students' more positive attitudes toward school. In such cases a pretest-posttest contrast of scores proves useful.

If the affective measure is a totally new one, and no pretest-posttest strategy is being employed, it is almost certain that we must gather a fair amount of real data before reaching a tentative, a very tentative, decision regarding what kinds of expectations to have for an affective measure.

ISOLATING THE ATTRIBUTE TO BE MEASURED

For the developer of an affective measure, the initial task involves isolating some current examinee behavior that will reflect that more general affective disposition in which we are interested. If you recall Chapter 9 where the procedures were set forth for creating a set of test specifications, we are at the very early stage when we need to consider alternative ways of measuring the more general attribute we're trying to assess. The first step, therefore, obliges us to create a variety of potential assessment schemes for review.

In several previous affective-measurement projects, my colleagues and I have had some success with a straightforward, step-by-step scheme for devising possible affective-assessment approaches.

In step one we try to discuss the general nature of the affective attribute we're dealing with so we understand it better. Then we try to imagine what an individual would be like who possessed (in a positive way) that affective attribute in a thoroughgoing manner. For instance, if we were trying to measure an individual's attitudes toward participatory athletics, we might think of a hypothetical attribute-possessor who lived and died just to get into the next game of softball, tennis, jai alai, golf, and so on. We then tuck this totally fictitious individual away for a while in a corner of our fantasy world.

Step two calls for the creation of a fictitious counterpart to the imaginary individual we conjured up in step one. Now we create a hypothetical attribute-nonpossessor who either is neutral toward participatory sports or finds them downright repugnant. This sort of person might watch a tennis match in person or on television but would never actually trot out on a court. Moreover, the idea of taking part in a sweaty, dusty, old softball game would be truly disgusting. This second fictitious person we also send flying around our heads in a holding pattern.

Now, in step three we attempt to think of many difference-producing situations—that is, situations in which our two hypothetical people would behave in a substantially different fashion. Maybe we'll come up with paper-and-pencil inventories, actually observe behavior in natural settings, behaviors in artificial settings, or products that might be generated in stress-laden settings. Here is where we engage in no-holds-barred and nonpunitive brain storming, preferably with other colleagues, so we get all sorts of ideas out on the table, the simple minded, the exotic, the super. Just let the ideas reel off and record them; we can sort out the winners from the losers later on. Often, at the end of step three, we have upward of a dozen or more potential measurement approaches.

In step four we survey the numerous measurement ideas, for that's what they really are—seeds of measurement approaches, generated in step three. We pick out the ones that are both likely to be valid and practicable. Practicality considerations should only be raised at this point, not in step three, since practicality is such a stultifying notion that we might lose some potentially valuable ideas. However, if a proposed scheme is too costly, takes too much examinee time, or too much teacher time, it just may not be sufficiently practical to employ.

Validity, of course, is a crucial commodity in any measuring device, and we want to be as sure as we can that we at least have a reasonable strategy for coming up with a valid measure. Ideally, we could select several substantially different ways of trying to isolate the general affective attribute we're going after with the hope that each of our different measures would snare a somewhat different facet of the affective attribute and that we would, in effect, triangulate in on the attribute more effectively. Since it's highly unlikely that a single affective measuring device will ever satisfactorily measure a complex affective attribute all by itself, the use of multiple affective measuring devices (with similar missions) is strongly recommended. However, if you're short on resources, one affective measure is surely better than none at all.

When developing affective measures, it is particularly important to eliminate any cues that might prompt the examinee to supply a socially desirable response. Measuring devices that fail to eliminate such cues are destined to be invalid. If examinees sense how they *should* respond—that is, how they think others would like them to respond—they often supply such responses instead of the ones they really might give without such influence. Clearly, the resulting data will be misleading.

To illustrate, returning to our little four-step strategy for a moment, suppose we were trying to create measures of children's attitudes toward the school program. Now in step three, one of the suggestions was that teachers ask pupils to raise their hands if they like the way they're being taught. We leave this inane suggestion in the eligible pool until step four when we quickly expunge it because it's cluttered by cues as to social desirability. Surely when a teacher asks pupils to raise their hands if they like the class, a good many youngsters will send fingers flying skyward because they don't want to hurt the teacher or, perhaps, because they fear potential

"There's just one problem with our affective measuring devices— the kids keep getting tangled."

grading recriminations. In any event, the social desirability cue would completely compromise such a test's validity.

One method for identifying socially desirable items is to include a set of items that are patently tapping socially desirable responses.[3] By using such a social desirability scale, we can see which other items in our affective measure correlate highly with the score on the social desirability scale, then eliminate them.

In step four we look hard at any cues to social desirability as well as any other factors, conceptual or procedural, that might influence a measurement scheme's validity. Having done so, we can rank a few affective measurement schemes in order of their merits and try to create several measures if our resources permit.

ASSESSMENT OPTIONS

The most common approaches to the measurement of affect involve the use of observations, ratings, and self-report inventions. In the previous chapter we considered observations and ratings. Let's spend a bit of time,

[3]See V. C. Crandall, V. J. Crandall, and W. Katkovsky, "A Children's Social Desirability Questionnaire," *Journal of Consulting Psychology*, 29,1(1965), 27–36.

therefore, analyzing the various sorts of self-reports that one might use in an effort to get a fix on an examinee's affective status. Before tackling self-report devices, however, let's recall that since in the affective domain we are anxious to get a fix on what an examinee *will do* (rather than *can do*), the use of observational techniques offers an especially powerful arsenal of valid affective-assessment ploys. The major reason that educators frequently opt for self-report devices over observational techniques is merely because of the practical difficulties associated with carrying out observations of individuals under normal or specially created circumstances.

High-Inference and Low-Inference Self-Report Devices

When we gather self-report information from examinees, we can do it in such a way that the responses require little or no high-powered logic chain to draw a conclusion regarding what they mean. These rather direct devices we can think of as *low-inference* self-report devices. There are other instruments, however, in which we secure data from which we must make pretty hefty logical leaps. These more exotic measuring devices we can think of as *high-inference* self-report measures.

The most typical form of affective assessment involves our soliciting examinees to answer a series of questions or to respond (such as agree-disagree) to a series of statements. Suppose the questions or statements are put forward in a relatively direct fashion so that, if the examinee responds truthfully, we can use those responses as an accurate reflection of a more general affective disposition. In such cases, since we don't have to make much of an inferential hop, we describe these instruments as low-inference self-report devices.

However, of course, the problem with low-inference measures is that the examinee may not be feeding us truthful responses. Since the purpose of a low-inference self-report device is relatively transparent, the respondent can readily manufacture answers that are not truthful. Even if we employ the traditional "respond anonymously" directions, we cannot be sure that examinees are delivering up truthful answers.

For such reasons, of course, measurement people have sometimes turned to less obvious data-gathering gambits. However, before dismissing them as too fakable to be used, let's recognize that sometimes we are not dealing with affective dimensions where examinees feel driven to be deceptive. If we ask people about their erotic fantasies, they may be inclined to conceal (or embellish). If we ask them about their food preferences, they just may tell us the truth. Besides, low-inference self-reports constitute such a readily gatherable source of data that we should often employ them, sometimes in concert with more esoteric data-gathering schemes.

Since low-inference self-reports are particularly susceptible to examinee faking, we sometimes want to employ less transparent ways of securing examinee responses. With less direct self-report schemes, however, we usually must make a larger inferential jump from the actual data we're getting and the affective dimension it allegedly reflects. Because the self-report inventory is less easily faked, we have more confidence in the candor of an examinee's responses. But the problem here, of course, is whether these more candid answers really tell us what we want to know.

Because of our occasional queasiness about the validity of responses to high-inference self-report devices, this is an ideal time to employ both a high-inference and a low-inference inventory dealing with the same dimension. At least one organization now distributes sets of affective measures dealing with students' attitudes toward school that contain parallel high-inference and low-inference self-report measures for a number of different affective dimensions.[4]

Commonly Employed Self-Report Devices

We can turn now to several of the more frequently employed types of self-report devices which will be of potential utility for the assessment of affect. For most of these self-report techniques, it is possible to create instruments which adhere to either a high-inference or low-inference model.

Thurstone scales.   In the late 1920s L. L. Thurstone and his associate, E. J. Chave, created a series of attitude scales at the University of Chicago. One of the schemes devised by Thurstone, known as an *equal-appearing interval scale*, has been used frequently since those days. When one reviews possible self-report scales, particularly to measure an individual's attitudes, the Thurstone scale should certainly be considered.

The first step in the assembly of a Thurstone attitude scale is to generate or collect a large number of statements which express varying degrees of negative, neutral, and positive views about an institution (for example, state government, universities, teachers unions), group (for example, Chicanos, blacks, school teachers), or some other object of interest (for example, U.S. history, justice, biology).

One way to gather such statements is to ask a number of folks to write a brief statement in which they express their personal opinions about the object or group of interest. Given a sizable number of people, it is likely that a goodly range of positive, neutral, and negative statements will be produced.

---

[4]"Attitudes Toward School Measures" (Los Angeles: Instructional Objectives Exchange, 1977).

Next, get a group of competent judges (the more judges, the better), for example, 100 judges, and ask them to sort each statement into one of eleven stacks on a continuum ranging from extremely favorable to extremely unfavorable. The judges are directed to rank the *statements*, not render their personal opinions. For instance, suppose you are constructing a Thurstone scale regarding teachers organizations and one of the statements to be ranked is the following: "Teachers organizations will ultimately benefit education immeasurably." Now suppose one of the judges was Mr. Kane, a school administrator who, having been burned at the bargaining table more than once by his district's teachers union, has an almost psychotic abhorrence of teachers organizations. Regardless of his personal values, Mr. Kane should place the statement in one of the positive piles, since it expresses an obviously positive opinion about teachers organizations. Thus, a judge's personal values are to be disregarded in the ranking process.

Although it is expected that different judges will rank statements somewhat differently, only those statements are retained which are ranked in a relatively consistent fashion by the judges. Somewhere between 20 and 45 of these statements are then used to create the scale. The statements are randomly ordered. Each statement is given as its value the mean score of the judges based on the sorting operation. For instance, if the mean rating of judges for a rather negative statement was 2.3, then that statement would be given a 2.3 value on the scale. A positive statement might, for example, receive a 9.6 value.

Examinees are presented with all of the statements (without statement values, of course), then asked to check all statements with which they agree. An examinee's score is the *average* of the items checked.

In Figure 14–1 is presented one of Thurstone's attitude scales, in this instance based on a six-point instead of an eleven-point scale. The item values, in parentheses, would be removed from the version presented to the examinees. You might enjoy going through the scale and checking the statements with which you agree. If so, disregard the item values. Later, compare the sorts of statements which received very high and very low values, for example, statement 27 versus statement 4.

Although simple to administer and score, Thurstone scales are fairly time consuming to develop. The difficulty of assembling many statements, securing sufficient judges, isolating statements on which most judges agree, and computing the required statistical operations is more laborious than with some less complex self-report devices.

Likert scales. Perhaps the most widely used of the various affective scales is the scheme devised by Likert in the early thirties.[5] Although it

---

[5]R. Likert, "A Technique for the Measurement of Attitude," *Archives of Psychology*, 22, 140 (1932), 1–55.

ATTITUDE TOWARDS MOVIES

This is a study of attitudes toward the movies. On the following pages you will find a number of statements expressing different attitudes toward the movies.

✓ Put a check mark if you agree with the statement.

✗ Put a cross if you disagree with the statement.

If you simply cannot decide about a statement you may mark it with a question mark.

This is not an examination. There are no right or wrong answers to these statements. This is simply a study of people's attitudes toward the movies. Please indicate your own attitude by a check mark when you agree and by a cross when you disagree.

LIST OF OPINIONS IN THE SCALE

1. (1.5) The movies occupy time that should be spent in more wholesome recreation.
2. (1.3) I am tired of the movies; I have seen too many poor ones.
3. (4.5) The movies are the best civilizing device ever developed.
4. (0.2) Movies are the most important cause of crime.
5. (2.7) Movies are all right but a few of them give the rest a bad name.
6. (2.6) I like to see movies once in a while but they do disappoint you sometimes.
7. (2.9) I think movies are fairly interesting.
8. (2.7) Movies are just a harmless pastime.
9. (1.7) The movies to me are just a way to kill time.
10. (4.0) The influence of the movies is decidedly for good.
11. (3.9) The movies are good, clean entertainment.
12. (3.9) Movies increase one's appreciation of beauty.
13. (1.7) I'd never miss the movies if we didn't have them.
14. (2.4) Sometimes I feel that the movies are desirable and sometimes I doubt it.
15. (0.0) It is a sin to go to the movies.
16. (4.3) There would be very little progress without the movies.
17. (4.3) The movies are the most vital form of art today.
18. (3.6) A movie is the best entertainment that can be obtained cheaply.
19. (3.4) A movie once in a while is a good thing for everybody.
20. (3.4) The movies are one of the few things I can enjoy by myself.
21. (1.3) Going to the movies is a foolish way to spend your money.
22. (1.1) Moving pictures bore me.
23. (0.6) As they now exist movies are wholly bad for children.
24. (0.6) Such a pernicious influence as the movies is bound to weaken the moral fiber of those who attend.
25. (0.3) As a protest against movies we should pledge ourselves never to attend them.
26. (0.1) The movies are the most important single influence for evil.
27. (4.7) The movies are the most powerful influence for good in American life.
28. (2.3) I would go to the movies more often if I were sure of finding something good.
29. (4.1) If I had my choice of anything I wanted to do, I would go to the movies.
30. (2.2) The pleasure people get from the movies just about balances the harm they do.
31. (2.0) I don't find much that is educational in the current films.
32. (1.9) The information that you obtain from the movies is of little value.
33. (1.0) Movies are a bad habit.
34. (3.3) I like the movies as they are because I go to be entertained, not educated.
35. (3.1) On the whole the movies are pretty decent.
36. (0.8) The movies are undermining respect for authority.
37. (2.7) I like to see other people enjoy the movies whether I enjoy them myself or not.
38. (0.3) The movies are to blame for the prevalence of sex offenses.
39. (4.4) The movie is one of the great educational institutions for common people.
40. (0.8) Young people are learning to smoke, drink, and pet from the movies.

In scoring the attitude scale, we cannot say that one score is better or worse than another; we can only say that one person's attitude toward the movies is more or less favorable than another person's. It is purely arbitrary that attitudes unfavorable to the movies have lower scale values than favorable attitudes.

Any individual's attitude is measured by the average or mean scale value of all the statements he checks. The person who has the larger score is more favorably inclined toward the movies than the person with a lower score.

For the purpose of comparing groups, the distributions of attitude in each group can be plotted, and it can then be said whether and how much one group is more favorable to the movies than another group.

FIGURE 14–1 An attitude-toward-movies scale. (Reproduced from L. L. Thurstone, *The Measurement of Values*, Chicago: University of Chicago Press, 1959, pp. 285–86, by permission of The University of Chicago Press.)

yields results about as reliable as the more elaborate Thurstone scales, the Likert method is more simple to construct and score.

Sometimes referred to as a *summated-rating scale*, the essence of a Likert scale is that a series of statements is rated, typically on a five-point continuum of agreement. Each statement, for example, is to be responded to according to the following scale: strongly agree (SA), agree (A), uncertain (U), disagree (D), strongly disagree (SD). Depending on the direction of the statement, a value of 5, 4, 3, 2, or 1 is given to each examinee's response. The values for all items are then summed to provide an overall score for the examinee. Let's see how we would go about creating a Likert scale.

First off, a number of positive or negative statements are written or gathered regarding the affective object of interest, for example, school, my family, myself, the United States. This preliminary set of items should have no neutral items and few items at the extreme end of the positive-negative continuum. These statements are then given to a large number of subjects who register their degree of agreement with each statement on a scale, such as the five-category scale given earlier. Sometimes a few more categories are used. With younger examinees, three, or even two, categories are employed. The (agree versus disagree) items are then scored, depending on the positive or negative direction of the statement, on a 5, 4, 3, 2, or 1 basis.

For example, if we were whipping up a Likert scale to assess adults' attitudes toward mandatory school busing, we might have statements such as the following:

SA   A   U   (D)   SD   1. The use of mandatory busing should be halted immediately.

(SA)   A   U   D   SD   2. Mandatory busing provides students with new social perspectives.

Assuming we were giving high scores to those who favor mandatory busing (the scale's designers could choose the other direction as well), the response to item one would get a four and the response to item two would get a five. In other words, the following scoring scheme is applied, depending on whether the statements are positive or negative:

For positive statements: strongly agree = 5, agree = 4, uncertain = 3, disagree = 2, and strongly disagree = 1.

For negative statements: strongly agree = 1, agree = 2, uncertain = 3, disagree = 4, and strongly disagree = 5.

For each item a correlation is computed between the item and the total score. Only items are retained which correlate strongly (negatively or positively) with the total score. The result is that the items finally selected are internally consistent. Not surprisingly, because of its method of item selection, a Likert scale will frequently yield higher internal consistency reliability coefficients than a Thurstone scale does.

In Figure 14-2 we see a 15-item Likert scale developed by Tidwell to gauge parental attitudes toward a school district's minimum competency program.

In addition to the advantages already noted, namely, ease of construction and scoring, Likert scales tend to yield more varied scores than do Thurstone scales. Their reliabilities, as noted, compare favorably with those of the Thurstone scales.

One must remember, however, that a good Likert scale cannot be churned out in milliseconds. A two-step operation is required in which one first creates potential items, then tries them out, and *on the basis of the tryout's results*, selects the final items for the scale. Without the initial tryout (in which one would necessarily employ more items than needed for the final scale), there is too much likelihood that the statements for the scale will be fashioned inappropriately. At least one revision, and preferably more, is required to create a first-rate Likert scale.

The semantic differential. Devised by Osgood and his associates in 1957, the *semantic differential* technique attracted considerable attention as an affective assessment tool in the sixties and early seventies.[6] Although interest in the semantic differential has declined in recent years, the procedure is now regarded as a standard assessment device for getting at affective dimensions. To use this approach, Osgood measured and portrayed concepts in three dimensions of meaning, that is, *semantic space*. The dimensions are *evaluation* (good-bad), *potency* (strong-weak), and *activity* (fast-slow). Because the evaluation dimension is the strongest of the three, it is generally recommended for use in semantic differential scales dealing with affect. The evaluation dimension contains 28 sets of bipolar adjectives

[6]C. E. Osgood, G. J. Suci, and P. H. Tannenbaum, *The Measurement of Meaning* (Urbana, Ill.: University of Illinois, 1957).

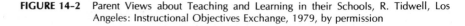

FIGURE 14-2   Parent Views about Teaching and Learning in their Schools, R. Tidwell, Los Angeles: Instructional Objectives Exchange, 1979, by permission

7.	My child is prompted from grade to grade even though the skills have not been learned.	1	2	3	4	5
8.	The teachers in my child's school believe it is essential to master the basic skills before a student graduates.	1	2	3	4	5
9.	My child looks forward to going to school each day.	1	2	3	4	5
10.	My child receives too little instruction in the basic skills.	1	2	3	4	5
11.	The type of classroom instruction my child gets will not really help my child to meet future needs.	1	2	3	4	5
12.	My child will have ample knowledge in the basic skills before receiving a high school diploma.	1	2	3	4	5
13.	My child is given assignments that can be completed with little effort or thought.	1	2	3	4	5
14.	The basic skills my child is learning are not adequate to enable an adult to function in society.	1	2	3	4	5
15.	My child is not given enough classroom and homework assignments to learn the basic skills.	1	2	3	4	5

FIGURE 14-2 *(cont.)*

which can be used to form a semantic differential scale. The 28 sets of bipolar adjectives in the evaluation dimension are the following:

Good-Bad	Beautiful-Ugly
Sweet-Sour	Clean-Dirty
High-Low	Calm-Agitated
Tasty-Distasteful	Valuable-Worthless
Kind-Cruel	Pleasant-Unpleasant
Bitter-Sweet	Happy-Sad
Empty-Full	Ferocious-Peaceful
Sacred-Profane	Relaxed-Tense
Brave-Cowardly	Rich-Poor
Clear-Hazy	Nice-Awful
Bright-Dark	Fragrant-Foul
Honest-Dishonest	Rough-Smooth
Fresh-Stale	Fair-Unfair
Pungent-Bland	Healthy-Sick

It is possible to use all or only some of these adjective pairs in creating a semantic differential scale. We should choose only adjectives with which examinees will be familiar. It is not necessary to mesh the adjective pairs with the concept being rated so that the adjectives "make sense." The semantic differential attempts to get at *connotative*, rather than *descriptive*, meanings. Indeed, it is a major advantage of the semantic differential that the ratings supplied are not based on obvious choices, hence are not as readily faked. For instance, here is a typical semantic differential scale for tapping youngsters' attitudes toward teachers.

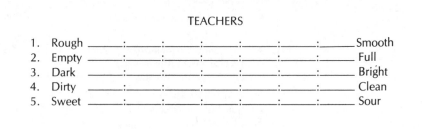

A seven-point scale is then interposed between the adjective pairs and subjects check the blank space which most closely corresponds to their feelings about the stimulus word or phrase (in this case, teachers). From one to seven points are then assigned for each response, depending on the direction of the adjective pairs. Note that in the TEACHERS example, the third and fourth adjective pairs are in a direction opposite to the other three pairs. In that example, therefore, score points would be assigned as follows:

Item	Score Values						
1.	7	6	5	4	3	2	1
2.	7	6	5	4	3	2	1
3.	1	2	3	4	5	6	7
4.	1	2	3	4	5	6	7
5.	7	6	5	4	3	2	1

Thus, scores on this five-item semantic differential scale could range from 5 to 35, with high scores reflecting a more favorable evaluation of teachers.

Other options.   In addition to the three affective scales described here, there are some other, less frequently used, self-report alternatives for securing affective data. For example, one can employ routine questionnaires in which one embeds (submerges) a few questions which really deal with the affective dimension of interest. While all of the items on the questionnaire are legitimate, hence no deception of the examinee is involved, the questionnaire developer's overriding interest may be in only a few questions, such as, "If you could do so legally, would you drop out of school today?"

The Q-sort technique, developed by Stephenson some three decades ago, is used occasionally these days.[7] An individual is given a set of cards containing statements, traits, or even pictures. The cards are then sorted into piles according to a particular continuum, such as "most like me" or "least like me." Ordinarily, the number of cards allowed in each pile is predetermined. Applications of the Q-sort technique are seen most frequently in the field of counseling and clinical psychology.

A type of scale which you might hear about occasionally is the Guttman scale.[8] A Guttman scale yields scores which permit one to assert that if an individual scores at a certain point on the scale, all other examinees who attain that score achieved it in precisely the same way. If we know an individual's score, we know that individual's response pattern. For instance, if we had a 100-item Guttman scale, anyone scoring 47 on the scale would have responded correctly (or positively) to the first 47 items and incorrectly (or negatively) to the remaining 53 items.

Guttman scales are of limited practical significance since they require items more reliable than can be produced by most mortals.

And, finally, as we saw in the previous chapter, there are some powerful ways of getting at student behaviors and products through ratings and observations that can provide us with highly useful insights regarding students' affective leanings.

INDIVIDUAL AND GROUP AFFECTIVE ASSESSMENT

In the case of cognitive and psychomotor tests, we typically use the test results to make decisions about individuals. For instance, we decide whether or not to admit Lee Smith to a graduate school on the basis of Lee's score on an aptitude test. Alternatively, choosing another common example, we reach a decision about Sally Sill's final grade in geometry on the basis of her performance on the end-of-course test.

Cognitive test results are thus employed to make decisions about *individuals*. Such results are also used to make decisions about *programs*, such as the effectiveness of a particular instructional program. We might see, for instance, whether the pretest-posttest gains after a special reading instruction program are sufficient.

[7]W. Stephenson, *The Study of Behavior: Q-Technique and Its Methodology* (Chicago: University of Chicago Press, 1953).
[8]L. Guttman, "The Cornell Technique for Scale and Intensity Analysis," *Educational and Psychological Measurement,* 7 (1947), 247–279.

In the case of affective measures, there are only a few instances in which we use test results to make decisions about individuals. Almost all of these occur in connection with educational counseling, such as when we attempt to isolate an individual's vocational interests for purposes of career counseling. There are also instances in which a school psychologist needs to pick up some affective information on a student's emotional status for counseling purposes. With any affective measure that will be used for making decisions about *individuals*, those measures need to possess the traditional sort of individual validity which we have always sought for cognitive tests.

However, with *most affective tests in education*, there are no individual decisions at issue. Instead, these measures are employed to make decisions about *programs*, not particular people. As a consequence, substantially different validity requirements exist for such measures. For instance, when we employ the results of students' scores on an attitude test regarding environmental pollution to evaluate the effectiveness of a schoolwide antipollution campaign, we will make decisions about the campaign, not particular students.

Since many affective-assessment results are never used for purposes of individual decision-making, it follows that those assessment devices need not produce valid data for individual examinees. If the tests can be employed to make valid decisions about groups of examinees, as is the case when we need to evaluate programs, then they will be quite serviceable for our needs.

Let's see how this kind of situation might occur. Suppose you had put together a really oblique questionnaire that you believed would work beautifully for the vast majority of your students but that might mislead a small number of them. What should you do? The answer is simple if you're only evaluating a program and not students, as is frequently the case in assessing affect. For your purposes, a test valid for *groups* of students will do the job nicely because the aberrant responses of a few examinees will be overwhelmed by the responses of the majority.

This is a rather significant point to be noted by developers of affective measures. It permits them to create ingenious measuring devices that might possess more validity, in part because the test developers don't have to satisfy the lowest common denominator. If we tried to build affective-assessment devices so that every living soul would be validly assessed, we'd surely end up with a bland battery of "please-tell-the-truth" self-report inventories. We'd be at the mercy of the individuals filling out the inventories whose honesty we'd have to accept because we'd have no other choice.

No, in many settings it makes more sense to build more clever assessment devices, sometimes rather convoluted in form, so we can be more confident in the meaningfulness of our data—even if we thereby render potentially invalid the responses of a small number of examinees. Make sure your assessment devices are valid for the decision context in which you will use them. More often than not, with affective instruments, that means a decision for groups rather than for individuals.

Measuring instruments that possess validity for individuals will, of necessity, possess validity for groups. The reverse, however, is not true. Let's examine some practical illustrations to see the implications of this point. Suppose you were developing a new affective paper-and-pencil self-report instrument which you thought would provide a reliable and valid estimate of how pupils felt about a certain set of values. The instrument was so well designed, in fact, that you believed it would provide for each learner an estimate of how that learner felt (believed) regarding the value question under consideration. Because the measure would provide valid data for each learner, it is clear that it would also provide a valid estimate of group performance. On the other hand, suppose you had devised a new attitude technique that, although it seemed likely to work for most learners, would probably be misconstrued by a few learners whose backgrounds (unknown to you) might cause them to interpret certain items atypically. Now even though you could not, therefore, use the measure to help you make decisions about individual learners, you still might use the device to help you decide whether an affective education program was working, as reflected by group performance.

Several years ago I found myself directing a project to develop affective measuring devices dealing with students' (1) attitudes toward school and (2) self-concept. There was precious little literature available for guidance regarding how to produce reliable and valid measures of pupils' self-concept and attitudes toward school. I worked closely with my good friend and colleague, John D. McNeil of UCLA. Our general approach was to assemble our development staff and in as permissive an environment as possible generate all sorts of techniques—standard or bizarre—to measure the affective dimensions of interest.

Early in these idea-generating sessions, however, a common problem began to recur. Just when someone had proffered an original but zany measurement ploy, another staff member would always say something like this: "Well, that would work well for most kids, but what about the kid who . . ." Thereafter would be recounted a description of one or more types of youngsters whose prior experiences would so distort their responses to the measuring device being proposed that the meaningfulness of the resulting data would obviously be vitiated. With resignation we would say, "That's right," and abandon the new approach to search once more for measures that would stand the validity test for all human beings.

We lost most of our good ideas during the early phase of that project, because we constantly steered clear of any measurement ploys that wouldn't work for everybody. Often, in an effort to satisfy this universal validity requirement, we ended up with the most drab self-report devices imaginable. Learners could fake them with ease but, at least if they answered truthfully, the measure would be valid for everyone.

And then, after weeks of sputtering, the insight came crashing through to us. We were trying to devise measures for educators working in the field of program evaluation. They weren't going to be using these measures to make decisions about individuals. Teachers weren't going to give Johnny an *F* if he did well on all cognitive tests yet had a poor self-concept. A teacher doesn't fail Martha if she can multiply like a magician yet doesn't like math. The teacher wants an estimate of the class's attitude toward math, not just Martha's. The measures we were developing, therefore, didn't have to be valid for every child. As long as there weren't too many aberrant responses, we could get a good group estimate and help evaluators make recommendations regarding a program's impact on groups.

The liberating impact of this understanding was enormous. We could return to developing clever little measurement devices designed to work with most, but not all, youngsters. The range of our assessment devices expanded accordingly. We were able to contrive instruments that although they might be invalid for a handful of learners, would most likely be far more valid for an entire group of learners than the bland self-report devices we had previously produced.

In selecting and/or generating affective measuring instruments, the evaluator should identify the decision-making context and if it concerns groups, rather than individuals, temper more customary conceptions of validity requirements.

When educators set out to assess affective dimensions, they soon will find themselves in the midst of an ethical quandary, since it is in this arena that covert, even deceptive, measurement schemes seem particularly appropriate. However, even though the educator's affective-assessment techniques are incredibly primitive and have rarely been employed on a wide-scale basis, educators must begin to confront the ethical issues associated with certain affective measurement strategies. Hopefully, an increasing technical sophistication in the field of affective assessment will be matched by an increasing awareness of the ethical issues facing those who would engage in affective measurement.[9]

[9]I have railed at some length elsewhere regarding affective measurement and ethics. If you are serious about ethics and affective assessment, please see W. James Popham, *Criterion-Referenced Measurement* (Englewood Cliffs, N.J.: Prentice-Hall, Inc. 1978), pp. 207–214.

PRACTICE EXERCISES

There's no practice quite as useful in the acquisition of a skill as performing the skill itself. Accordingly, one of the very best forms of practice for this chapter would be to create a range of affective-assessment instruments, particularly those stressed in the chapter, such as Thurstone scales, Likert scales, and the semantic differential. Try to create both low-inference and high-inference scales. If possible, try to get a colleague or fellow student to critique your efforts.

DISCUSSION QUESTIONS

1. Do you agree with the basic contention that whereas cognitive measures assess *optimal* performance, affective measures assess *typical* performance? Why?
2. What are the typical distinctions between high-inference and low-inference self-report devices?
3. In what sorts of situations would educators be apt to use affective measures for decision making regarding individuals? In what sorts of situations would educators be likely to use affective results for decisions related to groups?
4. Why do you think that one finds affective measures used so infrequently in the schools?
5. If you were asked to summarize for a high school faculty the ethical principles you believed important in the assessment of affect, what would you say?
6. What, in your view, is the relationship between affective variables, such as self-concept, and achievement variables, such as one's knowledge of history?

SUGGESTIONS FOR ADDITIONAL READING

CHASE, CLINTON I., "Assessing Personality Interests, and Attitudes," Chapter 12, *Measurement for Educational Evaluation*, pp. 258–291. Reading, Mass.: Addison-Wesley, 1978. Chase describes special problems associated with personality inventories, that is, their limitations, reliability, and validity.

EBEL, ROBERT L., "Personality, Attitudes, and Interests," Chapter 19, *Essentials of Educational Measurement* (3rd ed.), pp. 362–373. Englewood Cliffs, N.J.: Prentice-Hall, Inc., 1979. Ebel treats three main topics in this chapter, namely, personality tests, the nature of attitudes, and the measurement of interests.

LAKE, DALE G., MATTHEW B. MILES, and RALPH B. EARLE, JR., eds. *Measuring Human Behavior*. New York: Teachers College Press, 1973. In this volume systematic reviews of 84 different instruments for assessing human behavior are presented. Thirty-eight are oriented toward personality variables (of which nineteen are affective-motivational).

STANLEY, JULIAN C., and KENNETH D. HOPKINS, "The Assessment of the Affective Domain," Chapter 12, *Educational and Psychological Measurement and Evaluation* (5th ed.), pp. 282–302. Englewood Cliffs, N.J.: Prentice-Hall, Inc., 1972. Stanley and Hopkins offer an excellent description of many assessment procedures which can be used in connection with effective measurement, namely, rating scales, the semantic differential, Q-sort technique, and questionnaires.

TUCKMAN, BRUCE W., "Measuring Interests, Attitudes, and Personality Orientation," Chapter 14, *Measuring Educational Outcomes: Fundamentals of Testing*, pp. 408–441. San Francisco: Harcourt Brace Jovanovich, Inc., 1975. This chapter deals with the measurement of interests, attitudes, and personalities. The uses of published affective measures is discussed.

AND FOR THOSE WHO TIRE OF READING

Identifying Affective Objectives. Distributed by Vimcet Associates, Inc., P.O. Box 24174, Los Angeles, Calif. 90024. A four-step strategy for generating objectives in the affective domain is described in this thirty-minute filmstrip-tape program.

Instructional Tactics for Affective Goals. Distributed by Vimcet Associates, Inc., P.O. Box 24174, Los Angeles, Calif. 90024. Three tactics, namely, modeling, contiguity, and reinforcement, are described in this thirty-minute, illustrated filmstrip-tape program. These procedures are touted as useful in the modification of students' scores on affective measures.

part IV

USING
EDUCATIONAL TESTS

Now that we've seen how to evaluate and develop educational tests, it should follow that you're ready to use such tests. In this text's final three chapters we deal with a series of important considerations regarding the ways to employ educational tests most judiciously. After an initial chapter dealing with the assembly, administration, and scoring of educational tests, we turn to such provocative issues as standard-setting and grading. This volume on modern educational measurement concludes with an appraisal of the ways in which instructional and measurement specialists can collaboratively use testing devices to enhance the quality of an instructional enterprise.

15

We now face the practicalities of the educational testing world, for we must address the essential problems associated with assembly, administration, and scoring of tests. Such practicalities, of course, are tremendously important, since even if we possess a test which possesses really resplendent reliability and truly awe-inspiring validity, an ill-conceived administration of the test can yield meaningless examinee responses.

For instance, let's say we administered such a supertest under truly adverse physical conditions, for example, in an insufficiently ventilated, poorly lighted, overheated, and noisy school auditorium. Not surprisingly, we could anticipate many distortions in the responses of the examinees, that is, those who did not swoon during the test-taking period.

Although the situation just cited may seem somewhat far fetched and you would think that few educators would make such egregious errors in the selection of a test setting, there are more subtle, but nevertheless significant, practical errors which educators make as they ready tests, dispense them, and try to make sense out of their results. By being alert to such potential mistakes, educators can hopefully avoid them. Thus, since this text was designed to make you a flawless and facile user of educational

Administering educational tests

tests, prepare to plunge into the practical procedures of test administration.

Selecting or Constructing the Test

In Chapter 3 we described a series of evaluative criteria which can be used to decide whether a test is a winner or a loser. For most school testing programs, or district testing programs, decisions will need to be made regarding the sources of the needed testing devices. Whereas classroom teachers will typically generate their own tests for use in the day-to-day instructional programs, there are other choices when it comes to the acquisition of tests to use for such purposes as annual assessment, affective appraisal, and the determination of students' scholastic aptitudes.

The basic choice facing most educators who need tests is "buy 'em or build 'em." Now buying tests, of course, costs money. Building tests, at first blush, sounds less expensive. After all, the schools are staffed by a host of able teacher-types who could surely create a clever test or two. However, distressingly, local construction of tests usually turns out to be an assessment disaster, and badly built tests can prove far more costly than is typically thought.

For example, suppose that a school district builds its own basic-skills achievement tests and uses pupil performance on these tests to inform citizens of the schools' effectiveness. Let's say the tests turn out to be pretty shabby and, as a consequence, pupil-performance levels fail to rise, in spite of valiant efforts by teachers to boost pupils' exam performances. The public, dismayed by apparent ineffectiveness on the part of the schools, registers its dissatisfaction by defeating all subsequent school bond elections. The resulting loss in revenue to the district dramatically exceeds the modest funds which would have been required to buy an appropriate off-the-shelf test from a commercial publisher. Officials in our hypothetical school district were penny-wise, but pound-foolish.

A superior school testing program will serve a variety of decision-making functions, for example, norm-referenced aptitude tests, criterion-referenced achievement tests, affective inventories for purposes of program evaluation or counseling, not to mention a number of more specialized tests, such as those that are required in connection with federally or state-funded educational programs, for example, for special education. Moreover, perhaps most fundamentally, there are the myriad tests needed by classroom teachers as they do daily with the evil forces of sloth, ignorance and borderline villainy. Teachers need plenty of help in putting together top-flight tests.

For example, there's the rather prosaic problem of how to arrange the items on a teacher-made test if several different types of items are used. Measurement wizards usually recommend that test items be grouped in order of increasing complexity, so that a grouping in the following order would prove satisfactory:

1. Binary-choice items.
2. Matching items.
3. Short-answer items.
4. Mutiple-choice items.
5. Essay items.

Now, obviously, few tests will contain all five of these item-types. However, the general principle of arraying items from less to more demanding makes considerable sense.

Those who must decide whether the tests will be constructed locally and/or purchased will need to weigh all sorts of factors, such as cost, the congruence of the commercial test's mission with the needs of the local schools, the absence of cultural bias in the commerical test, and so on. After considerable deliberations, hopefully involving the numerous qualitative dimensions of educational tests that served as the theme of Part II in this text, let's assume that the tests have been acquired. Now we need to get ready to administer them.

Separate Response Sheets

In getting ready to use an educational test, one of the first matters to decide is, "Where will examinees respond?" For selected-response and short-answer tests, students can supply their answers by either marking on the test itself or on a separate answer sheet. There are economic advantages associated with the use of separate answer sheets, since the test booklet itself can be reused. In addition, separate answer sheets are typically easier to score since the scorer does not have to leaf through a series of pages in the test itself.

However, there is some evidence that first- and second-grade children's scores were lower when separate answer sheets were employed.[1] Apparently, it is distracting for younger children to transfer their responses from the test booklet to a separate answer sheet. In middle and later grades it would seem prudent to employ separate answer sheets with tests. Accordingly, of course, the directions to the examinee should make it clear that a separate answer sheet is to be used.

PREPARING EFFECTIVE TEST DIRECTIONS

Given the considerable energy that is devoted to the construction of test items, it is always a bit surprising to see how casually most teachers approach the task of devising directions for a test. Indeed, in some cases no directions at all are prepared, supposedly on the assumption that an alert examinee should be able to figure out what's called for by the items. Well, as experienced teachers know, not all examinees are alert. In fact, some students appear to have completed formal training in anti-alertness.

It is important, therefore, for test developers to fashion decent directions for their tests since, without those directions, many students will flounder on the exam due to confusion regarding the task at hand. A good set of directions for a test will include information regarding:

[1]V. M. Cashen, and G. C. Ramseyer, "The Use of Separate Answer Sheets by Primary Age Children," *Journal of Educational Measurement*, 6 (1969), 155–158.

1. The test's purpose.
2. Time allowance.
3. The basis for responding.
4. Method of recording responses.
5. Appropriateness of guessing.

The nature of the directions, particularly for classroom tests, will depend on such factors as the students' familiarity with the types of items on the test. To illustrate, if Mrs. Thomas has been dishing out weekly mutiple-choice vocabulary quizzes in her English class for the last fifteen weeks, her students will doubtlessly need little guidance in how to answer the questions on this week's quiz. Suppose, on the other hand, that a teacher is introducing an exotic new type of interpretive exercise in which students must first make sense out of a complicated map *and* a complicated graph, *then* respond to a series of matching items. Under such circumstances a detailed set of test directions is definitely needed.

The Test's Purpose

Although for many tests it is apparent what the intent of the test is, for some tests the purpose is more opaque. As a general rule, since it usually takes no more than a single sentence to do so, it is a good idea to include in the test directions a statement that describes the intended mission of the test.

Time Allowance

Directions should indicate how much time is being allowed for the total test. It is also helpful to suggest to examinees how they should allocate their time during an examination. If, for example, there are several sections on the exam, then the directions should estimate how much time should be spent on each section.

For tests consisting of essay questions, it is useful to provide question-by-question guidelines regarding appropriate time expenditures. At UCLA, for example, doctoral qualifying examinations usually consist of six questions, each of which is to be answered in about one hour by graduate students. Even with a reminder alongside each question that it is a "one-hour" question, some students use up too much of their time in responding to early items. Without such reminders, some students might never get beyond the first question. (Doctoral candidates are a decidedly verbose crew.)

The Basis for Responding

In some instances, such as with multiple-choice tests, all the directions need do is to indicate that students "should select the best alternative for each item." If possibilities for confusion are present, such as might be encountered with matching items where examinees would be uncertain as to whether responses can be used more than once, then such matters need to be clarified in the directions.

In particular, essay questions should provide students with cues regarding what their responses should stress, for example, particular facts or a synthesis of such facts.

For very young children it is frequently helpful to provide a sample test question which shows how a response should be made. Many nationally standardized examinations, in recognition of the value of a good model, provide such a sample question and oblige the test administrator to show examinees how the sample item should be completed.

Method of Recording Responses

As indicated earlier, if separate response sheets are used with the exam, students may need to be given directions about how to use the response sheets. If the answer sheets are to be scored by machine, it may be necessary to indicate precisely how the sheets are to be filled out. For example, many new machine-scorable response forms now consist of circles (or "bubbles") which must be darkened by examinees. Indeed, a new verb has been created by the educational testing industry during the past decade, because test directions now inform students that they are "to *bubble* in the correct answer for each item."

Appropriateness of Guessing

Later in the chapter we consider the pros and cons of employing correction-for-guessing procedures. If there is any special guidance which examinees should have regarding whether guessing is appropriate, the test's directions are an eminently suitable locus for such guidance. However, with respect to the wisdom of employing guessing-correction formulae, please hold off for a bit.

ADMINISTERING THE TEST

The two main factors to consider when administering the test are (1) the physical setting in which the testing takes place and (2) the nature of the test administrator's interaction with the examinees. If either the physical setting or the test administrator's instructions are unsatisfactory, examinees may end up with lower scores than they deserve.

The Physical Setting

When we think about the ideal testing room, particularly for important tests, our minds usually conjure up a delightful, well-lighted, properly ventilated classroom or cafeteria with ample workspace for each student. More often than not, of course, pupils are obliged to complete tests in their regular classrooms. Accordingly, teachers should strive to make certain that their classrooms possess all the virtues of an ideal testing room—at least on the occasions when those classrooms are to be used for significant examinations.

It is customary for test manuals of commercially distributed tests to urge that examinations take place in well-lighted rooms where desks or tables provide students with adequate workspace. Interestingly, at least one investigation suggests that pupils can adapt quite satisfactorily to less than optimum conditions of this sort. In a study of testing conditions, Ingle and DeAmico found that students who took standardized tests in a poorly lighted auditorium using lap boards, instead of desks, performed as well on the tests as did youngsters who took the tests in well-lighted classrooms with adequate workspace.[2]

However, even though children might be able to take tests on lap boards in near darkness, that doesn't mean that we should oblige them to do so. No, it just makes common sense to provide students with decent lighting, reasonable workspace, an acceptable room temperature, and air circulation.

Teachers should also be attentive to the number and magnitude of auditory distractions that may arise during a testing period. Not all students are bothered by loud noises, but some are.

I used to teach in a high school on the ground-floor level next to an expansive front lawn. It seemed that the school's custodian (who was also its gardener, mechanic, plumber, and painter) had access to special information regarding my exam schedule, since he invariably chose that day to mow the lawn. It would have been all right had he used a small lawn mower and finished the job quickly. However, our congenial custodian had rigged up an adapted tractor engine with the lawn mower. That engine, when running, sounded like the first stage of an Apollo space rocket. Furthermore, he kept going back and forth, back and forth, apparently wish-

---

[2] B. Ingle, and G. DeAmico, "Effects of Physical Conditions of the Test Room on Standardized Achievement Test Scores," *Journal of Educational Measurement*, 6 (1969), 237–240.

ing to give every blade of grass its fair share of shearing. Both I and my students suffered as a consequence of these mower- .essed exam periods.

The Test Administrator's Behavior

In most instances the test administrator will be the teacher. Certainly teachers will administer their own classroom tests. However, whether special test administrators or typical classroom teachers, there are a few guidelines which should be attended to when directing a testing session.

Avoid verbal or nonverbal behaviors which are likely to make examinees anxious.   Do not assert that the test is a "crucial" one or that evil will befall all those who fail it. Don't pace back and forth in the front of the testing room, looking up frequently at the clock. Don't "hover" over students, observing them with intensity as they make their answers.

Instead, try to reassure students that the purpose of the test is to help them, either to learn or to guide counseling decisions. Let them know that the time limits are adequate (assuming they are). In fact, the test administrator should deliberately try to *allay* anxiety, not foster it. Studies reveal that there are certain students who become so anxious during testing sessions that the quality of their performance is substantially depreciated. Even an adroit test administrator will not be able to transform such nervous students into tranquil test-takers. However, the administrator may be able to at least keep such students' anxieties within reasonable limits.

Don't talk unnecessarily before the test, and never talk during the test.
Some test administrators get carried away with the significance of the occasion, hence jabber on endlessly before actually dispensing the tests. Students are ready, but their time is being used up by a long-winded test administrator.

Similarly, some classroom teachers choose the moments prior to exams to comment about last week's activities or this week's assignments. Such diatribes probably won't be well attended to by students, and they certainly will annoy the students who are anxious to get going on the test.

After the exam gets underway, teachers sometimes interrupt for one reason or another to make announcements. Such interruptions should be avoided unless critically important (such as, for example, when a mistake in a test item has been discovered or the school is on fire). Some insensitive test administrators will carry on a loud conversation with a student during the examination. Test administrators should nurture their whispering prowess.

While on the subject of interruptions, try to reduce external interruptions. One helpful way of doing this in a classroom is to post a sign outside

"Every so often I wonder if we've gone a bit too far in providing a comfortable testing environment."

the door which says something like "Test in Session—Do Not Disturb." Some teachers, frustrated by excessive interruptions during their regular teaching schedules, may be inclined to post such signs on a daily basis.

Monitor for possible cheating, taking steps to discourage such behaviors. Teachers have to cope with the possibility of student dishonesty during examinations. By attentive proctoring, that is, alert surveillance by the test administrator of examinee activity during the test, much potential cheating can be forestalled. Alternate forms of the test can also be employed to discourage students from casual copying of the marks on others' answer sheets.

Ebel contends that the basic cure for cheating is relative to its basic cause. "Students and their teachers must recognize that cheating is dishonest and unfair and that it deserves consistent application of appropriate penalties—failure in the course, loss of credit, suspension, or dismissal."[3] Ebel argues that even if reports of cheating are prevalent, it should not be considered an acceptable harm which is inevitable and hence "must be accommodated as gracefully as possible."

[3]R. L. Ebel, *Essentials of Educational Measurement*, 3rd ed. (Englewood Cliffs, N.J.: Prentice-Hall, Inc., 1979), p. 186.

Do not give hints to students about individual test items. Certain students are more willing to ask about test items th ı are others. Perhaps they are cunning, or maybe they are merely outgoing. However, an experienced teacher will tell you that during an exam it usually turns out to be the same few students who approach the teacher with queries, such as, "On item 22, did you mean . . . ?"

Now it is perfectly reasonable to clarify ambiguous test items, if that is the kind of clarification needed. However, some astute students are really trying to secure hints as to the correct answer. Yet, teachers, wanting to be nice folks, sometimes succumb to these entreaties by dispensing little bits of insight that lead directly to the correct response.

However, test administrators should play the proctoring game with even-handedness. They should not reward a few aggressive students by giving them special information while withholding that information from less aggressive, but no less deserving, students. Avoid giving hints on test items, even if you're strongly tempted to do so.

When administering a standardized test, follow the directions explicitly. So far the discussion of test-administration practices has dealt with the kinds of tests that could be teacher-made *or* distributed by commercial firms. When using standardized tests, such as, for example, the *Iowa Test of Basic Skills*, there are always directions provided for test administrators. These directions include not only how much time to allow for the test and its subparts but often the explicit words to be read aloud when explaining how the test is to be completed.

Because the entire conception of a standardized test is premised on the extent to which it is administered, scored, and interpreted in a *standardized* manner, test administrators must adhere religiously to the directions provided.

SCORING THE TESTS

It would be nice if tests would score themselves. Scoring tests is so boring. However, distressingly, that little innovation is not yet at hand, hence we will need to face the problem of how to score tests after students have completed them.

Hand Scoring

In the classroom the bulk of tests are scored by hand, usually the teacher's hand. In a few cases teachers can have students exchange papers and score each other's tests, but because of the possibility of "mutual kindness" by pairs of students, this practice is rarely recommended for important examinations.

If tests must be hand scored, it is important to devise the most efficient method of scoring. For example, if short-answer tests are to be scored, it usually helps the teacher to write out a numbered list of the correct answers and have the list at hand during the scoring.

For selected-response answers, particularly those made on a separate response sheet, it is most effective to use a scoring stencil (or template) in which holes have been punched out over the correct answers. The teacher simply scores a student's answer sheet, marks with a colored pencil any missing answers, then totals the score. (A quick glance at the answer sheet to see that students weren't filling in too many responses is also recommended.) By returning the answer sheets to students (with errors marked in colored pencil), students can determine not only how many but what sorts of errors they made.

Several new hand-scoring procedures are now available, although not yet widely used. A *carbon booklet* provides two sheets, the bottom of which already has spaces for the correct answer provided. Students mark their answers on the top sheet and, because of the carbon treatment, simultaneously imprint on the bottom sheet. After the carbon booklet has been turned in, the teacher simply removes the bottom sheet and readily computes the number of correct answers.

In addition, a number of *latent-image* scoring schemes have been used, at least on an experimental basis. These latent-image procedures typically involve the use of a chemically treated answer sheet on which the student responds with a special writing instrument (such as a felt-tipped pen containing a chemical substance designed to interact with the chemicals on the answer sheet). When the student marks a response on the special answer sheet, a latent (hidden) image appears, and the student finds out immediately whether the response was correct or incorrect. In addition, because the latent image is now visible, the *number of incorrect attempts* made by each student can subsequently be counted.

With some carbon booklets, latent images, and comparable test-response approaches there is usually a scheme whereby students who wish to change an answer may do so.

Machine Scoring

For large-scale test scoring, there is no substitute for a well-trained machine. In this era of ever-increasing advances in electronics technology, recent years have seen a number of improvements in the machine scoring of tests. Most of these involve the use of some sort of optical scanning equipment which can be used to "read" a student's response sheet, then pump out a record of correct and incorrect answers. Sophisticated test-scoring machines will also produce a series of subscores, error patterns, and so on.

Optical scanning machines can be used to score single-response sheets as well as test booklets on which younger students write directly. The major variable in the cost of optical scanning machines is the number of sheets which can be processed in a given period of time. Whereas a machine that can score 1,000 sheets an hour might cost $30,000 to $40,000, a machine that can score 6,000 sheets per hour might cost two or three times that amount. We can expect continuing increases in the efficiency of such machines and, hopefully, a reduction in their cost.

Most large school districts now own their own electronic test-scoring equipment, so teachers in such districts will often find themselves administering tests that will be machine scored at the district office. One of the major impediments to effective use of machine scoring is the extensive turn-around time that sometimes delays a teacher's receiving test results until weeks after the test was administered. Such delays, of course, render test results somewhat useless for instructional purposes.

For districts which do not possess their own test-scoring machines, there are increasing numbers of scoring services being established throughout the nation. Typically, these scoring services can accommodate mailed-in batches of answer sheets and, depending on priorities and costs, provide fairly rapid turn-arounds. Some school districts and universities are even providing such test-scoring services at a nominal cost to other users.

CORRECTING FOR GUESSING

Because it is feared that if there are no penalties associated with guessing, some students might "blind guess" their way to unwarrantedly high scores, *correction-for-guessing* formulae are sometimes recommended for use in calculating a student's score on a test. The usual formula for this purpose is

$$\text{Score} = R - \frac{W}{n-1}$$

where R = number right
W = number wrong
n = number of alternatives

Thus, for a test consisting of binary-clause items the formula would be

$$\text{Score} = R - \frac{W}{2-1} = R - W$$

For multiple-choice items the formula would be different, depending on the number of options on the items.

$$\text{For 3 alternatives, Score} = R - \frac{W}{2}$$

$$\text{For 4 alternatives, Score} = R - \frac{W}{3}$$

$$\text{For 5 alternatives, Score} = R - \frac{W}{4}$$

Items which are *omitted* by the student are not counted as wrong.

To illustrate the use of the correction-for-guessing formula, let's consider the case of a student who completes a fifty-item multiple-choice exam on which each item has four alternatives. The student answers 27 items correctly, misses 18, and does not respond at all to five items. If we were only scoring the student's paper by number correct, then the student would get a 27. If, however, we apply our correction-for-guessing formula, then we would have

$$\text{Score} = 27 - \frac{18}{3} = 21$$

There are two fairly distinctive settings in which the correction-for-guessing formula might be applied. The first of these involves unspeeded tests, that is, tests for which most students have ample time to complete the test. The second, not surprisingly, involves speeded tests, that is, tests for which it is not thought that most students will be able to finish. To oversimplify, with speeded tests there appears to be some value in correcting for guessing, since such a correction (if announced in advance) can deter slower students from answering the final test questions on the basis of wild guessing.

For unspeeded tests, most measurement specialists advise against the use of correction-for-guessing formulae. Considerable research suggests that there is little advantage in using such corrections.[4] In general, scores that have been corrected for guessing will rank students in approximately the same relative positions as will uncorrected scores. In other words, in spite of the fact that their scores have been subjected to diabolical correction schemes, students usually end up with scores which rank them in the same way as would have been the case without any correction schemes.

For classroom tests, therefore, it is usually inappropriate to correct for guessing unless the test is speeded to the point that many students will be unable to complete all of its items. Under any circumstances, as suggested

[4]For example, see G. L. Rowley, and R. Traub, "Formula Scoring, Number-Right Scoring, and Test Taking Strategy," *Journal of Educational Measurement*, 14 (1977), 15–22.

before, the test's directions should make clear whether any penalties will be applied. It is generally good advice to suggest that students employ *informed guesses* if they are uncertain but have some sort of idea of a question's correct answer. For speeded tests it is helpful to urge students to work rapidly so they can complete as many items as possible (rather than suggesting they complete the test's final items by random marking of the answer sheet).

ADDITIONAL CONSIDERATIONS

There are several other issues to be considered in connection with test administration. Each of these can be treated briefly.

Differential Scoring Weights

Teachers will sometimes decide that because certain items are more significant, those items should be assigned double or even triple weighting. For instance, instead of giving every item one point, these special items might receive two or three points. Similarly, errors on such items carry heavier penalties.

Although differential weighting of items makes intuitive sense, this process rarely raises or lowers students' overall rankings to any appreciable extent. Differential weights do not improve or lower a test's reliability or validity. Just like correction for guessing, this process usually makes little difference in the way that students are ultimately ranked.

Even though differential weighting of items may make little difference in the rankings of students, it may substantially influence students' study efforts if they are aware that certain kinds of items will receive heavier weighting on major exams. Accordingly, since the quality of the exam is not affected adversely, teachers may wish to use differential weightings as a helpful emphasis guide for students.

RECORDING TEST RESULTS

Once tests have been scored, the necessity arises to record the results in such a way that they can be both stored and retrieved efficiently. This sounds more routine and simple than it actually is.

For instance, in any sort of large educational operation, such as a school district with several thousand pupils, the data storage space requirements are considerable. In addition, if someone wants access to a certain pupil's records, how will those records be plucked from the tens of thousands of student records that will accumulate even over a short span of years?

At the present, most of these student records are maintained at the school site in some sort of cumulative record folder during the period that the pupil is at the school. Upon graduation these cumulative record folders are shipped off to the district office where they are permanently maintained.

Sometimes special-purpose record forms are developed for use in programs, such as a school district's minimum competency program tied to high school graduation. An illustration of such a record form is provided in Figure 15-1.

In the future, surely, these records will be maintained by means of

NAME _____
(LAST)   (FIRST)

Semester	Teacher	Period	Room
Fall			
Spring			

STUDENT RECORD CARD:
Detroit Ninth Grade Objective-Referenced Testing Program

DIRECTIONS: Place Pretest score report here or use this space to write in results of individually administered Pretest.

Form of Test _____
Date of Testing _____

	READING SKILLS				STUDY SKILLS		WRITING SKILLS		
	WRITTEN DIRECTS.	WORDS IN CONTEXT	MAIN IDEA	INFER-ENCE	USING A DICT.	CATEG. LISTS.	CAPITALIZ. AND PUNCT.	SENT. CONST.	PARAG. ORGANIZ.

DIRECTIONS: Record Interim Test scores here. Write the percentage correct in each space. If desired, a symbol (*) can be used to represent mastery.

TEST FORM	READING SKILLS				STUDY SKILLS		WRITING SKILLS		
	WRITTEN DIRECTS.	WORDS IN CONTEXT	MAIN IDEA	INFER-ENCE	USING A DICT.	CATEG. LISTS.	CAPITALIZ. AND PUNCT.	SENT. CONST.	PARAG. ORGANIZ.
INTERIM (A)									
INTERIM (B)									

DIRECTIONS: Place Posttest — Part I score report here or use this space to write in results of individually administered Posttest.

Form of Test _____
Date of Testing _____

	READING SKILLS				STUDY
	WRITTEN DIRECTS.	WORDS IN CONTEXT	MAIN IDEA	INFER-ENCE	USING A DICT.

DIRECTIONS: Place Posttest — Part II score report here or use this space to write in results of individually administered Posttest.

Form of Test _____
Date of Testing _____

	STUDY	WRITING SKILLS		
	CATEG. LISTS.	CAPITALIZ. AND PUNCT.	SENT. CONST.	PARAG. ORGANIZ.

FIGURE 15–1 Excerpt from a Record Sheet for a High School Minimum Competency Testing Program.

electronic computers. Some larger districts, in fact, currently maintain all pertinent records in a district-operated student data file. Some of these computer-based data retrieval systems have all sorts of features associated with them, such as procedures for printing up special letters which inform parents of their children's progress on a subtest-by-subtest basis.

There is a decided tension existing between our wish to make records of student test scores available to those who need to use them and, simultaneously, to prevent those records from being seen by those who have no business with them. Recalling our discussion of confidentiality in connection with affective measure, it should be clear that we don't want every Tom, Dick, and Harriet browsing through records of student test scores. The trick is to set up a storage and retrieval system that provides requested data to authorized personnel while making certain that no unauthorized individuals can penetrate the retrieval system.

How should data be recorded for purposes of classroom instruction? Although measurement folks have lots of practice in setting up permanent records, they have scant experience in recording or portraying test results so that teachers can make the most use of them instructionally. In Figure 15–2 we see an attempt to represent student scores on a series of ninth-grade language arts tests used in the Detroit Public Schools. Note how the teacher has access to pretest scores as well as a series of ten-item interim tests measuring each of the nine objectives in the Detroit program.

In Chapter 17 we probe more seriously into the matter of how to use tests for purposes of instructional improvement. However, it is obvious that before we can use a test's results, those tests must be scored in such a way that we can effectively provide them for those who must use the tests. With schemes similar to the Detroit ninth-grade language arts model, we are beginning to make progress on this front.

TEST SECURITY

Should tests be kept from students after they have been used, or should the tests be returned to students in order to gain the instructional dividends that might accompany such an act? Although there is a division of opinion on this issue, it is my view that educators should *not* turn over important examinations to students since by that act the teacher is thereafter unable to use those exams again.

It's not that I don't want students to learn well. On the contrary, I've spent most of my professional life fussing around with methods of making students learn more, faster. However, teachers can construct only so many decent test items before they run out of ideas. If, after generating two

STUDENT PROGRESS RECORD

Satisfaction of District Proficiency Standards and Course of Study

STUDENT'S NAME _____   GRADE   7   8   9   10   11   12

SCHOOL _____   (Circle grades completed by the student.)

PROFICIENCY STANDARDS See master list for complete descriptions.	ASSESSMENT				PROFICIENCY STANDARDS See master list for complete descriptions.	ASSESSMENT			
	Performance					Performance			
	1st date:	2nd date:	3rd date:	Achieved + Not achieved o		1st date:	2nd date:	3rd date:	Achieved + Not achieved o

CONFERENCE TO DISCUSS NEED FOR INSTRUCTION IN BASIC SKILLS	Notification of Pupil	Notification of Parent or Guardian	Telephone attempt(s) to contact parent or guardian within 5 days of written notification (if necessary)	Date Conference Held & Name(s) of Participating School Personnel
	date:	date:	date(s):	
	date:	date:	date(s):	

SUBSEQUENT INSTRUCTION IN BASIC SKILLS

Type and Dates: _____

_____

_____

This student has met PROFICIENCY STANDARDS necessary for graduation. ☐ _____
(date)

This student has met the prescribed COURSE OF STUDY necessary for graduation ☐ _____
(date)

by: _____

_____

Prepared by the Instructional Objectives Exchange   February 1977

FIGURE 15-2   An Excerpt from the Record Card Used in the Ninth-Grade Language Arts Program of the Detroit Public Schools, 1978.

terrific exams in successive years, a drained teacher must then turn out a series of mediocre exams for years to come, think of the students who will be mismeasured.

No, teachers should devise the very best test items they can, refine them, then guard them with the diligence of an intelligence agent. Test security must be maintained! By maintaining secure tests, over the years a teacher will be able to build an increasingly fine file of test items to use in future exams. Items can be stored on cards along with results, for example, item-analysis data, p values, and distractor analyses from previous exams. By having more than the items needed for a given exam, the teacher will be able to select enough items from the item file to create different forms of the test each year, term, and so on.

For less important tests, such as weekly quizzes or easily generated tests, little is lost by turning over the test itself to the students. Tests of this sort can usually be churned out without much problem.

To reiterate, although there are loads of more exotic topics in educational measurement than the practical problems we've been tussling with in this chapter, without satisfactory resolution of these practical issues, the overall testing program is sure to fail.

PRACTICE EXERCISES

There were a number of separate issues treated in this chapter. A significant practice exercise would take place if you would coalesce these distinctive topics into a plan for an overall *school testing program*. Try to write out a description of the administrative side of an effective school testing program. Your description should at least address the following topics:

A. Test Directions
B. Test Administration
C. Test Scoring
D. Recording Test Results

Furthermore, add any factors you believe important to include in an effective school testing program.

Because it is impossible to provide a set of answers for this sort of exercise, please entice a colleague or classmate into critiquing your description.

DISCUSSION QUESTIONS

1. If you were asked to defend the proposition that test results and tests should be returned to students after all exams, how would you defend your case?

2. What sorts of test records do you believe would be most appropriate for classroom teachers to use in connection with instructional decisions?
3. Do you believe that correction-for-guessing formulae should be used with untimed tests? Why?
4. In what ways can student test anxiety be reduced?
5. How can teachers help students to increase their *testwiseness* so that they behave optimally on tests?
6. If you were a classroom teacher, how would you recommend dealing with instances of cheating on your exams?

SUGGESTIONS FOR ADDITIONAL READING

CHASE, CLINTON I., "The Test Taker and His Environment," Chapter 13, *Measurement for Educational Evaluation*, pp. 292–331. Reading, Mass.: Addison-Wesley, 1978. In this chapter motivation for test taking is considered along with such factors as test anxiety, the nature of the examiner, and examinee fatigue.

EBEL, ROBERT L., "How to Administer and Score an Achievement Test," Chapter 10, *Essentials of Educational Measurement* (3rd ed.), pp. 177–201. Englewood Cliffs, N.J.: Prentice-Hall, Inc., 1979. The ways to help students in developing skills in test taking are described in this chapter, along with routine problems encountered by test administrators, such as student cheating.

GRONLUND, NORMAN E., "Assembling, Administering, and Appraising Classroom Tests," Chpater 11, *Measurement and Evaluation in Teaching* (3rd ed.), pp. 249–278. New York: Macmillan, 1976. In this chapter Gronlund provides a series of highly practical suggestions regarding the assembly and administration of classroom testing devices.

HOPKINS, CHARLES D., and RICHARD L. ANTES, "Administration of the Test," Chapter 1, *Classroom Testing: Administration, Scoring and Score Interpretation*, pp. 1–18. Itasca, Ill.: F. E. Peacock, 1979. The authors explore psychological and physical conditions associated with test administration in this practical introduction to classroom test giving.

MEHRENS, WILLIAM A., and IRVIN J. LEHMANN, *Measurement and Evaluation in Education and Psychology* (2nd ed.), pp. 304–355. New York: Holt, Rinehart & Winston, 1975. A host of practical problems are treated in this chapter, including assembly, reproduction, administration, and scoring of classroom tests.

NOLL, VICTOR H., DALE P. SCANNEL, and ROBERT C. CRAIG, "The Measurement Program," Chapter 13, *Introduction to Educational Measurement*, pp. 402–435. Boston: Houghton Mifflin, 1979. In this chapter the authors explore the requisites for a successful measurement program, one major element of which is the effective administration of tests.

Today, more than at any previous time in the history of education, American educators are being obliged to set explicit performance standards for students. Educators have recently been asked, and sometimes required by law, to specify a precise level of performance below which a student will be considered deficient. Because few educators have seriously wrestled with the problems of setting standards and because so many educators must now do so, this chapter was prepared to assist those individuals who, in a practical setting, must come up with an answer to the question: "How good is good enough?"

What a Performance Standard Is

Since the dominant topic of concern in the following pages is performance standards, and how to set them, it seems only reasonable to spend a few sentences attempting to clarify the expression, *performance standard*. The interpretation most of us ascribe to *standard* is the following definition offered by the *Oxford English Dictionary*:

Setting performance standards

> *A definite level of excellence, attainment, wealth, or the like, or a definite degree of any quality, viewed as a prescribed object of endeavour or as the measure of what is adequate for some purpose.*

When we apply such an interpretation to education, and to student performance, we're clearly talking about a "measure of what (student performance) is adequate for some purpose." However, when educators are forced to set *measurable* performance standards, rather than talk about it, the game's stakes instantly skyrocket. And that, of course, is the situation today since legislative bodies, and the public in general, are demanding that educators describe measurable performance standards for students.

In situations where educators have merely been admonished to set general (and by implication, not necessarily measurable) performance standards, one can detect markedly increased tranquility in the educational establishment. Unmeasurable standards need be little more than rhetoric. However, where educators have actually been forced to measure students' mastery of performance standards, anxiety indices rise and a quest for sensible standard-setting procedures commences. This chapter is designed for those latter situations, that is, those in which educators must set honest-to-goodness measurable performance standards.

It is important to recognize that performance standards, in the sense that phrase is used here, apply to an *individual*, not a group of individuals. There are many instances in which we use a group's performance to help us make decisions, for instance, when a teacher decides whether to revise an instructional procedure for a group of students. However, the types of standard-setting dilemmas now facing educators are clearly focused on individual students, for example, "Should John Jones receive a high school diploma or should Mary Muggins be advanced to the next grade?"

On a similar note, today's preoccupation with standards is almost exclusively associated with performance in the cognitive domain, only occasionally in the psychomotor domain, and never in the affective domain. Although we might set some *group* standards in the affective domain, educators never set minimum requisites (for example, regarding a pupil's attitudes toward school) which, if not satisfied, would result in an adverse decision regarding an individual student. No, our concern here is chiefly with the establishment of performance standards in the cognitive domain. While the strategies to be described pertain to psychomotor skills as well, all of our examples will be drawn from cognitive pupil behavior.

Minimum Competency Testing

Although this is not the place to engage in an extensive probing of why it is that so many citizens are pushing educators to carve out performance standards, it's a certainty that the chief stimulus for the recent concern about setting performance standards stems directly from the so-called minimum competency testing movement.

A majority of states in the late seventies enacted laws or established regulations which required students to display minimum prowess in reading, writing, and arithmetic before being granted a high school diploma. These minimum competency programs, almost without exception, called for students to exceed a specified performance standard on a test of some type. Sometimes that standard was set at the state level for all the state's would-be high school graduates. Sometimes the standards were set by local school districts. However, under either condition, the minimum performance standards for high school graduates were to be made explicit, and that's just the problem. Most educators really didn't know how to go about setting defensible performance standards.

It is important to note, in connection with minimum competency testing programs, that there are at least two substantially distinct interpretations of the phrase "minimum competency." For some people that notion refers to the absolutely imperative skills that an individual must have in order to function satisfactorily in society. Individuals who hold this view typically equate the notion of minimum competency with the idea of *survival skills*. A major defect of this conception of minimum competency is that it often proves impossible to establish with any degree of confidence just what these minimum skills are, since for almost any "minimum" skill that we can identify, there are people who fail to possess it but somehow seem to get along in life.

A second, more readily defended, interpretation of minimum competency is to think of such competencies as the minimum skills that educators (or citizens) *are willing to accept* as satisfying one of the requirements for, say, high school graduation.

A Camouflaged Problem

Whichever way we interpret this key concept, there's no doubt that the enactment of minimum competency programs has forced into the open a problem about which educators have always fretted. Although educators have perennially been obliged to decide when a student "passed a test" or "passed a course," this obligation was discharged in private, behind closed classroom doors. With the requirement that students pass minimum competency tests as a precursor to high school graduation, the issue of what it means to *pass* minimum competency tests is clearly receiving spotlight attention. Yet, unlike some problems which when illuminated become less vexing, the recent highlighting of our standard-setting shortcomings has not been accompanied by the emergency of effective solution strategies.

Putting it simply, educators have always faced decisions about whether students' performances were good enough to pass the students, but those decisions were typically made individually and privately. Now, educators are being called on to deal *openly* with the question of standards. Moreover, instead of setting a passing level for each teacher's class, so that it affects only a limited set of student grades, educators are currently being asked to set passing levels for large collections of students, such as all seniors in a school district or even an entire state.

When teachers were tussling with the passing-standards problem in private, they could take solace in the fact that if some students were penalized because of the too-stringent standards in one teacher's class, those students would most likely benefit from another teacher's relaxed grading standards. Most of us remember classes in which our final grades seemed unwarrantedly low or, conversely, charitably high. Thus, educators could console themselves in the belief that grading inequities tended to cancel each other out over the long haul.

However, with minimum competency testing programs, this sort of compensation is unavailable to the student. If an excessively stringent passing standard is set on a district-wide high school graduation test, many students will be penalized irrevocably. There won't be numerous other opportunities wherein this error will be rectified because of unduly relaxed passing standards. Clearly, errors in setting an excessively high passing score on a high-stakes minimum competency test can have lasting consequences for many people, not just the students who are inequitably failed, but also their families and friends.

The flip side of that argument, of course, is that if we set standards that are too low, society is ultimately the loser. It is generally conceded that one strong motive underlying the enactment of minimum competency testing programs was to halt, both in the public's perception and in fact, a devaluation of the high school diploma. Clearly, if standards are set too low, the devaluation of high school diplomas will have been accelerated, not impeded.

It is apparent that educators have been historically plagued by the problem of how to set defensible passing standards but have thus far been unsuccessful in producing sensible solution strategies. Further, because passing standards were generally established in private by individual teachers, no large-scale attention has been given to this issue. The setting of standards has been a major, but well-camouflaged, educational problem for centuries. Chiefly because of the minimum competency testing movement, that problem is now decisively out of the closet.

The Arbitrariness Bugbear

It has been contended by some (for example, Glass, in 1977) that the act of setting a performance standard is *by its very nature* so arbitrary, mindless, and capricious that educators ought not to engage in that enterprise. However, such critics unwarrantedly equate caprice with human judgment. Admittedly, when human beings apply their judgmental powers to the solution of problems, mistakes will be made. However, the fact that judgmental errors are possible should not send us running from such tasks as the setting of standards. Judges and juries are capable of error, yet they do the best job they can. Similarly, educators are now faced with the necessity of establishing performance standards, and they, too, must do the best job they can.

That educational performance standards need to be set in order for instructional decisions to be made is indisputable. That those standards will, in the final analysis, be set judgmentally is equally indisputable. However, that all judgmental standards must be arbitrary is decidedly disputable.

Approaching the standard-setting task seriously, taking full cognizance of available data and the preferences of concerned constituencies, need not result in an enterprise which is arbitrary and capricious. On the contrary, the act of standard setting can reflect the very finest form of judgmental decision making.

To assert that the setting of educational performance standards in the past often has been mindless and arbitrary is accurate. To assert that many educators will continue to set mindless and indefensible performance standards is also accurate. To assert, however, that such caprice and arbitrariness are *requisite* elements of the standard-setting process is assuredly inaccurate. In the remainder of this chapter we consider procedures for reducing the potential arbitrariness against which educational standard setters must be on guard.

GENERAL CONSIDERATIONS

Before getting to the major elements that might go into standard-setting schemes, and a consideration of specific procedural alternatives, there are several preliminary considerations to which would-be standard setters should attend. We examine four such considerations.

Revisability

Because of the obvious reliance on human judgment in the setting of performance standards, everyone involved in the standard-setting enterprise should, early on, alert the world to the tentativeness of the standards being established. Standard setters should concede without debate that they may, in all likelihood *will*, make mistakes in the establishment of performance standards. That being the case, the expectation should be established that performance standards, once established, will be continually reviewed and, probably, revised.

With regard to revisability, it will typically be easier to raise than to lower widely publicized performance standards. Suppose, for example, that a state sets its high school graduation performance standards for a given mathematics test at the 80 percent correct level, then discovers that two-thirds of the state's youngsters can't pass the test at that level. There will be far more loss of public confidence if the state's educators "lower their standards" to the 75 percent level than if they had set an initial level at 70 percent and, after a year or so, "raised their standards" to 75 percent. There is a danger, of course, in playing it so safe at the outset that the initially set standards are far too low, thus inviting ridicule. Nevertheless, standard setters should be aware that it's decidedly easier to adjust standards up than down.

Quantitative Quicksands

Most educators would like to have a compact, portable, and perfectly reliable standard-setting machine that, with a crank or two would spit out simply splendid performance standards. However, although nearly all educators recognize the folly of looking for such a magic standard-setting machine, there are many educators who will settle for the next best thing: a quantitative standard-setting procedure. Americans just love quantitative decision schemes. We reverently genuflect in the face of numerically sophisticated formulae because such quantitative schemes smack of genuine authoritativeness. After all, if it has numbers in it, can precision be far removed?

Well, in spite of our commitment to number magic, even those quantitative standard-setting approaches just brimming with numbers and symbols must be appraised as rigorously as any nonquantitative schemes. Later, we consider some of these quantitatively oriented standard-setting schemes, and you will discover that, in all of them, there are key points where *human judgment* operates to set weightings, determine the significance of variables, and so on. Thus, even though a standard-setting scheme appears to be exclusively quantitative, and thereby to have dodged that messy commodity known as human judgment, you invariably find that judgmental operations have been slipped into the procedures. For standard setting, you won't be able to escape the necessity of making some tough judgments, all the numbers in the universe notwithstanding.

Experience-Based Standards

There have been several recent reports of states or major school systems that have attempted to set performance standards in the absence of *any* data regarding how students will actually perform on the tests being used. This is foolhardy. Preferably, standards would be set only after there has been a thoroughgoing tryout of the tests with the kinds of pupils for whom they are ultimately intended. At the very least, a sample of student performance should be gathered to guide standard setters in their efforts to isolate realistic expectations.

Time Requirements

There are so many time-consuming activities associated with the educational programs for which performance standards are required that educators sometimes try to race by the standard-setting phase of the program. "After all," they naively assume, "all we have to do is choose a few percentages."

Well, badly set performance standards can surely be set in a hurry; but decent ones rarely can. It takes plenty of relevant data, and time for reflection, if performance standards are to be set properly. For example, if local citizens have a stake in the decision at hand, such as setting high school graduation standards for a minimum competency testing program, they should be given ample opportunity to develop the meaningful sort of local "ownership" that in the long run will result in acceptance of the program *and its standards*. Attempting to rush the process will make the program's failure likely.

MAJOR FACTORS IN SETTING STANDARDS

Let's now explore four key factors which should be addressed when standards are to be set for individual learners. Throughout this analysis, it is assumed that some group of individuals, whether by designation or by default, is functioning as the standard setters. In some locales the standard setters are local boards of education. In other situations they are members of the state board of education. These standard setters will, with varying degrees of defensibility, discharge their responsibility to set performance levels that students must satisfy.

Factor One: Analysis of Decision Context

The first and most important factor to consider in standard setting flows directly from the decisions at issue and the situation in which those decisions are to be made. Standard setters must have a thorough understanding of just what's at stake if an individual fails to achieve the standards they're going to set. To illustrate, if we're merely setting standards for an end-of-unit test and the students who don't reach that standard need only repeat the two-week instructional unit, the stakes are lower than when a youngster's graduation from high school is in the balance. Thus, the magnitude of the *decision at issue* must first be comprehended.

There are typically *contextual considerations* which should, quite properly, be taken account of by standard setters. For example, suppose you are setting standards for a high school graduation program and you know that the first pupils to be affected by these standards have not been given sufficient instruction related to the competencies involved. In such a context, you might want to set somewhat more relaxed performance standards initially, planning to raise them later.

Alternatively, suppose, for a similar program, you knew that students who failed initially would have many opportunities to retake the proficiency examination and that ample remedial instruction would be available to them. In that kind of setting, you might lean toward more stringent standards.

There's also the problem of *false-positives* and *false-negatives*. Is it more serious to advance erroneously a student who hasn't mastered a competency than to hold back erroneously a student who has? If so, how will that difference impinge on the standards being set?

To illustrate the risks associated with false-positives and false-negatives, think first about a typical classroom situation in which a mathematics teacher administers a quiz to identify "masters" and "nonmasters," that is, those who respectively have and have not mastered the skills being promoted in a unit of instruction. Students who pass the quiz (the masters) will move on to a more advanced topic, while those who fail (the nonmasters) will be given more instruction in the skills being sought. In such situations, it would seem that the most serious risk is associated with the identification of false-masters, since students who haven't truly mastered the unit's skills will be in real trouble when they try to cope with more advanced topics. They are apt to become frustrated as they struggle with concepts beyond their capabilities. On the other hand, a false nonmaster will simply be held back too long in an already mastered unit. After all, giving children an added dose of instruction will do them good. Thus, in the classroom, since we wish to reduce the number of false nonmasters, we would tend to set the performance levels relatively high so that few nonmasters are erroneously moved on to more advanced topics.

In other settings, for instance, in situations where a high school student must pass a proficiency test prior to receiving a diploma, we may be more concerned about false nonmasters. Suppose, for example, that a true master is erroneously denied a diploma. The negative effects of not receiving a diploma on that person's life can be devastating. An individual might become stigmatized as a high school nongraduate. Accordingly, since false-negatives constitute a more critical problem in this instance, we might set lower passing standards.

Hopefully, these two illustrations will make clear how we must attend to the relative perils of false-positives and false-negatives. There are, of course, other considerations which should be attended to as one surveys the decision context.

Now, how do standard setters become aware of the *decision at issue* and the relevant *contextual considerations*? Well, one straightforward way of acquiring this sort of information is to create dialogue opportunities for those involved, so that such matters can be discussed openly. Standard setters should make certain that they set aside sufficient up-front time to clarify the decision context for which they're commissioned to set standards.

Factor Two: Clarity of Target Competencies

How would you respond with any kind of sense to the following question: "What level of minimal graduation skills should we set for high school seniors in mathematics?" There are, obviously, all sorts of uncertainties associated with that question which preclude a sensible answer. The most pivotal of these indeterminancies is the elusive nature of the skill for which the performance standard is actually being set, namely, "mathematics."

It is apparent, using this extreme and patently absurd example, that since you really don't have a good fix on what's involved in as broad and diffuse an entity as mathematics, it is impossible to establish minimum performance levels. There's a vast difference in our expectations for learners when we shift from asking them to add pairs of integers and, instead, demand that they solve simultaneous equations.

Although not so obvious, when standard setters attempt to pick a minimal level for pupil performance on most norm-referenced achievement tests (and some allegedly criterion-referenced tests), they are in a similar bind. Because, for a variety of reasons norm-referenced achievement tests are accompanied only by general, sometimes vague, descriptive schemes, it is next to impossible to set sensible standards for student performance on such tests. The standard setter can, of course, always consult the actual items on the test itself. In that event, the standard is being set less for a given skill, or set of skills, than for a particular set of test items and their idiosyncratic phrasings, distractors, and so on. Even so, this is preferable to attaching performance standards to the nebulous collectivities of heterogeneous test items represented by many standardized achievement tests.

For this reason, if no other, standard setters should typically eschew any Rorschach-ridden norm-referenced tests, preferring instead criterion-referenced tests which spell out with lucidity just what they're measuring. As implied earlier, not every test that is currently masquerading as a criterion-referenced measure does, in fact, provide an unambiguous description of the skill(s) being measured. Standard setters will be obliged to review such measures with care to be sure that they end up setting standards for competencies that are genuinely comprehended.

If you were asked to set a minimum performance standard for a completely unique skill, one which was totally foreign to your experience, you ought to be at a loss. Standard setters must rely on some sort of experience in deciding on expectations. For most tasks facing standard setters, there are several sorts of performance data which can prove useful. Performance data, in this sense, refer to the test scores of examinees on the measures actually being used to assess student mastery of competencies.

Standard setters will be able to set more defensible performance levels if they have access to performance data from individuals who have been (1) *uninstructed*, (2) *just-instructed*, and (3) *previously instructed*. Data from each of these three types of populations will provide different and useful insights regarding what might constitute a defensible performance standard for the skill in question.

To illustrate how these three categories of performance data might prove illuminating as we wrestle with the standard-setting problem, let's consider the case of establishing a passing level for a high school graduation minimum competency. More specifically, let's assume we're dealing with a competency that calls for students to discern the main ideas of commonly encountered reading selections. Since this illustration is fictitious, let's embellish it by assuming that the competency is to be measured by a marvelous criterion-referenced test, just bristling with descriptive clarity. In other words, there's no doubt in the minds of the standard setters what skill is involved. Their only task is to set a reasonable passing level that students must reach if they're going to get a high school diploma.

The uninstructed. Since this example involves a high school competency program, we could consider those pupils who are entering high school as uninstructed. We could administer our criterion-referenced test on main-idea comprehension to a sample of pupils during the first few weeks of their high school careers. Let's assume that those students average 70 percent correct on the test and that less than one student in twenty scores below 50 percent correct. Having access to such performance data, wouldn't standard setters be reluctant to set standards *lower* than this level?

However, you may be wondering, isn't it the case that at least regarding this particular competency, students entering high school are not totally uninstructed? Indeed, don't students receive the bulk of their instruction in reading during the early grades of elementary school, well before they troop off to high school? The answer, of course, is yes. And this illustrates a key procedural question regarding the accumulation of performance data from "uninstructed" students, namely, how uninstructed should they be? Theoretically, we could pretest infants as they're being wheeled from the delivery room, thereby being assured of low scores on most cognitive tests. But how long should we really wait? It's apparent that with respect to almost any competency that might be included in a high school graduation minimum competency test, some students will have received instruction prior to their entry into high school. That being the case, performance data from samples of students at several levels could be gathered, for instance, something like we see in Table 16–1.

The chief purpose of gathering performance data for uninstructed learners is to aid standard setters in isolating a lower limit for their expectations. Data, such as those presented in Table 16–1, should prove useful in that regard. For instance, it seems unlikely that on the basis of such data, standard setters would be strongly inclined to set a 12th-grade high school passing level for this skill below 50 percent or 60 percent correct.

On the other hand, let's assume we were looking at performance data, such as are presented in Table 16–2. It seems more likely that standard setters would see lower pass rates as at least eligible contenders.

The just-instructed. Carrying through with our example, we'd want some performance data regarding student skills at the close of high school. It is uncommonly helpful for standard setters to see how students "really are doing." Let's imagine we administered our criterion-referenced test to all, or a large sample, of a district's high school seniors during late April. Let's say that these students' average scores on the main-idea comprehension test turned out to be 83 percent correct. Further, the test data were displayed as seen in Table 16–3, indicating the percentage of students who would not receive diplomas, depending on where the passing level was set.

If you were a standard setter faced with the problem of pegging a passing level for our test in comprehending main ideas, wouldn't you benefit by having access to the kind of information presented in Table 16–3?

There is a considerable danger, of course, in being so influenced by the status quo that we let present performance blunt our aspirations for students. Clearly, what *is* must not be equated with what *should be*. The most likely interpretation of the Table 16–3 data is to say that the tabled percentages of pupils will be apt to fail if instruction does not improve. *But it should improve.* If standard setters can be realistically confident about a

TABLE 16–1   Fictitious Average Test Performance of Uninstructed Students

SAMPLE GROUP	n	% CORRECT
Beginning Fourth Graders	98	38
Beginning Seventh Graders	93	52
Beginning High School Students	104	70

TABLE 16–2   Fictitious Average Test Performance of Uninstructed
              Students

SAMPLE GROUP	n	% CORRECT
Beginning Fourth Graders	109	24
Beginning Seventh Graders	87	31
Beginning High School Students	111	42

school system's ability to augment its effectiveness, it would seem prudent
to raise expectations to some extent.

The previously instructed.   Most of the skills being isolated for
minimum competency testing programs are typically thought to be significant in an individual's future life. Thus, it would also seem useful to standard setters to see how well adults, at least postschool young adults, can
perform those skills. Let's imagine we had some performance data, such as
those presented in Table 16–4.

The performance of previously instructed groups is particularly informative as a sort of "reality check" to help standard setters discern
whether some of their aspirations for pupil performance are in any sense
consonant with the kinds of proficiency actually needed in the real world.
Further, since there is typically a certain degree of decay associated with
many of the skills in which we are interested, we can see how well they hold
up after a student has left high school.

In review, this fictitious example was intended to illustrate the general
proposition that if standard setters have access to a wealth of data regarding how various kinds of individuals can perform the skill under consideration, the standards set for these skills will tend to be more defensible.
Fictitious illustrations were provided for three major categories of relevant
performance data, namely, test results from the uninstructed, just-
instructed, and previously instructed.

TABLE 16–3   Fictitious Projected Failure Rates for High School Seniors
              at Varying Passing Levels, Based on 427 Seniors' Test
              Performances

% CORRECT PASSING LEVEL	PROBABLE % OF PUPILS FAILING
90	61
85	52
80	43
75	21
70	14
65	7

TABLE 16-4 **Fictitious Average Test Performance of Nonstudent Groups**

GROUP	n	% CORRECT
Students Graduated Two Years Earlier	114	79
Students Graduated Four Years Earlier	89	75
A Stratified Sample of Adults in Community	172	62
Members of the School Board	7	89

Factor Four: Preferences of Others

In addition to performance data, a useful sort of information for standard setters is the preferences regarding standards of various concerned groups. For example, suppose the standard setters in our previous example consisted of the local board of education. Beyond the previously described performance data, perhaps they wanted to see what other people's sentiments were regarding appropriate standards for high school graduates with respect to the comprehension of main ideas when reading. Let's say they directed the school district's research and evaluation office to come up with preference data, such as those seen in Table 16–5.

In a judgmental operation, such as the setting of performance standards, it is often beneficial to have on hand the preferences of other individuals. These other people can be called in either because they have a special stake in the action, such as parents of the students or business officials who will be hiring the high school graduates, or because they possess special expertise, such as district educators or university instruc-

TABLE 16-5 **Fictitious Recommendations from Various Clienteles Regarding an Appropriate Passing Standard for Comprehending Main Ideas**

GROUP	n	AVERAGE PREFERENCE
This Year's High School Seniors	497	71%
Graduates of Three Years Ago, Now in College	94	84%
Graduates of Three Years Ago, Not in College	119	65%
District Teachers	112	78%
District Administrators	32	83%
Parents of Ninth, Tenth, and Eleventh Graders	814	91%
Community People	119	79%
University Reading Specialists	18	75%

tional specialists. In general, since they typically express their preferences in the absence of any relevant performance data, these individuals are guided by an analysis of *the nature of the skill* for which a standard is being set.

Care must be exercised, of course, to be *guided* by such preferences, not controlled by them. It is still the standard setter's ultimate responsibility to decide how good is good enough. The standard setters must reckon with the fact that it may be in the interest of certain groups to recommend standards which are inappropriately high or low. Such biases must be recognized so that the resulting preferences of such groups can be considered in that light.

We have examined four major factors which can be attended to in the setting of performance standards. Let's turn now to some specific procedural alternatives for standard setting, recognizing that in many of these procedures one or more of the four factors cited here have been omitted.

ALTERNATIVE STANDARD-SETTING PROCEDURES

In describing the various standard-setting procedures which are currently available to educators, it must be stated at the outset that not all of these schemes are being offered with approbation. Indeed, aside from the first scheme to be described, the *Informed Judgment Model*, each of the other approaches seems to possess one or more serious deficits. Moreover, even the *Informed Judgment Model* is not without frailties.

The chief purpose in setting out these alternative schemes is to provide the reader with an opportunity to survey them and thus to decide whether there are elements in any which might be adopted. Some of the five models to be described are fairly fashionable; others are more obscure. Each will be explained in sufficient detail so that if one wishes to adopt that approach to standard setting, the requisite procedural specifics will be at hand.

The Informed Judgment Model

This standard-setting procedure is predicated directly on the foregoing analysis, namely, that since the setting of standards, is, at bottom, a judgmental enterprise, information-laden judgments will be preferable to informationless judgments. Informed judgments, since they are rendered by human beings, can still be in error. Nevertheless, informed judgments will generally be far superior to judgments made in the absence of relevant information.

The *Informed Judgment Model*, with myriad variations available, obliges standard setters to deliberately engage in five operations:

1. Analyze the decision context.
2. Clarify the competencies.
3. Acquire relevant performance data.
4. Gather pertinent preference data.
5. Set standards based on this information.

The first step calls for an analysis of the decision context, that is, the magnitude of the *decision at issue* and the *contextual considerations* in which that decision is to be made. This analysis can be engaged in by oneself, but it is often more effective if conducted in a group setting. Different individuals' views regarding the significance of the decision at issue, and the factors which should be considered in relationship to that decision can be highly informative.

For example, suppose that a district's current pupil performance was mediocre but that the district was going to make a major instructional improvement effort next year by pouring in substantial financial and personnel resources. Perhaps, in light of this knowledge, higher expectations for student performance might be made than would be based on an analysis of students' current prowess.

The second step, securing clarification of the competencies for which standards are being set, can be carried out in several ways. Most often this clarification comes from an analysis of the actual assessment devices being used to measure the competency. Ideally, there would be some sort of descriptive information accompanying the test, for example, a detailed delimitation of the competency being measured (plus sample test items), which would enable standard setters to become clear about the skills for which they're setting standards. The degree of consensus among standard setters regarding their understanding of the competencies can be verified in a number of ways. For instance, standard setters could be given different test items, some congruent and some incongruent with the competency to be measured, then asked (independently) to identify those which accurately assessed the competency under discussion. Disagreements could be analyzed.

The third and fourth steps of the *Informed Judgment Model* would oblige someone to present to the standard setters the type of information cited previously in Tables 16-1 through 16-5. For performance data, there would optimally be information from the uninstructed, the just-instructed, and the previously instructed. For preference data, the views of many concerned groups (because of interest or expertise) should be gathered.

Clearly, the acquisition of such information often carries a hefty price tag. For less significant standard-setting chores, of course, one would expend fewer resources in gathering such data than on high-stakes situations where indefensible performance standards would be more costly.

Finally, with the aforementioned information at hand, judgments must be made about where to set the performance standards. If a group is involved in the standard setting, it is helpful to have the various group members not only state their personal preferences regarding standards but also clarify the principal factors which guided them in their decision. Through consensus-promotion techniques or democratic vote, the group must make its judgmentally derived decisions.

The Borderline-Group Method

One fairly simple standard-setting approach involves the judgmental identification of students who are considered to be "at or near the borderline" with respect to mastery of the competency at issue. Individuals who are familiar with students (for example, teachers) select a fairly large number of such borderline students, then administer to them the test by which competency mastery is to be established. The median performance of the group becomes the performance standard for that competency.

The specific steps in the implementation of this approach are as follows:

1. Identify judges who are familiar with the student population involved.
2. Have judges discuss what constitutes minimally acceptable performance.
3. Have judges identify borderline students.
4. Administer test.
5. Compute median performance.

The identification of judges is clearly a key feature of this approach, since judges who are unfamiliar with students' actual functioning levels will be ill equipped to subsequently select the borderline students. Further, the judges must be genuinely conversant with the content of the competency for which a performance standard is being set, since they must, at least in general terms, employ an estimate of what it is that constitutes "minimally acceptable performance."

The discussion of the nature of minimally acceptable performance (step 2) can range in specificity from a rather general series of comments regarding what might be acceptable, to a very detailed effort to isolate instances of acceptable versus unacceptable student performance. Since a global estimate is being employed in the subsequent identification of students, it is difficult to tie down exactly how much specificity should be involved in this second step of the operation.

In the third step of the *Borderline-Group Method*, the judges provide lists of students whose performances are, in their view, so close to borderline that they cannot be clearly identified as having mastered or not mastered the competency in question.

Fourth, the test which will be used in connection with the performance standard is administered. Finally, based on the median performance of the "borderline" students, a performance standard is set.

One clear advantage of the *Borderline-Group Method* is its simplicity. It is important, however, to have enough borderline students involved so that a reliable estimate can be secured. Usually, a hundred or so students are needed for the sake of reliability. In small school districts this sometimes necessitates the accumulation of borderline students' test performances over a period of several years.

The Contrasting-Groups Model

In a way, the *Contrasting-Groups Model* is the converse of the *Borderline-Group Method* just described. In the *Contrasting-Groups Model* a group of judges isolates those who are *clearly* masters or nonmasters of the competency in question.[1] Borderline students are deliberately excluded. Tests are then administered to the students judged competent or incompetent, and the point where their scores overlap is considered the performance standard.

The steps in this procedure are as follows:

1. Identify judges who are familiar with the student population involved.
2. Have judges discuss what constitutes minimally acceptable performance.
3. Have judges identify students who are definite masters or nonmasters of the competency.
4. Administer test to both groups.
5. Plot performance curves for both groups.
6. Set the performance standard based on the intersection of the two curves.

The first two steps are identical to the *Borderline-Group Method* previously described. The third step calls for the judges to isolate individuals who, in their estimate, are absolute masters or nonmasters of the competency being considered. This does not oblige the judges to classify all students with whom they are familiar, only those for whom (in the judges' views) mastery is indisputably present or absent. The number of students in the two groups need not be the same, although there should be about a hundred or so in the smaller of the two groups to provide some stability in the estimate.

---

[1]L. Nedelsky, "Absolute Grading Standards for Objective Tests," *Educational and Psychological Measurement*, 14,1 (1954), 3–19.

The next step involves giving the test to both groups and then plotting their performance, similar to the two performance curves presented in Figure 16–1.

The point of intersection of these two curves, each representing the performance of the two groups on a twenty-item test, can be used to set the performance standard. It should be noted that this *Contrasting-Groups Method* can be readily modified if one is more concerned about false-positives than false-negatives. For example, note that in Figure 16–2 the standard has been set deliberately to reduce the possibility that false-positives, that is, false mastery of the competency, will occur. In Figure 16–3 a standard has been set which is deliberately designed to reduce the possibility of false-negatives.

It will be recalled from the earlier discussion of the decision context that concerns about false-positives and false-negatives should enter into the standards being set. This *Contrasting-Groups Model* provides quantitative data to guide one in such judgments.

Nedelsky's Method

The fourth procedure we will examine is based on a scheme recommended by Nedelsky in 1954.[2] The *Nedelsky Method* is to be used with multiple-choice tests and focuses on an analysis of the wrong-answer options in such tests. Probabilities associated with the likelihood that an item will be answered correctly constitute the key data in employing this scheme which has, until recently, received scant attention. With the current requirements to set performance standards, more attention has been given to Nedelsky's approach.

The steps necessary to implement the Nedelsky scheme are these:

1. Appoint judges familiar with both the competency and students' typical mastery of it.
2. Have judges consider the distractors (wrong-answer choices) for each item, and identify those distractors which a minimally competent student would recognize as being incorrect.
3. For each item, convert the responses *not* eliminated in step 2 (correct response plus uneliminated distractors) to a "correct-by-guessing" probability.
4. Sum these per-item "correct-by-guessing" probabilities for each judge, then average them across judges to obtain a standard of performance for minimally competent students.

The first step is the usual one, namely, enlist the aid of some judges who are conversant with the competency and with the youngsters. As in the

[2]R. A. Berk, "Determination of Optimal Cutting Scores in Criterion-Referenced Measurement," *Journal of Experimental Education*, 45 (1976), 4–9.

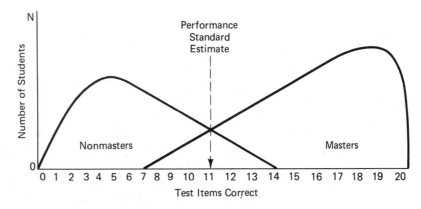

FIGURE 16-1 Intersection Point of Mastery and Non-Mastery Groups

two previously described standard-setting methods, it would be helpful if these judges spent some time discussing what they mean when they think of a "minimally competent student." The *Nedelsky Method* can be applied with very few or very many judges, but if more than one judge is used, such a discussion is important.

An item-response recording form can be duplicated along the lines seen in Figure 16–4 where the number of responses per item that a minimally competent student would *not* recognize as incorrect can be circled. The following sample form is for four-response multiple-choice tests. Modified forms can be used for three- or five-response multiple-choice tests.

Here's how such a form is completed. First, for each item a judge is to focus on the *distractors* and spot those that a minimally competent student ought to recognize as incorrect. (If a group of judges is involved in this

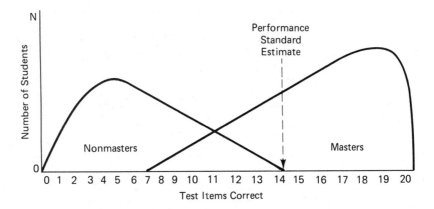

FIGURE 16-2 A Standard Set to Reduce False Positives

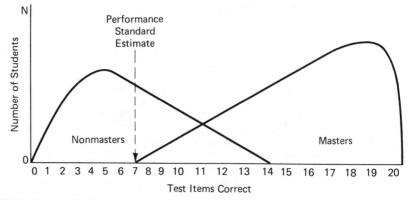

FIGURE 16–3 A Standard Set to Reduce False-Negatives

process and, if time permits, the judges can discuss any distractors on which there is a substantial amount of disagreement.) Let's say on item 2 that a judge believed one of the three distractors was so obvious that a minimally competent student would spot it as being wrong. That leaves two distractors *and the correct response*; so alongside item 2 in the recording form the judge would circle a 3, thus indicating that three responses (the two distractors plus the right answer) had not been eliminated.

If three responses for item 2 are thus thought to be choices that even minimally competent students must choose among, then it is assumed that merely by guessing a student has a one-out-of-three chance of being correct; hence, in the last column the correct-by-guessing probability for that

Item Number	Circle Number of Responses Not Eliminated	Correct-by-Guessing Probability
1	4 3 (2) 1	.50
2	4 (3) 2 1	.33
3	(4) 3 2 1	.25
4	4 3 2 (1)	1.00
etc.	etc.	etc.
	SUM = ☐	

FIGURE 16–4 Item Response Recording Form for the Nedelsky Method

item would be .33. Similarly, if for item 4 a judge had eliminated all three distractors as being too easily recognizable, then only the correct answer option would remain, and the correct-by-guessing probability would be 1.00.

The per-item correct-by-guessing probabilities are then summed (if many items are involved, a hand calculator, abacus, or quantitatively quirky colleague will come in handy), and that sum of item-by-item probabilities reflects an individual judge's recommended performance standard. For example, if the probability for a twenty-item test added up to 13.33, then the passing standard for that judge would be set at 13 items correct. A student who answered only 13 or fewer items correctly would fail. If more than one judge were involved, their summed probabilities would be averaged.

The *Nedelsky Method*, of course, appears to be highly quantitative, with probabilities (in decimal form) being summed and averaged. It should be recalled, however, that at bottom this method is a judgmental operation in which judges focus their attention only on the allure of wrong-answer options in a multiple-choice test, instead of a student's overall performance.

The Angoff Adaptation

Since the Nedelsky approach must be employed only with multiple-choice tests, the *Angoff Adaptation* was created to be used with any sort of test items, multiple-choice or not.[3] Angoff's approach is essentially similar to Nedelsky's except that judges are directed to make estimates of the likelihood that each item will be answered correctly by the minimally competent student. In other words, without considering the individual distractors in each item, judges simply move to the correct-by-guessing probabilities column from the *Nedelsky Method*.

If, using the *Angoff Adaptation*, a judge thinks that an item is so simple that a minimally competent student is almost certain to answer it correctly, then a probability of 1.00 is given to the item. If, on the other hand, the item is judged to be so difficult that it would be unlikely a minimally competent student would answer it correctly, then the judge might assign it a low probability, for example, .30.

Incidentally, since the *Angoff Adaptation* can also be used with multiple-choice test items, a judge should never assign an item a lower probability than would result from raw chance based on the number of options in the multiple-choice test. To illustrate, in a three-option multiple-choice test, the assigned probability should never be lower than .33 (one out of three).

[3]W. H. Angoff, "Scales, Norms, and Equivalent Scores," in *Educational Measurement*, ed. R. L. Thorndike (Washington, D.C.: American Council on Education, 1971).

Angoff's scheme calls for a judge to sum the probabilities for all items (and to average these sums if more than one judge is involved), then use that quantity as the passing standard. For tests judged to be very easy, since the estimated probabilities per item will hover near 1.0, the passing standard will be a high total test "percentage correct." For tests judged more difficult, the total test "percentage correct" will obviously be much lower.

As with the *Nedelsky Method*, the *Angoff Adaptation* lends itself to discussion and clarification when more than one judge is involved. For example, judges can make their probability estimates independently, then the judges giving the highest and lowest probability estimates can explain their reasons for those judgments. These reasons can be discussed by the total group of judges. Judges then may, but are not required to, alter their original estimates in light of the discussions.

APPRAISING THE ALTERNATIVES

It should be apparent from an analysis of the several standard-setting methods described here that judgmental operations are involved in all. In some cases those judgments are more visible than in others. Sometimes the addition of numerical trappings may lead us to forget that, as always, someone is making a judgment about "how good is good enough?"

In the case of the *Informed Judgment Model*, it is clear that human judgment is the dominant factor. The thrust of the approach is essentially to create more defensible judgments by securing more relevant information. Judgments are more global than in some of the other approaches, that is, the key judgment may be made only at the final stage of the game, such as when a "percent correct" passing standard is chosen.

The *Borderline-Group Method* is totally dependent upon judges' abilities to isolate truly borderline students. In a sense this method employs some circular logic since the standard is totally dependent on the group of students the judges select. If the students chosen do, in fact, represent youngsters who hover on either side of minimal competence, then the standard set on the basis of their median performance is defensible. But what if their performance hovers elsewhere? Then the resulting standard may be decisively at variance with what genuinely constitutes minimally competent performance. This approach, though perhaps the most simple to implement, depends heavily on the accuracy of the original student selections.

The *Contrasting-Groups Method*, since the students to be selected are at the extremes of a "competency continuum," makes the task of judges potentially more manageable. It is probably easier to isolate sure-fire winners or sure-fire losers than borderline students. Yet, the added confidence that comes from knowing that the right youngsters have been tossed into the data-gathering mechanism may blind one to the fact that the key decision choice, for example, the point where the performance curves intersect, is based on the performance of students who actually happen to be *borderline*, not clearly masters or nonmasters as the judges contended. The judges, therefore, are obviously capable of erroneous selections. If they selected nonmasters by using very stringent criteria, but chose masters using less stringent criteria, then this method will yield far different results than if the stringency of the criteria had been reversed.

In contrast to these four standard-setting methods which focus chiefly on the performance of groups of students, the *Nedelsky Method* and the *Angoff Adaptation* stress item-by-item judgments. Whereas the Angoff approach obliges judges to come up with estimates of how difficult the individual items are, Nedelsky requires judges to engage in distractor-by-distractor judgments. However, although these judgments are made regarding far more specific bits of data than in standard-setting approaches which focus on group data and group standard setting, a rash of mistaken judgments about individual items will not, when aggregated, suddenly be transformed into correctness. Considering these two methods, it is important to recognize that they are still both judgmental operations but that the judgments are being made about smaller slices of the performance pie.

There are several writers who have authored thought-provoking analyses regarding the difficulties of the standard-setting enterprise. Ebel, for example, has described several different approaches to the determination of passing scores.[4] His suggestions stress the importance of having judges not only consider the *difficulty level* of individual items but also the *importance* of the items themselves. He concludes that the best we can expect "... is that the basis for defining the passing score be defined clearly, and that the definition be as rational as possible."

In a stimulating essay that ultimately rejects the possibility of setting sensible performance standards, Glass describes, discusses, and eventually dismisses six methods of establishing a passing score.[5]

Millman offered an analysis of five types of information helpful in the setting of standards for tests with content-homogeneous items.[6] Meskauskas has appraised the merits of several standard-setting procedures, including several treated here, as well as a few more exotic approaches.[7] Zieky and Livingston provide a series of step-by-step suggestions regarding four

---

[4]R. L. Ebel, *Essentials of Education Measurement*, 3rd ed. (Englewood Cliffs, N.J.: Prentice-Hall, Inc., 1979).

[5]G. V Glass, "Standards and Criteria." Evaluation Center, Western Michigan University, Kalamazoo, Michigan, December 1977.

[6]J. Millman, "Passing Scores and Test Lengths for Domain-Referenced Measures," *Review of Educational Research*, 43, 2 (1973), 205–216.

[7]J. A. Meskauskas, "Evaluation Models for Criterion-Referenced Testing: Views Regarding Mastery and Standard Setting," *Review of Educational Research*, 46, 1 (1976), 133–158.

standard-setting procedures, as well as a number of useful observations regarding the factors to consider in setting standards.[8]

SEPARATE OR AGGREGATE STANDARDS

Another choice to be made by standard setters who are using measures of more than one competency is whether to set standards competency-by-competency or to set a composite, single-score standard. To illustrate, suppose the school board of a particular school district has endorsed five competencies in reading and four competencies in mathematics for a basic-skills graduation requirement. Suppose, further, that district educators have selected two commercially available criterion-referenced tests which coincide fairly well with these competencies and that these tests yield a competency-by-competency score per student. (For purposes of our illustration, district educators might just as well have constructed their own tests.) Should the district's standard setters opt for nine separate passing percentages (which may or may not be identical) or for two aggregate passing percentages, one for the math test and one for the reading test?

Let's consider the advantages and disadvantages of each choice. In favor of selecting the single, aggregate score, we have simplicity—both for processing the data and for communicating with the public. In addition, the greater number of items on the total test will undoubtedly induce a higher degree of reliability than would be the case with the shorter subtests.

On the other hand, a single test score for a group of essentially distinctive competencies can effectively mask the performance of students on particular competencies, since it is impossible to tell on which competencies a student scored high, low, and so on. Further, by opting for a single score, we do not encourage teachers to attend as carefully to the individual competencies comprising the test and thus fail to garner one of the instructional dividends typically associated with programs in which highly specific competencies are sought.

A middle position which may appeal to some is to set the standard for an overall test score but still report competency-by-competency performance for each pupil. Even though the single standard may be satisfied by a student's performing well on most competencies but doing badly on one or two, the teacher will be aware of which competencies have not been mastered.

If standard setters opt for a competency-by-competency approach, they still must decide (1) whether there will be any differences among the

---

[8]M. J. Zieky and S. A. Livingston, *Manual for Setting Standards on the Basic Skills Assessment Tests* (Princeton, N.J.: Educational Testing Service, 1977).

passing standards set for the several competencies and (2) whether a student must pass all or only a proportion of the competencies.

For simplicity's sake, it is inviting to set a single standard, say 75 percent correct, for each competency. Yet, in most instances there will be differences among the competencies, not only in the difficulty of mastering them, but also in the significance that their mastery may have in the student's future. For these reasons, it would seem prudent to at least give careful consideration to setting potentially different standards on a competency-by-competency basis. Those standards may, of course, turn out to be identical, even if they are set one at a time.

What about requiring the student to master all of the competencies or only a proportion? For example, some district educators have established standards which require students to pass "all but one" or "all but two" competencies. A district which has five reading, five math, and five writing competencies might, for instance, tie high school graduation to the student's mastery of at least four competencies in each of the three areas.

Now, supposing standard setters are contemplating this "all-or-a-proportion" choice, should they settle that issue before or after deciding on the passing percentages for individual competencies? It would seem sensible to make this decision *after* the individual competency standards have been set. If stringent standards appear to have been set for the individual competencies, a more relaxed approach might be dictated for the composite "all-or-some" decision. If, however, less stringent standards have been set for the separate competencies, local standard setters might plunk for the "all-or-else" position.

And how will standard setters decide whether the standards for the individual competencies have been set stringently or not? Why, they'll have to use their judgment!

This discussion of the choices involved in employing aggregate or separate standards should further demonstrate that determining defensible performance standards is a sticky and time-consuming business. Anyone who approaches the task simplistically or tries to carry it out in a hurry is apt to come up with decidedly indefensible standards.

Reprise

In review, this chapter has addressed the question of how to go about setting performance standards. If anyone initiated a reading of this chapter with the notion that the setting of standards was simple, hopefully, they have been disabused of that erroneous conception.

However, even though taxing, the setting of standards is an enterprise in which educators must often engage. That those standards will be set judgmentally should not intimidate us. Indeed, of the various approaches reviewed here, a preference was given to the *Informed Judgment Model*, which deliberately emphasized the judgmental operation.

Standards will continue to be set. Some will be set defensibly, and students will benefit. Some, though set defensibly, will still be "wrong." But even though judgmental errors may occur, as educators we are only culpable when we set standards by using procedures that are themselves indefensible.

PRACTICE EXERCISES

Part A

In the chapter, four key factors were considered in setting performance standards, namely: (1) *analysis of decision context,* (2) *clarity of target competencies,* (3) *relevant performance data,* and (4) *preferences of others.* In the following five vignettes, you will find educators engaged in activities primarily related to *one* of these key factors. Read each vignette, then decide which of the four factors is the fictitious educator's chief concern. (It should be a fairly easy exercise for you.)

1. A school board, charged by state law with the responsibility to set standards for a locally devised sixth-grade "exit exam," conducts a series of town meetings to gather the opinions of citizens, particularly parents, regarding where to set the cut-off score for the sixth-grade examination. At the school board meeting immediately following the series of town meetings, the board reviews results of these sessions, then chooses a cut-off score.

2. A state-level Advisory Commission on Basic Skills, obliged to recommend a performance standard on the statewide High School Graduation Competency Test, attempts to gather information regarding how many students are apt to fail if different performance standards are set. The commission also tries to discover what capabilities the state's schools possess to supply remedial instruction for those who fail the test. The commission carries out an additional survey among a sample of citizens to discover what the reactions will be of parents when children fail to pass the exam, hence, fail to graduate.

3. Prior to filling out a set of district-issued preference ballots regarding what standards should be used with the district's high school competency test, the district teachers' organization demands that each teacher be given (1) a copy of the test specifications which were employed to generate the test and (2) at least two sample items per competency. Officials of the teachers' organization believe that their members can't register preferences

about standards regarding competencies if they don't have "a good fix on what the competencies are."

4. Before seeking the preferences of citizens regarding a locally established cut-off score on a junior high school proficiency examination, administrators in a major metropolitan school district use a filmstrip-tape program at public orientation meetings to provide citizens with a lucid notion of the skills being measured by the examination.

5. Prior to establishing a cut-off score on a newly devised admissions examination, officials of a technical training institute administer the examination to samples of previous graduates, applicants, and instructors in the institute. They summarize their scores and review them prior to setting a cut-off score.

Part B

After considering the key factors to be used in setting standards, five different standard-setting schemes were described in the chapter, that is: (1) the *Borderline-Group Method*, (2) the *Contrasting-Groups Model*, (3) the *Nedelsky Method*, (4) the *Angoff Adaptation*, and (5) the *Informed Judgment Model*. To give you a bit of practice in recognizing these approaches, see if you can spot which of the five methods is being used in the following descriptions.

6. Judges identify students who are clear "winners" or "losers," that is, those who have and haven't mastered the district's competencies in basic communication skills. Based on the test performance of these two groups, more specifically the point where their plotted test-score distributions intersect, a cut-off score is established.

7. Judges are directed to identify any distractors in a multiple-choice test that a minimally knowledgeable student ought to identify as correct. The uneliminated responses form a "correct-by-chance" probability which is averaged and summed across items to reach a performance standard.

8. Items on a short-answer competition test are judged according to the possibility that a minimally competent student would answer them correctly. These probabilities are summed and averaged for the total test in order to guide the setting of a cut-off score.

9. The school board discusses implications of setting various cut-off scores on the high school proficiency test, analyzes the skills being measured, gathers actual test performance information from recent graduates and current students, seeks community and student advice regarding what standards to set, then establishes a set of "annually revisable" cut-off levels.

10. Teachers identify 155 students about whom they are truly uncer-

tain as to whether they can master the district's competency test. These students take the test. Their median performance constitutes the district's cut-off score.

ANSWERS TO PRACTICE EXERCISES

Part A

1. The school board was focusing its efforts on securing the *preferences of others* prior to making its decision.
2. The commission was trying to carry out an *analysis of the decision context* to see what the repercussions of different standards would be.
3. The teachers, although they are being asked to supply preferences, are most concerned with seeking *clarity of target competencies*.
4. Here again we find focus on promoting the *clarity of target competencies*.
5. The institute's officials were assembling *relevant performance data* prior to making their cut-off decision.

Part B

6. Contrasting-Groups Model.
7. Nedelsky Method.
8. Angoff Adaptation.
9. Informed Judgment Model.
10. Borderline-Group Method.

DISCUSSION QUESTIONS

1. As you review the alternative standard-setting techniques described in the chapter, which one do you believe is the most defensible? Why?
2. How might you combine one or more of the standard-setting procedures described to produce an even more defensible composite standard-setting procedure?
3. To what extent do you agree with the assertion that all standard-setting procedures must, by their very nature, be arbitrary, mindless, and capricious?
4. Suppose you were charged with the creation of a systematic standard-setting procedure for a large metropolitan school district in connection with a minimum competency high school graduation examination. What would be the specifics of your procedure?

SUGGESTIONS FOR ADDITIONAL READING

ANDREW, BARBARA J., and JAMES T. HECHT, "A Preliminary Investigation of Two Procedures for Setting Examination Standards," *Educational and Psychological Measurement*, 36, no. 1 (Spring 1976), 45–50. An experimental

study of two standard-study procedures is described in this report, namely, the Nedelsky and the Ebel methods. Substantially different standards were set when the two different standard-setting procedures were used.

BERK, RONALD A., "Determination of Optimal Cutting Scores in Criterion-Referenced Measurement," *Journal of Experimental Education*, 45 (1976), 4–9. A scheme for setting performance levels based on the differential performance of two criterion groups is presented in this essay. Berk discusses techniques for minimizing false-positives as well as false-negatives.

GLASS, GENE V, "Standards and Criteria," *Journal of Educational Measurement*, 15, no. 4 (Winter 1978), 237–262. A review of six methods for setting standards forms the basis of the author's conclusion that performance must necessarily be set capriciously. The journal issue in which the article appears contains a series of responses to Glass's thought-provoking essay.

JAEGER, R. M., "Measurement Consequences of Selected Standard-Setting Models," *Florida Journal of Educational Research*, 18 (1976), 22–27. One of the earlier essays on standard setting, Jaeger offers an insightful analysis of key issues associated with the setting of standards.

MESKAUSKAS, JOHN A., "Evaluation Models for Criterion-Referenced Testing: Views Regarding Mastery and Standard Setting," *Review of Educational Research*, 46, no. 1 (Winter 1976), 133–158. An exploration is provided of the underlying features of several models used to set standards for criterion-referenced tests.

MILLMAN, JASON, "Passing Scores and Test Lengths for Domained-Referenced Measures," *Review of Educational Research*, 43, no. 2 (Spring 1973), 205–216. Millman provides a thorough account of the factors which can be considered when determining performance standards. Millman also reviews two models for establishing test length. The relationship of performance standards and test length is discussed.

NEDELSKY, LEO, "Absolute Grading Standards for Objective Tests," *Educational and Psychological Measurement*, 14, no. 1 (Spring 1954), 3–19. A quantitatively oriented scheme for setting performance standards is described which involves estimates of individual-item difficulty. The Nedelsky method has received considerable attention in recent years because of the increasing necessity to establish performance standards.

ZIEKY, MICHAEL J., and SAMUEL A. LIVINGSTON, *Manual for Setting Standards on the Basic Skill Assessment Tests*. Princeton, N.J.: Educational Testing Service, 1977. This manual, designed for use with tests distributed by ETS, provides a lucid description of a number of standard-setting procedures.

In this, the final chapter of this text, we tackle the important issue of how educators should get the most mileage out of test results. More specifically, we look at two important applications of test results. The first of these centers on using test results in *grading* (sometimes called *marking*). The use of test results by teachers to render grades for students is, of course, a long-standing practice. Various ways of dispensing grades have been considered at length through the years. We look at several.

The second topic addressed in the chapter is the use of tests and test results in the *design and improvement of instruction*. That topic is less frequently encountered in measurement texts since measurement authorities have traditionally viewed educational tests as instruments to assess the *effects* of instruction, not tools to enhance the quality of the instructional process itself. However, as indicated at the very outset of this volume, it is both possible and profitable to regard well-constructed tests as catalysts for instructional improvement. In the concluding half of the chapter, therefore, we explore procedures for boosting instructional quality through the use of tests and test results.

Using the results of educational tests

GRADING

Teachers have been graders for almost as long as there have been teachers. When archaeologists find fragments of pottery from ancient Assyria with only single letters on them, the initial hypothesis should be that an Assyrian instructor was dishing out end-of-course grades, probably on a norm-referenced basis.

The reasons that grades are necessary, of course, are numerous. In general, people need to know how students performed in school and in particular courses. Included in the individuals who have a legitimate use for grades are students themselves, students' parents, persons involved directly with the education of students (that is, teachers, counselors, and administrators), prospective employers, and college admission officials.

Each of these groups has a high-priority reason for wanting to know how Melanie performed in her 11th-grade English class. We must devise schemes for supplying all such individuals with reasonable estimates of how well Melanie really did in the class, and that, obviously, tosses us right in the middle of grading.

Arguments to Abolish Grading

Lest it be assumed that there is universal support for the awarding of grades in school, it must be noted that there are plenty of individuals who have mounted strong, emotional arguments for the abolition of grades.[1] Proposals to do away with grades were actually proffered over a half century earlier.[2]

Although our systems for grading are fraught with frailties, to abandon them would be perilous. Indeed, as Moynihan observed when he stressed the value of the grading system as a democratic vehicle by which persons born to modest or lowly circumstances can be recognized for their worth:

> I have not the least doubt that this system is crude, that it is often cruel, and that it measures only a limited number of things. Yet it measures valid things, by and large. To do away with such systems of accreditation may seem like an egalitarian act, but in fact it would be just the opposite. We would be back to a world in which social connections and privilege count for much more than any of us, I believe, would like. If what you know doesn't count, in the competitions of life, who you know will determine the outcomes.[3]

The fact that an enterprise has imperfect aspects should not incline us to abandon that enterprise in its entirety. Our task should be to strengthen the quality of our grading systems, not chuck them out.

Reliance on Test Results

Teachers exercise power when they dispense students' grades. One of the most serious defects of the grading enterprise is that teachers often exercise this power cavalierly. High grades are given to students who court the teacher's favor. Low grades are given to class cut-ups, no matter how much they know about the course content. Yes, it must be conceded that far too

---

[1]See, for example, W. Glasser, *Schools Without Failure* (New York: Harper & Row, 1969) or J. Holt, *How Children Fail* (New York: Pitman, 1968).

[2]H. M. Dadourian, "Are Examinations Worth the Price?" *School and Society*, 21 (1925), 442–443.

[3]P. Moynihan, "Seek Parity of Educational Achievement, Moynihan Urges," *Report on Educational Research*, 3,5 (March 3, 1971), 4.

many teachers use grades as an omnipurpose tool for rewarding or rebuking students on other than academic grounds. However, just because something *is* done, does not mean that it *should* be done.

One effective way of discouraging teachers from using petty personality differences with students as a factor in grading is to rely heavily, perhaps exclusively, on the results of educational tests in deciding what grade the student should receive. As usual, when we speak of educational tests in this context, we refer to the whole gamut of assessment devices we have discussed in this text, such as observations of classroom performance and ratings of oral presentations. We certainly do not mean only the teacher's end-of-unit or end-of-course written examinations.

By relying on documented evidence of this sort (typically compiled in the teacher's gradebook), teachers will be less likely to succumb to uncontrolled subjectivity. Mabel will be less apt to get a high grade chiefly because "she is always so neat, punctual, and well-balanced." Mary Jane will be less likely to pick up a low grade because "at least once per week she is a horrible hellion, disrupting class with her unruly behavior."

By relying on a systematically amassed set of test scores, project ratings, and classroom observations, teachers will more likely be able to use grades as the indicators most people believe them to be, namely, as an accurate indication of the student's academic performance in a class.

Now there should be a way for teachers to register their reactions to the positive and negative qualities of students. If Mabel is an angel and Mary Jane is a scurrilous child, these points can be made in a grading system which also allows teachers to enter comments regarding the pupil's sociopersonal development. However, such factors should not be unthinkingly merged with grades that supposedly reflect academic attainments. By rooting their grades in students' test results, teachers can more readily move in the direction of defensible grade giving.

Conventional Grading Systems

The most widely used system of grading is the use of a single letter grade (A, B, C, D, or F) to describe a student's performance. Sometimes teachers will be permitted to employ a plus or minus in connection with their letter grades, so that students can get a $C+$ or an $A-$. By so doing, of course, teachers move from a five-point scale (the five letter grades) to a fifteen-point scale (the five letter grades as well as a plus and minus variant of each).

Since most teachers grew up in settings where traditional single-letter grades were awarded, it is not surprising that they persist in using such grades themselves. We do what we know. However, even within the confines of a traditional grading system, there are substantially different ways of determining who gets an *A* or who gets a *C*. Let's consider the most common of these.

Relative grading.   Here, the focus is on giving grades to students on the basis of their performances relative to each other. To award a grade to a student on the basis of how that student stacks up with other students is by all odds the most common way of granting grades. There is the problem, however, of deciding which group will be used as the reference (or comparison) group for the student. For instance, is it only this term's classroomful of students, or is it perhaps an inferred district or national sample of such students? More often than not, the comparison group employed to make grading decisions is "the group existing in the teacher's head." In other words, most teachers carry around a mental image of how well students typically perform on the kinds of tasks encountered in their classes. It is this experience-based conception of the typical student against which relative comparisons are usually made. Such notions of the typical student are often accumulated by teachers over a period of many years.

Clearly, it is more equitable for teachers to use a generalized notion of typical student performance than to reference grades directly to a particular classroom's students. For example, suppose that the bulk of this year's class is academically deficient. If grades are assigned on the basis of this year's inferior class, then even a weak student might end up with an *A* since, *in comparison to the rest of that class*, the student appears to be strong. Contrarily, if the class turns out to be flooded with near geniuses, then pity the poor pupil who will get an *F* because of a poor *relative* standing.

If teachers call on their experience to form a more generalized estimate of a reference group, such injustices are less likely. The larger the reference group, the more defensible the assignment of grades on a relative basis.

The system of assigning grades on a relative basis is, of course, entirely consistent with a norm-referenced approach to testing. Sometimes this approach is referred to as "grading on the curve." However, grading on the curve does not mean that a teacher is obliged to force a class grading distribution into a normal curve where a certain proportion (for example, 5 to 7 percent) of the class must get *F*s and a similar proportion *A*s. More commonly, grading on the curve merely means that the teacher is using the relative performances of that year's class in the calculation of grades.

If a teacher truly graded according to the normal curve and allocated proportions of high and low grades on the basis of the normal curve's properties, such a grading scheme would be truly reprehensible. Such procrustean proclivities should be expunged.[4]

---

[4]Procrustes was a fabled Greek giant who stretched short captives or lopped off parts of tall captives to make them fit his unisized iron beds. One must view Procrustes' standards as somewhat absolute.

Absolute grading.   Well, if there is a *relative* approach to grading which is essentially *norm-referenced*, it would seem to follow that there should be an *absolute* approach to grading which is *criterion-referenced*. And there is—more or less.

As we saw in the last chapter, the problem of determining "how good is good enough" can get genuinely vexing at times. To come up with reasonable expectations of students, that is, to decide what levels of student performance are required for an *A*, *B*, and so on, will almost always involve the grader's reliance on some sorts of comparative data. Without a rough idea about how the student population in general behaves, we are in a bind when it comes to deciding on grading levels. Thus, when we describe a set of skills or a body of knowledge that we expect students to master in order to achieve a certain grade, our decisions are invariably influenced by normative considerations.

Mehrens and Lehmann report an incident in which a parent was discussing grades at a school board meeting.[5] The parent asserted emotionally, "My children are different, and I don't want them being compared to anyone." Mehrens and Lehmann speculated on how parents can ever know their children are different without somehow comparing them to someone.

However, even though we may arrive at a set of grading standards by means of normative comparisons, what we do with those standards *at that point* helps us distinguish between absolute and relative grading standards. Graders who are relativists will be markedly influenced by the performance of this year's crop of students. Graders who are absolutists tend to be less influenced by the performance of current students. In other words, when a criterion-referenced grader has chosen mastery of particular skills as requisites for certain grades, then students either must master those skills or expect a lower grade. There's much less bending once an absolutist grader has decided on standards for grading.

Achievement based on aptitude.   I once learned that, according to Aristotle, achieved potential constituted a metaphysical good. Being particularly enamored of Aristotle's insights (and a devotee of Greek food), I always remembered that. When I became a high school teacher and grading requirements rolled around for the first time, I tried to carry out my task in a somewhat Aristotelian manner. That is, I attempted to judge my students' academic attainments in relationship to their potential.

My plan did not prosper. I really had no clear idea of what my students' potentials truly were. No doubt Aristotle could have discerned what

---

[5]W. A. Mehrens, and I. J. Lehmann, *Measurement and Evaluation in Education and Psychology* (New York: Holt, Rinehart & Winston, 1975).

his students would be capable of performing—but Popham certainly could not.

The chief difficulty associated with grading students' achievement on the basis of their aptitudes is that teachers have inadequate bases on which to make accurate estimates of their students' potentials. It is because teachers miss one of the key pieces of the puzzle that Stanley and Hopkins assert that "achievement in relation to aptitude is an untenable basis for marking, despite the obvious appeal that the idea has for many educators."[6]

Pupil growth. In a related vein, some teachers find the notion of student growth an appealing one as the foundation of a grading method. At first blush, it would seem to make sense if we award students who make the best strides in achievement. For example, if Johnny scores only 20 percent correct on a pretest at the first of the term but scores 85 percent correct on an equivalent form of that test when the term is over, then Johnny has experienced a gain of 65 percent. Joe, on the other hand, ends up with a perfect score on the test, but his pretest score was already 90 percent correct. Hence Joe only gained 10 percent. Surely Johnny's 65 percent jump is more worthy of a high grade than Joe's meager 10 percent increase. But wait a minute, if we only look at the final exam results, Joe scored 100 percent correct and John only scored 85 percent correct. Is it really fair to give John an *A* and Joe a *B* or *C*?

If this sort of dilemma were not enough, and it ought to be, there is the reliability of gain scores themselves. Harris has shown that, even with well-honed testing devices, gain scores are highly unreliable.[7] With the sorts of tests that most teachers are obliged to use, unreliability multiplies exponentially. In fact, basing grades on pupil growth poses even more formidable problems than using achievement based on aptitude. Basing grades on student growth is not a defensible scheme.

Pass-Fail Grading Systems

During the late 1960s and early 1970s the use of *pass-fail* grading procedures became rather popular at a number of colleges and universities. In part, perhaps, the initiation of pass-fail grading was due to the same factors that led to the well-documented *grade inflation* of that period in which nationwide surveys indicated that the grade point averages of college students rose more than 0.4, mostly during a five-year period starting around

[6]J. C. Stanley, and K. D. Hopkins, *Educational and Psychological Measurement and Evaluation*, 5th ed. (Englewood Cliffs, N.J.: Prentice-Hall, Inc. 1972).
[7]C. W. Harris, ed., *Problems in Measuring Change* (Madison Wis.: University of Wisconsin Press, 1963).

1968.[8] Since it is difficult to conclude that during this period college students "got smarter," we assume that college professors became more lenient in their grading practices.

One suspects that college students of the sixties became much less acquiescent than their predecessors and that the resulting pressures on faculty members led both to the grade-inflation phenomenon and to the installation of the pass-fail grading option for many classes. However, irrespective of its origins, a pass-fail grading system now constitutes another alternative which teachers, grades K through postgraduate, can consider.

At the college level a pass-fail scheme is applied to a total course. For example, students may sign up for specified courses (or, in some colleges, for any course) so that they receive no letter grade, only a pass or a fail. In general, of course, students who do so reduce the likelihood of receiving a low grade (for instance, a *C* or *D*). Moreover, since results of pass-fail courses do not count on the student's grade point average, it is much safer to take difficult courses on a pass-fail basis.

But how about elementary or secondary schools? Can pass-fail systems be used there? Yes, they can, but not in the same way as is seen at the college level, that is, not as a total course grade. Instead, we now see the emergency of grading systems in a few public schools where students receive pass-fail marks, but on a skill-by-skill (or objective-by-objective) basis.

To illustrate, during the movement toward minimum competency testing requirements in the late seventies, many school districts isolated a number of competencies (in reading, writing, and mathematics) that it was assumed a minimally competent student should possess. However, rather than testing the student's mastery of these competencies and then awarding a letter grade based on the student's overall prowess, systems of mastery-nonmastery on a competency-by-competency basis were employed. In essence, a number of pass-fail decisions were made competency-by-competency. Typically, a final decision was made about each student with respect to high school graduation or between-grade promotions by summing the number of pass-fail decisions per competency.

Millman has proposed that educators move toward a criterion-referenced grading system. This would require the use of criterion-referenced report cards in which particular accomplishments of the students would be set forth on a skill-by-skill basis.[9]

There are some measurement authorities, however, who view pass-fail systems with disfavor. Ebel, for example, argues that "pass-fail grading

---

[8]For example A. E. Juola, *Grade Inflation (1960–1973): A Preliminary Report* (Unpublished monograph, Michigan State University, East Lansing, Michigan, 1974).

[9]J. Millman, "Reporting Progress: A Case for a Criterion-Referenced Marking System," *Phi Delta Kappan*, 52,4 (December 1970), 225–230.

removes much of the immediate motivation and reward for efforts to excel." He believes that whereas a modest number of courses, such as those in the appreciation of art, music, or literature, might be offered on a nongraded basis, most courses should be accompanied by the awarding of traditional grades. Ebel concludes his repudiation of pass-fail grading systems with the following observation:

> Most of us want to be valued as persons. Most of us don't particularly want to be evaluated. But we can't enjoy the first without enduring the second. The weakness of pass-fail grading is that by doing a poor job of evaluating it keeps us from doing a good job of valuing.[10]

Yet, in spite of such criticisms (Ebel was chiefly attacking pass-fail systems for total course grades), variations of the pass-fail grading system continue to be tried out in the schools. In many cases these pass-fail schemes are employed chiefly with the subskills in a course which contributes to the overall grade. That overall grade, not surprisingly, still is awarded on a letter-grade basis.

Report Cards and Supplementary Reporting Schemes

When my father was growing up, the report cards used in the schools were rather rudimentary. I ran across his old report cards the other day while cleaning out a drawer. The cards had been saved by his mother and by my mother. In view of my dad's rather poor performance in mathematics classes, perhaps the cards should have been "lost." However, the report cards of the 1920s were rather lean in what they reported. At the high school level, in each course he received an *E* (Excellent, above 90), a *G* (Good, 80 to 90), an *F* (Fair, 70 to 80), or a *U* (Unsatisfactory, below 70). At the elementary school level, the report cards were even more global, with the same four-letter grading scheme being applied to only three dimensions, namely, "scholarship, deportment, and application." I must confess that I don't know how my father ever pulled a *fair* in application at Sunnyside Elementary School in the third grade. He always seemed to apply himself rather well.

In Figure 17–1 we see a copy of my father's third-grade report card; and in Figure 17–2, one of his high school report cards. The attentive reader will note that he was advanced to the fourth grade "on trial." I am pleased to report that he made it.

While yesteryear's report cards were succinct, today's report cards often resemble a set of income tax forms. In recent years my children have

---

[10]R. L. Ebel, *Essentials of Educational Measurement*, 3rd ed. (Englewood Cliffs, N.J.: Prentice-Hall, Inc., 1979).

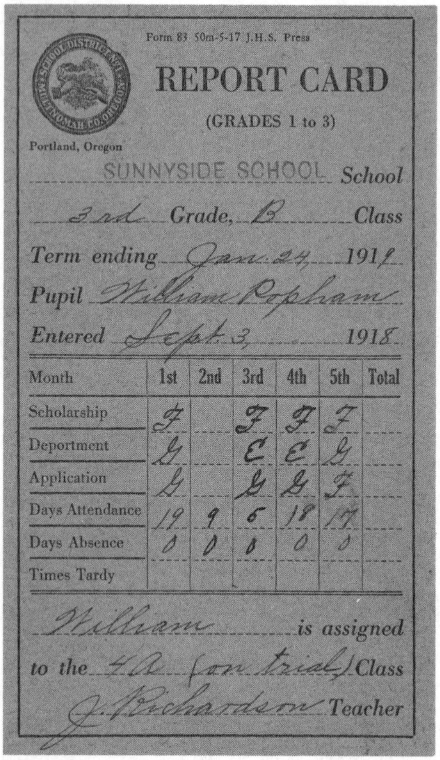
Form 83 50m-5-17 J.H.S. Press

SCHOOL DISTRICT No. 1 MULTNOMAH CO. OREGON

REPORT CARD

(GRADES 1 to 3)

Portland, Oregon

SUNNYSIDE SCHOOL School

3rd Grade, B Class

Term ending Jan. 24, 1919

Pupil William Popham

Entered Sept. 3, 1918

Month	1st	2nd	3rd	4th	5th	Total
Scholarship	F		F	F	F	
Deportment	G		E	E	G	
Application	G		G	G	F	
Days Attendance	19	9	6	18	17	
Days Absence	0	0	0	0	0	
Times Tardy						

William is assigned to the 4A (on trial) Class

J. Richardson Teacher

FIGURE 17–1 A 1919 elementary school report card of the father of a textbook writer (by permission of surviving son, also a textbook writer).

brought home report cards that dealt with so many dimensions it almost required two evenings and a paid consultant to figure them out. Instead of grading only academic progress on a subject-by-subject basis, each of the academic subjects is broken down in considerable detail. There are, for example, four distinct grades associated with different skills in reading. Moreover, when it comes to nonacademic behavior, designers of these modern report cards really went wild. It seems that I not only have a grade report on my son, Chris, but almost a complete psychosocial clinical report. I marvel at (or sympathize with) teachers who have the patience to fill out these near-endless sets of student evaluations. Apparently, today's educators are moving toward more elaborate *multidimensional report cards* which provide pupils and parents with ample information about all important aspects of a student's accomplishments.

Letters to parents. To supplement final report cards, some teachers rely on the use of less formal letters to parents in which the unique strengths and weaknesses of each pupil can be described. Given the distinctiveness of each child, such letters provide teachers with an opportunity to be as particularized as they wish in communicating with parents about a child's special potentials, shortcomings, and so on.

The major drawback with such letter reports is the enormous time it takes to prepare a letter for each child. A few school districts with access to adequate clerical-stenographic resources have provided teachers with dictating equipment so that such report letters can be dictated, then transcribed by secretarial personnel. However, most don't.

As indicated in Chapter 15, some school districts also have access to fairly sophisticated computer equipment which can be programmed to provide parents with somewhat more individualized pupil-progress information than is available even in multidimensional teacher-prepared report cards.

Parent-teacher conferences. Particularly in the early elementary grades, another supplement to the standardized report card is the parent-teacher conference. In such conferences teachers have a more extended opportunity to describe a child's progress, or lack of it, on a face-to-face basis with the child's parents. As with letters to parents, such supplementary reporting activities can be highly useful but extremely time consuming.

Not only is there the actual time the teachers must spend in the conferences themselves, but there's also the time spent in arranging the conferences. Besides that, not all parents want to know how their children are doing in school; at least they don't want to know so intently that they're willing to make a special trip to school. Accordingly, for some children,

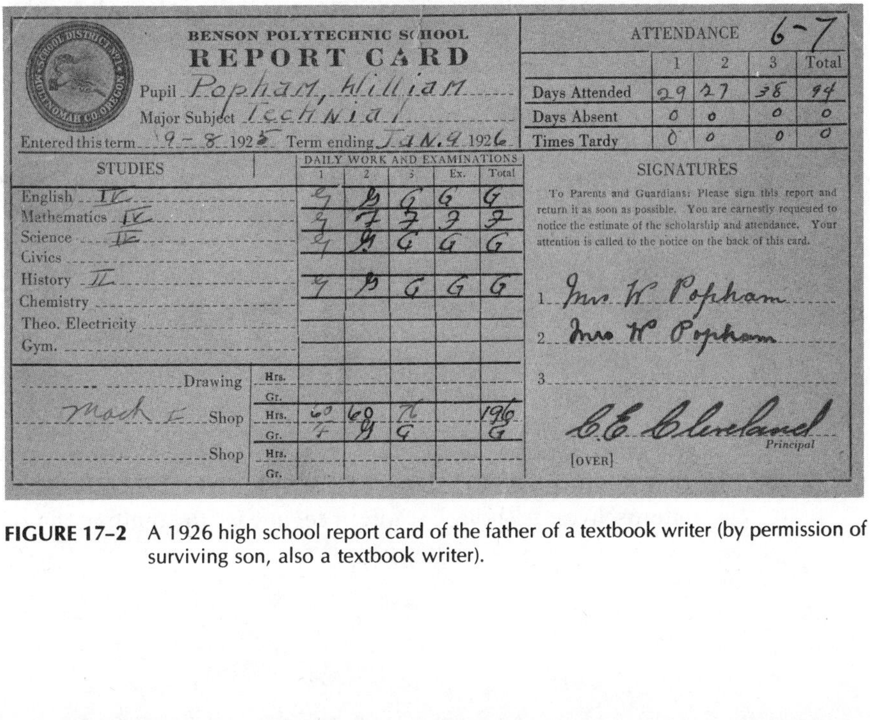
BENSON POLYTECHNIC SCHOOL
REPORT CARD
Pupil Popham, William
Major Subject Technial
Entered this term 9-8-1925 Term ending Jan. 4 1926

	ATTENDANCE 6-7			
	1	2	3	Total
Days Attended	29	27	38	94
Days Absent	0	0	0	0
Times Tardy	0	0	0	0

STUDIES	DAILY WORK AND EXAMINATIONS 1	2	3	Ex.	Total
English IV	G	G	G	G	G
Mathematics IV	G	F	F	F	F
Science II	G	G	G	G	G
Civics					
History II	G	G	G	G	G
Chemistry					
Theo. Electricity					
Gym.					
Drawing Hrs.					
Gr.					
Mach I Shop Hrs.	60	60	76		196
Gr.	F	G	G		G
Shop Hrs.					
Gr.					

SIGNATURES
To Parents and Guardians: Please sign this report and return it as soon as possible. You are earnestly requested to notice the estimate of the scholarship and attendance. Your attention is called to the notice on the back of this card.
1. Mrs W. Popham
2. Mrs W. Popham
3.
C. E. Cleveland
Principal
[OVER]

FIGURE 17–2 A 1926 high school report card of the father of a textbook writer (by permission of surviving son, also a textbook writer).

"Mr. Rath really does dispense his final grades with a flourish."

teachers will be unable to arrange conferences with the parents. In spite of the practical difficulties associated with parent-teacher conferences about grades, many teachers swear by them. (Some overworked teachers, it must be reported, also swear *at* them.) For the lower elementary grades, parent conferences appear to have sufficient dividends that we can anticipate their continued use in the schools.

Amalgamating Test Results

As teachers move through the academic year, they typically assemble a fairly hefty set of grade-relevant data for pupils. These will be weekly quizzes, end-of-unit exams, ratings of written projects or oral reports, and so on. One of the problems associated with grading is how to combine these different results sensibly. In Chapter 7 we spent a fair amount of time discussing standard scores. It turns out that the use of standard scores offers us an excellent procedure for amalgamating different test scores in an equitable manner.

Equitability is an important consideration in grading, of course, because unfairly awarded grades can have a decisively adverse effect on students' lives. Although it might seem easy to combine the results of different tests (for instance, by simply adding together the point-totals associated with each), it doesn't turn out to be that straightforward. We can use either z or T scores to obtain a mean of students' scores on different tests. This is done in order to obtain a more representative estimate of a student's total relative position than we could gain merely by summing raw score points. The advantage of standard scores is illustrated in Table 17–1, where two girls' scores on four quizzes have been compared with respect to both raw scores and standard scores.

Whereas Mary has obtained more total points from the four tests, Joan has the higher z-score total. This disparity results from the greater contribution of points on examination 4 to Mary's total score. Joan, in the other three tests, exceeds Mary's scores by marked differences in standard deviation units, that is, in the quality of their respective performances on three individual tests. Many educators have found that using average standard score estimates of performance yields a more representative picture of student attainment than is available by using total points.

It is also possible when adding together several examination performances to ascribe varying degrees of importance to different examinations by simply multiplying (weighting) the standard score for a given exam by two, three, and so forth.

Grading and Guilt

Anyone who grew up under the influence of some sort of religious training ought to be beset occasionally by *guilt*. Guilt, or so it seems, is one of those universal human characteristics that, given the right (wrong) kind of early assistance, really blossoms full-blown in adulthood. Many teachers, realizing that the dispensation of grades is a nonscientific and intuitive enterprise, often suffer guilt pangs during and after the grading process.

How do we defend, for example, the decisions we make about borderline cases? Oh, it's always easy and usually satisfying to award As to outstanding students. It's even easy and sometimes satisfying to toss an F at a student who didn't try during a course and failed every single exam. But

TABLE 17-1   A Comparison of Two Students' Raw Scores and Standard Scores on Four Quizzes

QUIZ	$\bar{X}$	S.D.	JOAN'S X	MARY'S X	JOAN'S z	MARY'S z
1	130	22	152	141	1.00	0.50
2	75	10	70	60	−0.50	−1.50
3	38	7	59	38	3.00	0
4	200	60	140	320	−1.00	2.00
Mean			105.25	139.75	2.50	1.00

how about all those in-betweeners? Can the teacher always make the right grading decision with such students? The answer is, distressingly, *no*.

Teachers must anticipate that they'll mess up more than a few grades. However, thank heaven, over the long haul, students who get short-changed in one course will be benefited in another. This point was made in the previous chapter. Teachers, in recognition that they're working with an imprecise, value-laden operation that is subject to all sorts of human error, should do the best grading job they can, then shed any guilt.

THE DESIGN AND IMPROVEMENT OF INSTRUCTION

The last topic to be treated in the book might well turn out to be the most important one, since it constitutes a substantial departure from what one typically encounters in your run-of-the-median measurement text. What we'll be considering in this final section are the ways that educators can use tests and test results to organize and improve instructional sequences so that those sequences are really effective.

Back in Chapter 1, a distinction was drawn between two orientations to measurement, namely, measurement as *status-determination* and measurement for *instructional improvement*. The more traditional of these orientations, of course, is that of status-determination. Through the past half-century in this nation, most measurement specialists have believed it was educational measurement's mission to discern what the status of a student was (typically in relationship to other students).

Only in recent times do we find many educators viewing measurement as an intervention that might *improve* the quality of teaching and learning. Instead of thinking that tests are developed *after an instructional sequence* to see whether learners picked up the intended skills and knowledge, these more modern measurement folks see teachers and test developers collaborating to create tests *prior to instruction* and to design instructional schemes that help learners succeed on those tests.

A Matter of Attitude

Perhaps the key notion is *collaboration*. In the past testers and teachers have pretty much functioned in separate worlds. Teachers would whip up an instructional storm, then testers would swoop in to see how much students had learned. Teachers were often obliged to administer tests in whose development they had no hand. Testers ended up assessing the effects of instructional activities about which they knew nothing.

However, the title of this text is *Modern Educational Measurement*, and in modern times educational measurement is too important to be left to measurement specialists. Too many significant educational policies are being shaped as a consequence of test results. Too many decisions about the educational effectiveness of teachers are being based on pupils' test scores. Too many citizens are forming their views about public education as a consequence of published test results. In other words, the educational stakes are terribly high. Educators must become not only more knowledgeable regarding measurement matters in general, they must also play an active role in shaping the nature of educational tests and in *profiting* instructionally from their applications.

This means that neither teachers nor measurement experts can afford the luxury of becoming specialists only in one area. A teacher can no longer "leave those matters to the measurement people." A measurement specialist can no longer view instructional considerations as "tasks for the classroom teacher." Both testers and teachers are going to have to expand their knowledge base, and do so in a hurry.

For the past two decades or so we have seen the roles of state departments of education expand rather dramatically. It is quite clear that state department of education staff members can and *do* play a major role in the nature of a state's educational operations. Moreover, in the more heavily populated of our states, some of these department of education staffs are both extremely large and highly qualified. Sad to say, however, in many instances those staffs consist of highly qualified *specialists,* that is, specialists in *either* instruction *or* measurement.

I wish I could describe for you the innumerable times I have dealt with state department of education staffs as they wrestled with significant education problems and discovered that the instruction people and the measurement people were really functioning in two separate worlds.[11] It is as though they had set up well-insulated enclaves, almost with different language systems for each. Instructional specialists were often intimidated and threatened by the measurement crowd. The measurement people viewed the instructional folks as "softheads who think a *median* is someone able to communicate with spirits." As you can gather, the operative mentality was *isolationism.* Curriculum people played curriculum games, and measurement people calculated means and modes. Beyond a few cordial greetings in the corridors, these two sets of professionals rarely interacted on a meaningful basis. However, for the well-being of students, such situations are truly tragic. Such situations must be altered.

---

[11]Although I am using the distinction between *measurement* and *instruction* specialists here, please think of this separation as a more encompassing one. In one camp, think of individuals who are involved in measurement, research, evaluation, and so on. In the second camp, include folks who are specialists in curriculum and/or instruction, both generalists as well as special subject matter experts (for example, in mathematics or reading). Classroom teachers, of course, would be members of the second camp.

I have dwelt somewhat on the distressing schism between instruction and measurement that I have personally witnessed in many state department of education staffs because such splits are a reflection of the educational world at large. Whether at the national, state, or local level, instructional personnel and measurement personnel tend to travel their separate trails. Rarely does one find a situation in which there is a genuine spirit of collaboration between these two camps. More often than not, there is indifference or even antipathy between instructional people and measurement people. Now if nobody was being harmed by the separation of instructional and measurement specialists, we could simply laugh off this situation as an amusing instance of bureaucratic territorialism. However, sadly, children are being short-changed when instructional people and measurement people fail to cooperate. The resulting quality of education will be lower than would have been the case if the two camps had interacted meaningfully.

Well, how should this situation be rectified? It must be recognized that a chief impediment to collaboration is *ignorance*. If people are ignorant about someone else's operation, they often fear it. At the very least, they try to stay clear of that operation. Thus, one way of breaking down the barriers between instruction people and measurement people is to make each group more conversant with the other's enterprise. Instructional personnel must acquire more technical knowledge regarding measurement. Measurement people must learn the ins and outs of instruction. Vocabularies must be expanded. Knowledge must be added. Technical processes must be understood. With a reduction of ignorance and the adoption of a collaborative orientation, we can expect exciting and effective instructional plans to emerge from the *joint* efforts of measurement and instructional professionals.

Selecting Teachable Testing Targets

As we saw in Chapter 9, the specifiers of educational tests typically have considerable latitude in deciding whether to test a student's mastery of a given skill or attitude with, for instance, assessment strategy *x* or assessment strategy *y*. It is usually the case that those key assessment decisions are made by measurement folks who are oblivious to the extent to which a given skill or attitude can reasonably be taught. Yet, in many cases it would be so simple to choose an assessment strategy that would be both a valid index of the attribute to be measured and also an index that was amenable to achievement through well-designed instruction.

In the original isolation of targets for teaching, that is, the selection of the assessment schemes which will serve as the intended outcomes for teaching, it is *imperative* that measurement experts employ an instructional as well as a testing mentality. If you're creating a new test, ask yourself seriously whether there's a reasonable chance for good teachers to promote learner mastery of the test. Hopefully, if you've taken seriously the plea expressed in the previous section, you'll know enough about instruction yourself to render these judgments. If not, be sure to call in some experienced teachers or other instructional experts. Don't set out instructional targets that no one can hit.

Designing Effective Teaching Sequences

This is a book about measurement. It is not a book about instruction, hence we can't spend an inordinate amount of time discussing principles of teaching. However we're going to expend a few paragraphs in that manner because, frankly, measurement people sometimes get intimidated by teacher-types. Not understanding teachers' terminology or tactics, measurement people sometimes conclude that "the teaching of reading is an esoteric art, comprehensible only to those who can tell the difference between a diphthong and a consonant blend." However, the design of instruction is really less opaque than that. To illustrate that fact, we're going to consider four high-powered, yet understandable, principles of instructional design. Hopefully, having encountered these principles, the reader will conclude that the realm of instructional design is indeed capable of being mastered, hence will set out to do so without delay.

Rather than review the almost unending galaxy of instructional principles that one could dredge up from the research literature and from the experiences of veteran teachers, we're going to focus on only a handful of instructional principles. However, they are extremely powerful principles because they are principles rooted in the effective use of testing instruments and test specifications. Adherence to these principles, whether for an initial or remedial instructional sequence, will markedly increase the likelihood that your instructional program will be a success.

As with all instructional interventions, of course, the proof of the pudding is not in its appearance but in its edibility. In other words, even the most elegantly designed instructional programs may or may not be effective. They may or may not be effective even if they are predicated on sound instructional principles. We must attend to the *outcomes* of these programs, that is, the proportion of youngsters who attain the intended outcomes, in order to judge whether the instructional designs were good ones. Fortunately, by adhering to the following four principles, you'll be more apt to put together a successful instructional program.

For purposes of this discussion, let's focus on instructional designs intended to promote a student's mastery of well-explicated *competencies*, that is, cognitive skills. Other, somewhat different, principles should be used for the promotion of affective or psychomotor aims.

Competency comprehension. Teachers can teach better that which they understand well. This simple assertion packs a ton of instruction potency, far more than is generally recognized. We can refer to this notion as the principle of teachers' *competency comprehension*. First off, it's vastly easier to explain something you really understand. Teachers who comprehend the nature of a competency—its main elements and its nuances—will be in a position to provide lucid exposition regarding the competency in question. Without question, students will have a better chance to master a skill if that skill has been clearly explained to them.

Secondly, it is imperative that teachers understand a competency well enough so that they can decide which of the numerous instructional activities they might choose for students are truly on-target. Teachers who only have a murky notion of the skills they're trying to promote often select instructional activities which bear only tangential relevance to the actual task at hand. Poor comprehension on the teacher's part leads to poor instructional design.

For both these reasons, it is important for anyone involved in instructional design or delivery to master the specifics of the competency being promoted. In most cases this can best be done by consulting descriptive materials that are available regarding the competency. Usually, since the students' performance on the competency test really operationalizes the competency, the best source of clarity regarding a competency is the test itself. Since teachers should not "teach to the test" in the sense that they are teaching the particular items on a test, if the rules used to generate test items are available, that is, the *test specifications*, then those rules should be studied intensively by everyone involved in the instruction. Obviously, if ill-defined competencies and a fuzzy test have been chosen during earlier stages of the game, this will be impossible. However, for the sake of optimism, let's assume teachers have access to a fairly detailed set of test specifications for each competency, that is, specifications which really tie down fairly well the nature of the learner behaviors that constitute each competency.

Teachers should read these specifications, attempt to master them, then share their understandings with other teachers. For example, a staff session could be set aside during which different teachers took turns describing instances of student behavior which were or weren't congruent with the behaviors set forth in the competency specifications, then allowed other teachers to judge which behaviors fit the competency. Discussions and clarifications of disagreements will usually prove illuminating to all concerned.

There are other procedural ways, of course, to get educators to better comprehend the nature of the competencies they are responsible for promoting. However, by whatever means seem to suit best the local situation, be sure you build in some activities which heighten staff conversance with the competencies to be promoted. This sort of competency comprehension is an indispensable element in an effectively designed instructional program.

Task description. A second powerful principle for the design of instruction is that of *task description*, namely, letting the learners know what is expected of them. In this context the principle can be translated to mean that educators must apprise students, in no uncertain terms, of the nature of the competencies they're expected to master.

On moral, if not instructional grounds, it is important to clarify students' expectations regarding the commpetencies being promoted. Competency-oriented instructional programs should not be a setting where educators shroud their expectations in vague generalities, merely informing students that they'll have to become proficient in "practical life skills of reading." No, there are far too many ways to measure such an ill-defined batch of skills. Students who are told no more than this won't know what sorts of competencies they're really expected to master.

If, on the other hand, students possess a really good idea of what the skills are that they're supposed to acquire, they can focus their intellectual energies on trying to accomplish those skills. Rather than spending wasted effort trying to "outpsyche" the teachers, students can really attempt to accomplish some well-staked-out competencies.

Generally speaking, the detailed test specifications or skill descriptions (that teachers might use for instructional design purposes) will prove too technical for students. Consequently, these more detailed competency descriptions typically must be recast into language more understandable to students. An example (or examples) of the kinds of test items to be employed should always be provided to students. However, sample test items, although helpful, are insufficient. An attempt should be made to spell out in student language the precise nature of the sought-for competencies, then share these with the students—often. In particular, task descriptions are useful at the *beginning* of an instructional sequence.

In a sense, the principle of task description is, for students, analogous to the principle of competency comprehension for teachers. But are teachers and students the only folks who can profit from knowing what's expected of learners? No, there's another group who, if knowledgeable regarding our competency expectations, might be most helpful in a minimum competency program—and that's the parents. Why not let parents or guardians know what the competencies are that their children are striving to master? There might be situations at home, and plenty of them, when parents could supply a bit of real life practice for students, practice that because of its obvious reality could prove potent indeed. Imagine that a youngster's mother and father had discovered an unbalanced bank account or an error in their insurance bills. These situations, when shared with their children, could prove both motivating and instructive. The schools need all the help they can get.

Appropriate practice. One of the most potent of all instructional principles is that of *appropriate practice*, wherein we give learners an opportunity during instruction to engage in the class of behaviors called for in the competency. Some researchers refer to this as the variable of *time-on-task*, and a number of recent empirical investigations have solidly confirmed the commonsense notion that the more time students spend on practicing a skill, the more likely they are to master that skill.[12]

Given clear descriptions of the target competencies, it is possible to put together some practice exercises for students, since those exercises will be identical to the test items themselves, except that provisions will be provided whereby students can judge the accuracy of their answers. It is essential in such practice exercises to incorporate mechanisms through which students can gain *knowledge of results* regarding the responses to practice exercises. There are many ways to provide such feedback schemes. For example, the correct answer can be presented immediately following each practice item, but set off in some way, for example, by a shaded box, so that students do not inadvertently see the correct answer prior to responding to the practice exercise.

Teachers often require assistance in securing the sorts of practice exercises needed to capitalize on the appropriate practice principle. Here is where an adroit school administrator will expend some resources to help teachers live the good pedagogical life. Teachers, perhaps assisted by outside consultants, could be given summer or after-school stipends to work together and collaboratively create some practice exercises that could be shared by all.

But no matter how, plenty of practice opportunities must be included in an effectively designed instructional program. If students receive ample

---

[12]R. S. Marliave, C. W. Fisher, and M. N. Dishaw, "Academic Learning Time and Student Achievement in the A–B Period," *Technical Note VI–A*, Beginning Teacher Evaluation Study (San Francisco, Far West Laboratory for Educational Research and Development, December, 1977).

time-on-task prior to their being tested, odds are they'll do well on the competencies. If, on the contrary, they receive little practice, they're apt to fail. Whether for initial or remedial instruction, appropriate practice will decisively enhance the quality of an instructional program.

Progress monitoring.   The final instructional principle to be considered involves our effort to find out how students are doing as they wind their ways toward proficiency. We refer to this principle as *progress monitoring* because, cleverly, it involves our monitoring of the progress that students are making.

In essence, this principle urges teachers to find out, as often as practicable, just how youngsters are doing with respect to particular competencies. This is done so that if any students are having difficulties, special instructional attention can be given to those students. Conversely, if students display mastery of a particular skill, there's little or no need to keep pounding away at that skill. An implication of progress monitoring is that when students have made sufficient progress, we can hop off their backs.

It is important to find out *when to stop teaching* a particular skill in order to avoid the very real danger that minima may become maxima, that is, we will allow less profound instructional aspirations to crowd out higher-level aspirations for students. By keeping track of a student's progress and providing higher-level targets for those who have mastered the minimums, we can hope to avoid this error.

We have now considered four instructional principles which, if skillfully blended into an educational program, should enhance the likelihood that the instructional phases of the program will be successful. However, let's say that we have saturated our program with these four principles. Is that enough? If we had an instructional program that was loaded with competency comprehension, task description, appropriate practice, and progress monitoring, would we have a certain winner? Unfortunately, the answer to that question is no.

Beyond these four powerful, *but not sure-fire*, instructional principles, educators will still be obliged to bring all their ingenuity and zeal to bear on the task of instructional design. Too many local factors preclude one's detailing a certain-to-be-effective recipe for instructional design. Maybe, for example, on a school's staff there is a teacher who not only loves to individualize instruction but thrives on the teaching of remedial skills. In such serendipitous situations it may make sense to build a total remedial laboratory around this pedagogical powerhouse. In other settings totally different elements may incline teachers in other directions.

But no matter what the directions, strive to incorporate the four principles described here. While they're not a guarantee of success, they really put the odds in the teacher's favor.

Formative evaluation takes place when we assess the merits for an instructional program in order to ameliorate its deficits. In contrast to *summative evaluation,* which is an end-of-the-road appraisal of a program's merits for purposes of reaching a go or no-go decision, formative evaluation has a far more striking *improvement* concentration.[13]

As indicated in the concluding discussion of the four principles of instructional design, even by following them faithfully, there is still the chance that an instructional program might turn out to be a loser. What's to be done then?

Well, surprisingly enough, here's where measurement folks can once more play a prominent role. In the first place, of course, it will often be because of test results that an instructional program is judged to be defective. However, once having discovered that an instructional sequence isn't working, educators can turn to testing folks for some assistance.

One of the most useful things that test developers can do for teachers is to design tests which measure the key *en-route* (*enabling*) skills that learners must master on their way to acquisition of the terminal skill. Teachers and testers together can carry out a *task analysis* in which the most important of these *en-route* skills are identified. The most direct way of undertaking a task analysis is to focus on the terminal skill (for example, an end-of-course objective), then ask, "What does the learner need to be able to do in order to perform this skill?" Having identified a precursive *en-route* skill, then focus on the skill and once more ask, "What does the learner have to be able to do in order to perform this (*en-route*) skill?" Do this until a reasonable choice of *en-route* skills has been isolated.

Then the task of the test developer is to construct sets of items measuring each of these key *en-route* skills. Such a test, when administered to students who have completed instruction judged to be ineffectual, will usually help teachers identify the *en-route* skills which students have failed to master. In revising the instruction, therefore, the teacher now has access to some cues regarding the improvement of the instructional sequence, namely, to emphasize more strongly or explain more lucidly the content associated with the *en-route* skills which are troubling students.

Other useful data to improve a weak instructional sequence include results of affective inventories that we saw treated in Chapter 14. We can

[13]For a further peek into the mysteries of educational evaluation, including these two roles of evaluation introduced by Michael Scriven, please read every page (with diligence and awe) of W. James Popham, *Educational Evaluation* (Englewood Cliffs, N.J.: Prentice-Hall, Inc., 1974).

often pick up helpful insights into the efficacy of an instructional program by discerning its affective impact on students.

In all these formative evaluation activities, the measurement specialist can play a significant role because the data-gathering tools to be used will have been created by that measurement person. It is important for measurement people who construct such tests to identify with the instructional designers by devising tests whose results will have clear implications for *decisions*. To shape up a beleaguered instructional program, we need decision-relevant test results, not just test results that are "interesting" or "nice to know."

Matching the Testing Strategy to the Task

Part I of this text focused on the importance of selecting appropriate tests for particular sorts of educational purposes. This is no less true when we attempt to design effective teaching sequences and to salvage those that are floundering. Because the key to astute instructional design and instructional amelioration is the *clarity* with which instructional designers and formative evaluators comprehend the skills (attitudes, knowledge, and so on) being sought, this will generally call for the use of criterion-referenced measures.

This is not to suggest that norm-referenced tests would be entirely feckless in instructional contexts, for certainly test results of any sort are better than none at all. However, criterion-referenced tests would prove superior.

For other sorts of educational purposes, and there are tons of such purposes, norm-referenced tests can provide information that is most significant. For purposes of instructional design and formative evaluation, however, criterion-referenced tests, and the greater lucidity they bring regarding the behaviors being assessed, should invariably be preferred.[14]

We can conclude this excursion into educational measurement more or less where we came in, namely, with the observation that educational tests can be of enormous value to those who must carry out educational operations. That value, however, will depend directly on how well the users of educational tests match the assessment device to the purpose at hand.

[14]Not all measurement maestros share your author's inspired insights on this issue. In 1978, for instance, I participated in an enjoyable and, hopefully, thought-provoking debate with Bob Ebel on this topic. See R. L. Ebel, "The Case for Norm-Referenced Measurements" and W. J. Popham, "The Case for Criterion-Referenced Measurements" in *Educational Researcher*, 7,11 (December 1978), 3–10.

Part A

It may be a bit of an oversimplification to view grading practices as based on a norm-referenced or criterion-referenced conception (since we saw that with respect to grading, teachers must rely on some sorts of normative notions in reaching their grading decisions). Nevertheless, to help clarify the distinction between these two orientations, decide whether each of the teachers in the following episodes is chiefly using a *norm-referenced* or a *criterion-referenced* approach to grading.

1. A high school teacher of chemistry has evolved a grading system over the years whereby students who perform a specified number of successful experiments during the semester receive a preset grade. For instance, if the students successfully complete at least fourteen of the experiments described by the team at the beginning of the semester, they receive an *A*.

2. Wendy Hiller is an English instructor in a junior high school which, she says, seems to be, "smack in the middle of the city's ethnic migration trail." Since the student population in her classes shifts so dramatically from year to year, Wendy waits each year to base her grade-assignment decisions on the particular students with whom she is working.

3. Based on normative data gathered during the early years of his teaching experiences, Joe Jergens has established some clearly defined expectations for his history students. For a series of term projects, Joe knows exactly what it takes to get an *A*, *B*, and so on. If one year's group of students fails to achieve up to the standards he has set, Joe shrugs off their poor performance and assigns no *A*s, and sometimes no *B*s, to the students.

4. Sally Smith grades "on the curve" for her classes, comparing student scores to those of other students in the class before deciding how many students get grades of *A*, *B*, *C*, *D*, or *F*.

5. In spite of the fact that he has read about the dangers of basing grades on growth scores or on relationship to student potential, a fourth-grade teacher at Creston School attempts "to grade students on their growth from pretest to posttest as a function of their potential." Those students in each year's class to show the best growth in relationship to their aptitude get the highest grades, and vice versa.

Part B

Imagine that you are a teacher in a district that is embarking on a minimum competency testing program in communication skills. Fourteen such communication skills have been identified. You have just attended a Saturday morning staff-development workshop designed to help you (and the 55 other teachers in attendance) become more conversant with the kinds of instructional strategies that will help your district's students master the skills imbedded in the minimum competency testing program.

The director of the workshop has just distributed a set of practice exercises dealing with four instructional principles she has been describing. Your job is to complete the exercise as directed below.

Listed below are four guidelines for effective instruction. (Notice the subtle similarity between these and the four treated earlier in the chapter.) Briefly review them, then read each of the following five instructional vignettes and decide which, if any, of the guidelines has been followed by the teacher.

> Guideline One: *The more clearly a teacher comprehends the skills being sought, the more likely students will achieve those skills.*
>
> Guideline Two: *The teacher should describe a target skill to learners early in an instructional sequence.*
>
> Guideline Three: *Students should be supplied with ample opportunity to practice the behavior called for in each target skill.*
>
> Guideline Four: *Monitor students' progress toward skill mastery so that additional instruction can be given to those making insufficient progress.*

6. Gil Jones, a veteran instructor at Cooley Junior High, has been reviewing sets of communication skills test specifications in his new *Teacher's Handbook* during the summer months. Many times Gil's friends have asked him to join them in one of their customary fishing excursions, but he always declines, saying: "I'd like to go with you folks, but I'm too interested in understanding these fourteen communication skills competencies." Gil's friends privately discuss his emotional stability, since he has never in the past refused a fishing trip opportunity.
At the start of the school year, however, Gil's familiarity with the fourteen skill descriptions astonishes his colleagues at Cooley. He can flawlessly describe the major ingredients in each of the fourteen skills, as well as the key subskills for all fourteen.

Early in the fall semester, Gil presents a remarkable brief, yet illuminating, description of all fourteen communication skills to his ninth-grade students. Along with this description he stresses the practical significance of each of the fourteen skills. At the conclusion of his descriptive excursion, all of his students appear to be really excited by the new testing program—all except those who missed school to go fishing.
Which, if any, of the guidelines did Gil clearly follow?

7. Three sixth-grade teachers at Rhoda St. School decide to pool their efforts in order to create a series of supplemental practice exercises which will be seen by their students as truly relevant. Each of them selects

the top two students in their classes, thus forming a committee of six student "test writers." For each of the six reading competencies, the student committee creates fifteen new practice items which should be of interest to local sixth graders. For example, the students use a good many items based on currently popular rock groups in the city. The students also try to incorporate some humor in their items so that students will be interested in reading the items. Each of these fifteen-item pools is organized into a set of practice exercises for pupils who have trouble in mastering particular skills. On the first page of each set of exercises, the teachers provide a clear description of what they believe to be the heart of that competency, so that the students completing the exercise packet won't be confused about what is expected of them. Answers to all practice exercises are provided at the close of the packet.

Which, if any, of the guidelines did the three teachers clearly follow?

8. For the last several years, Joan Taylor has become increasingly impatient with her ninth-grade students at Northeastern. They seem to be, in her words, "Going downhill on a well-waxed toboggan!" When a new minimum competency testing program was announced, she became intrigued with its potential implications for her own teaching, hence looked forward with genuine anticipation to the distribution of descriptive materials regarding the new program.

Because the ten competencies for the program resulted in ten relatively distinct skills, Joan saw this as an ideal opportunity to individualize her instruction. She set up her classroom operations so that they were based on a galaxy of self-paced instructional materials and activities. She initiated an elaborate peer-tutoring program whereby more advanced students worked with less advanced students. In sum, she created a flexible and individualized instructional environment for her students. By the end of the first semester, Joan's classes were the topic of conversation during many coffee breaks at Northeastern. During one of those sessions, she commented, "Well, at least I've scraped some of the wax off the toboggan."

Which, if any, of the guidelines did Joan clearly follow?

9. Josie Green is a humanistically oriented English teacher at Cody Middle School with two seventh-grade classes in which a new criterion-referenced testing program in social studies will be used. After surveying the various components of the testing program, she decides that she is going to design her instruction so that the students (1) know what's expected of them and (2) know how they're doing with respect to the seven social studies skills.

First off, she spends a fair amount of time with the *Teacher's Handbook* in order to be completely conversant with each of the seven skill descriptions. She figures that she must have this kind of knowledge of the skills in order to adequately describe them to her students. Next, she carefully explains each of the seven skills to her students prior to an introduction of that skill's instructional unit. Finally, she uses the two sets of interim tests (provided with the system) to assess each student at least once, and usually twice, during the instructional unit treating each skill. Students are informed of their progress so that they can concentrate on skills with which they are having difficulty.

Which, if any, of the guidelines did Josie clearly follow?

10. English faculty members at Western have decided to coordinate their efforts in promoting learner mastery of the six communication skills embedded in the new twelfth-grade language arts testing program. They persuade their department chairman and principal to provide a certain amount of backup support to aid them in preparing for the schoolwide installation of the new testing program. More specifically, by means of some exotic accounting transactions, school financial resources are used to support a departmental wine-and-cheese party every Thursday afternoon during which the staff discusses instructional strategies and creates practice exercises to supplement those available with the testing system. The teachers also spend a substantial amount of time trying to understand precisely what is covered in the six skills being assessed.

Although not all of the English faculty at Western commenced this one-semester activity as wine enthusiasts, after seven or eight meetings there was a marked increase in each teacher's enthusiasm and alcoholic consumption. The principal, noting the substantial increase in weekly expense reports, attributes this to an intensified professional commitment.

At the close of the semester, the English faculty had created three additional sets of practice exercises for each of the six skills. For some undisclosed symbolic reason, the three sets of exercises were referred to as Chablis, Burgundy, and Rosé. Several teachers questioned the principal regarding whether it was legitimate to include cheese and wine rations as elements in future contract negotiations.

Which, if any, of the guidelines did the English faculty clearly follow?

ANSWERS TO PRACTICE EXERCISES

Part A

1. Criterion-referenced
2. Norm-referenced
3. Criterion-referenced
4. Norm-referenced
5. Norm-referenced

Part B

6. Gil was clearly following guidelines one and two. There is, this instance notwithstanding, no clear evidence that enthusiastic acceptance of the communications program will induce emotional instability.

7. The three teachers clearly followed guidelines two and three. They also exhibited keen managerial skills in getting help from high-powered students.

8. Well, although she individualized up a storm and it seems probable that her students benefited, Joan didn't *clearly* follow any of the guidelines. If you thought she was, you ought to curb your tendencies toward excessive generosity or you may find yourself on Joan's toboggan.

9. Josie gets credit for three of the four guidelines. (That's 75 percent correct and surely passing.) She clearly used guidelines one, two, and four. We don't know if Josie also provided relevant practice, thus following guideline three. She seems like a decent sort, however, so odds are that she did.

10. It appears that the English faculty was following guidelines one and three (at least they created the necessary practice exercises). It would be an interesting research hypothesis to gauge the impact of the Thursday wine-and-cheese orgies on the quality of Friday morning classes.

DISCUSSION QUESTIONS

1. If you were asked to describe a fair grading system for elementary or secondary grade students, what would it be like?

2. What sorts of influences are encountered by teachers as they set out to award grades? Can any of these be countered? If so, how?

3. Suppose you were delivering an address to a graduating class of public school teachers on the topic: *The Relationship Between Testing and Teaching.* What would you emphasize in such an address?

4. Try to conceptualize a school district system in which measurement really contributed to instructional decision making. What would be the chief elements of that system?

SUGGESTIONS FOR ADDITIONAL READING

BUNDA, MARY ANNE, and JAMES R. SANDERS, eds., *Practices and Problems in Competency-Based Measurement.* Washington, D.C.: National Council on Measurement in Education, 1979. This volume contains a series of first-rate articles, many of which deal with the instructional correlates of measurement.

CHASE, CLINTON I., "Assessing and Reporting on School Programs," Chapter 14, *Measurement for Educational Evaluation*, pp. 312–340. Reading, Mass.: Addison-Wesley, 1979. A description is provided of schemes for grading and for reporting to parents the use of test data in the broader context of evaluation.

DEMBO, MYRON, "Standardized and Teacher-Made Evaluation Instruments," Chapter 9, *Teaching for Learning*, pp. 345–381. Santa Monica, Calif.: Goodyear Publishing Co., 1977. In this chapter consideration is given to educational tests as they relate to instructional approaches.

EBEL, ROBERT L., "Marks and Marking Systems," Chapter 12, *Essentials of Educational Measurement* (3rd ed.), pp. 227–257. Englewood Cliffs, N.J.: Prentice-Hall, Inc., 1979. In this chapter a discussion is provided regarding the virtues of "marks and grades" in spite of their many shortcomings. Quantitative schemes are suggested for application of grades.

GRONLUND, NORMAN E., "Marking and Reporting," Chapter 19, *Measurement and Evaluation in Teaching* (3rd ed.), pp. 511–536. New York: Macmillan, 1976. The author offers a series of suggestions for better disposition of grades. Alternative schemes, some of them quantitative in their orientation, are provided.

HOPKINS, CHARLES D., and RICHARD L. ANTES, "Criterion-Referenced Interpretation," and "Norm-Referenced Interpretation," Chapters 7 and 8, *Classroom Testing: Administration, Scoring, and Score Interpretation*, pp. 112–147. Itasca, Ill.: F. E. Peacock, 1979. Chapters 7 and 8 include schemes and analyses of norm-referenced and criterion-referenced conceptions of student evaluations.

KARMEL, LOUIS J., and MARYLIN O. KARMEL, "Grades and Report Cards," Chapter 17, *Measurement and Evaluation in the Schools* (2nd ed.), pp. 440–448. New York: Macmillan, 1978. The purpose underlying grades provided the focus of this brief chapter on grading procedures.

LINDEMAN, RICHARD H., and PETER F. MERENDA, "Pupil Evaluation: Marketing and Reporting," Chapter 6, *Educational Measurement* (2nd ed.), Glenview, Ill.: Scott, Foresman, 1979. In this chapter the authors treat the use of test results for (1) grades and (2) reporting of pupil status and progress.

LINDVALL, C. MAURITZ, and ANTHONY J. NITKO, "Planning for Instruction and Evaluation," Chapter 2, *Measuring Pupil Achievement and Aptitude* (2nd ed.). New York: Harcourt Brace Jovanovich, 1975. Lindvall and Nitko consider measurement in the context of instructional design. In particular, Chapter 2 deals with instructionally relevant tests, noting how measurement plans and instruction are intertwined.

MILLMAN, JASON, "Reporting Student Progress: A Case for Criterion-Referenced Marking System," *Phi Delta Kappan*, 11, no. 4 (December 1970), 226–230. In this brief essay the author advocates the use of criterion-referenced report cards as opposed to the more traditional normative varieties report-card schemes.

TUCKMAN, BRUCE W., "Getting the Most from the School Testing Program," Chapter 15, *Measuring Educational Outcomes: Fundamentals of Testing*, pp. 442–471. San Francisco: Harcourt Brace Jovanovich, Inc., 1975. Tuckman discusses how to get the most from a school testing program, including individual and classroom applications of results.

Index

A

Accuracy, of content, 291–92
Achievement based on aptitude, 404–5
Achievement tests, 33–34
AERA (*See* American Educational Research Association)
Affective assessment:
  educational counseling and, 346
  group, 345–48
  individual, 345–48
  options, 335–45
  program evaluation and, 346
  validity requirements of, 346
Affective domain, 328–31
  levels of, 330–31
  organization in, 331
  performance standard and, 372
  responding in, 330
  valuing in, 331
Affective measures:
  defensible scoring key in, 332
  definition of, 328
  practicality considerations in, 334
  social desirability cues, eliminating, 334
  step-by-step scheme for, 333–34
  validity, 334
Age-equivalent values, 317
Algorithms, 219
American Educational Research Association (AERA), 100
American Psychological Association (APA), 99–100
Analysis in cognitive domain, 330
Anecdotal records, 313, 315
  advantages of, 315
  disadvantages of, 315
  objectivity in, 315

Angoff adaptation, 391–92
  appraisal of, 393
APA (*See* American Psychological Association)
Aptitude tests, 33–34
  construct validity of, 118–20
  criterion-related validity of, 112
Army Alpha, 17–18
Army Beta, 18
Assessment options, range of, 205–6
Assessment schemes, alternative, 212–16
Attributes:
  isolating, 333–35
  response, 216, 221–23
  stimulus, 216, 218–21

B

Bayesian statistical model, 54–55
Bayesian statistical strategy, test length and, 304
Behavioral objectives, 57
Behaviors, 309–10
  cognitive, levels of, 207–8
  products and, distinction between, 267–68
Bias, linguistic definition of, 181
Bias, test (*See* Test bias)
Binary-choice format, modified, 257
Binary-choice items, 236, 241–47
  dividends and deficits of, 242–43
  problems in writing, 243
  use of, 241
  weakness of, 242
Binomial model, 54–55, 304–5
Black Intelligence Test Counter-balanced for Honkies, 181–82

Black Intelligence Test Cultural Homogeneity, 181–82
Borderline-Group Method, 386–87
  advantage of, 387
  appraisal of, 392
  steps in, 386
British Civil Service Commission, 15

C

Carbon-booklet, 362
Centiles, 162
Central tendency errors, 322
Changing-alternatives scales, 320
Cheating, 360
China's Examination Hell, 13
Civil Service Board, 15
Civil Service Commission, 15
Civil Service Examinations:
  British, 14
  Chinese, 11–15
  United States, 15
Class intervals, 70–71
Clues:
  grammatical, 329
  unintended, 239–40, 257, 258
Coefficient:
  correlation, 67
  reliability, 68
Coefficient alpha, 145, 148
Cognitive Abilities Test:
  on internal consistency estimates, 148–49
  on standard error of measurement, 150, 152
Cognitive domain, 328–31
  application in, 329
  comprehension in, 329
  evaluation in, 330
  knowledge in, 329
  levels of, 329–30
  performance standards and, 372
  synthesis in, 330
Cognitive measure, definition of, 328
Cognitive tests, 33–34
  individual decision in, 345
  item-writing guidelines, 244–47
Competencies:
  clarification of, 379, 385
  expected, 417
  verification of apprehensive consensus on, 385

Competency assurance, 6
Competency comprehension, 416–17
Competency testing, minimum, 372–73
  problems with, 373–74
Concurrent validity, 109–11
Confidence-band, 147
Constant-alternatives scale, 320
Construct:
  legitimacy of, 114
  psychological definition of, 113
Constructed-response behaviors, classification of, 267
Constructed-response items:
  measurement mission of, 269
  preparation of, 269
  response structure in, 270
  and selected-response items, comparison of, 268–71
Constructed-response tests, 266–85
  criterion-referenced test specifications for, 226–28
Construct effective cognitive functioning, 119
Construct validity, 113–18
  assembly of, 113–14
  correlations with intelligence tests, 119
  differential-population studies, 114–15
  effective cognitive functioning in, 119
  evidence of, 114
  intervention studies, 114–15
  related measures studies, 114–15
  targets for, 116
Content:
  accuracy of, 291–92
  defining attributes of, 219
  selection process, 104
Content-behavior, 102
Content categories, 207–8
  listing of, 209–11
Content coverage, adequacy of, 108
Content validity, 100, 101–8
  commercially published tests and, 104–5
  conception of, 103
  criterion-referenced tests and, 105–6, 121–23
  definition of, 101–3
  IOX Basic Skill tests and, 121–23
  norm-referenced tests and, 103–5

Contextual considerations, 377
  magnitude of, 385
Contrasting-groups method, 387–88
  appraisal of, 392–93
  modification of, 388
  steps in, 387
Correction-for-guessing:
  formulae, 363–64
  penalties, application of, 365
  procedures, 357
Correctness, gradations of, 260
Correlation coefficient:
  computation of, 89–92
  cross products, 90
  deviation score formula, 89–92
  Pearson product-moment, 87–89
  rank-order, 93–95
  Spearman's, 93
Criterion, defined, 27
Criterion-as-desired-behavior concep-
      tion, 27
Criterion-as-a-level conception, 27
Criterion-referenced measurement,
      24–41
Criterion-referenced tests:
  construct validity of, 117–18
  content validity of, 105–6, 121–23
  criterion-related validity of, 112–13
  definition of, 27
  description of measured behavior
      in, 48–50
  distinction of, 26–28
  domain-referenced tests and, 29
  equivalence of, 134
  instructional design and diagnosis,
      37
  internal consistency estimates of,
      145–46
  interpretation of, 32–33
  item analysis for, 300–303
  judgmental item-improvement
      schemes for, 288–89
  norm-referenced tests and, 31, 134,
      206
  objective of, 217
  objectives-based tests and, 28
  percentiles versus percentage cor-
      rect, 32–33
  proficiency level for, 28
  specifications, 211–30
  stability of, 130–32
  superiority of, 421

Criterion-related validities, 108–13
  aptitude tests and, 112
  concurrent validity and, 109–11
  criterion-referenced tests and,
      112–13
  definition of, 109
  norm-referenced tests and, 111–12
  predictive validity, 109–11
  reading tests and, 120–21
Culture-Fair Intelligence Tests, 184,
      186–88
Culture-fair tests, 184–90
  nonverbal material in, 188
Curve:
  normal, 74
  smoothing, 73–75

D

Data:
  comparative, 60–61, 156–80
  interval, 94
  normative, 157
  preference, 383–84
  reliability, 148–52
David-Eells Test of General Intelligence,
      184–86
Decision at issue, 377
  magnitude of, 385
Decision-consistency, 130–31, 149
Decision context, analysis of, 377–79,
      385
Descriptive-graphic rating, dimension
      of, 320
Descriptive-graphic rating scale, 320
Deviations, 80–81
  squaring, 81–82
Differences:
  pretest-posttest, 300–301
  uninstructed versus instructed
      group, 301
Differential Aptitude Tests, construct va-
      lidity of, 119–20
Difficult levels, influences of, 298
Difficulty, median, 303
Difficulty disparities, 133
Difficulty indices, 294–95
Directions:
  information in, 356
  preparing effective, 355–57
Dispersion of scores, 80

Dispositional assessment, 332
Distractor analysis, 299–300
Distractors:
  plausibility of, 259
  undemanding, 254
Distributions:
  bimodal, 78
  frequency, 68–71
  negatively skewed, 74–75
  normal, 74, 158–60
  positively skewed, 74–75
  trimodal, 78
Documentary evidence, quality of, 62
Domain-referenced tests, 29
  content validity of, 108
Domain-selection validity, 122

          E

Educational accountability, 5
Educational effectiveness, demanding
  evidence of, 5–6
Educational measurement:
  compatibility of functions, 18–19
  consistency of, 59
  criterion-referenced, 24–41
  educational specializations and, 4–5
  fixed-quota settings, 35
  fundamental concepts in, 5
  history of, 10–18
  instructional-improvement, 9, 19,
    412
  norm-referenced, 24–41
  program evaluation, 36–37
  requisite-skill settings, 35–36
  selection decisions, 34–35
  status-determination, 9, 18–19, 412
  strategy and mission, 34–38
  two-category schemes of, 235
Educational tests:
  achievement tests, 33–34
  administering, 353–70 (*See also* Test
    administration)
  affective tests, 33–34, 332
  applications of, 6–9
  aptitude tests, 6, 33–34, 112, 118–20
  choices of, 353–55
  classroom tests, 46–47
  cognitive, 33–34, 244 (*See also* Cog-
    nitive tests)
  comprehensiveness of, 31–32

  constructed-response, 266–85 (*See
    also* Constructed-response tests)
  creating, 202–350
  description of measured behavior,
    47–50
  domain-referenced tests, 29
  evaluating, 44–65
  factors to judge quality of, 45–63
  functions of, 9–10
  instructional improvement and, 400
  multiple-choice (*See* Multiple-choice
    items)
  objectives-based, 29
  psychomotor tests, 33–34, 345
  purchasing, 354–55
  purposes of, 2–41
  school district tests, 46
  selected-response (*See* Selected-
    response tests)
  theoretical continuum of descriptive
    clarity for, 229–30
  true-false (*See* True-false tests)
  using, 352–427
  validity of, 98–125 (*See also* Test va-
    lidity)
  valuative factors, 47–61
Elementary and Secondary Education
  Act of 1965 (ESEA), 7–8
Empirical item-improvement schemes,
  286–89
En-route skills, 212, 420
Equal-appearing interval scale, 337
Equitability in grading, 410–11
Equivalence:
  criterion-referenced tests and, 134
  norm-referenced tests and, 133–34
  reliability and, 132–34
  stability and, 134–35
Equivalent test forms, 135
Equivalents, grade (*See* Grade equivalents)
ESEA (*See* Elementary and Secondary
  Education Act of 1965)
Essay items, 236, 274–82
  dividends and deficits of, 276–77
  item-writing guidelines for, 277–82
  optional questions, 278–79
  for program evaluation, 277
  restricted-response form of, 278
  scoring of, 276–77
Evaluation:
  formative, 420

Evaluation (*cont.*)
  statistical concepts in, 66–97
  summative, 420
Evaluative review, 62–63
Evidence-gathering mechanisms, 6
Examination process, validity and justice of, 280
Examinee(s):
  item-improvement questionnaire for, 293
  judgment, 289–90, 292–93
  response data, 287
  task, 277–78
Examiner(s):
  demeanor of, 194
  positive actions of, 194–95
  racial match of, 194
Extended-response questions, 275

F

Face validity, 102
False-masters, identification of, 378
False-negatives, 54, 304
  problems of, 378
  standard set to reduce, 390
False-nonmasters, concerns about, 378
False-positives, 54, 304
  problems of, 378
  standard set to reduce, 389
Five-point continuum of agreement, 340
Fixed-quota settings, 35, 112
Frequencies, cumulative, 69
Functional Literary Test, 209–10

G

General description, in test specification, 216–18
Generalizability, 122, 213–15
Generosity errors, 322–24
GPA (*See* Grade point average)
Grade equivalents, 170–72
  problems with, 171–72
Grade inflation, 405
Grade point average (GPA), 299
Grades, single letter, 402–5
Grading, 400–412
  abolition of, 401

absolute, 404
according to potentials, 404–5
conventional system of, 402–5
equitability in, 410–11
guilt and, 411–12
pass-fail system, 405–7
pupil growth and, 405
relative, 403
value of, 401
Grading-on-the-curve, 403
Guessing:
  appropriateness of, 357
  blind, 242
  coping with, 243
  correcting for, 363–65 (*See also* Correction-for-guessing)
  informed, 242, 365
Guttman scale, 345

H

Halo effect, 324
Handwriting rating scales, 318
Histograms, 318

I

Individual assessment, 6–7, 19
Inferential jump, 336–37
Informed judgment model, 384–86
  appraisal of, 392
  operations of, 385–86
  performance data in, 385
  preference data in, 385
Instructional design, 37, 412–21
  principles of, 415–19, 423
Instructional diagnosis, 37
Instructional impact, 270
Instructional improvement, 412–21
  catalysts for, 8–9
  collaboration in, 412–13
  status determination and, 20
Instructional Objectives Exchange, 216
Intelligence tests, group, 17–18
Internal consistency, 107, 135, 141–46
  estimates, 145–49
  split-half technique, 142
Interpretations, validity of, 98–99
IOX Basic Skill Test in Reading, on stability estimates, 149–50

IOX Basic Skill Test in Reading Competency, reliability data for, 151
IOX Basic Skill Tests, content validity of, 121–23
IPAT Cultural Fair Intelligence Testing, 187
Item analysis:
  discrimination efficiency of, 296
  external criteria, 298–99
  internal criteria, 298–99
Item bias, 292
Item-difficulty index, 294–95
Item discrimination indices, 295–99
  computation of, 296–98
  influence of difficulty levels and, 298
Item-discriminators, 296
Item form, 29
Item homogeneity, 302–3
  chi-square statistical analysis and, 302
  determination of, 302
Item-improvement:
  approaches to, 286–89
  questionnaire for examinees, 293
Item-specifications congruence, 290–91
Item scoring (*See* Scoring)
Item-types, choosing, 270–71
Item writers:
  communication with, 231
  moral responsibilities of, 237
Item-writing:
  accuracy, degree of, 273
  clues, unintended, 239–40 (*See also* Clues)
  directions, unclear, 237–38
  false reference, 238–39
  guidelines:
    binary-choice items, 243–47
    cognitive tests, 244–47
    essay items, 277–82
    matching items, 248–51
    multiple-choice items, 254–61
    short-answer items, 272–74
  lean sentence structure, 240
  negative and double negatives, 245
  obstacles to, 237–41
  phrasing technique in, 244–45
  single concept per statement, 246
  syntax, complicated, 240
  terminology, polysyllabic, 240

verification of questions' quality, 279
vocabulary and, 240–41

J

Judgment, qualitative, 310, 315
Judgmental data, 287
  sources of, 289

K

Kuder-Richardson method, 142–45
  formulas, 148–50

L

Latent-image scoring schemes, 362
Latent trait models, 137
Learning outcomes:
  assessment of, 271
  measures of, 275
Leiter International Performance Scale, 184
Letters to parents, 408–9
Likert scales, 338, 340–41
  developed by R. Tidwell, 342–43
Limit-focus measurement, 211–12
Logistic difficulty scale, 138
Logit:
  defined, 138
  values, 138–40
Logit value difficulty, 138–40
  adjusting down, 140
Lorge-Thorndike tests, construct validity of, 119
Loss ratio, 54, 304

M

Marathon testing, 136
Marking (*See* Grading)
Masters, identification of, 378
Mastery and non-mastery groups, intersection point of, 389
Matching items, 236, 247–51
  describing basis for, 251
  dividends and deficits of, 248
  heterogeneous lists, 249
  homogeneous lists in, 299–50
  item-writing guidelines of, 248–51
Mean, 76–77
  deviations from, 80–81

Mean (*cont.*)
  formula for, 76
  median, mode and, relationship of,
    78
Measured behavior, description of,
    47–50
  criterion-referenced tests and,
    48–50
  determining adequacy of, 50
  instructional design and, 49
  norm-referenced tests and, 48
  program evaluation and, 49
Measurement, practicality of, 122
Measure Treasure Unlimited (MTU),
    232
Median, 77
  advantage of, 77
  mean, mode and, relationship of, 78
Minimum competency:
  criterion-referenced tests and, 379
  interpretation of, 373
  norm-referenced tests and, 379
Mode, 77–78
  mean, median and, relationship of,
    78
MTU (*See* Measure Treasure Unlim-
    ited)
Multiple-choice items, 236, 251–62
  allure of, 261–62
  alternatives, 251, 256
  best-answer approach, 252, 255
  correct-answer approach, 252, 255
  direct-question format, 252
  distractors, 251 (*See also* Distractors)
  dividends and deficits of, 253–54
  flexibility of, 253
  foils, 251
  item-writing guidelines of, 254–61
  reliability of, 253
  response sets and, 253
  stem, 251 (*See also* Stem)
  weakness of, 254

N

National Council on Measurements
    Used in Education (NCME), 100
NCME (*See* National Council on Mea-
    surements Used in Education)
Nedelsky method, 388–91
  application of, 389
  steps in, 388

Nelson Reading Skill Test, 120–21
Nonmasters, identification of, 378
Normal curve, 157–60
  characteristics of, 158
  percentages of, 169
Normal curve equivalents (NCE), 168
Normative data:
  assembly of, 175
  criteria for judging, 176–78
  quality of, 61
  samples of convenience and, 175
Norm group, 172
Norm-referenced measurement,
    24–41
Norm-referenced tests:
  construct validation for, 116–17
  content validity of, 103–5
  criterion-referenced tests and, 31,
    134, 206
  criterion-related validity of, 111–12
  definition of, 26
  description of measured behavior
    in, 48
  distinction of, 25–26
  empirical item-improvement
    schemes for, 288–89
  equivalence coefficients for, 133–34
  internal consistency estimates of,
    145
  interpretation of, 32–33
  normative tables, 32
  percentiles versus percentage cor-
    rect, 32–33
  quality indication of, 298
  resource allocation, large scale, 38
  stability of, 129–30
  test specifications of, 206–11
  weaknesses for program evaluation,
    37
Norms, 172–78
  clarification of, 176
  local, 174–76
  national, 174–76
  standard and, 172
Norm tables, 32, 172–73, 177

O

Objectives, amplified, 230
Objectives-based tests, 29
Objectives-referenced tests, 29

Observations, 205, 309–25
  anecdotal records, 313–15
  checklist, 313–14
  ratings and, 310–11
  systematic, 311–15
  tools and techniques in, 312–13
Observed events, descriptions of, 313
Observers:
  task of, 310–11
  training of, 312
Optical scanning machines, 362–63
Optimal performance measuring, 34
Optional questions, 278–79
Otis Quick-Scoring Mental Ability Tests,
  186
Otis test, 17
Oxymoron, 321

P

Paper-and-pencil schemes, 205
Parent-teacher conferences, 409–10
Penmanship, treatment of, 280
Percentage column, cumulative, 69
Percentile equivalents:
  normalized z scores and, 167
  table of, 163
Percentiles, 160–62
  computation of, 161
  definition of, 160–61
  normal curves, standard scores and,
    170
  percentile ranks and, 160
Performance:
  minimally acceptable, 386
  optimal measuring, 34
Performance data, relevant:
  just-instructed and, 380–81
  previously instructed and, 380,
    382–83
  uninstructed and, 380–81
Performance domain of interest, defi-
    nition of, 102
Performance standards:
  aggregate, 394–96
  alternate procedures for, 384–92
  Angoff adaptation, 391–92
  considerations on, 375–77
  contrasting-groups method, 387–88
  definition of, 371
  determining defensible, 395

  experienced-based, 376
  informed judgment model, 384–86
  judgmental decision making and,
    374–75
  major factors in, 377–84
  minimum competency testing and,
    372–74
  Nedelsky method, 388–91
  separate, 394–96
  setting, 371–99
  time requirements, 377
Personal-bias errors, 322–24
Polygons, frequency, 72–73
  graphic-display techniques, 72–75
Practice, appropriate, 418–19
Predictive validity, 109–11
Predictors of future acts, 331
Procrustean proclivities, 403
Products, 309–10
  appraisal of examinee-created, 205
  behaviors and, distinction between,
    267–68
Proficiency, level of, 53, 303
Program evaluation, 7–8, 36–37
  missions, 19
  test results, 8
Progress monitoring, 419–21
  implication of, 419
Psychomotor domain, 328–31
  performance standard and, 372
Psychomotor measure, definition of,
    328
Psychomotor tests, 33–34
  individual decision in, 345
Punctuation, treatment of, 280
Purposes, description of, 356

Q

Q-sort technique, 345
Quartile, 162

R

Range, 80
Range restriction, reliability coefficient
    and, 130
Ranking, 321
  application of, 321
Rasch-equated test form, construction
    of, 140

Rasch model, 135, 137–41
  advantage of, 141
  unidimensionality, 141
Raters, training of, 324
Rating errors:
  halo effect, 324
  instrumental, 321
  procedural, 321–22
  rater personal-bias, 322–24
Rating forms (*See also* Rating scales)
  teacher, 319
  two-dimensional, 316
Ratings, 309–25
  administrative, of teacher effective-
    ness, 323–24
  for affective assessment, 335
  after-the-event, 311
  behavior, 315–17
  product, 317–18
  qualitative gradations in, 319
Rating scales, 316
  changing-alternatives scale, 320
  common, 317–21
  constant-alternatives scale, 320
  descriptive-graphic, 320
  graphic, 319–20
  handwriting, 318
  numerical, 317, 319
Raven's Progressive Matrices, 184
Raw score distribution, z score distri-
    bution and, 164
Raw score formula, for product-
    moment correlation coefficient,
    92–93
Reading tests, criterion-related validity
    of, 120–21
Record cards, 368
Record folder, cumulative, 366
Record forms, special-purpose, 366
Record sheets, 366
Relationship:
  curvilinear, 88
  direction of, 87
  indicators of, 85–95
  linear, 88
  magnitude of, 87
  negative, 86–87
  positive, 86
  strength of, 87
Reliability, 126–55
  approaches to determining, 135
  consistency and, 126

equivalence and stability, 134–35
  equivalence coefficient of, 132
  estimate, 142
  internal consistency, 141–46
  stability and, 126, 128–32
  standard error of measurement,
    146–48
  validity and, 126–28
Reliability coefficient, 128, 130, 143
Report cards, 407–10
  multidimensional, 408
  1919 elementary school, 408
  1926 high school, 409
Reporting schemes, supplementary,
    407–10
Requisite-skill settings, 35–36
Resource allocation, large-scale, 38
Responding, basis for, 357
Response evaluation, anonymous, 280
Response form, 270
  machine-scorable, 357
Responses:
  classification scheme of, 236
  constructed, 221–22
  extended, 275–76
  recording methods of, 357
  restricted, 275–76
  selected, 221
  selected versus constructed, 236
  trial, 222, 279
Response set:
  examinees', 260
  item writers', 260
Response sheets, separate, 355
Restricted-response questions, 275
Results, knowledge of, 418
Reviewers:
  checking on judgments of, 291
  independent, 289
  nonexaminee, 290–92
Reviews, systematic, 292
Revisability, 375–76
  public confidence and, 375–76
RST (*See* Nelson Reading Skill Test)

S

Sample item, 216, 218
  format variations and, 218
  purposes of, 218
Sample test questions, 357

Scale(s):
  interval, 93–94
  ordinal, 93–94
  ratio, 93
Scope of measurement, 56–58
  broad-scope tests, 56–58
  narrow-scope tests, 56–58
  specificity and utility, 57
  test developers, role of, 56
  test evaluators, role of, 56
Score consistency, 130
Score interval, midpoint of, 161
Scores:
  analyzing, 69
  average, 76
  cut-off, 131–32
  determination of passing, 393
  dispersion of, 80
  T (*See* T scores)
  Z (*See* Z scores)
Scoring, 269–70, 361–63
  analytic, 280–81
    advantages of, 281
  carbon-booklet, 362
  consistent evaluation in, 280
  ease of, 62
  equipments, 363
  by hand, 361–62
  holistic, 280–81
    advantages of, 281
  latent-image, 362
  by machine, 362–63
  methods, 204–5
  objective, 268
  optical scanning equipment for, 362
  stencil, 362
  subjective, 268, 270
Scoring keys, function of advanced, 279–80
Scoring weights, differential, 365
Security, need for, 133
Selected-response answers, handscoring for, 362
Selected-response items:
  constructed-response items and, 268–71
  improving quality of, 262
  measurement mission of, 269
  response structure in, 270
Selected-response tests, 235–65
Self-report inventions:
  for affective assessment, 335–44

high- and low-inference, 336–37
  validity of responses, 336–37
Semantic differential scales, 341, 343–44
  advantage of, 344
Settings, physical, 358–59
  auditory distractions, 358
  lighting, 358
  room temperature, 358
  work space, 358
Severity errors, 322, 324
Short-answer items, 236, 271–74
  ambiguous, 253
  answer space, 274
  blank placing, 273–74
  completion form, 271
  concise response, 273
  direct question form, 271
  dividends and deficits of, 271–72
  item-writing guidelines, 272–74
  legibility in, 272
  purposes of, 271
  scoring of, 272
Short-answer tests, handscoring for, 362
Skewen, 74
Skill listings, 209–11
Social desirability, identification of, 334–35
Social desirability scale, 335
SOMPA (*See* System of Multicultural Pluralistic Assessment)
Spearman-Brown prophecy formula, 142
Specification supplement, 216, 223
Spelling, treatment of, 280
Spiritual domain, 329
Stability, 126, 128–32
  criterion-referenced tests and, 130–32
  norm-referenced tests and, 129–30
Stability coefficient, 128
Stability estimates:
  consistency-of-decision approach, 149
  illustrated, 149–50
Standard:
  cut-off, 131
  definition of, 371
Standard deviation, 80–85
  meaning of, 82–85
  notation schemes of, 82
Standard error of estimate, formula for, 147

Standard error of measurement, 146–48
  illustrated, 150, 152
  significance of, 148
  split-half analysis, 152
Standardized achievement tests, 17
Standardized-observation system, 311
Standardized testing, origins of, 16–17
Standardized tests, administering, 361
Standard scores, 162–63
  normal curves, percentiles and, 170
  normalized, 165–68
  raw scores and, 411
  standard deviation units and, 162
  transformed, 165
Standard-setting procedures, 384–92
Standards for Educational and Psychological Tests, 100–103, 109, 113, 148
Stanford-Binet Intelligence Scale
  construct validity of, 114–15
  correlations with construct validity, 119
Stanine(s), 168–70
  values, 169
Statistical descriptive techniques, 67–68
Statistical model, Bayesian, 54–55
Statistics:
  central tendency indicators of, 75–78
  class intervals, 70–71
  cumulative frequencies, 69
  cumulative percentage column, 69
  frequency distributions, 68–71
  function of, 66–68
  graphic displays, 71–75
  graphic representations, 85–89
  indicators, 67
    of relationship, 85–95
  measurement scales, 93–95
  theoretical limits, 70
  variability, 79–85
Status determination:
  instructional improvement and, 20
  missions, 18–19
  oriented, 9
Stem:
  grammatical consistency with alternatives, 257–58
  negatively stated, 255–56
  self-contained, 254–55
Subskills, measuring, 51

Subtests, 51–52
Summated-rating scale, 340
Swiss cheese items, 274
System of Multicultural Pluralistic Assessment (SOMPA), 189–90

T

Task, examinee's, well defined, 277–78
Task analysis, 420
Task description, 417–18
Taxonomy of Educational Objectives, Handbook I: The Cognitive Domain, 207, 329–30
Teachability, 122, 215–16
Teaching sequences, designing, 415–19
Technical Manual of the Cognitive Abilities Test, construct validity of, 118–20
Terminal skills, 420
Test administration, 353–70
  factors to consider, 357–61
  physical setting, 358–59
Test administrators:
  behavior of, 359–61
  surveillance by, 360
Test bias, 181–99
  in administration, 193–95
  connotations, similar, 192
  cultural, 62
  definition of, 182–83
  evaluating for, 190–97
  examinees, 195
  examiners, 194–95
  instructional shortcomings, 183–84
  in interpretations, 195–97
  in items, 191–93
  judging, 190–91
  normative samples and, 196
  quota system for, 196–97
  racial, 181–82
  relevancy, 192
  settings, 195
Test blueprints, 207
Test developers, task of, 355
Test development effort, size of, 287–88
Test equating, 135–41
  approaches to, 136–37
  equivalent difficulty, 136–37

Test evaluation, 45–64
Test evaluators, job of, 49
Testing targets, selecting, 414–15
Test interpretations, racial variables
    in, 196
Test items:
    binary-choice (*See* Binary-choice
        items)
    classification of, 268
    difficulty level of, 393
    empirical improvement of, 286–88,
        293–305
    essay (*See* Essay items)
    function similarity, 302
    grouping, 354
    homogeneity of, 106–7
    improving, 286–309
    indispensable elements of, 220
    judgmental improvement of, 286–
        88, 289–93
    long-answer, 268
    matching (*See* Matching items)
    multiple-choice (*See* Multiple-choice
        items)
    number of, 303–5
    practicality in preparing, 236–37
    prototypic, 302
    recognition of, 268
    revision of, 288
    short-answer (*See* Short-answer items)
    significant dimensions of, 220
    trial, analysis of, 220
Test length, 53, 204, 305
    problems, 54–55
Test planning:
    constraints of, 204–5
    item grids and item generation proc-
        ess, 209
Test reliability, 58–59
    internal consistency, 59
    stability, index of, 59
Test results:
    amalgamating, 410–11
    computer-based data retrieval sys-
        tems, 367
    confidentiality of, 367
    influence of, 412–13
    recording, 365–67
    reliance on, 401–2
    use of 400–427
Test-retest coefficient, 128
Test review form, 63

Tests:
    affective, 33–34, 332
    scoring machines, 363
    standardized, 16–17, 361
Test security, 205, 367, 369
Test specifications, 203–34, 416
    criterion-referenced tests and,
        211–30
    functions of, 230–32
    norm-referenced tests and, 206–11
    quality of, 230
    selection factors, 213–16
    teachability, 215–16
Test users, communication to, 230
Test validity, 59–60
    establishment of, 98–125
    guiding literatures for assessment
        of, 99–100
    variation of, 101
Thurstone scales, 337–39
Time allocation, suggestive, 356
Time allowance, 356
Time limit, 278
Time-on-task, variable of, 418
True-false items:
    acquiescent response set, 246
    ambiguous, 238
    difficulties with, 242
    item-writing guidelines of, 243–47
    modification of, 243
    opposite version, 244
    parallel version, 244
    supporting basis of, 243
    with syntax, complicated, 240
True-false tests, 235
    binary-choice items in, 241
T scores, 165
    normalized, computation of, 167
Typical performance measuring, 34

U

University examinations, 15–16
    England oral examinations, 16
    Louvain scheme, 16
    Ratio Studiorum, 16

V

Validation study, quality of, 111

Validity:
  actual focus of, 99
  assessment factors, 122
  construct, 100, 113–18
  criterion-related, 100, 108–13
  descriptive, 105, 122
  predictive, 109–11
  reliability and, relationship between,
      126–28
  social desirability cues and, 334–35
Variables:
  affective, definition of, 331
  continuous, 295
  criterion, quality of, 110
  dichotomous, 295
Variance, 85

W

Weighting, specification of, 278
Wrong-answer options:
  analysis of, 388
  identification of, 221–22
  nature of, 221

Z

Z score distribution, and raw score,
      transformation of, 164
Z scores, 163–65
  disadvantage of, 164
  normalized, calculation of, 166–67
  standard deviation units and, 163